A Cognitive Approach to Learning Disabilities

McGraw-Hill Series in Special Education

Robert M. Smith, *Consulting Editor*

A Cognitive Approach to Learning Disabilities

D. Kim Reid
School of Human Development
University of Texas

Wayne P. Hresko
Associate Professor of Education
Division of Special Education
North Texas State University

McGraw-Hill Book Company

New York   St. Louis   San Francisco   Auckland   Bogotá   Hamburg
Johannesburg   London   Madrid   Mexico   Montreal   New Delhi
Panama   Paris   São Paulo   Singapore   Sydney   Tokyo   Toronto

This book was set in Times Roman by The Total Book (ECU/BD).
The editor was Phillip A. Butcher; the production supervisor was Diane Renda.
The cover was designed by Antonia Goldmark.

A COGNITIVE APPROACH TO LEARNING DISABILITIES

Library of Congress Cataloging in Publication Data
Reid, D   Kim.
   A cognitive approach to learning disabilities.

   (McGraw-Hill series in special education)
   Bibliography: p.
   Includes index.
      1. Learning disabilities.   2. Cognition in Chil-
dren. I. Hresko, Wayne P., joint author. II. Title.
LC4704.R44   371.92   80-18428
ISBN 0-07-051768-1

From each to the other

Contents

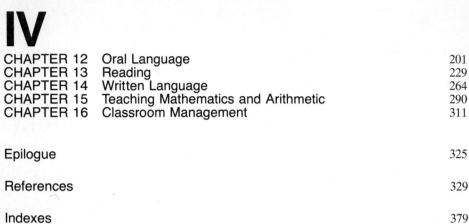

IV

Preface

This book is designed for preservice and inservice teachers, school psychologists, speech and language specialists, and students and professionals who have an interest in the field of learning disabilities. As professors, we became aware that most textbooks in learning disabilities either present a review of historical approaches or discuss current practice. Critical analyses of historical perspectives leave the reader with little direction for intervention. Discussions of current practice leave the reader vulnerable. Without knowledge of previous theoretical and intervention approaches, the reader cannot benefit from the knowledge that has accrued and is therefore suseptible to rediscovering, often enthusiastically, practices that have not been demonstrated effective. This text presents the historical framework and, where appropriate, both the prevailing orientation and alternatives that are still in keeping with the mandates of P1 94-142.

Part One of the book provides an introduction to learning disabilities and discusses implications that current research and theory have for the instruction of learning disabled children.

Chapter 1 provides an analysis of the definition of learning disabilities and a discussion of prevalence and causative factors. It also addresses the question of the impact that learning disabilities have on persons of various ages.

Chapter 2 presents an overview of hyperactivity and explores both the overlap between learning disabilities and hyperactivity and the distinctions between them. Both suspected causes and popular treatment methods are critically evaluated.

Chapter 3 describes an approach to learning and teaching that has gained increasing support from research in learning, cognition, metacognition, reading, and language. It is a view of the learner as active in his/her own learning and of the teacher as a person who provides experiences from which children learn. Contrasts between what we are calling a *cognitive approach* and the process and behavioral models so well known to special educators are discussed. Emphasis is on higher-order executive or control functions rather than the representational systems of perception and associative memory.

Because learning disabilities are defined in terms of "disorder in one or more of the basic psychological processes" and because the field of learning disabilities has been dominated by assessment and intervention practices directed at measuring and training these psychological processes, Part Two is devoted to an examination of the traditional approaches to defining, measuring, and training basic processes once thought to be prerequisite to academic achievement. Research related to the effectiveness of these orientations is reviewed and points of departure from modern theories of knowing are delineated. Finally, implications of current research findings from teaching children who exhibit disorders in one or more of these basic processes are explored.

Chapter 4 presents evidence that learning disabled children tend to have significant problems with memory. Modern models of memory are presented along with a discussion of the developmental aspects of memory and metamemory. Implications that recent research findings may have for instructional design are explored.

Chapter 5 defines preception and discusses the theories and programs of the early perceptual-motor theorists who dominated the field of learning disabilities. Research findings related to the effectiveness of their interventions are reviewed.

Chapter 6 presents models of attention and vigilance and notes the developmental nature of these functions. The rather extensive body of literature on attention and selective attention in learning disabled children is reviewed and put into the perspective of the larger body of literature in psychology that deals with attention and vigilance. Strategies for increasing attention both through modification of children's behavior and modification of instructional design are examined.

Chapter 7 deals with affect. Although the discussion of social and emotional development leads to the conclusion that affective development should constitute an important curriculum goal, it currently receives little such consideration. It was for this reason that we chose to include the discussion of affect with other psychological functions. Three major topics are addressed in this chapter. First, the relation between learning and behavior problems and the possible sources of these problems are presented. Second, characteristics of learning disabled children, their schools, and their families that appear to facilitate or hinder social/emotional development are reviewed. Finally, current intervention practices are delineated and critiqued.

Part Three addresses issues related to assessment and instructional planning. Its intent is to make the reader aware of important issues related to evaluation and to recommend the use of different assessment strategies for diagnosis and teaching.

Chapter 8 reviews the purposes and considerations of assessment, including reliability, validity, normative data, evaluation models, and issues related to nondiscriminatory testing.

Chapter 9 describes and critiques early identification and screening practices. Tests that measure correlates of learning as well as direct measures of early academic functioning are described and evaluated.

Chapter 10 presents a comprehensive approach to individual diagnostic testing based on data collected from nine sources; observational data, other available data, language assessment, educational assessment, specific abilities measures, adaptive behavior scales, medical/developmental data, personality data, and measures of intellectual functioning. Both formal and informal tests which are widely used in the field of learning disabilities are described and evaluated. A sample psychoeducational evaluation is presented.

Chapter 11 is devoted to individual educational plans, service delivery systems, and a critical evaluation of mainstreaming. New roles which learning disabilities professionals are likely to fulfill within the next several years are described as are suggestions for meeting the demands of those roles.

Part Four is devoted to curriculum areas. Discussions of the nature of the abilities/content to be learned are followed by descriptions of the traditional and cognitive approaches to teaching them.

Chapter 12 compares approaches to language that have stemmed from the early underlying abilities model psycholinguistics and from current behaviorial approaches and cognitive approaches using behavioral technology. Instructional practices that emphasize flexibility and generalization are recommended.

Chapter 13 reviews the research on the nature and possible causes of reading problems, with particualr attention to specific developmental dyslexia. Traditional approaches to reading instruction (including whole word, phonic, and multisensory methods and their variants) are described and evaluated. These traditional approaches are contrasted with the psycholinguistic approaches to reading advocated by F. Smith and Y. & K. Goodman. Finally, an interactive model of reading is offered as a synthesizing, middle-ground position. Recommendations for instruction are based not on questions of whether phonics or comprehension should dominate instruction, but on how "top down" orientations might contribute to a comprehensive instructional plan.

Chapter 14 covers several topics in written language instruction, including spelling, handwriting, and composition. Both informal assessment and instructional procedures are outlined.

Chapter 15 examines problems children have with mathematicas and arithmetic computation. Traditional approaches to instruction in mathematics are contrasted with methods based on a cognitive approach. Once again, both informal assessment procudures and instructional strategies are provided.

Chapter 16 contrasts two models of classroom management. One is a behaviroal approach which emphasizes control by the teacher and the second is a more humanistic model based on helping children make decisions for themselves. Although some persons may prefer one model and some the other, it is helpful for teachers to be familiar with both so that they have a variety of intervention techniques at their disposal to deal with difficult children.

Although many of the recommendations for instruction that are made in this book are rather new and unproven, they are founded on currently accepted theory and research. As noted in Chapter 3, many of the more traditional practices in special education are both untested and based on assumptions that *(a)* children are passive learners, and that *(b)* learning and motivation can be externally controlled. Considerable research in developmental and cognitive psychology, reading, and psycholinguistics challenges these assumptions. It is our opinion that it is far better to attempt new approaches with some theoretical merit than to continue using practices known to be minimally effective.

We are convinced that effective instuction amounts to problem solving in which intelligent, well-trained teachers take into account the interests and abilities of the learners, the nature of the abilities or content to be mastered, and available instructional materials and strategies. For this reason, we have perhaps presented more theory than is customary in textbooks on learning disabilities. It is clear, however, that the way a person operates in the world, views problems, and solves them is dependent on what he or she thinks the world is like. If one thinks reading is primarily a visual skill, one becomes concerned with "teaching" perception. If one thinks children learn in a logical, hierarchical manner, one will select behavioral-objectives sequences to guide teaching interventions.

One need only to observe naturalistic learning in children, however, to recognize that children are self-directed, self-motivated, and generally holistic in their approaches to learning tasks. Just a few years ago many four-year-olds sang *supercalifragilisticexpialidocious*—a word with no meaning, no conerete referent, and incredibly difficult to pronounce. Those children didn't say just a single, simple part of that very complex word. They said it all—just as well as they could. Learning in naturalistic settings is holistic and progresses from initial, often cumbersome attempts to increasingly accomplished approximations. Since there is no evidence in the research literature that more traditional instructional interventions are reducing the incidence of learning problems in schools, perhaps it is time to adopt a formulation of educational principles that stresses active learners, long-term acquisitions, and the validity of educational goals.

There are many people who deserve thanks for the support and assistance they offered during the preparation of this manuscript. First, we are indebted to our students at New York University for asking the questions and raising the issues that led to our own search for a better way. We are also indebted to Virginia Bruininks, Joseph Torgesen, John Wilde, and Eric Brown (who reviewed all or parts of the manuscript) for their helpful and very insightful criticisms that undoubtedly made this a better book. To Bill Talkington and Phil Butcher, our editors at McGraw-Hill, our sincerest thanks. It is with deepest appreciation that we thank our typists, Mary Benderoth and Cynthia Slayton, who managed pleasant smiles even while working round the clock to meet deadlines. For their encouragement and willing help with a variety of domestic problems that arose during the writing of this book, we thank Carol and Jim O'Malley, Vera and Don Lawson, and Mom and Dad Reid. We are especially grateful to Annette Bodzin, our production editor, for her good humor and unfailing diligence. Finally, we owe an enormous debt to Bryan and Bridget, Kellie, and especially John who taught us about meaningful learning in kids.

D. Kim Reid
Wayne P. Hresko

Part One

Learning disabilities is probably one of the least well understood labels used in education today. When learning disorders are severe, they can be diagnosed with some assurance. But most people thought to be learning disabled, experience mild although pervasive and long-lasting problems. Professionals who work in the field come from a variety of disciplines and bring with them their own perspectives on the problem. Pediatricians, for example, tend to be concerned with organic symptoms, especially those related to central nervous system dysfunction. Psychologists tend to be interested in social and emotional development and intellectual potential, while teachers stress academic strengths and weaknesses. Speech and language professionals, physical and occupational therapists, and allergists all contribute different emphases and strategies for intervention. The field is consequently rich and interesting, but often confusing. What makes the understanding of learning disabilities even more difficult is that many approaches to the field, though tried and found to be of questionable use, retain adherents who continue as hopeful of their merits as they were when those strategies were new and untested. Even more striking is that as one discipline tests its theories, assessment devices, and intervention strategies and rejects them, other related disciplines often claim these as their own.

Because learning disabilities are by definition primarily school-related, the

Photo on facing page: Reading about Monsters and Trolls.

1

orientation in this book is one that incorporates data contributed from a wide variety of disciplines into an instructional approach. The first chapter examines the current definition of learning disabilities and attempts to highlight the complexities related to understanding its operational parameters, its causes, and its prevalence. The second chapter is devoted to a discussion of hyperactivity, because (1) hyperactivity tends to be equated in many people's minds with learning disabilities, (2) it appears to share many of the hypothesized causes of learning disabilities, and (3) management of hyperactive children is often the responsibility of learning disabilities professionals. The final chapter in this section of the book discusses the need for a *cognitive* approach to the education of learning disabled persons. A cognitive approach is one which stresses that learners must be active participants in the construction of meaning, that learners must be made aware that they are responsible for their own learning, that only strategies that lead to long-term acquisitions are valid, and that psychological processes and academic abilities must be considered unitary for the purposes of teaching.

Chapter 1

An Introduction to Learning Disabilities

INTRODUCTION

The field of learning disabilities has been plagued with definitional problems from its conception. The purpose of this chapter is to present an integrated definition of learning disabilities that is consonant with both professional opinion and with mandated legislation. In order to do so, a number of topics will be addressed. First, the standard definition of learning disabilities will be discussed in terms of recent legislative changes. Second, the areas of commonality across a number of definitions will be clarified. Next, the problem of calculating the prevalence of learning disabilities will be explored in order to identify potentially intruding factors. Fourth, the categories of organically based causes and environmentally based causes will be examined. Fifth, as a means of explaining the seeming confusion of the field, the chapter briefly reviews the history of the field. Finally, the chapter addresses the question of the meaning of learning disabilities across the life span.

DEFINITION

The term *learning disabilities* emerged from a need to identify and serve a group of children who were failing in school, but did not fit the existing categories of exceptionality. Since this group of children, however, exhibits a wide variety of problem behaviors and requires the services of professionals from a number of disciplines, there is often little agreement as to what exactly constitutes a "learning disability." The most widely used and legally accepted definition is that devised by the National Advisory Committee on Handicapped Children (1968):

> Children with special learning disabilities exhibit a disorder in one or more of the basic psychological processes involved in understanding or in using spoken or written languages. These may be manifested in disorders of listening, thinking, talking, reading, writing, spelling, or arithmetic. They include conditions which have been referred to as perceptual handicaps, brain injury, minimal brain dysfunction, dyslexia, developmental aphasia, etc. They do not include learning problems which are due primarily to visual, hearing or motor handicaps, to mental retardation, emotional disturbance or to environmental disadvantage.

Although considerable debate has centered on the adequacy of a definition by exclusion, the authors have chosen to use the legal definition as a point of departure for two reasons: (1) it defines the limits of the population for whom funding is available to support special education services, and (2) it provides a broad framework under which most other definitions can be subsumed.

This same definition has been reconfirmed and somewhat clarified by the passage of Public Law 94-142 (*Federal Register,* August 23 and December 29, 1977). Although the regulations continue to recognize the illusive character of specific learning disability (*Federal Register,* December 29, 1977), specification of the criteria evaluation teams must use to determine the presence of a learning disability have helped in part to clarify its nature. Those criteria stipulated under the law are: (1) that the child fails to achieve commensurate with his or her age and abilities when provided with appropriate educational experiences in the areas of oral expression, listening comprehension, written expression, basic reading skill, reading comprehension, mathematics calculation or mathematics reasoning, or (2) the child evidences a severe discrepancy between achievement and intellectual ability in one of those areas. (Both or either of these two criteria are often referred to as constituting a discrepancy model.) In learning disabled children, intellectual ability, most often determined by a score on an intelligence test, is average or above average. Children with below-average scores are labeled as learning disabled only when the testing profile suggests that, for some reason, test scores are depressed and the child does, indeed, possess average or better intellectual capacity.

A wide variety of definitions emphasize various aspects of the problem (adapted from Reid, 1977). Some, for example, limit the definition to children with perceptual disorders. Others use hyperactivity and/or emotional lability as the criterion. Still others argue that the problems are due to difficulties in the acquisition and use of language. Some postulate a developmental problem, a lag in the maturation of the central nervous system, that affects various aspects of behavior at different times during the child's growth (first, perception, then, language, etc.). Still others define the problem in terms of skills and equate a learning disability with a reading disability or perhaps a problem with mathematics. Most recently, complex thinking skills have come into question. Perhaps, as Grossman (1978) suggested, the lack of a clear definition is the result of no one school of thought having clear superiority in the field. Despite these differences of opinion, there are five characteristics that most professionals would regard as necessary to a diagnosis of learning disability: (1) difficulty in school learning; (2) uneven performance across a variety of tasks; (3) physiological correlates; (4) disruptions in basic psychological processes; and (5) exclusion from any other previously established categories of disability (Chalfant & King, 1976).

Difficulty in School Learning

The primary concern in identifying children as learning disabled is to establish that they have problems in one or more academic skills. No matter what other symptoms associated with learning disability a child may have, if he or she does not exhibit problems in school learning, the learning disabilities label is inappropriate.

Uneven Performance across a Wide Variety of Tasks

Another indicator of a learning disability is a discrepancy within the child's own levels of performance. A child may have superior skills in reading and yet be unable to comprehend mathematical calculations or express himself appropriately. Tests are often used to reveal a discrepancy between the child's potential (IQ or aptitude) and his or her academic performance.

Physiological Correlates

The inclusion of constitutional (or physiological) correlates in the definition of learning disability is related to the assumption that there is a disorder of basic processes and prohibits the labeling of children on the basis of poor instruction, cultural difference, and the like. Problems arise when one begins to attempt to describe these correlates or to determine conclusively that they exist in every case. Some children with learning disabilities have clear signs of brain injury such as irregular patterns of brain waves, failure to develop or loss of certain abilities following a head injury, or prolonged fevers or convulsions. For others, brain dysfunction must be inferred on the basis of a neurological examination. The neurological examination reveals more subtle symptoms, often called "soft signs." These include performance on tests of neurological functioning at levels that would be perfectly normal for a younger child (Kinsbourne, 1973a). The neurological examination also reveals awkwardness, distractibility, hyperactivity, and/or a relative lack of impulse control when compared to age-mates. Some children, especially those with developmental dyslexia, exhibit none of these symptoms. Their problem, nonetheless, is widely accepted as neurological in nature (cf. Critchley, 1970; Critchley & Critchley, 1978).

It is not uncommon for such children to be characterized as having "minimal brain dysfunction." This term reflects the inability to demonstrate that *damage* to the brain has occurred and suggests, instead, a *malfunction* of the central nervous system. Physiological problems may result from genetic variations, biochemical irregularities, malnutrition, and a variety of illnesses and injuries. It is important to note, however, that only a portion of children with known brain damage or dysfunction actually experience problems in school learning and can, therefore, be considered as learning disabled. Figure 1-1 represents that relation between medically diagnosed dysfunction (circle A) and educationally defined learning disability (circle B).

Problems in Basic Psychological Processes

This component of the definition of learning disabilities probably causes the most difficulty. As Hammill (1974) in his analysis of the National Advisory Committee definition indicated, little agreement exists as to what those basic psychological processes are, how to identify them, or what their significance is. Most major texts in the field, however, include disorders of perceptual-motor functions, attention, memory, language, and emotionality. Although a great deal of energy has been expended in attempting to remediate disorders of psychological processes deemed prerequisite to academic learning, these attempts (e.g., perceptual or psycholinguistic training) have consistently failed to improve children's academic performances, and there is no clear evidence that these processes exert a *causal* influence on children's ability to learn. In this text, basic psychological processes will mean those variables under the control of the executive systems that have been identified by psychological research to be important aspects of learning: (1) attention and vigilance; (2) perception; (3) memory; (4) language; and (5) social/emotional development. These processes are clearly integrated, with some being more complex and subsuming others.

Figure 1-1 The relation of learning disabilities to other educational problems.

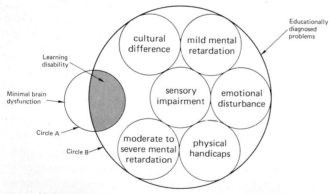

Note: Medically diagnosed problems related to minimal brain dysfunction are represented by Circle A. All educationally diagnosed problems, including those related to behavior disorders, sensory impairment, mental retardation, cultural differences, etc., are represented by Circle B. Using a strict interpretation of the definition of learning disabilities, the intersection between the circles (shaded area) would represent the relatively small proportion of those individuals with educationally diagnosed problems who would be classified as learning disabled.

Exclusion From Other Categories of Disability

Nearly all definitions agree in their exclusion of children with primary problems of sensory impairment (such as blindness and deafness), motor handicaps (cerebral palsy, muscular dystrophy, and the like), and moderate-to-severe mental retardation. There are those who take issue, however, with the exclusion of children who are primarily emotionally disturbed, mildly retarded, or culturally disadvantaged. Many authorities (cf. Kirk, 1963) argue that it is extremely difficult to tell which is primary, the emotional or the learning disability, since they occur together with such frequency. Some (cf. Hallahan & Kaufman, 1976) refer to the extreme overlap among the populations of the learning disabled, the educably mentally retarded, and the emotionally disturbed which prohibits clear differentiation for the purposes of instruction. Others (cf. Hallahan & Cruickshank, 1973) contend that, since the culturally disadvantaged exhibit many of the same symptoms and learning problems as the learning disabled, they should be included under the definition.

Although no clear operational definition exists, one potentially fruitful endeavor for clarifying the characteristics of the learning disabled population is the research project being conducted on marker variables in learning disabilities (Keogh, Major, Omori, Gandara, & Reid, in press; Keogh, Major, Reid, Gandara, & Omori, 1978). The project is attempting to establish "a set of core variables which are collected in common by those conducting research . . ." (Keogh et al., 1978, p. 6). Viewed as background characteristics, the marker variables would allow comparisons of research findings across studies. Two potential problems, however, must be noted. First, characteristics can be described only for preexisting populations. Since these populations were circumscribed by using a variety of existing definitions, current controversies and confusions are likely to confound the marker-variable data. Second, such a project is likely to lead to lists of correlates that may or may not constitute defining characteristics of learning disabilities.

PREVALENCE

Because there is so little agreement about definitions, it has been difficult to estimate the number of people who are learning disabled. Prevalence figures are subject to fluctuations due to such factors as how encompassing a definition is employed, the type of academic area or areas examined, whether the population is rural, suburban, or urban, the age groups studied, the level of performance required on given evaluation devices, and sociocultural factors. As a result, estimates of the number of learning disabled vary from 1 percent to 30 percent of the school-aged population (Lerner, 1976). In an attempt to suggest a prevalence figure, the National Advisory Committee on Handicapped Children (1968) suggested that the prevalence of the learning disabled in the school-aged population is somewhere between 1 percent and 3 percent. This figure (though conservative) has been the standard by which most state and local school districts have been guided.

A number of researchers have concluded that the prevalence of learning disabilities exceeds the 3 percent figure. Myklebust and Boshes (1969) used the relation of the child's current educational achievement to his assessed potential as criterion. They found prevalence figures to be between 7 percent and 15 percent, depending upon whether the cutoff was a 15 or 10 percent discrepancy between achievement and potential. Similarly, Meier (1971) determined the range to be between 4.7 and 15 percent, depending on criteria selected. Bruinincks and Weatherman (1970) suggested a prevalence figure of 5.8 percent. These figures, ranging from 4.7 percent to 15 percent are clearly in excess of the suggested National Advisory Committee's recommendations.

With the passage of The Education for All Handicapped Children Act of 1975, Public Law 94-142, Congress attempted to legislate a solution to the prevalence question. Under the regulations of this law, a state would not have been able to count more than 2 percent of the school-aged population as learning disabled. No more than 12 percent of the school-aged population would have been eligible to be counted as handicapped and of that, only one-sixth could be classified as learning disabled. Ringelheim (1978) attempted to justify the 2 percent cap on the learning disabled population from the standpoint that it would decrease the incidence of incorrect labeling. He further noted that removal of the cap and a lack of clarity in definition would have the effect of allowing incidence figures to vary upward toward 15 percent and that such an upward trend would lead to serious economic considerations. The Federal Office of Education encouraged public and professional input prior to the issuance of the final regulations. As a result, in December 1977, the Office of Education removed the 2 percent limit on learning disabilities. Their reasoning was that:

> It is generally agreed by parents and professionals alike that the isolation of various labels used by different theorists, as cited in the legislative history, are overlapping and represent assumptions about conditions which cannot with current technology be successfully determined or discretely categorized. Other categories of handicapping conditions as defined have no cap. Since there may, in fact, be more than two percent of the school-age population in some States that are handicapped by specific learning disabilities, such a limitation is inequitable. Such a procedure would not help provide a basis for the determination of whether a child has a specific learning disability, and would not provide assistance in helping to resolve questions of appropriate diagnosis or placement in the event of due process hearings. *(Federal Register,* 1977, p. 65085.)

In removing the limit and noting the lack of a clearly established and conceptually sound definition of learning disabilities, the Office of Education recognized that prevalence depends upon definition. As the definition becomes more exclusive, prevalence declines and when a position is taken which views learning disabilities as "learning problems found in children who have traditionally been classified as mildly handicapped, whether it be emotionally disturbed, mentally retarded, or learning disabled" (Hallahan & Kaufman, 1976, p. 28), then prevalence increases to, at maximum, the totals of the handicaps involved.

It should be noted that the argument for generic classification is both a practical and a theoretical one. Little data exist which either support or challenge the efficacy of grouping mildly handicapped children for instruction. Becker (1978) has demonstrated that performance differences exist which discriminate among the groups, but no one has as yet shown that the heterogeniety of a combined group increases instructional complexity.

The question arises as to what constitutes an acceptable prevalence figure for learning disabilities. When a concerted effort is made to exclude those children whose problems are not really *handicapping,* as well as those who are more appropriately conceptualized under other categories of handicapping conditions, the 1 percent to 3 percent prevalence estimate seems quite satisfactory. Current practice tends toward the use of a 50 percent discrepancy, although all discrepancy formulas are at present considered controversial (Algozzine, Forgnone, Mercer, & Trifiletti, 1979; Hanna, Dyck, & Holen, 1979).

CAUSES OF LEARNING DISABILITY

There are two general classes of causes of learning disability: organically based (symptoms of suboptimal neurological functioning) and environmentally based (arising from circumstances in experience which limit or inhibit the acquisition of basic skills). Included in the first category are usually problems related to brain injury (genetic as well as prenatal, perinatal, and postnatal) and biochemical disorders. Environmentally based disorders include poor nutrition, lack of early stimulation, and it is argued by some, emotional disturbance. In truth, however, whatever the etiology, the behavioral manifestations are frequently similar and it is often impossible to determine whether a particular problem is organically or environmentally based.

Organically Based Causes

Mykelbust and Boshes (1969) compared the results of neurological examinations in learning disabled and normal groups of children. Hard signs of neurological impairment (convulsions, motor involvement) occurred in 75 percent of the learning disabled children, but in only 25 percent of the normal group. The presence of soft signs (distractibility, awkwardness, impaired perception, and spatial orientation) was nearly equal in the two populations. It is clear that, although these signs are prevalent among the learning disabled, they do not constitute a discriminating characteristic.

When one considers the complexity of the human brain, this state of affairs becomes understandable. Although the structure and function of different areas of the brain are clearly differentiated, it is inaccurate to assume that mental functions are "localized" in specific cell groups. Luria (1965) explained that even very basic neural functions, such as sensation or perception and movement, are reflex processes resulting from constant interaction between the organism and its environment. Since this view of mental function involves dynamic systems consisting of long and complex neural pathways, one can expect that trauma might result in the disruption of many, sometimes heterogeneous, processes rather than in the loss of a single function and that one complex function might be disturbed by lesions in various parts of the cortex. Furthermore, the effect of a lesion depends on the duration and severity of the trauma, the extent of the area affected, and the age of the person afflicted (Gardner, 1975).

One additional factor, seldom considered in educational texts, is that the effects of a lesion will also depend on the level of performance a person has developed in the disturbed skill. Luria explains, for example, that since students just beginning to learn to write must concentrate both on the acoustical components of words and the choice and construction of each letter, writing is made up of a series of discrete motor acts. The experienced writer, on the other hand, has developed "firmly entrenched auditory-motor stereotypes" that enable writing to become an automatic process based on different psychological mechanisms from those needed by the beginner. At these different stages of development, writing "involves the activity of different dynamic systems involving different cortical structures" (p. 693). Hence, the exact same lesion would have different effects during the beginning stages of writing and at more advanced stages.

Some forms of learning disability, particularly developmental dyslexia (Critchley, 1970) and learning disorders that overlap with hyperactivity (Cantwell, 1976), are often thought to have a genetic component. Attempts to support such a hypothesis have examined the transmission of chromosomal anomolies from parents to children (Warren, Karduck, Bussaratid, Steward, & Sly, 1971), the manifestations of an inherited, innate disease form in both parents and siblings (Steward, 1970), the presence of "maturational lags" in family members (Silver, 1971), higher incidences of psychiatric illness in the parents of identified children (Cantwell, 1975), and, of course, a higher incidence of learning problems (de Hirsch, 1974). Results of the studies investigating physiological factors, such as chromosomal anomalies, have been generally negative. Those looking for a higher incidence of psychological and learning disorders have generally found the increased relation, but the findings could be equally supportive of an environmental explanation: parents with serious difficulties might be expected to provide home environments in which stress and inconsistency are commonplace (Dubey, 1976).

The final explanation of organic causes, the hypothesis that biochemical irregularities exist in learning disabled (especially hyperactive) children, constitutes the strongest rationale for the use of psychoactive drugs in the management of learning and behavior problems (Lambert, Windmiller, Sandoval, & Moore, 1976). Several possibilities have been suggested: (1) that certain "trace" elements are lacking in the central nervous systems of such children and must be replaced (Ellingson, cited in Ladd, 1970); (2) that these children cannot metabolize certain of the central nervous system neurotransmitters, such as serotonin, dopamine, or norepinephrine (Silver, 1971; Wender, 1971); and (3) that ingestion of toxic levels of lead (David, 1974; David, Hoffman, McGann,

Sverd, & Clark, 1976) constitutes a causative factor. Only the hypothesis regarding toxic lead levels seems to be supported at this time (Dubey, 1976).

Environmentally Based Causes

Of the environmentally based causative factors, perhaps the role of nutrition is the most widely researched, and yet the least well understood. Its role is poorly understood because malnutrition is an "ecological outcome" (Cravioto & Delicardie, 1975, p. 27) inextricably linked with various factors (e.g., poverty, ignorance, disease, cultural deprivation) which themselves contribute to the possibility of learning problems. Protein-caloric deficiency is the name of the syndrome that results from the inadequate ingestion or utilization of proteins. Marasmus is the disease entity which refers to a gradual emaciation, while kwashiorkor, the result of a carbohydrate diet, possibly high in calories, but low in protein, is characterized by swelling of the extremities and the appearance of discolored blotches on various parts of the body. These two diseases represent malnutrition in its extreme forms. Zinc, magnesium, and calcium deficiencies have also been implicated as well as toxic and allergic reactions to the ingestion of certain foods (Mayron, 1978).

The effects of malnutrition are dependent upon several variables: the age of onset, its duration and intensity, and sociocultural conditions. Malnutrition in a pregnant woman generally has little effect on the development of the fetus, because metabolic properties enable the fetus to obtain proteins at the mother's expense. During the first six months after birth, however, when brain cells are dividing, malnutrition can lead to a permanent reduction in their number and to irreversible effects. The effects of malnutrition that occur after that time, when cells are increasing in size rather than dividing, seems to be reversible with an adequate diet (Winick, 1969). When, however, a severely malnourished condition has persisted for several months in early childhood, even children who have been treated and cured show evidence of developmental lags in motor behavior, hearing, speech, social-personal behavior, problem-solving ability, eye-hand coordination, and categorizing skills. The magnitude of the deficits after rehabilitation appear to be related to the intensity and duration of the earlier malnutrition (Cravioto & Delicardie, 1975). When children who had survived such episodes were compared to their classmates and their siblings on school tasks (Richardson, Birch, & Hertzig, 1973), both they and their siblings did less well than other class members on tests of reading, spelling and arithmetic. That there were no differences between the scores of the survivors and their siblings suggests the effects of sociocultural variables. When median grades across school subjects, however, were studied, siblings' grades did not differ from those of their classmates, but the median grades of survivors continued to be significantly lower. Although methodological problems in studies of nutrition are overwhelming (because of the close interrelations between malnutrition and other variables), it is clear that these variables taken together as a measure of environmental deprivation affect constitutional well-being and may have a devastating effect on school performance.

As noted above, lack of early stimulation is a condition often closely associated with malnutrition. In fact, a marked reduction in exploratory behavior is a constant outcome of infant malnutrition (Cravioto & Delicardie, 1975). Very often both malnutrition and stimulation deficit are associated with the more global problems of mental retardation and cultural deprivation. Whether impoverished children should be included within the learning disability category is an issue which has seen considerable debate (see Symposium No. 9. "Disabled or disadvantaged: What's the difference?" *Journal of Learning Disabilities*, 1973, *7*, 381–421, and Cruickshank, 1977 for an overview of the arguments involved). No one disputes the fact that a lack of stimulation can lead to deficits in school-related functions. The question becomes whether the effects of the early stimulation deficit have affected overall potential, or whether their effect has lead to a reduced proficiency in the processing of information, while other areas of functioning have remained intact.

Other ecological variables have also been studied. Mayron (1978) suggested that electromagnetic radiation (including fluorescent lighting and television) *may* induce both learning and behavior problems. Although it is not often recognized, he argued that coal, petroleum, and natural gas derivatives may also be implicated.

The final environmentally based cause of learning disability to be examined here is an equally controversial one and, perhaps, in fact, begs the question of "the chicken and the egg" (Bender, 1968). Some authors argue that the emotional problems and psychological stress of the child result in and can be viewed as the cause of learning problems. Anxiety, for example, may lead to biochemical changes that are exhibited through behavior change (Mayron, 1978). Others argue the reverse, saying that the child's learning problems are the basis for the emotional problems and are the cause of any psychological stress. The controversy over which came first has created something of a dilemma for educators. Most operational definitions of learning disabilities attempt to make a distinction between *primary* and *secondary* emotional factors, that is, whether the emotional problems are the cause or the result of learning problems. The feasibility of making such distinctions with accuracy is, however, open to question.

Awareness of the interaction between behavior and learning problems is critical, because there is some suggestion that both factors may interplay in creating bias in the referral process. The ratio of boys to girls in special education classes is approximately 3 to 1 with some estimates running as high as 10 to 1 (Gold, 1979). Although there is considerable evidence that physiological traits are responsible for this preponderance of males, many (cf. Cruickshank, 1967; Hall & Keogh, 1978; Naiden, 1976) believe that female children are generally less threatening to teachers and so, although their learning problems may be equally severe, are not referred for special education placements. The differences in the ways that teachers and others in charge view boys and girls may, therefore, constitute a "cause" of learning disabilities. Oftentimes, behavior which, in general, is viewed as sick (e.g., excessive dependence) is seen as normal for female children. As Wheatley (1972) has pointed out, however, relatively little attention has been given to one of the most prominent characteristics of special education: the prevalence of males.

HISTORICAL LEGACY

No one who currently works in the field of learning disabilities would be apt to deny the wide variety of often conflicting opinions about what constitutes a learning disability, the goals and the nature of the interventions appropriate for use with learning disabled children, and who should be responsible for intervention, i.e., professionals from what fields. Until one examines the diverse orientations from which approaches to learning disabilities have arisen, the field appears to be in a state of chaos. But, like most apparent chaos, there is an underlying order which at least begins to explain some of the most readily identified trends. The trends were identified by Wiederholt.[1]

The Oral Language Thread

Much of the work that eventually blossomed into a concern for learning disabled children and youth stemmed from the investigation of adult, brain-damaged patients. In the early 1800s, several physicians, often neuropathologists, became interested in disorders of spoken language. Their efforts were largely directed toward charting the localization of speech functions in the human brain and in differentiating and characterizing various types of aphasic disorders. Gall, who is credited with being one of the first to investigate localization of brain functions, was eventually discredited as a charlatan because of his bias toward phrenology. Bouillaud and Broca, who separately continued to search for localized functions, argued that Gall had been mistaken in his identification of the specific areas of the brain responsible for speech functioning. Bouillard favored the frontal anterior lobes, while Broca recognized that the right and left hemispheres of the brain function differently and argued that disorders of spoken language were related to damage of the first and second temporal convolutions and the angular gyrus in the left hemisphere. Jackson took issue with Broca's findings, but agreed that the two brain hemispheres functioned differently and that damage to one (data had been collected to suggest that it could be either one) hemisphere could render a person speechless. He furthermore defined emotional versus intellectual speech and divided intellectual speech into internal and external language.

While these physicians were debating the nature and causes of aphasia, a number of prominent English and German physicians were developing *models* of language functioning. Bastian, for example, divided speech problems into two main types. He called the first amnesia, which referred to a type of speech

---

[1]Wiederholt (1974) summarized the historical antecedents of the field from the 1800s until 1960. This brief summary is heavily indebted to his work. The intent of the summary is to provide an overview of the significant influences in the field. Important issues are addressed at length in subsequent chapters.

disorder in which thinking was also implicated. Bastian differentiated amnesia from problems in which speech was affected without any concomitant loss of general intellectual functioning. Wernicke postulated four brain centers for speech disorders and suggested that aphasia resulted from disruptions in the neural pathways that connect auditory and motor speech areas in the brain.

Marie raised serious questions about both the work of Broca and Wernicke, and left the field in a somewhat chaotic state. Head's two volumes on aphasia attacked the popularly held beliefs that (1) the defects which characterized aphasia (e.g., motor, auditory, visual, and sensory) corresponded to components of the speech act itself, (2) that complex functions (e.g., speech, reading, writing, etc.) corresponded to particular locations in the brain, and (3) that speech-disturbing lesions would affect nonlanguage functions. He argued that the motor correlates of learning disorders were not related to the same kind of higher-order processing as language and that difficulties with the use of symbols (words, numbers, etc.) were specific and would not necessarily affect other aptitudes.

Like the results of any scientific endeavor, many of these postulates have served only as stepping stones from which more defensible hypotheses have been generated. It is the building of this foundation, as well as the time-honored findings, that make these contributions important to the field.

Concerns with spoken language continued through what Wiederholt called the *transition phase,* (the era 1930–1960 which spanned the early interest in etiology) and the *integration phase,* in which concern grew for the establishment of school programs for learning disabled children and youth. The focus was on using the etiological frameworks as the bases for the development of standardized tests and remedial programs.

Osgood's model, which will be more fully described in Chapter 8, was used as the basis for the development of the Illinois Test of Psycholinguistic Abilities (Kirk, McCarthy, & Kirk, 1968), a test which had a profound effect on the direction the field of learning disabilities was to take. The test was designed to fill the gap left by tests designed for classification purposes (such as IQ tests) by diagnosing strengths and weaknesses in specific, remediable, and educationally relevant abilities. Kirk and Kirk, as well as a number of other psychologists and educators (cf. Bush & Giles; Karnes; Dunn & Smith; Minskoff, Wiseman, & Minskoff; and Rupert) devised training programs to ameliorate the deficits defined by Osgood's model. Other, though somewhat less influential, tests of specific language abilities were based on a similar model developed by Wepman and his colleagues. One was a test of language modalities and the other a test of auditory discrimination. Eisenson developed a test for use with adolescents and adults who experienced language loss after normal language had been acquired. Myklebust labeled the problems of the children with whom he worked as psychoneurological learning disabilities. This was an important step in the field of learning disabilities, because it fostered the assumption that neurological dysfunctions of some kind underlay learning problems. McGinnis is best known for the development of a remedial program in which she taught the understanding and utilization of spoken language. Again, although many of these approaches currently persist, they are often more important for their having enabled other workers to go beyond them than for their own direct contributions.

People involved in the assessment and remediation of oral language skills became interested in the growth and development of programs for intervention in the 1960s. To expand upon Wiederholt's review, the present authors would like to suggest that two influences from psychology have affected these professionals and divided them. The first and earlier influence was behaviorism. The second was a combination of Chomskian psycholinguistics and cognitive psychology. Miller (1965) has used the term cognitive-psycholinguists to refer to persons of this persuasion.

The behaviorists reacted against the widespread use of hypothetical constructs as the sin qua non of conceptualization and intervention in learning disabilities. They decried theory and argued for the use of direct and continuous measures of behavior taken in situ as the basis for instructional programming. The behaviorists are unconcerned with labeling children. They argue, instead, for describing the strengths and weaknesses of children vis-à-vis academic disciplines. Haring and Bateman (1977), for example, argue that one should task-analyze the components of the oral language (or any other) process, find out which of them the child is capable of, and teach the remaining enabling functions until all have been mastered. The assumption is that oral language proficiency will emerge from mastery of its component skills.

The cognitive-psycholinguists, on the other hand, argued that language could not be taught directly, i.e., that one cannot list the rules for competent language usage and then teach them systematically to youngsters. They viewed language as being deduced by children from the examples that they hear around them. Rules are thought to be implicit rather than explicit. In fact, language is thought to be computed and recomputed rather than stored. Part of being competent in language usage, therefore, is the ability to select appropriate sentence structure, content, and the like, under a variety of constantly shifting circumstances. Chomsky (1965) noted that one of the critical factors in language acquisition is the ability to construct and understand sentences never heard before. It is this generative aspect of language that is difficult to teach using behavioral technology. The behaviorists view learning as additive, that is, one piece of information added to another, and to another, and to another, until ultimately, knowledge is acquired. The cognitive psycholinguists, on the other hand, view learning as the modification of existing knowledge. What is learned is, therefore, dependent on the child's competence to abstract what is meaningful. A child of about two and one-half, for example, may be instructed that "Daddy went to work." "Yes," he might agree, "Daddy goed to work." "No, daddy *went* to work." "Yes, he goed." The child seems unable even to hear the word "went." His implicit rule tells him that the past of *walk* is *walked,* that the past of *want* is *wanted,* and so he deduces that the past of *go* is *goed.* Nothing anyone else has to say convinces him that *went* sounds any better. If children select what is to be learned and construct their own knowledge, then, argue the cognitive-psycholinguists, behavioral assessment and intervention cannot constitute the most effective approach to teaching. The implications that such thinking has for education will be discussed in Chapter 3.

The Written Language Thread

Returning to Wiederholt's history, interest in the disruption of written language abilities (reading, writing, spelling, and arithmetic) began about the turn of the century among physicians whose patients could not read although vision, speech, and intelligence remained intact. They referred to this condition as *word blindness*. Hinshelwood, who had initially studied adult brain-damaged patients who had lost the ability to read, noticed similarities in the behavior of reading disabled children and, consequently, coined the term *congenital word blindness*. Hinshelwood noticed that his young patients recognized the letters of the alphabet, but were unable to remember words. He, therefore, diagnosed the problem as one of visual memory and articulated an intervention program which consisted of: (1) memorization of the letters of the alphabet, (2) spelling words aloud to force the use of intact auditory capacities, and (3) intensive practice in storing the visual memory of words.

Another important influence arose when Orton refuted Hinshelwood's hypothesis that a defect in the angular gyrus of the dominant hemisphere affected reading ability. Orton argued that reading was a complex activity requiring the interplay of a number of areas of the brain. Orton was convinced that normal adults used only one side of the brain in reading and that part of the brain was not important to vision, only to word pictures. Orton taught that the dominant side of the brain was determined by hereditary and environmental factors. He thought that reading disorders resulted from the inability of some children, which he estimated to be about 10 percent, to establish a pattern of one-sided dominance in brain control. He also noted that children with reading disorders were often poor speakers and spellers. These beliefs clearly influenced the direction his principles of remediation were to take. At the time the predominant approach to initial reading instruction was the "whole word" method. Since children with what Orton labeled "strephosymbolia" were not able to retain word pictures, Orton argued that they would need to be taught to read by the blending of the phonetic equivalents of printed letters. In addition, he advocated that all available linkages among vision, audition, and kinesthesis be taught, with emphasis on the kinesthetic components. Fernald, Monroe, Kirk, Gillingham, and Spalding extended the work of Orton by developing variations of multisensory intervention procedures which differed primarily according to the sensory system emphasized. Multisensory approaches dominated Wiederholt's transition phase.

Like the oral language thread, however, written language concerns fell under the influence of the behaviorists and the cognitivists, during the period following 1960, while intervention programs were being extended. The behaviorists devised reading programs that emphasized the sequential achievement of enabling behaviors. The cognitivists argued that reading is neither an aggregation of specific skills nor best learned as a logical, sequential progression of letter sounds and letter-sound combinations.

The Perceptual-Motor Thread

Interest in perceptual-motor processes has dominated the field of learning disabilities since its inception. Wiederholt traces its antecedents back to the work of Kurt Goldstein who worked with brain-injured soldiers during World War I. Goldstein, unlike the professionals working in oral and written language, was interested in total behavior. He noticed that his patients suffered from general symptoms, which included disruptions in attention, interpersonal relations, and the utilization of compensation. He described the inadequate and inconsistent behavior of the brain-damaged patient as a "catastrophic reaction," that frequently resulted in the patient's "shrinking" his environment to a manageable size and becoming excessively orderly.

At the Wayne County Training School in Northville, Michigan, Alfred Strauss and Heinz Werner studied brain-injured, mentally retarded (and later, nonretarded) children and confirmed that the characteristics noted by Goldstein in his adult patients could also be found in children—especially distractibility and distortion of figure-ground perception. Strauss noted, however, that there was one fundamental difference between Goldstein's adult patients and the children. Adults had lost a variety of specific abilities; the children never had had them at all. Furthermore, the perceptual, conceptual, and emotional problems which characterized the behavior of these children interfered with learning.

During the transition phase, many workers developed assessment and intervention techniques based on the findings of Strauss and Werner. A number of professionals devised tests and/or programs designed to detect and ameliorate perceptual problems, especially visual perception. Prominent among them are: Kephart, who viewed cognitive development as dependent on perceptual competence and developed a system of instruction designed to enhance perceptual-motor readiness; Getman, an optometrist who developed a remedial system parallel to Kephart's; Lehtinen, whose remedial principles focused on the organization of stimuli from a variety of sense modalities; Frostig, who developed a test and companion remedial program; Barsch, whose preoccupation with perceptual-motor functions lead to the development of a "movigenics" curriculum; and, finally, Cruickshank, who implemented four educational principles derived directly from the work of Strauss and Lehtinen: (1) reduction of extraneous stimulation, (2) confined space, (3) structured programming, and (4) increased saliency in instructional stimuli.

Because this approach to learning disabilities has little appeal for the behaviorists who eschew hypothetical constructs, they and the perceptual-motor theorists have been cast as two opposing camps. Mann (1979) is both ardently and eloquently opposed to the training of processes such as perception and memory. He suggested that these approaches found favor because special education consisted primarily in the making of potholders and popsicle bird nests (p. 538). Clearly, Mann (and other behaviorists) prefers to teach reading directly, rather than to focus on processes that are thought to lead at some later time to the ability to read. There has in fact been an upsurgence in interest in teaching cognitive processes, especially thinking skills (cf. Feuerstein, 1980). The National Institute of Education (1980) has even issued a request for proposals to researchers interested in evaluating the numerous approaches to teaching thinking that are now on the market. Although the newer approaches tend to be considerably more sophisticated than the static models currently popular in special education, the danger exists that once again the energies of both teachers and children will be diverted from the goals of schooling—reading, writing, and arithmetic—that this society has established. The present authors do not believe that one has to choose between teaching thinking or arithmetic, perception or reading, or memory or writing. Instruction in reading, writing, and arithmetic should make use of everything we know about cognitive processing (especially in terms of how children think and how they go about learning) and should necessarily lead to improved cognitive functioning.

Summary

Wiederholt's review has shown the field of learning disabilities to be influenced by three separate sets of professionals: those concerned with oral language, those interested in written language, and those coming from a perceptual-motor tradition. All three derivative approaches were evident in the early 1960s when the need to devise and implement programs for the learning disabled became apparent. The present authors have noted two additional influences that have affected and continue to affect each of the historical traditions: behavioral and cognitive psychology. Behaviorism is basically aimed at an objective view of human functioning, whereas cognitive psychology is directed toward learning about what happens in people's minds. Many writers who have been influential in the field of learning disabilities have begun to synthesize these two apparently contradictory approaches (cf. Bandura, 1977; Meichenbaum, 1977). These syntheses tend to view people as both active and reactive: as both responding to the environment and to transforming it through cognitive mediation (Berman, 1978). Mahoney (1977, p. 7) includes the following principles in his summary of the results of the cognitive-behavioral synthesis: (1) people respond primarily to what they "see" as the environment, rather than to some objective environment per se, (2) the way the environment is represented is a function of learning, in its broadest sense, and of the processes of learning, and (3) thoughts, feelings, and behaviors are causally related. It is the continued dialectical conflict between the behavioral and cognitive approaches which promises to characterize the field of learning disabilities over the next several years.

LEARNING DISABILITIES ACROSS THE LIFE SPAN

At each developmental level (preschool, elementary, adolescence, and adulthood), the concept and the ramifications of what constitutes a learning disability change. At no level is the exact nature of the learning disability clear or the result trivial. What is necessary, though often difficult, is to be aware of the overlap and the continuity of problems which exist throughout the life span of the learning disabled and the new ones that occur at different ages.

The Meaning of Learning Disabilities at the Preschool Level

At the preschool level, it is, by definition, inaccurate to use the term learning disabled to characterize children who are achieving at a lower level than their abilities would suggest or at a lower level than their peers. They have not "failed" nor have they shown a lack of ability to achieve in school content areas. For such immature children, growth rates may vary considerably. A very wide range of performance in any of a number of areas noted by PL 94-142 as precursors of learning disabilities—social, emotional, cognitive, motor, and perceptual—would be the rule rather than the exception. It is not until after indications that a low level of performance has been sustained well beyond normal limits that a child is thought to be deviant. Furthermore, diagnostic instruments and screening devices have tenuous predictive ability for mildly impaired children when used at the preschool level to predict later academic achievement. Yet, early consideration and intervention is a necessity. Rather than use the term learning disabled to describe the preschool population, the terms "high risk" or "vulnerable" are more accurate, since differential diagnosis is extremely difficult, and more appropriate, since those terms connote tentativeness.

Since academics have yet to enter the preschooler's life, the areas of concern for designating vulnerable children are different from those of older children. Of interest are the child's social development (interactions with both peers and adults), emotional development (appropriate affect and behavior), motor development (both fine motor and gross motor), cognitive development (practical problem-solving abilities and basic concepts), and language development (articulation, appropriate vocabulary, and syntax, and the ability to use language to achieve a variety of goals). These areas provide the foundation for later development.

With respect to this preschool population, PL 94-142 is, at best, a "flawed mandate" (Cohen, Semmes, & Guralnick, 1979). Whether or not preschool children (between the ages of three and five) receive special services is totally dependent upon the existing state educational regulations. Therefore, if a state does not have educational programs for preschool handicapped children or for nonhandicapped preschool children, then the state is not committed to the establishment of programs for the preschool handicapped.

The Meaning of Learning Disabilities at the Elementary School Level

At the elementary school level, what constitutes the focus of learning disabilities changes. The topics of concern in the preschool vulnerable child expand to include academic functioning in the content areas—reading, writing, and arithmetic. The term learning disabled becomes synonymous with difficulties in the acquisition of academic skills. Our concerns narrow from a general concern for overall functioning to a rather restricted view of functioning. The more focused nature of the learning disabilities label often places the school at the focal point of the child's life (and very often, the parent's lives). During the elementary years, the concern for learning disabled children becomes more intense. Specific diagnoses are developed, proper remedial programs are sought, and attempts are made to remediate the disabilities before the child leaves the elementary school.

For some children, the interventions employed at the elementary school level will be successful. Other children will not be given the proper remedial attention, will be missed in screening, or will not respond to interventions. The learning disabilities of these children will continue to exist into the high school years and usually throughout adult life.

The Meaning of Learning Disabilities at the Adolescent Level

The transition from elementary school to junior high and high school often proves extremely difficult for the learning disabled child. The child is expected to utilize the basic skills developed in the elementary school to learn new content. For the child who lacks basic skills, this can be devastating. The learning disabled adolescent must now cope with the necessity to acquire or improve basic skills, to learn additional content material, and at the same time, cope with increased social pressures (dating, peer approval, etc.), physical and emotional changes (pubescence), and preparation for adult life. Instruction and remediation for the learning disabled may take on a new look. Although many secondary programs continue to emphasize basic skills, other programs shift to vocational and/or similar survival skills (Wiederholt & McEntyre, in press).

Assessment of learning disabilities becomes difficult. Most tests have as their upper limits the beginning of adolescence and most diagnosticians have developed expertise primarily with younger children. The same is true of most learning disabilities teachers, since over two-thirds of the programs for the learning disabled are at the elementary school level (Martin, 1972).

Difficult as the life of the learning disabled adolescent may be, many will succeed in school through their own diligence, that of their families, and that of concerned school personnel. Changes are occurring (D'Alonzo & Miller, 1977). Many colleges are now recognizing the problems admissions tests pose for learning disabled youth and are developing special admissions procedures and special programs of study for them. A list of colleges offering such programs can be obtained from the Association for Children with Learning Disabilities. Still, many with aspirations to further schooling will be thwarted. Many will lack preparation. Many colleges still lack facilities to accommodate their needs. It is inevitable that learning disabled youth with little interest in vocational programs will find themselves in them. Many, however, will continue to remain unaided throughout adolescence.

At sixteen, children in most states can leave school and many learning disabled children are among those who leave. There has been considerable speculation about the prevalence of juvenile delinquency among this population. Research indicates that learning disabled youth commit the same *kinds* of crimes as do normal achievers, but the learning disabled commit more of them. It has also been suggested that the repercussions for having committed a misdemeanor are more stringent for those youth who are known to have concommitant learning problems (Keilitz, Zaremba, & Broder, 1979). It seems that judges respond more favorably to youths who commit crimes, but do well in school. It is as if school achievement constitutes a redeeming quality.

The Meaning of Learning Disabilities at the Adult Level

Adulthood will mean freedom for many of the learning disabled. The end of schooling will mean an end of having to signal to the world that they are unable to accomplish what most of the population can. But, for the most part, the effects of the learning disabilities will still remain. Trouble in filling out job applications, difficulty in making change, poor language, and a lack of knowledge about science and social studies do not disappear. Most will cope. They will seek their own level in society, living, working, and contributing to their communities in accordance with their abilities. Some will be able to come to terms with their disabilities, and some will fail to understand themselves and will continue seeking evaluations, diagnoses, and remedial instruction. Some, especially in rural areas where the technocracy is not so pervasive, will succeed in achieving their life goals.

SUMMARY

Although the field of learning disabilities has lacked an adequate definition from which to work, the definition of the National Advisory Committee on Handicapped Children (1968) has provided a framework which is acceptable to many professionals. The definition is primarily a definition by exclusion, since little consensus has been reached regarding criterion characteristics. The writers of PL 94-142 reexamined the definition, but adopted essentially the same definition that had been offered by the National Advisory Committee in 1968.

Across all definitions, there appear to be a number of common elements. These include reference to difficulties in school learning, uneven performance, physiological correlates, involvement of basic psychological processes, and exclusion from other categories of exceptionality. Although there is little disagreement about school learning and uneven performance, how to define the other three criteria is still controversial. Physiological correlates are often not easily demonstrable, and many professionals are against relying on inference from behavior to presume physiological impairment. With regard to the basic psychological processes, there is little agreement as to what they are, how they should be defined and evaluated, and what their importance is to academic achievement. Finally, there are those who would argue that it is extremely difficult to distinguish accurately between categories of mild exceptionality. It is no wonder then that prevalence figures vary from 1 percent to 15 percent or more, depending upon the criteria set for inclusion.

The specific causes of learning disabilities were separated into two very broad categories, those which are organically based and those which are environmentally based. Organically based causes involve neurological functioning, and include damage, dysfunction, maturational lag, genetic transmission, and biochemical disorders. Environmentally based causes include malnutrition, lack of stimulation, and psychological stress.

The final portion of the chapter suggested that the nature of learning disabilities changes with respect to the developmental level of the individual. Thus, the preschool child encounters a different set of problems than the adolescent, or for that matter, the elementary school child or adult.

Part of the diversity in definition, as well as in approach to the field can be explained by the routes professionals traveled to develop a concern for learning disabled persons. Some have training in the area of oral language, some in written language, and others in perceptual-motor skills. Early in the development of what was later to become the field of learning disabilities, came speculation, mostly on the part of physicians about the nature of the various problems. Later, about 1930, a new era began in which professionals began to measure and remediate skills and abilities hypothesized to be deficient in learning disabled persons. Beginning about 1960, we entered into a new phase: development of programs for management and intervention. This last phase has been influenced by at least two major movements in psychology: behavioral and cognitive psychology. Although behaviorism currently permeates most thinking in regard to conceptualization and intervention, the effects of cognitive psychology are beginning to become steadily more evident. Although the major thrust in this book is toward incorporating elements of that growing emphasis into special education programming, it would be misleading to present our view as totally cognitive. We do not, and this is a very important distinction, advocate that cognitive processes (thinking, including conservation, class-inclusion, and other abilities related to Piaget's research tasks; perception; memory; attention; etc.) become the goal of instruction. We are firmly committed to employing all of the knowledge we have about how children think and learn to devising better ways of teaching them (Duckworth, 1979). We are equally committed to teaching learning disabled children to master basic skills. What is unclear to us is how reading, writing, and arithmetic *can* be taught without regard for thinking, memory, etc. We see cognitive processes as the major ingredients of any education, not as ends in themselves. Our emphasis, therefore, on the cognitive approach stems from our having to counter the significant foothold that behavioral orientations have enjoyed in special education for decades.

SUGGESTED READINGS

Critchley, M., & Critchley, E. A. *Dyslexia defined.* Springfield, Ill.: Charles C Thomas, 1978.

Part B, Education of the Handicapped Act, **42** *Federal Register,* Aug. 23, 1977, 42473.

Supplemental procedures for evaluating specific learning disabilities. **42** *Federal Register,* Dec. 29, 1977, 65082.

Wiederholt, J. L. Historical perspectives on the education of the learning disabled. In L. Mann & D. A. Sabatino (Eds.), *The second review of special education.* Philadelphia, Pa.: JSE Press, 1974.

Chapter 2

Hyperactivity

INTRODUCTION

Hyperactivity has had a long and intimate relationship with learning disabilities. This relationship is based upon common knowledge of the links between hyperactivity and brain damage, and brain damage and learning disabilities. Because of this intervening link, many people believe hyperactivity and learning disability are the same problem. There is no evidence to suggest either that all learning disabled children are hyperactive or vice versa. The purpose of this chapter is fourfold. First, the need for a definition which is explicit and meaningful from a practical standpoint and allows for both qualitative and quantitative considerations will be addressed. Second, the various categories of suspected causes are delineated. Third, considerable space has been given to a discussion of the most widespread forms of treatment for hyperactivity, especially drug therapy. Included are considerations of diagnosis, treatment, and treatment outcomes. Finally, the chapter concludes with a discussion of treatments or interventions which are educationally oriented. The chapter is not meant to be exhaustive in its treatment. More extensive coverage is given in the list of suggested readings at the end of the chapter.

DEFINITION

Hyperactivity is a term which, unfortunately, is often used interchangeably with many other terms, for example, minimal brain dysfunction, hyperkinetic syndrome and, of course, learning disabilities. Such cavalier use of already vague terminology has clouded the concept of hyperactivity, its relevance to learning disabilities, and the selection of research and treatment procedures. It has, in addition, led many people to view hyperactivity as a disease like measles or pneumonia.

Hyperactivity is *not* a disease. It is a complex set of symptoms. Indeed, a diagnosis of hyperactivity is based on the accumulation of information related to a variety of manifestations. In defining hyperactivity, reference must be made to both the qualitative and quantitative aspects of behavior. Defining hyperactivity purely on the quantitative levels, is at best tenuous, since levels of *normal* activity have not been established either for children or adults. In addition, a quantitative definition of hyperactivity neglects questions related to the situational acceptability of the behavior, that is, the qualitative aspect (Koupernik, MacKeith, & Francis-Williams, 1975). Relevance, goal directedness, and appropriateness are three crucial factors in formulating a definition and diagnosis of hyperactivity. medical term not Educational

Ross and Ross (1976) describe the hyperactive child as one who "consistent-term! ly exhibits a high level of activity in situations in which it is clearly inappropriate, is unable to inhibit his activity on command, often appears capable of only one speed of response, and is often characterized by other physiological, learning, and behavioral symptoms and problems" (pp. 11–12).

Although there are persons who view hyperactivity and learning disabilities as synonymous, there is, in fact, no one-to-one correspondence. Although hyperactive children nearly always have learning problems, the majority of learning disabled children are *not* hyperactive. Furthermore, since the definition of learning disabilities requires that the learning problem itself be primary, specific, and unexplained by other classifications or labels, some authors argue that hyperactive children constitute a different population altogether. Knowledge of hyperactivity is needed by learning disabilities professionals who often must teach these children, so that they can ask the right questions, monitor referrals and treatment, and understand classroom behaviors. One must guard against the assumption, however, that a diagnosis of hyperactivity in any way determines the educational program. Hyperactivity is a *medical*, and *not* an educational classification. Similarly, parents and teachers must be careful to differentiate between excessive, undirected behavior and healthy, productive, and acceptable activity.

Most children, at some stage in their development, exhibit some of the characteristics of hyperactive children. In healthy children, however, these behaviors are limited both in their intensity and duration and they are directed toward some end. Koupernik and colleagues (Koupernik, MacKeith, & Francis-Williams, 1975) have listed occasions on which there might be a recognition of *overactivity* without a diagnosis of hyperactivity. These include: (1) children having either a chronological or mental age of two to three, (2) children who are especially bright and have a strong exploratory drive, (3) children reacting to environmental influences, such as deprivation or nagging, (4) troubled children suffering from depression or anxiety and, finally, (5) children suffering from infantile autism, epilepsy, etc. A diagnosis of hyperactivity should be reserved for children who evidence a high level of activity that serves no useful purpose, for children who resist training, and for cases where overactivity is accompanied by impulsivity, explosiveness, and variable moods.

CAUSES OF HYPERACTIVITY

Should one assume that a child's inability to deal with intense environmental stress (Bettleheim, 1973) or sociocultural, inner-city situations (McNamara, 1972) are at the root of the hyperactive behavior, the type of intervention strategy recommended would be quite different than if one assumes brain damage or dysfunction (Laufer & Denhoff, 1957). Competing etiological theories will be considered because of the treatment procedures they have spawned.

The competing causative theories are numerous and include neurological dysfunction, maturational lag, genetic factors, biochemical imbalance, lead poisoning, radiation stress, child rearing, learned behavior, food additives and allergies, and maternal smoking and drinking. Because of the controversial nature of drug therapy in the treatment of hyperactive children, and because of the emergence of educational strategies for educating hyperactive individuals, these topics will be dealt with in separate sections.[1]

Neurological Factors

One of the most widely held beliefs among educators is that brain damage underlies most cases of hyperactivity. A short digression into the historical events leading to this belief is in order. The position that brain damage could be inferred solely on the basis of observed motor behavior is thought to be the result of work done by the Frenchman, Ernest Duyere (Koupernik, MacKeith, & Francis-Williams, 1975). In his work of 1925, Duyere postulated that motoric behavior disorders (in his words, *débilité motrise*) were the result of specific brain lesions and that the existence of such lesions could be inferred from overt behavior. This somewhat tenuous relationship was furthered by the classic work of Strauss and Lehtinen (1947) in which tentative links were established between hyperactivity (as the overt behavior) and brain damage. In their 1955 work, Strauss and Kephart went one step further and asserted that brain damage could be inferred from the behavioral symptoms of hyperactivity. In addition, they suggested that the term *minimal brain damage* be used to describe the condition.

---

[1]The authors have avoided the terms *hyperactive syndrome* and *hyperkinetic syndrome* because considerable controversy has been raised concerning their appropriateness (Ross & Ross, 1976; Sroufe, 1975).

The effect, now over twenty years later, is that many tend to equate hyperactivity with brain damage, though that was not the original intent. Fewer than one out of ten children referred for hyperactivity, however, have medical histories indicating possible neurological involvement (Steward & Olds, 1973).

The intent here is not to deny the coexistence of hyperactivity and neurological impairment or even the possible causative nature which neurological dysfunction may play in hyperactivity. It is rather to stress that hyperactivity, in and of itself, is insufficient evidence upon which to develop a diagnosis of brain injury (Benton, 1975).

The role of central nervous system dysfunction in hyperactivity is, nonetheless, an important area of consideration and an area of considerable theory building. Although a diagnosis of brain damage can seldom be substantiated, many researchers are seriously entertaining the possibility that some type of *brain dysfunction* is implicated in hyperactivity. Some interesting possibilities have been identified. Gellner (1959) proposed that a malfunction of the midbrain structures may interfere with hyperactive children's ability to process certain types of incoming stimuli and may, therefore, render them understimulated. Such children may engage in increased tactile and motor behaviors as a means of compensation. Other possibilities include the inability to balance excitory and inhibitory response mechanisms (Flynn & Hopson, 1972) and fixation at a motor-tactile stage of development (Zaporozhets, 1957).

Biochemical Disorders

Perhaps the most complete theory of why such brain dysfunction may occur is that developed by Wender (1971, 1972). He supports the idea that hyperactivity results from the brain's inability to balance inhibitory and excitory responses. Specifically, Wender argues that chemicals which act as neurotransmitters in the inhibitory system, specifically noradrenaline, are lacking in sufficient quantity in hyperactive children. Since the neurotransmitters provide the medium through which the impulse must travel from the presynaptic to the postsynaptic neuron, children with deficient quantities of such chemicals would be expected to have difficulty inhibiting behavior. A more active level of behavior would result, since there would be a lack of balance between inhibitory and excitatory systems.

Although Wender's theory is interesting, it has been demonstrated only with rats. Wender has provided evidence that as an organism matures, an increase in monoamine output is noticed. This finding at least tentatively gives an explanation for what appears to be a decrease in hyperactive behavior with increasing age. A disturbing aspect of Wender's theory, however, is that it depends upon the assumption of a paradoxical drug effect, which is, itself, a questionable concept. The role of theory builders is a difficult task at best and although Wender's position is one of the best articulated, it is still open to considerable question (Sroufe, 1975).

Maturational Lag

Another explanation for hyperactivity is maturational lag. This concept suggests that there is no brain damage, no malformation, no deviation of brain structure.

It suggests that findings are abnormal only in function and only with respect to the child's age. If the child were younger, the "findings would be regarded as normal. They indicate a relative delay in some aspect of neurological maturation as a result of slowed evolution of cerebral control of the relevant activity" (Kinsbourne, 1973a, p. 268). Basic to the notion of maturational lag is the idea that the older hyperactive child is performing at a level commensurate with that exhibited by or expected of younger nonhyperactive children. Studies of the development of hyperactive children do indeed show significant lags in development, when these children are compared to normal children of similar chronological and mental age.

There is, in the maturational lag hypothesis, an implicit assumption that as the hyperactive child matures, the hyperactive behavior will decline. The general finding has been that although some of the symptoms change, hyperactivity persists into adolescence. The prognosis for remission of symptoms and increased school achievement is poor (Mendelson, Johnson, & Steward, 1971; Prout, 1977; Weiss, Minde, Werry, Douglas, & Nemeth, 1971). Not all studies, however, report the continued existence of developmental delays. For example, Houghton and Tabachnick (1979) investigated the responses of normal and hyperactive children (boys) with respect to the classic Muller-Lyer illusion in which the child is asked to state which of two apparently unequal line segments is longer ⇌. By age eight to nine, no significant differences were evidenced between the groups, though the peak age for the illusion was six for the nonhyperactive children and seven for the hyperactive children.

Maturational lag has been offered as an explanation for learning disabilities in general, and is not restricted to hyperactivity. Hyperactivity constitutes only one possible manifestation of development lag. Specific learning problems may constitute another. As with most neurological explanations, it is difficult to isolate maturational lag (because it must be inferred) as a *cause* of either learning disabilities or hyperactivity. There is considerable evidence, however, to substantiate the co-occurrence of delayed functioning and learning disabilities.

Genetic Factors

Of increasing concern is the possibility of some type of genetic transmission of hyperactivity. This transmission may take the form of predisposition towards hyperactivity, or the transmission of conditions known or thought to be related to hyperactivity (e.g., chemical imbalance). The question addressed here is not *what* is transmitted, but rather *whether* genetic transmission is a viable hypothesis.

Current thinking is that a polygenic model of genetic transmission is the most adequate explanation of available data (Cantwell, 1976). This conclusion follows considerable testing of the competing theories to be discussed. These include chromosome anomaly, simple autosomal dominant links, simple autosomal recessive links, and sex linkage. Warren, Karduck, Bussaratid, Steward, and Sly (1971), in what appears to be the only study to date investigating the chromosomal characteristics of hyperactive children, failed to find any signs of chromosomal anomaly. Sex-linked genetic transmission refers to transmission by means of a single recessive gene. Investigations of the simple autosomal recessive gene model (Cantwell, 1972; Morrison & Steward, 1971; Omenn, 1973) fail to support recessive transmission. A recessive gene model would predict that neither of the parents would manifest the disorder while 25 percent of the offspring of the hyperactive children would be hyperactive. The excessive number of parents of hyperactive children who are, themselves, hyperactive, places the observed percentages at variance with the model. Thus, neither a recessive model nor a sex-linked model appears valid.

The argument for a simple autosomal dominant gene would suggest three criteria: (1) one of the parents *must* exhibit the disorder; (2) no sex preference should be indicated; and (3) the disorder should not skip generations. Since each of these criteria is violated, the data do not support a dominant transfer theory (Cantwell, 1975, 1976).

Polygenic inheritance refers to genetic transmission when more than one gene is involved. Transmission is dependent upon the presence of either the correct number of genes or the correct combination of genes. Perhaps the best-known trait attributed to polygenetic transmission is intelligence. Like intelligence, traits that result from polygenetic transmission are thought to be normally distributed in the population. Polygenic models, however, are difficult to verify and only one study is available which supports the theory of polygenic transmission (Morrison & Steward, 1971). Perhaps the search for a genetic cause, although currently preferred, may be misleading. It may well be that future investigations will find that hyperactivity is genetically determined in only a subgroup of the hyperactive population or will lead to the discovery of several genetically distinct subgroups (Cantwell, 1976).

Child Rearing

Hyperactivity may be stress-related. That is, the demand of environmental situations may be such that the child is unable to cope effectively. The source of the child's problems would be bidirectional in the sense that, while the environment impinges on the child, the child affects the environment.

In the eyes of some researchers (cf. Bettleheim, 1973), the source of the impinging stress is the child's parents. The child's stress is the product of having had demands placed to which, because of possible constitutional factors, the child is unable to respond in an appropriate manner. In response, the child is driven to hyperactivity. This kind of argument is one-sided; the child is the victim of the environment, but never the antagonist. This view neglects the influence of the child on significant others in the environment.

A difficult child has the capability of alienating even his parents by setting up a situation where understanding begins to wane and where emotional support is not guaranteed (Thomas, Chess, & Birch, 1968). The parents, in their confusion, become less responsive and so, in turn, does the child, again disturbing the parents and increasing the distance between them. A point is reached where the child no longer has emotional support, and may lose what few effective strategies for dealing with stress he or she previously had available. The initiation of such relationships may actually be the work of the child. It may be that the child's problem brings about the poor relationship and not that the child falls victim to the poor relationship (Huessy, 1967).

The effects of any relationship are rarely one-sided. There is no reason to assume that the problem of family stress with the hyperactive child is one-sided either.

Learned Behavior

Within recent years, interest in hyperactivity as an adaptive, learned behavior has been increasing. Hyperactivity appears to be a means of control. It sometimes appears to be a way of manipulating the behavior of others and sometimes a way of stimulating one's self.

Hyperactive behavior appears to be a powerful means of control, especially over family members. Much of a family's energy and resources are often directed toward a hyperactive child. Because they are so difficult to manage, these children often get considerably more attention than their siblings and classmates. When a problem becomes too difficult to solve, the hyperactive child has a built-in excuse for not succeeding. There are, consequently, many privileges that accrue to hyperactive children.

Another way of viewing hyperactivity as learned is to view it as seeking stimulation (Gellner, 1959; Zentall, 1975). Zentall (1975) has named this approach the *optimal stimulation theory:*

> The increase in activity typically associated with the hyperactive child may well be an attempt to increase insufficient stimulation, rather than being a consequence of overwhelming stimulation. Using this model, activity can be seen as a regulator which maintains optimal stimulation for the child. (p. 552).

Such an approach has the benefit of looking at hyperactive behavior from a positive viewpoint. The behavior takes on a meaningful connotation.

A third type of "learned" hyperactivity may result from the child's having observed others who are hyperactive. Children will modify their behavior to emulate a very active model (Bandura, Ross, & Ross, 1961, 1963; Kaspar & Lowenstein, 1971). Still another type of learned behavior is the response to failure (Cunningham & Barkley, 1978). The hyperactive behavior noted in some children may be their response to continued failure in the classroom. Increased off-task behavior may be the result of reduced expectations of reward. Hyperactivity (off-task behavior) becomes the response of the child. Rather than engage in the class-related work, the child behaves in an aversive manner. As Cunningham and Barkley (1978) suggest, this has the effect of being cyclical in nature with off-task behavior leading to less reward which, in turn, leads to more off-task behavior.

Control, stimulation seeking, modeling, and avoidance all appear as viable hypotheses to explain hyperactivity. Each may require essentially unique treatment, for while operant conditioning may be effective to reduce activity acquired through modeling, another technique may be required to reduce behavior which constitutes optimal stimulation. The types of learned behaviors may characterize different subgroups of hyperactive children.

Lead Poisoning

In one of its mild manifestations, the ingestion of lead (either directly or indirectly) may lead to hyperactive behavior, and to retardation and death in its more severe manifestations (Vaughan, McVay, & Nelson, 1973). The sources of lead are primarily lead paint (though now banned for use), industrial waste, and gasoline emissions. That elevated lead levels coexist with hyperactive behaviors has been established. Baloh and Strum (1975) found significantly more hyperactivity in children with elevated lead levels than in normal children. Baloh, Strum, and Landrigan, and Whitworth (1975) and Perino and Ernhart (1974) noted perceptually oriented problems in children with elevated lead levels.

Questions arise concerning the idea of "normal" lead limits, and the treatment of the levels. First, let us consider the idea of "normal." As pointed out by Lin-Fu (1972), the laboratory idea of normal is that, "the lowest unit blood lead level diagnostic of clinically manifest lead poisoning . . . is the upper limit of normal" (p. 22). Any elevated lead level, however, may have an effect on the individual. Perhaps a continuous range of lead levels is the most appropriate conceptualization. David (1974) and David, Clark, and Voeller (1972) suggest that the predisposition of the host body may effect the idea of individual toxicity. Referred to as the body's "lead burden," this could account for behavioral anomalies in children below toxic levels. David and his colleagues hypothesized that low-level lead (nontoxic region) over a long period of time may cause hyperactivity and minimal brain dysfunction. They also indicated that another possible explanation would be that lead must be present in the body for hyperactive behavior to occur. Children who had received lead-level therapy and whose hyperactive behavior had subsided were noted again to have increased lead levels when behavioral manifestations of hyperactivity reoccurred. It may very well be that the hyperactive child has some type of constitutional predisposition to collect lead.

Lead toxicity is treated by removing the existing lead from the body. The individual is given a chelating agent which has the effect of acting like a magnet and removing lead atoms from the kidney and liver. The most common chelating agent is known as penicillamine. After ingestions of penicillamine, blood samples and urine specimens are analyzed for traces of lead. If the treatment has gone well, high levels of lead should be noted in the samples. With early detection, the widespread damage of lead poisoning can be averted.

Radiation Stress

The idea of radiation stress is at least as old as color television. The fact that "soft x-rays" are given off by the cathode of the color TV has been a concern since the federal government placed a restriction on acceptable leakage under the 1968 Radiation Control Act. Similar effects may result from exposure to fluorescent lights (Ott, 1974). In a series of studies (Mayron, Ott, Nations, & Mayron, 1974; Ott, 1976), numerous indices of remission of symptoms were found when the fluorescent lights were shielded. At this time, the data on radiation stress is meager. Until further research is done on both the sources of stress and the type of child affected, the findings remain speculative.

Allergens

A number of related topics will be discussed in this section. Although considerable publicity has been given to the effects of food additives and some naturally occurring food compounds, other topics are of equal importance. These include the influence of vitamin deficiency and the effects of hypoglycemic reactions. In addition, evidence is growing which suggests a link between the more usual types of allergic reactions (such as mold spores and pollen) and hyperactive behavior. It is well documented, for example, that mood and general behavior changes (dysphoric manner, irritability, etc.) accompany an individual's reaction to allergens. These types of reactions may quite readily be interpreted by teachers, parents, and others as "hyperactive." The following discussions will focus on the major issues in seeking relationships between hyperactivity and allergens (food compounds and additives, vitamins, and hypoglycemia).

The Feingold K-P Diet   Feingold (1976) proposed that some children's hyperactivity is a behavioral manifestation of an allergic reaction to food additives, primarily those involving colors and flavorings. The diet proposed by Feingold has been referred to as the K-P Diet (after the Kaiser-Permanente Medical Center). The thrust of the diet is the elimination of *all* salicylate-containing food, both natural and artificial, and other items such as aspirin and toothpaste or toothpowder. Natural salicylate-containing foods include almonds, cherries, cucumbers, oranges, strawberries, tea, and tomatoes. Parents' supervision of the diet is essential and parents are encouraged to create substitute foods at home.

The evidence regarding whether the diet works has been relatively inconclusive. Few studies have been conducted, and results seem to indicate equivocal findings. One of the biggest controversies concerns the extent of success claimed. Feingold's original success figures indicated 50 percent of those involved showing complete remission, while 75 percent improved enough to discontinue drug therapy (1975). In his 1976 article, his figures for success are somewhat lower, reported in the 30 percent to 50 percent range. Though support for the diet has been found in research conducted by both Feingold and others (Connors, Goyette, Southwick, Lees, & Andrulonis, 1976; Cook & Woodhill, 1976; Food Research Institute, 1976), the significance of the data is under question. Spring and Sandoval (1976) question the interpretation of the findings of the Connors et al. study. In the Connors' study, only one of fifteen hyperactive children showed very significant improvement, while four children were rated as moderately improved. Connors tentatively concluded that there may exist a subcategory of hyperactive children who do, in fact, respond to the K-P Diet. In the study reported by the Food Research Institute (1976), no significant changes in school behavior were evident, though some changes in parent and teacher ratings did occur. Even when gains are demonstrated, they are nowhere in the range of 30 percent to 50 percent suggested by Feingold. There are some exceptions to the low response rate. Rapp (1978) reported that eleven of seventeen hyperactive children continued to show marked behavioral improvement after food and dye alteration to their diet. These improvements were noted to be exhibited some twelve weeks after the initiation of the program. The evidence suggests a mild, positive effect, but until further research establishes consistency of results and some attempt is made to identify, in advance, children who will respond favorably, the diet should be implemented with caution.

Concerns arise over the effect of the diet upon the family constellation. The K-P Diet requires strict adherence, to the point where a restructuring of the family may be necessary. The burden of success rests with the parent. As indicated by the Nutrition Foundation (1975), "there can be no question but that the total regimen significantly alters the structure and dynamics of the families. . . ." Questions persist not only for the efficacy of the diet, but also for the effects of implementing the diet on others in the environment.

Clearly, the controversy of the treatment, and of the theory in general, continues. Adler (1978) has called for continued research in this area, stressing the meager knowledge of the effects of metabolism and nutrition on human behavior. The government policy on research with hyperactive children (Lipman, 1977) suggests that "the review of completed and ongoing research vis-à-vis the Feingold hypothesis is characterized as 'inconclusive,' but the weight of evidence is taken as indicating that the 'question' is worth additional study."

In May 1979, the American Council on Science and Health issued a pamphlet in which the following statement was contained (p. 5):

> Hyperactivity will continue to be a frustrating problem until research resolves the questions of its cause, or causes, and develops an effective treatment. The reality is that we still have a great deal to learn about this condition. We do know now, however, that diet is not the answer. It is clear that the symptoms of the vast majority of the children labeled "hyperactive" are not related to salicylates, artificial food colors, or artificial flavors. The Feingold diet creates extra work for the homemakers and changes the family lifestyle . . . but it doesn't cure hyperactivity.

Hypoglycemia and Hyperactivity   In a related area, Hawley and Buckley (1974) noted that hypoglycemic conditions have been related to hyperactivity. Their contention is that some hyperactive children consume excessive amounts of sugar and starch and that this could be a causative factor in hyperactivity.

Although much has been written in the press and popularized in magazines, questions still exist regarding the effect of antihypoglycemic diets on the metabolic system. The recent research fails to support the effectiveness of the low carbohydrate antihypoglycemic diet (Kershner & Grekin, 1976). In fact, Kershner (1978) hypothesized that this diet may have adverse effects rather than positive ones.

Megavitamins Another area which has come to the fore recently has been the use of megavitamins for the control of learning disabilities and hyperactivity. Kershner (1978) is rather outspoken in opposition to this procedure. Two important arguments can be made against the use of megavitamins, both of which deal with the feasibility of the theory. First, the theory rests upon the belief that there exists a substantial number of people who are vitamin-dependent, that is, they are in need of quantities of vitamins in excess of the rest of the population. Kershner questions this hypothesis, because the evolutionary process would not have allowed for this possibility: natural selection would have eliminated this vitamin-dependent population. Second, with the status of available research, the only way in which such a theory could be developed is through inference of prior causal relations, since diagnostic procedures for identification prior to initiating therapy do not exist. Kershner (1978) therefore questions the theory in the "absence of a valid diagnostic procedure which would enable clinicians to identify the vitamin-dependent . . . child and which would lead to realistic estimates of the actual incidents of such disorders," (p. 14).

Clearly, consensus does not appear to be forthcoming in the immediate future concerning the relationship of allergens, hyperactivity, and learning disabilities. Perhaps the only area of consensus at this time is in the call for additional research.

Maternal Smoking and Drinking

In their review, Ross and Ross (1976) elaborated upon an area of concern which, until recently, has failed to be identified. They reported that both smoking and drinking during pregnancy can lead to permanent, irreversible damage of the fetal central nervous system (CNS). In addition to physical and mental anomalies, the effects of smoking may decrease the amount of oxygen to the fetal tissue during pregnancy (Denson, Nanson, & McWatters, 1975). At any rate, a higher incidence of hyperactive children was found among mothers who smoked heavily. It is important to note, however, that the linkage between smoking and hyperactivity is, at this time, correlational and not causative.

Maternal drinking has been researched by Jones, Smith, Streissguth, and Myranthopoulos (1974). They have estimated that one-third of the children of mothers who drink heavily during pregnancy will evidence some type of CNS, physical, or mental trauma. Because of the extreme vulnerability of the fetal brain, many of these children do not survive. Many of those who do appear to exhibit hyperactive behavior.

Summary

The preceding has suggested a number of possible causes for hyperactive behavior. Only one thing remains certain after all the research is reviewed: the available findings can lead to few reliable conclusions. At best, the research has given us direction for future research and may serve to stimulate the concerted effort on the part of research scientists, educators, psychologists, and medical personnel that will be needed to solve such a complex problem.

TREATMENT OF HYPERACTIVE CHILDREN

Until now, our discussion of hyperactivity has been devoid of any consideration of the possible treatment programs related to the area. The subsequent discussion of treatments will focus on two rather large areas: drug therapy and educational strategies used to control or modify hyperactive behavior.

Drug Therapy With Hyperactive Children

Although the use of psychotropic drugs precedes this discussion by some thousands of years, the first recorded use of medication in the control of hyperactivity which concerns us is the study of Bradley (1937) on the use of stimulant drugs to effect change in hyperactive children. Although Bradley is given the credit for discovering that stimulant medication has some effect on the hyperactive child, two other researchers, Molitch and Eccles, published similar findings in the same year. Bradley's discovery has been both a source of joy and anguish for the past forty years. Questions have arisen as to the proper medication, the dosage, the type of child for whom the medication works, and the explanation given for the effect noted.

This discussion will be limited to the effects of stimulant drugs used for the control of hyperactivity. Other drugs, however, including tranquilizers and anticonvulsants, are also used singly or in combination, for the control of hyperactivity, but they constitute a minor part of therapy programs. Table 2-1 has been provided for easy reference and contains the following information: trade name, generic name, the use for which the drug is normally given, and the side effects usually noted.

The two most widely used stimulant drugs are dextroamphetamine (Dexedrine) and methylphenidate (Ritalin). The first, dextroamphetamine, is the drug originally used by both Bradley and Molitch and Eccles, in 1937. It is usually given to the child in the form of a tablet (limited time of duration) or a capsule (time-release type). The dosages vary, but usually begin with 5 mg being given at each of three meal times. The drug is usually not given before bedtime in the belief that the child will be unable to sleep. Recent work by Kinsbourne (1973b), however, suggests that quite the opposite is true. The child who is *not* given the medication before bed may, in fact, undergo mild withdrawal symptoms. He, therefore, suggests that the medication be continued around the clock.

The side effects which have been noted for dextroamphetamine include insomnia, diarrhea, headache, skin rash, dizziness, loss of appetite, weight loss, and depression. In addition, long-term effects which have been noted include growth suppression and disturbances in heart rate.

The second drug, methylphenidate (Ritalin), is very similar in effect to dextroamphetamine. Whereas the scheduling of the dosages is relatively the same, methylphenidate appears to be the less potent drug (Ross & Ross, 1976). In addition to the effects related to the use of dextroamphetamine, methylphenidate also has the possible side effects of nervousness, nausea, and abdominal pain.

Perhaps the most confusing aspect of drug usage is the determination of the precise effect that the drug has on the organism. Bradley's original work described the stimulant effect as calming in the hyperactive. This effect was considered "paradoxical," because the same substance appeared to "speed up" the responses in adults and nonhyperactive children. The paradox, if you will, is based on behavioral manifestations which have been interpreted as indicating that the drug is acting differently on hyperactive and nonhyperactive individuals. The behavioral manifestation, however, should not be construed as evidence that the drug is having a differential *pharmacological* effect (Ross & Ross, 1976). Only *one* study has ever been completed that directly compared stimulant effects in both normal and hyperactive children (Shetty, 1971). Both groups manifested the *same* side effects, the *same* improvement in performance, and the *same* favorable drug response when brain activity was measured. No evidence of enhanced cognitive or learning performance was noted in any of the populations under investigation. The effect of the drug is associated with producing a better integrated response, thereby giving the *impression* of increased mental capabilities. No evidence indicates a decrease in activity level per se.

The idea of the "paradoxical effect" appears, therefore, to be suspect on at least two counts: (1) there is no evidence that the hyperactive population is affected in a way different from other populations; and (2) the effect of the drug has more to do with the ability of the individual to respond in an integrative manner than with sedation of activity level.

> Until a definitive experiment is conducted, it is a misnomer and is detrimental to progress in the field to use the term *paradoxical* to refer to the more appropriate and better integrated responses that occur in some hyperactive children as a function of stimulant medication, because it suggests a difference in brain functioning of the hyperactive child that has not been established (Ross & Ross, 1976, p. 117, italics theirs).

Effectiveness of Stimulant Therapy

Though questions remain about the nature of the effects and side effects, drugs are nonetheless in widespread use. A general question which must be considered is how drug therapy becomes the method of choice for a given child. "The presence or absence of neurological abnormalities have been found to be unreliable predictors of the response of the child to medication" (Lerer & Lerer, 1977, p. 223). No reliable predictor of success *is* currently available regarding the

Table 2-1 Drugs Used in Control of Hyperactivity

	Stimulants		
Trade name	**Generic name**	**Use**	**Side effect**
Cylert	Pemoline	Control of minimal brain dysfunction symptoms	Insomnia, anorexia
Dexedrine	Dextroamphetamine	Control of minimal brain dysfunction symptoms, i.e., short attention span, distractability, impulsivity, or hyperactivity. Used in some types of depression.	Palpitation, dizziness, anorexia, weight loss, diarrhea, headache, rash
Ritalin	Methylphenidate	See above	Suppressed growth, insomnia, anxiety, nausea, dizziness, anorexia, abdominal pain, weight loss
Tofranil	Imipramine	Control of symptoms of depression	Nervousness, skin rash, nausea, vomiting, fatigue, constipation, convulsions, drowsiness
	Major tranquilizers		
Trade name	**Generic name**	**Use**	**Side effect**
Compazine	Prochlorperazine	Control tension and anxiety	Drowsiness, dizziness, blurred vision
Haldol	Haloperidol	Control of psychotic disorders and Gilles de la Tourette's syndrome	Anorexia, nausea, & vomiting, diarrhea, constipation, hypersalivation, blurred vision
Trade name	**Generic name**	**Use**	**Side effect**
Mellaril	Thioridazine	Management of psychotic disorders, depression, agitation, hyperactivity, or aggressiveness	Drowsiness, nausea, vomiting, nasal stuffiness, blurred vision

selection of drug therapy as a treatment, although Kinsbourne, Swanson, and Herman (1979) have been developing procedures for evaluating the responsiveness of children in a brief period of time. Kinsbourne (1973b) has also found that children who respond favorably to the medication respond differently on learning tasks when they are under the effect of the drug than when they are not.

Once drugs have been selected as the treatment method, the children must be watched very carefully to determine whether they will have adverse reactions to the drug. The range of reported positive response without adverse side effects

Table 2-1 *(continued)*

Stelazine	Trifluoperazine	Management of psychotic disorders, anxiety, tension, or agitation	Drowsiness, dizziness, rash, dry mouth, insomnia, fatigue, blurred vision, anorexia
Thorazine	Chlorpromazine	Management of psychotic disorders, agitation, hyperactivity, or aggressiveness	Similar to above
Pheno-barbital	Phenobarbital	Control convulsive states	Rash

Minor tranquilizers

Trade name	Generic name	Use	Side effect
Librium	Chlordiazepoxide	Control of anxiety and tension	Drowsiness, dizziness
Valium	Diazepam	Relief of anxiety, tension, agitation, and apprehension	Drowsiness, fatigue, skin rash, headaches

Anticonvulsants

Trade name	Generic name	Use	Side effect
Dilantin	Diphenylhydantoin	Control of seizures	Slurred speech, mental confusion
Tegretol	Carbamazepine	Control of seizures	Dizziness, drowsiness, nausea, and vomiting
Pheno-barbital	Phenobarbital	Control convulsive states	Rash
Benadryl	Diphenhydramine	Antihistimine, antiemetic, sedative	Drowsiness, confusion, nervousness, restlessness, vomiting, nausea, stuffiness

is between 30 percent and 70 percent (Conrad & Insel, 1967). Most studies, however, indicate a positive response rate of between 30 percent and 50 percent (Fish, 1969). Another 10 percent to 20 percent have positive responses, but suffer some side effects. Ten percent have what might be classified as negative responses. Given that some children will respond more favorably than others to the medication, and that the diagnosis of who will and will not respond is unreliable, how does such widespread prescription of drugs take place?

Both the diagnosis of hyperactivity and the selection of drug therapy as the method of treatment are made subjectively (Neisworth, Kurtz, Ross, & Madle,

1976). The physician has to rely upon the reports of parents and teachers, which we might say places hyperactivity in the eyes of the beholder. The physician must rely upon relatively inaccurate and subjective rating scales (Poggio & Salkind, 1979) and is often faced with less than adequate monitoring systems. In sum, the main source of information regarding the child's need for medication and the child's response to medication is outside the control of medical personnel. Most physicians are restrained in their dispensing of medication, but some have had a tendency to dispense drugs without careful implementation and monitoring of drug therapy (Ross & Ross, 1976).

The communication system between the physician and the teacher of the child is rarely optimal and, in most cases, is nonexistent. Teacher/physician communication occurs adequately between 15 percent (Okolo, Bartlett, & Shaw, 1978) and 18 percent of the time (Weithorn & Ross, 1975), while 27 percent of the time, a total lack of communication exists (Weithorn & Ross, 1975). Though only a small percentage of teachers received requests for evaluative reports, most thought that they had important information which should have been shared with the physician (Okolo, Bartlett, & Shaw, 1978). Though the teacher is with the child for the major portion of the child's day in school and observes firsthand the effect of the drug on the child's behavior in class, it is the school nurse who has the most contact with the physician. In fact, 66 percent of the nurses surveyed reported being contacted by the physician at the start of the drug therapy, while 76 percent indicated that they received requests for evaluative reports (Okolo, Bartlett, & Shaw, 1978). Although the attending physician might assume he or she is getting information from the teacher through the nurse, in view of the teacher's direct contact with the child, it is likely that more accurate and informative reporting could be obtained directly from teaching personnel.

Given that a child is placed on medication, what is the effect on subsequent learning? If we talk of learning in general, and seek evidence regarding improvement, the evidence is predominantly negative. Sroufe (1975) pointed out that studies involving the establishment of drug therapy to improve problem solving or achievement in academic settings have been conspicuously absent. A review of 120 drug-related investigations on hyperactivity (Barkley & Cunningham, 1978) revealed that only 17 studied measures of academic performance (with 52 different tests and measures used). The performance of hyperactive children on 82 percent of these measures was unaffected by the use of stimulant drugs.

Regarding the amount of activity and appropriateness of behavior, the degree of improvement is directly related to the demands of the situation and the person evaluating the children. For example, while little research supports the contention that activity level, per se, is decreased, there are indications that in situations in which a demand for compliance is high (such as in a highly structured classroom) the behavior of the hyperactive child is better controlled (Hoffman, Engelhardt, Margolis, Polizos, Waizer, & Rosenfeld, 1974; Knights

& Hinton, 1969). Similarly, extraneous activity and irrelevant behavior decrease even within playroom settings (Rapoport, Lott, Alexander, & Abramson, 1970). At the same time, no evidence of decrease in free play or unstructured situations has been found. Apparently, the improvement in behavior is situation specific.

An area open to question, but which is of great importance, is that of state-dependent learning. (This refers to learning which occurs under a certain condition, such as medication, the effects of which are evidenced only under that condition.) If state-dependent learning occurs with hyperactive children on medication, long-term drug treatment programs would be indicated (Kinsbourne, 1973b).

In sum, research is just now beginning to answer questions regarding the prediction of children who will benefit from drug treatment, management procedures, and the necessary duration of treatment and its effects. "While the drugs seem to facilitate the short-term management of hyperactive children, they have little impact on long-term, social, academic, or psychological adjustment of these children" (Barkley, 1977, p. 158).

Educational Treatments

A more recent approach to the management of hyperactive children has been to make the educator responsible for intervention. This trend appears to be a reaction against (1) the idea that hyperactivity is solely a medical problem (environment could play a significant part), and (2) the medical profession's failure to make significant headway in dealing with hyperactivity. Even when drug therapy is successful in controlling behavior, it does not teach the child self-control, nor does it guarantee that learning will improve. The problem of *teaching* hyperactive children is, in the end, a problem that must be dealt with by educational personnel.

The major educational strategies used to manage hyperactive children are: (1) structured environment, (2) operant conditioning, and (3) cognitive behavior modification. Psychotherapy and biofeedback training have also been used (Freidman, 1978), but to a more limited extent.

Psychotherapy   Since psychotherapy is, at best, only moderately associated with classroom intervention, let us deal with that issue first. Although under some circumstances, psychotherapy has been judged to be effective (Ross & Ross, 1976), the majority of the available research indicates findings in the other direction. For the subpopulation of hyperactive children whose hyperactivity stems from stress and anxiety, psychotherapy may be a viable therapeutic technique (Marwit & Stenner, 1972). However, it appears that the hyperactivity itself interferes with the psychotherapeutic process. In that case, psychotherapy would be appropriate only after some other form of treatment was used to control the behavior (Eisenberg, Gilbert, Cytryn, & Molling, 1961).

Biofeedback   With regard to biofeedback techniques, few positive findings have been noted. Biofeedback refers to the monitoring of physiological processes with the expectation that once conscious of these processes, the individual can bring them under voluntary control. In one of the early studies, biofeedback training was found to be beneficial for some children, but not for others (Wall, 1973). Later studies found improvement in the control of muscle behavior (Simpson & Nelson, 1974) and reduction of muscle tension (Braud, Lupin, & Braud, 1975). In all of these studies, samples were very small and the judgments concerning improvement subjective. At present, "there is insufficient evidence to support the clinical utility of EMG (electromyographic) feedback in hyperkinetic children" (Bhatara, Arnold, Lorance, & Gupta, 1979, p. 186). Cautions against continued research without further analysis of the possible effects of biofeedback have begun to emerge (Gargiulo, 1979). Biofeedback may further weaken the inhibitory mechanisms of highly aroused children rather than effect a positive change.

Structured Environment   Perhaps the most widely known educational method of controlling hyperactive children is that of stimulus reduction (Cruickshank, Bentzen, Ratzeburg, & Tannhauser, 1961). Relying on the earlier theoretical position of Strauss and Lehtinen (1947), Cruickshank and his colleagues proposed that by reducing the amount of stimuli impinging upon the child in the classroom, they could reduce the distractible behavior of the child and thereby obviate the hyperactivity. To date, there is no convincing evidence for the efficacy of the minimal stimulation classroom (Ross & Ross, 1976, p. 193). One variant of the low-stimulation classroom has been having children work in study cubicles. Such isolation, however, has not proven beneficial. Having a brain-injured or hyperactive child spend his study time in a separate booth has no effect whatever on achievement (Rost & Charles, 1967).

An intervention strategy which appears to have some support is the use of a highly structured classroom (Hewett, Taylor, & Artuso, 1969). Such classrooms structure both the time and the activity in which the child is engaged (Krauch, 1971) and the space of the environment and the physical objects (Cermark, Stein, & Abelson, 1973).

Operant Conditioning   Regarding the use of operant techniques, a substantial body of literature does exist that indicates that behavioral interventions are successful in shaping behavior when using tangible and social rewards (Haring & Bateman, 1977), token systems (Patterson, Jones, Whittier, & Whittier, 1965), and an outside consultant model (Weissenberger & Loney, 1977). These techniques have been criticized because of: (1) limited generalizability, and (2) lack of permanency. Still, the operant techniques provide an alternative which appears to be as viable as drug therapy.

Cognitive Behavior Modification Many believe that hyperactive children can overcome the absence of spontaneous controls (Wunderlich, 1970), if they are taught to direct their own behavior (Palkes, Stewart, & Kahana, 1968). Considerable success has been reported both with the child's use of verbal self-directions (Palkes, Stewart, & Freedman, 1972; Palkes, Stewart, & Kahana, 1968; Weithorn & Kagen, 1979) and a combination of modeling and verbal self-direction (Meichenbaum & Goodman, 1971). The success of these methods which consist of having the children talk themselves through tasks and/or use verbal commands, such as *stop, look, listen, think,* have important implications. The amount of time given by teachers to focusing children's behavior can be reduced. In addition, children gain proficiency in using a strategy which makes them self-reliant and can be generalized beyond the classroom setting. Because this technique is currently being extended for use with children with attentional deficits, more extensive discussion of cognitive behavior modification is presented in Chapter 6.

SUMMARY

Hyperactivity and learning disability are two terms that mean very different things and, therefore, cannot be used interchangeably. In defining hyperactivity, it was noted that the term does not refer to a disease, but to a constellation of symptoms which cover both quantitative and qualitative aspects of behavior. The term itself is a medical one, though the behaviors which it describes are of educational concern. It is in the classroom that the behaviors must be dealt with and where educational decisions must be made. Also, in considering a definition of hyperactivity, it was noted that not all hyperactive children are learning disabled, nor do they all have learning problems. Not all learning disabled children are hyperactive; in fact, relatively few are. A distinction must be made between those children who have healthy, high activity levels and those who are hyperactive.

A number of potential causes of hyperactivity were discussed including neurological dysfunction, maturational lag, genetic factors, biochemical imbalance, lead poisoning, radiation stress, child rearing, learned behavior, food additives and allergies, and maternal smoking and drinking. All are potentially viable explanations. Few reliable conclusions, however, can be drawn, and the need for continued research is evident.

Of the treatments for hyperactivity, the most frequently employed are drug therapy, structured environment, operant conditioning, and cognitive behavior modification. There is some concern about the generalizability and permanency of these treatments. Serious questions arise as to which children should be chosen for drug therapy—the most widely used treatment—the monitoring of children receiving medication, the length of time children should receive medication, the long-term effects and side effects of medication, and the exact nature of what the medication accomplishes. If some educational interventions are shown to be as effective as drug therapy (which appears to be the case), then educational intervention would be the method of choice.

SUGGESTED READINGS

Barkley, R., & Cunningham, C. Do stimulant drugs improve the academic performance of hyperactive children? A review of outcome research. *Clinical Pediatrics,* 1978, **17**(1), 85–92.

Kershner, J. R. Leeches, quicksilver, megavitamins, and learning disabilities. *Journal of Special Education,* 1978, **12**(1), 7–15.

Sroufe, L. A. Drug treatment of children with behavior problems. In F. Horowitz (Ed.), *Review of child development research,* Vol. 4. Chicago: University of Chicago Press, 1975.

Ross, D. M., & Ross, S. A. *Hyperactivity: Research, theory, and action.* New York: Wiley & Sons, 1976.

Chapter 3

A Cognitive Approach to Instruction

INTRODUCTION

For the most part, all of special education has been dominated by two views of human behavior. The first, an additive model, has focused on observable, repeatable, and countable behaviors and events. That view is commonly known as behaviorism. It assumes that learning occurs as the result of associations built up through experience. Such an orientation was very attractive to people who wished to intervene in the usually very poor or very difficult learning of exceptional children. Behaviorism enabled special educators to focus on the teaching of bits of information that were hierarchically sequenced so that the first could be integrated into more complex behaviors. It also enabled specification of a curriculum suitable for nearly all children, because it assumes that knowledge exists as an objective reality and that learning is achieved when a copy of the external reality is stored internally, that is, when what we know accurately matches the objective reality. Furthermore, behaviorism offers a convenient formula for teaching: when the response is not the one that is desired, the teacher must change the stimulus. If the new stimulus does not lead to the desired response, the teacher should try yet another stimulus and yet another. And that is pretty much what instruction for many learning disabled children has been like. Instruction begins with small bits of information thought to be easiest, and as they are mastered, other easy bits are introduced, and then more difficult ones. If the child does not produce the desired response, practice is continued—usually with some variation in approach or instructional materials. Once that target behavior has been mastered, another is introduced and so on.

For the behaviorists (or behavior modifiers) intervention means direct involvement with reading skills, arithmetic computations, etc. For others, and these persons constitute the second dominant influence in special education, the primary, significant behaviors to be acquired are "underlying" abilities. If, for example, a child evidences problems in reading, it is assumed that there must be difficulties with more fundamental abilities, such as visual discrimination or visual memory. This orientation constitutes something of a "building blocks" model in which some processes, such as perception, are thought to be the foundation upon which higher abilities, such as conception, are based. Those specific underlying abilities become the focus of the remedial intervention. The aim of instruction in this view is to *teach* the underlying processes so that they can be integrated into more complex functions, specifically academic abilities. In this chapter we will give a summary of the research literature pertinent to these two positions, but more in-depth discussions will be given in subsequent chapters throughout the text. For now it is enough to stress that neither of these orientations emphasizes the integrated nature of cognitive functions.

THE NEED FOR A MORE COMPLEX APPROACH
TO THE STUDY OF HUMAN BEHAVIOR

Bruner's (Bruner, Goodnow, & Austin, 1956) book on the study of thinking redirected American psychology and education, because it reclaimed covert cognitive processes as a legitimate domain for study. One of the earliest and most scathing rejections of behaviorism was Chomsky's (1959) review of B. F. Skinner's book *Verbal Behavior*. The most damaging of Chomsky's criticisms was his demonstration that complex sequences of behavior require something more than hierarchically organized associations. They require *control processes*. Language, argued Chomsky, is not simply stored and reproduced. It is reconstructed, recreated in infinite variety.

Since then several other writers have enlarged upon Chomsky's objections. First, the view of man as a *passive responder* who is at the mercy of environmental influences is no longer tenable. The sciences of biology and neuropsychology have demonstrated that the relation between the human organism and its environment is one of constant *interaction*. The learner selects what he or she is to learn. Furthermore, how what is learned is then understood depends on what the learner already knows. Consider a child who observes a teacher boil water and condense it to illustrate how rain occurs, and then the child goes home singing the teacher's praises because the teacher can "make rain."

Mathematics also demonstrates the limited explanatory power of behaviorism, since it exceeds the boundaries of reality. A mathematician can meaningfully manipulate numbers that have no relation to any objective reality at all. Finally, people do not store *a copy of reality* in their minds. They transform and enrich reality through their own constructions. Even infants contribute to the construction of reality by interpreting events. A baby may begin to cry, for example, when an adult stands up, because the child interprets that action as the adult's preparing to go away (Piaget & Inhelder, 1969, pp. 24–25).

An approach to the study of behavior based on animal psychology (as behaviorism) could be dangerously misleading. "Trivial features may be unduly emphasized, while crucially important aspects may be postponed, neglected, or even entirely overlooked" (Miller, 1965, p. 11). Much of what occurs in language learning, for example, cannot be described as discrimination learning or the formation of associations. Learning theory does not account for interrelations. Yet language, to continue the example, cannot be adequately understood without consideration of the relations among words, sentences, and paragraphs.

The need for the understanding of *interrelations* is clear in all human psychological functions (Flavell, 1977). It is impossible, for example, to discuss perception without mentioning (directly or indirectly) such cognitive processes as *relevance, meaning, logical consistency, inference, strategies, problem solving, knowledge,* and *intelligence.* Perception, however, is not a special case. If one were to discuss reasoning, imagery, classification, or any other function, one would be obliged to recognize that all others affect it and are affected by it (Frijda, 1972)—a phenomenon the underlying abilities model failed to take into account. Neither behaviorists nor specific abilities adherents can account for these interrelations. More complex views of human behavior are needed.

Flavell (1972) suggested that a synthesis of information processing models and of Piagetian theory is probably the direction psychology (and education) will take. Information processing models grew out of the synthesis of two developments: information theory and computer technology (Loftus & Loftus, 1976). They treat humans as machines that act on information in the environment in accordance with the programs available to those machines. Piagetian theory has been contributing information about the way such programs develop. Information theory focuses more consistently on how the programs are used to process information.

In his speech before the first national conference of the Division for Children with Learning Disabilities Hammill (1979), who has been a forceful opponent of the underlying abilities model, stated:

> I suspect that the rampant interest in Skinnerianism, the behavioral objectives, the skills-based programs, and the behavior mod programs has peaked and that we're moving very slowly but very deliberately into an age that is rediscovering cognitive principles (Transcript of the speech, p. 3).

Many in the field of learning disabilities have begun to recognize that we are in the beginning stages of a paradigm shift in which a new vision of education is emerging. Some call it *holistic* (Hammill, 1979), some call it Deweyan or *experience methodology* (Iano, 1978), and some call it *cognitive* (Ausubel, Novak, & Hanesian, 1978; Wittrock, 1978), but all its proponents agree that it is child-centered rather than curriculum-centered and recognize that complex skills cannot be dismembered into component parts and still retain their integrity. Because it is child-centered, the cognitive approach to instruction must begin to recognize the role of higher-order control processes in learning. The next section will present one integrated view of knowing which will help to make clear what is meant by higher-order functions.

COGNITIVE APPROACH TO WAYS OF KNOWING

Anderson (1975) has developed a framework for understanding how we know. His view is representative of modern cognitive positions. This brief overview of Anderson's position is not meant to be exhaustive, but is intended to give the reader an indication of the concerns of cognitive theories of knowing and learning.

Cognitive theories of knowing acknowledge that there is no simple answer to the question of how one knows. Important to any study of knowing and learning are: (1) the process of transducing physical energies into nervous impulses at the sensory surfaces, (2) imposing preliminary organization on these nervous impulses, (3) establishing contact between incoming patterns of activity and memory, (4) altering memory, and (5) constructing and evaluating alternative courses of action.

The human organism is viewed as *adaptive.* It is able to change and/or nullify the effects of environment. The human uses the processes of assimilation (incorporating information into an already existing structure) and accommodation (modifying one's internal state to correspond with environmental factors) to produce an ever-dynamic, "elastic" fit between itself and its environment. In short, a human being is viewed as a complex *interactive* system. In such a system learning is viewed as the "capacity to fix a temporary pattern of internal states" (p. 16). Some learning is *dependent upon experience.* Other learning, generated internally, is considered to be *the product of thought.*

Cognitive theories so heavily emphasize what the individual child brings to the learning situation (in the form of both what was experienced and what meaning was constructed from those experiences) that Ausubel, Novak, and Hanesian (1978, p. iv) preface the second edition of their textbook on educational psychology with the following:

> If I had to reduce all of educational psychology to just one principle, I would say this: The most important single factor influencing learning is what the learner already knows. Ascertain this and teach him accordingly.

Because the human is a complex system, there must be some organization imposed on the parts of that system, such that there is the mutual influencing of part and whole. That hierarchical organization consists of two functional systems: *the representational system* and *the executive system* (Anderson, 1975).

The representational system consists of *primary perception, secondary perception,* and *associative memory.* Primary perception refers to the system through which information "is received by the senses, processed by a variety of analyzers, and formed into an analogue model of the world" (p. 25). The information selected by primary perception is controlled by a person's range of sensitivity and attentional control. People do not hear the blood rush past their ears, for example, because they are not sufficiently sensitive. But to some extent, we do control what we hear by attending, for example, to a person's voice rather than to the air conditioner or the noise of passing traffic.

Secondary perception refers to the selection and combination of features which were "roughed out" by primary perception and the relation of these refined features to memory. Secondary perception is dependent on learning. What requires conscious learning initially, often later becomes automatic.

Associative memory adds meaning to perceptions. It is the result of experience and is automatic. Associations are extremely difficult to inhibit. If one says *salt,* for example, nearly everyone responds with *pepper.*

These ways of representing what we know—primary and secondary perception and associative memory—are not enough to explain behavior. *There has to be some way to explain the human's ability to plan and to monitor its behavior.*

Anderson and many other cognitive psychologists employ the notion of a homunculus in explaining this control process. They posit that there is a "little man" who pulls the strings, who guides and directs behavior. Anderson suggests the example of asking people the opposite of *ebony.* Seventy-two percent of the people surveyed reported that the first thing they thought of when they heard *ebony* was *black* (the association). Yet nobody said *black.* In fact, 74 percent of the people answered *white* and 10 percent *ivory.* The "little man" intervened. Even though people thought of the word *black,* they monitored their behavior, resisted saying *black* because it was inappropriate, and delayed responding until a reasonable response was generated. What is important is that the human organism is an adaptive, ever-changing system in which the relations among the parts are monitored by an "executive," a higher-order control system that both edits and directs behavior. This editing function seems to be disturbed in learning disabled children. One very common report of teachers is that learning disabled children seldom seem to have any idea whether their answers are right or wrong—sometimes even with preposterous responses such as the case in which a child adds 13 and 17 and gets an answer of 1,000. Normally, recognition of a correct response occurs early in learning (Peterson, 1967), so that people can begin to judge whether the responses they generate are correct. Editing is one function of the executive system that has been ignored in traditional approaches to teaching.

The executive system is also responsible for the goal-directedness of behavior. The executive system organizes behavior and thought into meaningful, sequential units that permit the accomplishment of complex behaviors. Miller, Galanter, and Pribram (1960) represented this organization as the TOTE (test-operate-test-exit) function. If, for example, one were interested in baking a cake, one would develop a plan and check each aspect of that plan in sequence. First, one might check to see whether the oven was set to preheat (the initial test). Seeing that it was not, one would then set it (operate) and check the setting's accuracy (test). Finding it correct, one would then go on (exit) to another aspect of the preparation—perhaps taking the ingredients out of the closet and another TOTE system would be carried out.

The executive system is thought to be divided into one superordinate and at least two subordinate systems. The superordinate system is thought to operate by willing, whereas the subordinate systems operate automatically. The superordinate system appears to operate in consciousness; the subordinate systems seem to be outside of consciousness. The superordinate system appears to operate serially on one thing at a time, whereas the subordinate systems operate in parallel, accomplishing several tasks at a time.

Plans are formed in the superordinate system and are executed in that system during early stages of practice. What requires conscious learning initially, often later becomes automatic. Driving, for example, initially requires our full attention. We must concentrate on various elements of driving, such as steering and accelerating or braking. Later, with practice, the skill becomes automatic and we hardly have to give it a thought. When functions become automatic, they are turned over to the subordinate systems, so that the superordinate system is freed. We are able to drive while holding a conversation or listening to the radio. The same is true of academic learning. Recall from Chapter 1 that all energy in writing is initially directed toward the formation of letters or the spelling of words. Only gradually do those functions become so automatic that one can concentrate on creating a message or a story.

This progress from superordinate to subordinate control is also apparent in the course of cognitive development. What is in the superordinate system is new. What is in the subordinate systems is old and well learned. The reason for suggesting that there are at least two subordinate systems is that one system refers to information and procedures that were once conscious. The second system is composed of functions that have never been conscious.

One common misinterpretation of the distinction between the representational and executive systems is that the representational systems are nonverbal, whereas the executive system is verbal. That is not the case. Both the representational and executive systems have both verbal and nonverbal aspects. Although a considerable body of literature has been amassed that investigates the control function of language, little has been accomplished to date to aid our understanding of the nonverbal controls of the executive function.

Until recently nearly all responsibility for executive functions in learning settings have been assumed by the teacher. Teachers and curriculum materials, for example, have decided on what the elements of a particular lesson would be. Teachers, and not children, have traditionally task-analyzed lessons to determine what should be learned and in what order. Teachers have assumed the role of the omniscient in determining for children which answers are correct and which are incorrect. A cognitive approach to instruction recognizes that learning to plan, organize, check, and recheck is an integral part of the learning process. It is what renders the information acquired useful.

A COGNITIVE APPROACH TO EDUCATION

A large number of psychologists and educators have been active in the cognitive movement in education. A few very familiar names would include Anderson, Ausubel, Bandura, Bruner, Cronbach, Dewey, Gagné, Greeno, Neisser, and Snow. Their position is generally that it is important to consider what happens *internally* to the person who is learning and to view learning as *construction*. It is the *learner* who is the most important element in the teaching-learning situation; not materials, lessons, teachers, or other factors external to the learner.

Effective instruction provides activities (in the broadest sense) to facilitate the *learner's ability to construct meaning* from experience. People learn not only by acting and experiencing the consequences of their actions. People learn by observing others, by imitating models, by watching television, by seeing a demonstration, by discussing issues, even by listening to a lecture, sometimes without practice, without reinforcement, and without overt action. Cognitive elaborations, such as inferences, images, memories, and analogies, influence their learning and understanding. Learners often construct meaning and create their own reality, rather than respond predictably to the sensory qualities of their environments (Inhelder, Sinclair, & Bovet, 1974; Wittrock, 1978).

Here is just one example of how the learner controls what is learned, i.e., how a learner constructs meaning from instruction. Kaufman, Baron, and Kopp (1966) told learners that they would be reinforced on a particular schedule (either a fixed-interval schedule or a variable-ratio schedule). In fact, they reinforced the learners on a variable-interval schedule. They found that the *instruction* controlled the response rate and *not* the reinforcing contingencies which were actually operant in the training condition.

Another important aspect of a cognitive approach to education is that it is vital for the learner to understand that he or she must be active in his or her own learning. A considerable body of research has been amassed to indicate that those children who believe that they are in control of their own lives and learning are the children who appear to be most successful as learners (cf. DeCharms, 1976; Paton, Walberg, & Yeh, 1973). Recognition of the need for children to feel responsible for their own achievements has led teachers to permit children to play a greater role in selecting their own topics for study and to encourage children to help devise approaches to learning.

A third important characteristic of a cognitive approach to learning is that its goal is focused more clearly on maintenance of information in long-term rather than short-term memory. Most of the procedures currently employed in education, and especially in special education, use techniques (such as practice, drill, and rehearsal) effective in ensuring that the information will be understood and maintained for a short period of time. Teachers frequently voice concerns about children's forgetting what they have learned, even in reading and mathematics. A major thrust of cognitive approaches is helping children transform or elaborate new information or abilities, so that the likelihood of their being transferred to long-term store is increased. Long-term storage is effected through the use of assignments which require discussions, summaries, topic sentences, recall of previous experience, drawing inferences, drawing pictures, viewing illustrations and diagrams, and deriving analogies, metaphors, and rule statements. These activities can be inductive or deductive, but they are always child-centered. They are designed to encourage the child to generate relevant relations between the new information and past experience. When we study models of memory in Chapter 4, we will see how important these relations and the continued processing of information really are.

A cognitive approach to education also recognizes that:

> . . . the mental representations which are used during perception and comprehension, and which evolve as a result of these processes, have a holistic character which cannot be understood as simple functions of their constituents (Anderson, 1977, p. 418).

Learning is a process of elaborating what the child already knows (Reid, 1978), not a process of accumulating bits of information or skills. Children learn by successive approximations, by coming closer and closer to what is accepted as objective reality, by consistently enriching and elaborating past knowledge. A new acquisition is not appended to prior knowledge in the sense that a new bit of clay might sit upon an already formed ball. Rather, new abilities and information serve to revise and/or expand what was already known. To extend the analogy, the new bit of clay is worked into, enlarges, and changes the previous ball.

Since what have come to be known as "executive" processes affect our perception and comprehension of new information from the very beginning, many educational innovations have been directed toward capitalizing on their usefulness. Much emphasis has been put on considerations of context and relevance in teaching. Consequently, more and more often educators and psychologists are calling for the holistic presentation of material to be learned. Few are advocating, for example, that instruction in reading begin with phonics. Phonics and other methods of analysis and synthesis are viewed as important interventions *after* children have begun reading, after they understand that reading (or mathematics, or spelling, or writing, etc.) has purpose and is functional. A cognitive approach assumes that children possess an "umbrella" concept so that when details are presented, the children have a way of organizing them into that overall concept. Individualized instructional plans are viewed as approximate and tentative guidelines from which to begin instruction. The assumption is that the immediate goals will change as the child acquires new information or skills or interests (Iano, 1978).

SUMMARY AND CONCLUSIONS

Many, without justification, have argued that learning disabled children cannot profit from a cognitive approach to instruction. It has not been demonstrated that learning disabled children or adults learn in a way that is fundamentally different from other persons (Reid, 1978). It is clear, instead, that their learning is less efficient and apparently developmentally delayed (Hall, 1980; Loper, 1980; Reid, Knight-Arest, & Hresko, 1980; Wong, 1979). An approach that focuses on the child's ability to construct meaning, to feel responsible for learning, to transfer information to long-term memory, and which also recognizes the unitary character of both psychological processes and academic skills is clearly not incompatible with inefficient learning. Totally new teaching strategies are not required. A cognitive approach assumes only that those we have developed will be used more effectively and that stress will be given to assisting the learning disabled in structuring their own approach to learning.

More and more frequently, research and instructional approaches in learning disabilities are beginning to concentrate on this executive (or control) system. Hall (1980), for example, has suggested that information processing theories may be very useful for studying learning disabled persons, since it is clear that production deficiencies, especially in strategizing, often exist in this population. When a person has an ability, but fails to use it in an appropriate situation, he is said to have a production deficiency (Brown, 1975; Flavell, 1970). One critical aspect of a production deficiency is that the person can use the behavior if instructed to do so. Learning disabled children who have mastered phonics skills, for example, often do not use them spontaneously, but they can use them when the teacher instructs them to do so (Spache, 1976).

Both behavioral and underlying abilities models tend to focus on whether a child *can* do something rather than on whether he or she *does* do it. The assumption has been made that acquisition of the skill is enough. Yet, what appears to differentiate learning disabled from normally achieving persons is their lack of spontaneous access to these abilities and functions, as well as their ability to coordinate them (Hall, 1980). Control processes (rather than external contingencies) seem to be implicated in the learning problems experienced by these persons.

A perusal of conventional educational strategies, particularly in the field of learning disabilities, indicates that nearly all of our efforts have been directed to the levels of primary and secondary perception and associative memory, i.e., the ways of representing information. Only recently has educational technology been directed toward affecting better control by the executive system. Emphases on representational aspects of learning have led to a preoccupation with performance (rather than competence), have viewed error as an interference mechanism in learning, and have assigned responsibility for executive functions to the teacher (Reid, 1979b).

The neglect of higher-level functions has led to a distortion and some confusion regarding the information processing capabilities of the learning disabled. These distortions have, in some instances, led to recommendations for remediation which have failed to affect the child's academic functioning. The seeds of discontent are apparent among professionals in the field. More and more frequently, books and journal articles (cf. Algozzine & Sutherland, 1977; Newcomer & Hammill, 1976; Torgesen, 1977; Vellutino, Steger, Moyer, Harding, & Niles, 1977) are raising serious issues related to the justification of current educational practices. As the attention of many professionals shifts from an emphasis on perception to a consideration of cognitive and linguistic factors affecting learning disabled children and adults, an impact from psycholinguistic theory and cognitive theory in general is being felt. The following chapters will reflect this shifting emphasis. Whenever appropriate, cognitively oriented and traditional special education approaches will be presented. Many will recognize a number of the behaviors considered important in the cognitive approach as "study skills" (Brown, 1978). As noted earlier, a cognitive approach to education does not necessitate a complete "turn around" in educational practice. It means a reordering of emphases and priorities.

SUGGESTED READINGS

Anderson, B. F. *Cognitive psychology: The study of knowing, learning, and thinking.* New York: Academic Press, 1975.

Anderson, R. C., Spiro, R. J., & Montague, W. E. (Eds.) *Schooling and the acquisition of knowledge.* Hillsdale, N. J.: Lawrence Erlbaum Associates, 1977.

Gallagher, J. M., & Reid, D. K. *The learning theory of Piaget and Inhelder.* Monterey, Calif.: Brooks/Cole, in press.

Part Two

Perhaps no other aspect of the learning disabilities definition has caused so much confusion and controversy as the phrase "basic psychological processes." There has been considerable speculation that if these processes are indeed basic, they must be remediated before successful teaching can be accomplished. This underlying abilities approach, which is really a movement incorporating the work of many professionals from a number of disciplines, predominated in the early days of the field. Although one still finds vestiges of these "building block" theories, they are currently far less popular. For the most part, the underlying abilities approaches were replaced by a behavioral orientation which dictated that one teach simple academic skills to have a child learn to read or write. Prior remediation of basic processes was not viewed as necessary or even desirable.

There is currently a resurgence of interest in the basic psychological processes, but (as the next several chapters will point out) from a very different perspective. Since learners are now coming to be viewed as active in their own learning, researchers and educators are interested in finding out how children learn reading, or writing, or arithmetic that enables them to progress successfully. Brown (1978) has compared this movement to a renewal of interest in what we previously thought of as *study skills*. How can the materials be structured to provide maximum learning? How should the child organize the material? How

Photo on facing page: Learning about the World.

55

should he or she approach the learning task? How should the child study to make certain that he or she does not forget? These are the questions learning disabilities professionals are now asking that may be answered by a better understanding of basic psychological processes. Chapters 4, 5, and 6 treat memory, perception, and attention and vigilance, respectively. Chapter 7 is concerned with social and emotional factors in learning.

Chapter 4

Memory

INTRODUCTION

It is widely recognized that the learning disabled have deficits in memory. Two of the six major areas of disability described by Myers and Hammill (1976) and all of the basic learning abilities described by Valett (1969) involve memory. Many other writers (Chalfant & Scheffelin, 1969; Doehring, 1968; Johnson & Myklebust, 1967; Kirk, 1966) have also reported that the learning disabled experience difficulties with one or another memory tasks. Some experimenters have found problems among learning disabled children on tasks of visual memory (Altwit, 1963; Bryan, 1972; Matheny, 1971; Stanley & Hall, 1973) and others have found deficits on auditory memory tasks (Aten & Davis, 1968; Badian, 1977; Richie & Aten, 1976; Van Atta, 1973). Additionally, there is some evidence to suggest that the problems of the learning disabled may lie in transferring information from short- to long-term store (Marshall, 1976) or in shifting information back and forth between the stores (Spring, 1976). Several studies have also pointed to learning disabled children's inability to organize material and have suggested that this lack of organizational ability is causally related to problems in memory (Bender, 1976; Freston & Drew, 1974; Parker, Freston, & Drew, 1975; Ring, 1976; Torgesen, 1977).

It is rather interesting, in light of these reports, that the present authors were unable to find any carefully controlled series of studies which investigated aspects of memory functioning in learning disabled children. There appears to be a general consensus that memory constitutes a problematic area for the learning disabled, but there have been only isolated attempts at discovering where in the memory process these problems might occur. As Torgesen (1978–79) indicated in his review of research on the memory skills of poor readers, the research is not only scattered and unsystematic but also task-oriented and nontheoretical. Perhaps that is because most work in learning disabilities has approached memory from either an underlying abilities or behavioral, associationist perspective. As will become clear later in this discussion, adherents of the underlying abilities model tended to view memory as a unitary capacity which was impaired in learning disabled children as a result of neurological involvement (Torgesen & Kail, 1980). From the behavioral standpoint, memory has been viewed as the establishment of a link between units of experience by contiguity and repeated associations. Once a link is formed, reactivation of one unit leads to the reactivation of the unit or units with which it had been associated.

Currently, memory is what we call the set of capacities that enable us to interact with incoming information in order to make sense of our environments. It is a multifaceted skill dependent on a variety of subskills. For individuals working with the learning disabled, understanding of the memory process is important, because it provides the backdrop against which memory problems can be understood. Our intent is to introduce some of the terminology frequently used and to describe current thinking about memory and its development. The status of our knowledge of memory processes among learning disabled persons will be reviewed. Educational strategies and teaching implications will be suggested.

MODERN THEORIES OF MEMORY

Multiple Store Models

Atkinson and Shiffrin (1971) described a two-component model of memory. Information enters the system through the sensory registers. It then becomes lost or flows into the short-term store. In short-term store relevant associations with the long-term store may occur and thinking is conscious.

> Because consciousness is equated with the short-term store and because control processes are centered in and act through it, the short-term store is considered a working memory: a system in which decisions are made, problems are solved and information flow is directed (Atkinson & Shiffrin, 1971, p. 83).

The control processes that affect retention of information include rehearsal, coding (information to be remembered is put in the context of additional, easily retrievable information), imaging, decision rules, organizational schemes, retrieval strategies, and problem-solving techniques.

Modern psychologists differentiate two types of long-term memory: episod-

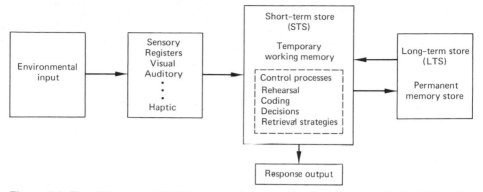

Figure 4-1 The Atkinson and Shiffrin model of memory. *(R. C. Atkinson, & R. M. Shiffrin. The control of short-term memory. Scientific American, 1971, 225, 85–90. © 1971 by Scientific American, Inc.)*

ic and semantic memory. Episodic memory is the receiving and storing of information about temporally dated episodes or events, and temporal-spatial relations among these events (Tulving, 1972, p. 385). Episodic memory is thought to be important to academic tasks because in early reading memory for grapheme-phoneme correspondences is essentially episodic. Furthermore, Brown (1975) has argued quite convincingly that the use of efficient memory strategies is more important to the successful completion of episodic rather than semantic tasks. Semantic memory is necessary for the use of language. It includes the organized knowledge "a person possesses about words and other verbal symbols, their meaning and referents, about relations among them, and about rules, formulas, and algorithms for the manipulation of these symbols, concepts and relations" (Tulving, 1972, p. 386). The semantic system, unlike episodic memory, permits the retrieval of information not directly stored in it. It allows one to use old information to construct new ideas. It is also less susceptible to forgetting than episodic memory.

Descriptions of the organization of semantic memory show the strong influence of computer technology (Collins & Quillian, 1969; Kintsch, 1970; Meyer, Schvaneveldt, & Ruddy, 1975; Quillian, 1969; Winograd, 1975). Some depict semantic memory as an intricate network (Loftus & Loftus, 1976). A network shows the interrelations among concepts with "nodes" representing properties that are intrinsic to them. Connections between nodes define relations. The *semantic distance* between any two concepts is affected by the order in which a person has learned the particular concepts, and the logical connections between them. People usually learn that a *salmon* is a *fish*, and that a *fish* is an *animal*. Since *salmon* is a subset of *fish* and *fish* is a subset of *animal*, *fish* should be stored between *salmon* and *animal*.

To decide whether a salmon can swim, one need only examine the properties stored. However, to decide whether a salmon has fins, one must examine the next level in the network (the *fish* node). It should take more time to retrieve the information about fins than about swimming. It should take even

Figure 4-2 An example of organization in semantic memory. *(Adapted from Collins & Quillian, 1969, as cited in G. R. Loftus & E. F. Loftus,* Human memory: The processing of information. *Hillsdale, N.J.: Lawrence Erlbaum Associates, 1976.)*

longer to move up two levels than to search an adjacent level (Collins & Quillian, 1969).

A slightly different approach to the organization of semantic memory has been taken by Smith, Shoben, and Rips (1974). Their model emphasizes process rather than structure. The essential process is the comparison of features. The Smith, Shoben, and Rips model distinguishes two types of features which may describe an item: "defining features" and "characteristic features." Defining features are considered to be necessary for the item to be in a particular class or category. Defining features of the concept *robins* would include *living, have feathers,* and *have red breasts* (Loftus & Loftus, 1976). Characteristic features are those which describe robins, but are not necessary to define the class. Examples would be *harmless* and *tree-perching.* To decide whether or not an item belongs to a particular category (e.g., is a robin a bird?), the individual performs a general comparison of the defining and characteristic features for both the instance (e.g., robin) and the class (e.g., bird). If the similarity between the two sets is high, the response is affirmative, i.e., a robin is a bird. If the correspondence is low, the response is negative. When the results of the initial comparison are unclear, a second stage of the process occurs in which only the defining features of both classes are compared. Neither of these models can be considered *theories* of memory, but are sets of principles which have been incorporated into theoretical frameworks.

Depth of Processing Models

Depth of processing models of memory (Craik & Lockhart, 1972) are also information processing models. They are concerned with the way people operate on bits of information, rather than with the formation of stimulus-response associations. Although the multistore models are appealing and empirically

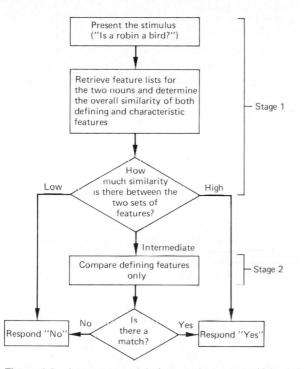

Figure 4-3 A process model of semantic memory. *(Adapted from Smith, Shoben, & Rips, 1974, by Loftus & Loftus, 1976.)*

verifiable, none clarifies the manner in which information is transferred from one store to the other, nor explains how control processes (rehearsal, coding, imaging, etc.) work. Stimuli may be encoded in a variety of ways. For example, sometimes a word might be encoded in terms of its visual features, sometimes its phonemic features, sometimes its semantic features. Alternatively, the same word may, on another occasion, be stored in terms of its verbal associates or a visual image. There is also evidence that the duration of the memory will vary with the type of encoding (Craik & Tulving, 1975).

The analysis of incoming information generally includes perceptual recognition of its physical features (size, brightness, loudness, and pitch), the extraction of meaning, and pattern recognition (matching the input against previously stored information). Further elaboration of the stimulus may also occur, because the stimulus may trigger a variety of ideas and images which are integrated with past knowledge (Tulving & Madigan, 1970).

Some domains of processing must necessarily precede others: for example, some sensory processing must precede semantic analysis (Craik & Jacoby, 1975), but, in general, processing need not occur in some fixed sequence. Memory processing, therefore, should not be viewed as occurring in discrete stages It is rather a continuum of analysis. The duration of the memory is related to the depth of processing given to the incoming information. Duration is accounted for neither by the repetition of the association, as in association theory, nor by rehearsal, as in the multistore models. Rather, duration is thought to be affected by the degree to which the stimulus input is *integrated* with previously stored information. It is possible in the depth of processing approach to maintain information in memory by means of rehearsal, but rehearsal will not strengthen the memory trace unless additional processing takes place. Learning activities that focus on repetition and drill may therefore be of questionable value.

What is meant by primary memory is not a storage structure but rather the "activation of some part of the perceptual analyzing system by the process of conscious attention" (Craik et al., p. 175). Rehearsal does nothing to improve memory performance. Elaborative rehearsal, however, which relates the new information to what was previously known, involves a reorganization of the material and thereby increases the probability of later retrieval (Craik & Watkins, 1973). Depth of processing models include a central processor—something like the homunculus described by Anderson (1975)—which selects and applies encoding procedures according to the nature and meaningfulness of the stimulus material and the demands of the task (Craik & Lockhart, 1975).

A Combination Model

One attempt to synthesize the multistore and depth of processing models into a more comprehensive framework is presented in Figure 4-4. In this system, an item is subjected to a series of analyses, but higher-order analyses may start working on the products of lower-order analyses before the lower-order analyses are complete. It is, therefore, quite probable that the higher-order analyses may influence the lower-order analyses (Bjork, 1975) in such a way that what we see or hear becomes a function of our expectations (Bruner, 1957).

The input traces are subject to the central processor, which acts as a homunculus in the system. It is involved in the control processes (attention, rehearsal, organization, and retrieval) but may execute only one function at a time and is consequently a bottleneck in the system.

Short-term store contains the output of the central processor. This output may be a stimulus trace, a previously stored item retrieved from long- or short-term store, or a new item constructed in combination with information previously stored. Information enters long-term store only after it has been related to previous knowledge. Items are not transferred from store to store as in the multistore models. The information stored in long-term memory is constructed, in the sense that it is modified or elaborated in some way as it is integrated with previous knowledge. That same information is simultaneously modified in short-term memory in the same way.

Summary

What is critical about these models is that they view memory as an active, multifaceted process. Links between past and present experience are not

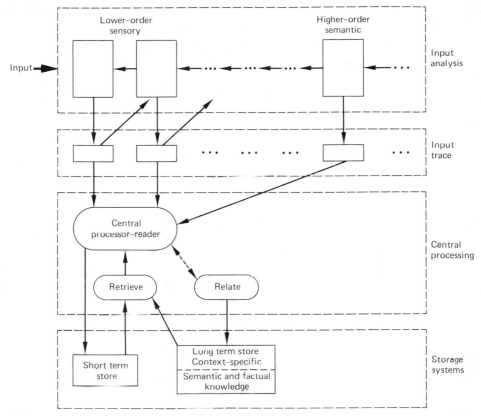

Figure 4-4 A depth of processing model featuring multiple memory stores *(Adapted from Bjork, 1975.)*

explained as the product of associations based on repeated stimulation provided by the environment. The individual is seen as selective both in terms of the features of the environment to which he or she will attend and in terms of the operations (or control processes) he or she will carry out on the incoming material (e.g., rehearsal, coding, imaging, etc.). One additional—and very important point for educators—is that a copy of the stimulus is never what is stored. The integration of new information with past knowledge changes the nature of the information. Furthermore, it is important to recall that rehearsal alone will not ensure that an item is transferred from short- to long-term store.

DEVELOPMENTAL ASPECTS OF MEMORY

There are marked changes in memory from preschool through adolescence (Brown, 1975; Flavell, 1970). The developing child increasingly uses cognitive and verbal skills in the storage and retrieval of information (Hagen & Kail, 1975;

Ritter, Kaprove, Fitch, & Flavell, 1973). One aspect of memory not studied until quite recently is the development of encoding processes: What features of stimuli are important to their categorization in memory?

Encoding Processes

Encoding results from a complex interaction between events in the real world and what an individual already knows. A number of developmental changes occur in the manner in which external events are represented. One source of age-related differences in encoding is, therefore, the child's semantic and conceptual knowledge. A child's cognitive and linguistic competence determines the features he or she may encode, as well as the network into which they are integrated. A developmental change may also occur in the rate of processing with faster reaction times with increasing age. Finally, the older person may be more adept at extracting signals from noise (Gibson, 1969) and will therefore encode a greater number of semantic features (Torgesen & Kail, 1980).

It has become clear that encoding is not a process of matching a stimulus to a preexisting internal "carbon copy." It is, instead, the *extraction* of what are deemed to be important features and the *interaction* of those features with prior knowledge (Kail & Siegel, 1977). The semantic information conveyed in a sentence goes well beyond that contained in the words individually. Similarly, the meaning and memory of several sentences is greater than the meaning and memory of the individual sentences (Bransford & Franks, 1971). Adults do not remember individual sentences or words. They abstract semantic relationships and spontaneously produce inferred relations within and between sentences. Children as young as five years old also demonstrate this semantic integration phenomenon (Barclay & Reed, 1974; Paris & Carter, 1973; Paris & Mahoney, 1974).

According to the depth of processing models, retention is positively related to the depth to which events are processed. Semantic and cognitive encoding results in longer-lasting memories than sensory and perceptual encoding. In a review of recognition memory tasks, Hagen, Jongeward, and Kail (1975) indicated that young children were more likely to recognize falsely acoustically related words, while older children were more apt to recognize falsely semantically related words. These findings were interpreted as evidence of a developmental shift from encoding words on the basis of acoustic to semantic features. For six-year-olds and perhaps for even younger children, however, there is evidence that the processing of meaning (semantic/cognitive encoding) should be considered as "obligatory" if the words are within the child's vocabulary (Geis, 1975; Geis & Hall, 1976). Age-related differences in retention can only be attributed to a small degree to differences in this automatic encoding in normal children. Instead, age differences in memory are found when *voluntary* encoding is needed. Types of encoding which are voluntary include "constructing images, organizing by superordinate categories and constructing sentences or story contexts" (Geis & Hall, 1976, p. 59).

Development of Strategic Behaviors

Memory is influenced by the cognitive strategies and organizations of the individual. Developmental changes occur in the selection of voluntary encoding procedures, or strategic behaviors. Early models of memory dealt almost exclusively with the specification of distinct stores and attempted to relate memory problems to a defective short-term store (Ellis, 1963; Spitz, 1973). In contrast, current formulations assume that young children are deficient in the use of strategic behaviors. The store itself is not believed to be defective (Brown, 1973).

Torgesen (1978–79), however, suggests that several studies of memory in reading disabled children revealed deficits in the structural aspects of memory. Problems have been found with both speed of processing and the synchrony of processing within auditory and visual short-term memory. Torgesen cautions, however, that the relative roles of structural and functional (requiring control processes) features are still unclear. On the one hand, the development of structural features may enable or encourage the use of control processes. On the other hand, speed and automaticity may be the result of practice, overlearning, and/or effective study habits.

When children enter school, they have a great deal of information which is, in large part, the involuntary result of intelligent interaction with the environment rather than any deliberate attempt at remembering (Brown, 1975). Flavell (1970) has characterized memory as a type of problem solving in which activities are deliberately undertaken to store and retrieve information, while recall constitutes the goal. The development of the strategic behaviors necessary to voluntary memory is gradual. Performance on a memory task is often dependent upon a variety of factors, such as the intent to remember the task, and the availability and application of strategies. Tasks which are not enhanced by strategic interventions (e.g., recognition and search) are relatively insensitive to age differences. When the cognitive and/or linguistic systems are tapped, however, developmental differences are expected, because the systems are the framework within which new material is organized. Not only do higher-order processes influence what is added to memory, but what we have already stored in memory changes as we become more developmentally advanced (Liben, 1977; Piaget, 1967; Torgesen & Kail, 1980). We recode what is in memory in accordance with our greater cognitive maturity. In addition, deeper levels of automatic encoding (more varied connotative meanings and the encoding of denotative meanings) are evident in older children (Geis & Hall, 1976).

The "plan to form a plan," which constitutes the work of the executive system, develops with age. Flavell (1970) regards the plan to form a plan as a general factor which reflects the intention to engage in some mnemonic activity. Young children and others who are developmentally young do not seem to be active in forming plans (Butterfield & Belmont, 1975). Little information exists, however, to explain why they do not seem active and deliberate in selecting strategies for remembering. It may be that the central processor (that homunculus also sometimes referred to as the executive function) becomes informed about which strategies foster retention through *metamemory,* i.e., an awareness of its own memory processes (Flavell & Wellman, 1977). Certainly knowing what is relevant to storage should help in the monitoring and selection of strategic behavior. Torgesen (1977) in his discussion of nonspecific factors in the performance of learning disabled children stressed the effect that *meta* variables may have on children's performance in specific settings and called for research examining them. What few studies have been carried out with learning disabled children (generally defined by normal intelligence but low reading scores) will be reviewed in the next section.

RESEARCH FINDINGS THAT SUGGEST EDUCATIONAL STRATEGIES

In studies dealing with the effects of *organization* upon long-term memory, it was found that the imposition of a superstructure tended to enhance retention over a prolonged period of time, regardless of the child's level of development (Geis & Lange, 1976; Hall & Pierce, 1974; Ornstein, Naus, & Liberty, 1975; Rogoff, Newcombe, & Kagan, 1974). Brown (1975), for example, investigated memory for order and items in a paired-associate learning task. She found that kindergarten children were unable to profit from the logical temporal ordering of material (unlike second and fourth graders) until instruction regarding the sequencing of events was explained. Some evidence exists (Torgesen, 1977b; Torgesen, Bowen, & Ivey, 1978) to suggest that learning disabled children are less likely to use categorizing to aid recall. These studies as well as others (cf. Freston & Drew, 1974; Parker, Freston, & Drew, 1975; Ring, 1976) suggest that children with reading problems may use less efficient strategies when approaching memory tasks. There is the possibility that these differences result from deficits in linguistic knowledge, but this explanation seems unlikely, because with minimal training group differences can be eliminated. These studies tend to support instead the Torgesen (1977) hypothesis that learning disabled children fail to adopt an active, planful, and organized approach to the task. The problem is clearly one of a production deficiency rather than of a structural deficit.

Streufert (1973) has indicated that there is a need for *relevance* in the information that is presented if deeper processing and retention are to occur. This position has also been supported by the research of Epstein, Phillips, and Johnson (1975). They demonstrated that recall is facilitated by semantic relationships which have a special meaning for the individual. Samuels (1976) also concurred with this notion. She found that recall was facilitated by matching the level of reasoning that an action required with that of the child to be tested, thus confirming the need for relevance as well as organization.

Another method of increasing retention and retrieval of information is related to the use of labeling and rehearsal techniques. Several studies (Denckla & Rudel, 1976a, b; Kastner & Rickards, 1974; Spring & Capps, 1974; Torgesen & Goldman, 1977) have indicated that learning disabled children neither label stimuli nor rehearse as frequently as do normally achieving children. Again, these data could be interpreted to suggest that the learning disabled children were unable to supply verbal labels. In the Torgesen and Goldman study, however, all of the learning disabled children could name the stimuli. It appears then that these children are less apt to apply rehearsal strategies spontaneously. In the Spring and Capps and Denckla and Rudel studies, however, there is evidence that learning disabled children have difficulty labeling stimuli *rapidly*. This may suggest, like the studies reviewed by Torgesen (1978–79), that structural as well as functional deficits characterize these children. Further evidence which may support a structural deficit hypothesis may be derived from a Perfetti and Goldman (1976) study in which poor readers were found to differ in the way they encode linguistic information. It may be that the verbal skills needed for strategies to be implemented are simply lacking.

Questioning students has also been found to have a facilitative effect on recall. Shavelson, Berliner, Ravitch, and Loeding (1974), investigating the type and positioning of questions for a prose selection, found that those students with low vocabulary scores would score significantly better when assigned to textual material that had higher-order questions (those requiring deeper processing, such as comprehension, application, or analysis) positioned after the passage. Consequently, it was found that the kinds of questions posed had a direct effect upon the responses elicited. LaPorte and Voss (1975) have indicated that the retention of prose over a one-week period is enhanced by the presentation of completion-type questions and feedback immediately following the presentation of information to be learned. In contrast, Rickards (1976) found that conceptual prequestions for prose material provided the best method for facilitating delayed recall of events and the organization of information to be maintained within the structure of memory. Wong (1979) found similar improvement in the delayed recall of learning disabled children when questions were embedded in the text to alert them to the important information. Since these activities can be used during a single presentation, it would seem prudent to utilize a combination of these questioning techniques.

Spring's (1976) study of the memory span of dyslexic children has linked their speech-motor encoding ability and verbal stimuli deficits to their impaired memory span. One implication of this finding is that the *presentation rate* of material to be taught should be at a level which is slower than normal if long-term retention is to be maintained. Zippel (1975) has suggested that the amount of material that an individual can handle in terms of categorical arrangement is on the average of three pieces of information. Broadbent (Kennedy & Wilkes, 1975) has lent support to this position in his theoretical conceptualization of memory. Additionally, Ehrlich (1975) has indicated that the progressive introduction of one or two elements into a "kernel group" of information will help children create very strong, well-organized structures which will lead to better retention. A study that has utilized a combinational approach (Keith, Axelrod, Anderson, Hathaway, Wood, & Fitzgerald, 1973) investigated the effects of types of spelling word presentation rates upon recall ability in a final weekly review test. On the basis of their results, Keith et al. suggested that students do best when they receive and are tested on a portion (five words) of the words each day rather than on a twenty-five-word list. Postmen, Kruesi, and Regan (1975) and Bjork and Whitten (1974) have made similar suggestions.

Summary and Conclusions

Research into means of enhancing the storage of information in long-term memory has indicated that the following factors influence retention: (1) the organization of the material, (2) its relevance, (3) labeling and rehearsal, (4) questions, and (5) presentation rate. Although there is some suggestion that some of the difficulties associated with memory in learning disabled children *may* have a structural basis, the preponderance of the research suggests difficulties in the use of control processes. The major support for such an assertion stems from the findings that when minimal training efforts are undertaken, group differences between learning disabled and normally achieving children are typically eliminated. It seems reasonable then to assume that as long as teachers are careful not to frustrate the learning disabled children with whom they work, much can be gained from teaching learning disabled students to use effective strategic and study behaviors.

SOME SUGGESTIONS FOR TEACHING

Memory is undoubtedly an *active* coding system that requires the following steps: first, one must decide what is relevant and important about the information to be stored. Second, one must decide where to store it in terms of one's previous knowledge. Third, one must determine how to encode the information. Finally, a plan for retrieval of the information must be adopted. Several of these steps may, of course, be carried out simultaneously. How can we help learning disabled children with these processes? The following are some illustrations and suggestions. Teachers are limited only by their own resources and inventiveness.

Organization

Organization is an important factor in presenting lessons to children. One way to use it is to impose or ask children to impose a superstructure on what they are trying to remember. Such a superstructure may involve the use of spatial or temporal series, categories, hierarchies, or other structures. It is not sufficient, however, to be present. Children must be told that it is there. Suppose you were asked to remember *retirwepyt*. That string of letters has an order imposed, but it cannot help you unless you know what it is. Teachers as a whole tend to be very highly organized people and their lessons tend to be quite well organized. What frequently happens, however, is that teachers fail to share that organization, to make it explicit to their pupils. Children, especially those with memory deficits, tend not to discover and impose structure for themselves. The following brief examples relate directly to many classroom concerns: It is important for children to know that $3 \times 3 = 9$ and $3 \times 4 = 9 + 3$. That is, they must understand $\times$ to mean repeated addition: 3×4 is simply increasing the number of times that 3s have been added together. Another example might be the use of the final, silent *e* in changing mat to mate, bat to bate, hat to hate, etc. Even when the words created do not have meaning, the concept is still regular and can be easily reconstructed.

Another reason to make organization explicit is that planfulness is age-related and young as well as learning disabled children do not spontaneously organize stimuli. They must be taught to do so. For example, when asked to remember lists of words such as hat, belt, tree, flower, dress, grass, shoe, and bush, most people remember those words by grouping them into categories of plants and clothing. When they repeat the list, they rearrange the order of the words and usually give words from one category before giving words from the other. This is called clustering. Young children and learning disabled children do not cluster. They do not categorize or impose rules on what they are trying to remember.

Teachers can help children to understand the importance of strategizing. They can assist children in discovering what kinds of strategies might be useful and in learning when to employ them. One way to encourage children to impose rule structures is by asking them to label items such as isosceles triangles, right triangles, etc. Another method is to ask them to make a statement about relations. For example, children might be asked how 1492, Indians, and the Atlantic Ocean might be related. (All too often that relation is presented to the children by the teacher!) Using a variety of presentations such as B, b, $\mathcal{B}$, $\mathscr{b}$, etc. is also helpful. Finally, rhythm can be a powerful tool in remembering. Notice, for example, how often television commercials and pop songs take advantage of rhymes and rhythms. Many of us find ourselves driving our cars and singing the plumber's phone number! Children are also responsive to these techniques.

Relevance

Arousal is a term which is usually employed to refer to a physiological state on a continuum from sleep to wakefulness. Typically, drugs are used to alter the child's levels of arousal, but there are educational manipulations that may also be tried. Children become more aware, more awake, if you will, when they are highly motivated, when they find things interesting, meaningful, worth getting excited about. Knowing that Washington's army camped on the creek in which the child plays after school makes the study of the Revolutionary War much more real. The *Glass Menagerie* is a play that adolescents usually find compelling, because they can identify with Laura's self-consciousness as she walks down the school aisles with her limp. Little children become considerably more excited about addition when they realize that 1 and 1 is not only the addition of numerals, buttons, or bottlecaps, but is also putting 1 cup of flour and 1 cup of milk together to make a cake—or similarly, that losing the button off your shirt is a form of subtraction. Mathematics is, after all, a system for measuring and recording the major operations of life.

But, to be remembered, information must also be relevant in the sense that it is understood. How can one make decisions about what is relevant, where and how to store information, and develop plans for getting that information back, if memory is rote? It was mentioned in passing that the code itself changes over time. It has been shown, for example, that when children are shown a series of sticks of graduated lengths which are arranged in series, they draw or otherwise reproduce the series in accordance with the way they understand it. Very small children, for example, may draw several series with two or three sticks in each. Older children might draw two ordered series or perhaps a single series which has fewer sticks than the model. These children are unable to integrate the two series or the additional sticks into a single series. The important point is that the children cannot reproduce what they have actually seen. What it is they have understood about the sticks is what is recorded in memory, not the actual configuration. When the children were asked several weeks or months later to remember what they had seen (they were not shown the sticks again), surprisingly, they drew configurations which were the same or *better* than their original drawing. What the children remembered had actually improved as their level of cognitive functioning improved (Liben, 1980; Piaget & Inhelder, 1973).

Rehearsal Strategies

Rehearsal often constitutes a simple repetition of what is to be remembered. If a telephone number must be remembered from the restaurant table to the telephone booth, for example, we usually repeat the number over and over again to ourselves along the way. If we must remember a visual presentation, perhaps the license number of the car that hit us, we usually transfer the visual image to an auditory one and again repeat the number over and over again to ourselves until we can write it down or otherwise report it. Learning disabled children do not appear to rehearse spontaneously. Conscious rehearsal is often needed to retain unfamiliar information for short periods, but learning disabled children do not always recognize that verbal repetition is a strategy they can use in maintaining the information. They must be taught to rehearse.

Another way to aid children who do not rehearse spontaneously is to contrive situations in which the need for rehearsal is at a minimum. Research has indicated that little effort is needed to remember information which is related to what is already known. The more relevant, interesting, and better organized the presentation of the information is, the less the child must depend upon rehearsal strategies. When rehearsal is necessary, however, the sooner the information can be used, the better. When you stop at a gas station, for example, and ask directions, the sooner you get back in the car and start driving, the better able you will be to remember whether you make two right turns, a left turn, and then two rights, or whether you make two right turns, two left turns, and then a right.

Questioning and Presentation Rates

Reviews should be carried out frequently, perhaps every two or three days, and cover rather small amounts of information. Recall that spelling words were better remembered when only five were introduced and practiced at a time, rather than the usual twenty. In the end just as many words were remembered and they were remembered better. Reviews should also be well organized, so that children are encouraged to relate ideas and skills to each other.

Questioning, both before lessons (what constitutes a form of advanced organizer as described by Ausubel, 1968) and after lessons has been shown to enhance memory. In fact, it was noted that children who had difficulty with vocabulary profited from higher-order questions which forced them to organize the material they had read and to relate it to past experience. Questions related to specific information, comprehension, application, and analysis are all useful. The only prerequisite is understanding!

STUDY SKILLS

No discussion of memory would be complete without some mention of study skills. These are essentially plans children develop for approaching and mastering their assignments. The nature of study skills changes somewhat with the age and competence level of the child. Organizational skills, which depend on the child's ability to establish relationships, are encouraged and cultivated throughout the school years. Early in schooling, they are rather restricted to simple categorizing skills (e.g., separating characteristics according to the story character they describe), but as the children advance, they become more complex (e.g., outlining, summarizing, and synthesizing). Early aids to recall include having primary-level children read for a certain prespecified purpose and then checking the child's ability through asking questions. Later, although these practices are often continued, children are encouraged to use associative techniques (jingles, rhymes, composing a sentence that uses the initial letters of the words to be remembered, etc.).

Most important SQ3R techniques are introduced during the intermediate school years. (SQ3R stands for survey, question, read, recite, review.) Surveying refers to glancing over the entire article (book, magazine) to get a sense of the information it contains. During the survey, students read the title, headings, graphs, introduction (the abstract of a research article), and summary. In the second step the students raise some questions in their own minds about what to expect from paragraphs under certain headings. Having asked themselves those questions, they begin reading. Now they can read with purpose—to answer those questions they have raised. After reading, they answer their own questions and self-monitor to make certain that the answers make sense. They can proceed through the passage paragraph by paragraph, page by page, or section by section. Once the entire article has been read, the final step of the SQ3R method is followed: review. Reviewing usually is accomplished by a second survey—this time with the details filled in. Teaching learning disabled children such study strategies can provide them with important direction to enable them to go about learning and remembering.

SUMMARY AND CONCLUSIONS

Little systematic information about the memory processes of learning disabled children is currently available. What there is suggests that they may have problems with both encoding strategies and the use of strategic behaviors. In general, it is fair to say that their performances on recall tasks tend to approximate those of younger, normally achieving children. As Torgesen (1977) has suggested, they tend to be passive, inefficient learners. Recommendations were made for teachers to assist learning disabled children in the use of strategic behaviors and the application of effective study skills. Some suggestions were also given for encouraging teachers to use techniques such as organization and questioning.

It should be clear, however, from the foregoing discussion, that memory is not a unitary capacity that exists apart from the content to be remembered (Hammill, 1979; Reid, 1979a). It is, consequently, inappropriate for memory to become the goal of instruction. The approaches recommended here are intended to provide means for improving the presentation and mastery of content so that its retention will be facilitated.

SUGGESTED READINGS

Atkinson, R. C., & Shiffrin, R. M. Human memory: A proposed system and its control processes. In K. W. Spence & J. T. Spence (Eds.), *The psychology of learning and motivation (Vol. 2)*. New York: Academic Press, 1968.

Loftus, G. R., & Loftus, E. F. *Human memory: The processing of information*. Hillsdale, N. J.: Lawrence Erlbaum Associates, 1976.

Norman, D. A. *Memory and attention: An introduction to human information processing*. New York: Wiley, 1976.

Torgesen, J. The role of nonspecific factors in the task performance of learning disabled children: A theoretical assessment. *Journal of Learning Disabilities,* 1977, **10,** 27–34.

Torgesen, J., & Kail, R. V. Memory processes in exceptional children. In B. K. Keogh (Ed.), *Advances in Special Education*. Greenwich, Conn.: JAI Press, Inc., 1980.

Tulving, E., & Donaldson, W. (Eds.). *Organization of memory*. New York: Academic Press, 1972.

Chapter 5

Perception

INTRODUCTION

One of the most prominent characteristics of the field of learning disabilities has been the overriding concern with perceptual abilities. This concern, growing out of the work of early theorists in the field (Kephart, Cruickshank, Frostig, and others), is reflected today in the numerous perceptual testing and remedial programs widely available. The perceptual-deficit hypothesis continues to enjoy wide popularity even though research has failed to support efforts to identify, train, or remediate perceptual abilities (Arter & Jenkins, 1977). But, we are jumping ahead of ourselves. For the teacher of the learning disabled, questions need to be explored, such as: "What is perception? How does it develop? What is the relationship between academic proficiency and perceptual problems? What do we mean by remediating perceptual problems?"

WHAT IS PERCEPTION?

Though most of the professionals involved in the field of learning disabilities would classify themselves as developmentalists, most are of a specific ability tradition. To these individuals, perception and cognition form a developmental hierarchy. Many suggest that the development of higher-level functions is dependent upon prior acquisition of lower-level processes. Following this line of reasoning, perceptual deficits are viewed as contributing to inadequate cognitive performance and must be corrected before academic achievement can occur.

Since perception was viewed as the basis for later cognitive development, methods of determining what aspects of a child's perceptual functioning were at deficit needed to be developed. Perception was consequently viewed as an entity which could be subdivided into component parts for both assessment and subsequent remediation. Components such as figure-ground perception, auditory and visual closure, spatial relations, and position in space were identified as discrete elements of perception. Once these components were identified, tests were built to measure them and remediation strategies divised to teach them.

Two serious questions arise concerning these tests and remedial devices. First, is perception prerequisite to cognitive ability? Second, can perception be parsed into discrete elements?

Perception as the Basis of Cognition

The idea that perception is the basis of adequate conceptual ability receives little support from either current cognitive-developmental theorists or from information-processing theorists. Perception is probably best viewed as a process of information extraction (Forgus & Melamed, 1976) or information processing (Schiff, 1980). It is not a composite of discrete skills. It is, instead, the analysis of relations, sequences, classes, categories, objects, and symbol systems. Perception is an active, person-centered process. It is not the passive reception of stimuli.[1]

Piaget's theory has often been inaccurately interpreted as support for the notion that perceptual abilities underlie later cognitive development. Reid (1978) has summarized the arguments against this interpretation:

> First, citing Piaget's work as support for the argument that the child until ages 6 or 7 is predominantly a perceptual being (cf. Hallahan & Cruickshank, 1973) is to ignore his emphasis on activity (Piaget, 1977a). . . . Secondly, but related to the first issue, is the lack of understanding that the child's level of development affects his perception (Inhelder, Sinclair & Bovet, 1974, Piaget, 1969). . . . Finally, the understanding of topological space precedes mastery of Euclidean forms (Piaget & Inhelder, 1967, pp. 8–10). Neither Piaget's theory nor current information-processing theories support the assertion that early perception is the basis of later cognition (p. 205).

Interaction between Perception and Cognition

Perception is "a continuing process that varies from events which are of a simple, elementary nature to those of greater complexity which require more active learning and thinking" (Forgus & Melamed, 1976, p. 5, see Figure 5-1). There is obviously a great deal of separation between orientations which view perception and cognition as being hierarchically arranged and those which view perception

---

[1]Although we focus on the conscious analysis of information as perception, some have noted that there is an automatic perceptual system (Schiff, 1980) which is an unconscious and involuntary registering or storing of information. This level of perception does not become conscious until we are required to respond to it.

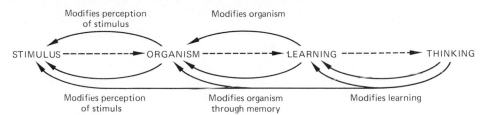

Figure 5-1 Interactive nature of the components of information extraction. *(Adapted from R. H. Forgus & L. E. Melamed,* Perception: A cognitive-stage approach. *New York: McGraw-Hill, 1976, p. 5.)*

as information extraction and suggest that cognitive strategies are the organizational factors of perception (see especially the Bjork model in Chapter 4).

Kolers and Perkins (1975) indicated that perception cannot be separated from cognition:

> Physical events never recur exactly. What we call the same object or event is different in some respect on a later occasion from what it was on an earlier one. When we "recognize" something, our perceptual apparatus ignores or reconciles the disparity between former and present appearances, to treat difference as sameness (pp. 228–229). . . . [so that perceptions] are not dictated by the optical array, but are the result of skills, dispositions, structures, and the like, interacting with it (p. 264).

PERCEPTUAL AND MOTOR THEORISTS

There are a number of perceptual-motor theorists who have had a significant impact upon the field of learning disabilities. Their orientation is predominantly developmental, with interests focusing on the visual components of learning and the development of adequate motor skills. The work of the most prominent of these theorists (Kephart, Getman, Frostig, Cratty, Barsch, and Doman and Delacato) will be discussed below. The intent of this section is to provide the reader with an understanding of the basic tenets of their respective systems. Though the usefulness of most of these programs has come under question, an understanding of the historical antecedents of the field is important to understanding current controversies being discussed in the literature (cf. Vellutino, 1978; Fletcher & Satz, 1979).

Newell C. Kephart

A hierarchical theorist, Kephart (1960, 1963) believed that at the basis of adequate school learning was the successful development of four patterns of motoric ability: (1) balance and maintenance of posture, (2) locomotion, (3) contact or motor activities, (4) receipt and propulsion. Balance and the maintenance of posture reflect the ability of the child to be able to orient and maintain position in space. Locomotion refers to the child's ability to move through space. Contact or motor activity is a generalization of body schema which relates to the child's ability to manipulate objects. Receipt and propulsion are related to the ability to coordinate movements of objects with simultaneous movements of the body. These *four motor generalizations* result from three successive stages of motor development.

The first of these stages, the practical stage, occurs during infancy and is characterized by exploration of movement. This movement, of both objects and body parts, forms the beginning environmental understanding necessary for later cognitive development. During this stage, two of the motor generalizations occur, balance and contact. The development of body schema leads to an understanding of directionality (consisting of verticality and laterality). Also occurring at this time are the beginnings of the child's awareness of the motor-temporal system, which consist of ideas of synchrony (simultaneous movements), sequence, and rhythm. At the second stage of development, the subjective stage, the motor generalizations of contact and locomotion appear to be of primary concern, with the child beginning to develop movement patterns. Kephart stressed the necessity of the perceptual-motor match (i.e., the integration of perception with motor activity) as the motor-spatial system develops. This match gives the child facility in exploring the world. At the third and final level, the child engages in complex motor generalizations coordinating his body with objects around him, and gaining facility in the ideas of receipt and propulsion. This last level involves the perception of direction, relations, spatial configuration, and form perception.

Kephart's (1968) basic intervention plan consists of the child's engaging in four groups of activities, including chalkboard activities, sensory-motor training, ocular control training, and form-perception training. The effectiveness of this program and its relation to academic skills will be noted in a subsequent section.

Gerald N. Getman

Gerald N. Getman is probably best known for viewing vision as the basis for adequate intellectual functioning (1961, 1962a, b). He firmly believed that good perception was basic to academic success. Note the following four statements by Getman, Kane, Halgren, & McKee (1968, p. iii) concerning vision and learning:

> **1** Academic performance in today's schools depends heavily upon form and symbol recognition and interpretation.
> **2** There are perceptual skills which can be developed and trained.
> **3** The development of perceptual skills is related to the levels of coordination of the body system, i.e., the better the coordinations of the body parts and body systems the better the prospects are for developing perception of forms and symbols.
> **4** The child whose perceptual skills have been developed and extended is the child who is free to profit from instruction and to learn independently. The greater the development of the perceptual skills, the greater the capacity for making learning more effective.

Believing that adequate visual perceptual ability was necessary for achievement, Getman proposed a six-level hierarchy of development which has a corresponding five-level training program. The six levels of Getman's program are: (1) general movement patterns, (2) special movement patterns, (3) eye movement patterns, (4) communication, (5) visualization patterns, and (6) visual perceptual organizations. His training procedures consist of practice in general coordination, balance, eye-hand coordination, eye movements, form recognition, and visual memory. Getman's theory has been criticized by numerous individuals (cf. Hagin, 1965; Silver, 1965) and has failed to be substantiated by research.

Ray Barsch

Ray Barsch is concerned with the human being as not only a visual organism, but as a visual organism operating within a spatial environment. Barsch's theory (1965b, 1967) of movigenics is the synthesis of ideas from numerous theorists. It rests upon ten basic ideas concerning people in spatial environments (Barsch, 1967):

1 Efficiency of movement is necessary for life.
2 People depend upon movement efficiency for survival.
3 Efficient movement depends on selection of relevant stimuli.
4 People process information through a percepto-cognitive system.
5 Movement occurs in space.
6 People move toward maturity as a function of natural development.
7 Stress is necessary for movement development.
8 Feedback is necessary.
9 The development of movement patterns expands through hierarchical movement.
10 Language allows the communication of movement efficiency.

These ten postulates form the basis for the development of the movigenics curriculum. This curriculum consists of twelve dimensions. The first four (muscular strength, dynamic balance, body awareness, and spatial awareness) constitute the group known as *postural-transport orientations.* The middle four dimensions (tactual dynamics, kinesthesia, auditory dynamics, and visual dynamics) constitute the *percepto-cognitive modes,* while the last four dimensions (bilaterality, rhythm, flexibility, and motor planning) are referred to as *degrees of freedom.* The curriculum is intended to improve academic functioning. As with other perceptual-motor programs, research has not been kind to the movigenics curriculum. The results of training studies are referred to in subsequent sections.

Bryant J. Cratty

Cratty (1967, 1969a, b, 1972, 1973) wrote that motor training is a valuable undertaking in and of itself, whether or not it influences school-related tasks. For Cratty, there are outcomes of motor training (physical activity) that are beneficial because they improve self-confidence, balance, grace, agility, and physical well-being. In addition, a teacher's knowledge of motor development is useful for understanding the requirements we make of children in classes, the relation of motor movement to other components of development, and the freedom that adequate motor ability gives a child.

Cratty's suggestions to educators revolve around a three-level theory of perceptual-motor learning. These levels include *general behavioral supports, perceptual-motor ability traits,* and *task specifics.* Within this framework, Cratty suggests a number of activities to improve body perception, balance, locomotion, agility, throwing, and catching. All are component parts of Cratty's screening test (1969a). Since Cratty does not claim that these activities improve academic skills, his program has not come under the same fire as the others.

Marianne Frostig

Perhaps one of the most well-known names in the field of learning disabilities is that of Marianne Frostig. Frostig's Developmental Test of Visual Perception (DTVP) is one of the most widely used tests in the field of learning disabilities. Frostig's interest in defining strengths and weaknesses within children's perceptual capabilities formed the basis for the development of her test (1967, 1972a, b, 1973, 1976). She believed that since information is gained primarily through the visual mode, deficits in visual perception would limit children's learning.

The DTVP (Frostig, Maslow, Lefever, & Whittlesey, 1964) subtests are: visual motor coordination, figure-ground, form constancy, position in space, and spatial relations. Chosen primarily because of their perceived relevance to school learning, early development, and neurological functioning, the subtests also form the basis for the remedial program developed by Frostig and Horne (1964). (The program consists of both games and activities, and worksheets.)

Both the DTVP and the related training program have been researched extensively. In general, the findings indicate poor subtest reliability, but good overall reliability (Frostig et al., 1964), ranging from .69 to .98. The test correlates with other tests of visual perception between .52 and .75. The subtests do not appear to be measuring separate entities, however, as noted by correlational (Hammill & Wiederholt, 1973; Larsen & Hammill, 1975) and factor analytic studies (Boyd & Randle, 1970; Cawley, Burrow, & Goodstein, 1968). As noted in subsequent sections, the training program appears to lack the power to improve visual perception *or* increase academic skills.

Glen Doman and Carl Delacato

Doman and Delacato, working from the theory of Temple Fay, developed what was to be referred to as the theory of neurological organization. This theory rests upon the belief that the well-functioning child develops "full neurological organization." Suggesting that children go through certain sequences of development, Doman and Delacato believed that if a child did not pass through the sequence, faulty neurological development would occur. Through appropriate testing, the child's development could be ascertained and activities prescribed that would lead to full neurological organization (Delacato, 1959, 1966).

The theory was based upon three assumptions: (1) ontogeny recapitulates phylogeny (the development of the individual proceeds in the same sequence as the development of the species); (2) brain functions are localized; and (3) laterality is a necessary prerequisite to adequate academic functioning. These assumptions were severely criticized by Robbins and Glass (1969) and Freeman (1967) who presented evidence that all three of the assumptions were not upheld by current knowledge.[2]

Doman and Delacato instituted a program of intervention strategies for use with children thought to have failed to develop full neurological organization. The remedial strategies included physical activities thought to induce correct neurological growth. For children unable to participate independently, the limbs were externally manipulated, often by teams of adults. These manipulations were referred to as "patterning" and were typically carried out on an extremely rigid schedule.

The Doman and Delacato techniques came under serious attack for both the assumptions and the training techniques utilized. In 1968, numerous professional organizations censured the Doman and Delacato treatments. Among these organizations were the American Academy for Cerebral Palsy, the American Academy of Physical Medicine and Rehabilitation, the Canadian Association for Children with Learning Disabilities, the National Association for Retarded Children, and the Canadian Rehabilitation Council for the Disabled. Though criticism still abounds, the program continues to thrive with institutes throughout the United States. *Individuals* attest to cases where treatment was of benefit, but the efficacy of the technique has never been established through any type of controlled study. To date, the organization which provides the Doman and Delacato treatment has refused to allow outside evaluation of their treatment programs.

Summary

The above individuals are by no means the only ones who have attempted to intervene in the perceptual or motor development of children with learning disabilities. They have, however, had the greatest impact upon the field. Their contributions should be remembered not for what they failed to do, but for the catalytic force they provided for research into the functioning of the learning disabled child. As Torgesen and Kail (1980) have noted, however, the field must move beyond their legacy—a legacy that suggests that basic psychological functions have been disrupted in learning disabled children by (inferred) brain dysfunction. It is now time to probe for greater explanatory power.

PERCEPTUAL DISABILITIES

Studies of the performance of learning disabled children on traditional tasks of perceptual functioning have established a number of consistent, negative

---

[2]The interested reader is referred to these works for a complete analysis of the controversy surrounding the Doman and Delacato approach.

findings. The area of visual processing has received the most attention, because most of the early theorists in the field of learning disabilities were visually oriented (not to mention historically relevant researchers such as Strauss and Werner) and most academic functioning was thought to be related to the processing of visual material. Reading, for example, appears intuitively to be a visual task and impaired perceptual functioning was thought to be related to impaired reading ability. (The soundness of this view is discussed at length in Chapter 13.)

Visual Perception and Visual-Motor Ability

One point that has not been addressed explicitly in the foregoing discussion is that the systems bear no resemblance to the cognitive systems first described. The area of visual perception has usually been researched using variables such as eye-hand coordination, position in space, form constancy, spatial relations, and closure. Nearly all of the tests confound visual perception with motor ability (by requiring the child to trace, draw, etc.). They are more properly described, therefore, as tests of visual-motor integration. Interestingly, few studies are available that build a data base for establishing the validity of these types of visual perception or the visual-motor errors characteristic of learning disabled children. Most of the available data come from correlational studies examining the relation of academic skills to the perceptual and perceptual-motor abilities of children with reading problems. There are a number of excellent reviews summarizing the literature with respect to visual perception and visual-motor functioning and academic skills (Bortner, 1974; Hammill, 1972; Hammill & Wiederholt, 1972; Larsen & Hammill, 1975). This section will summarize these studies in order to present a synthesis of relevant information.

Perhaps the most important conclusion to be drawn from the correlational literature on the relation of visual perception and visual-motor skills to academic subjects is that the correlations are generally not large enough to be considered useful for educational purposes (Hammill, 1972; Larsen & Hammill, 1975). Hammill (1972) reviewed post-1955 studies, but found only eleven acceptable statistically. Five of the eleven reported nonsignificant correlations. Of the three studies having correlations greater than .50, two used fewer than twenty-five subjects and two did not partial out the effects of IQ. Three of the studies reported correlations, which though statistically significant, were between .30 and .49. A growing literature suggests that not only do the correlations between various perceptual tests and academic skills remain below the significance level, but also that the functioning of disabled and nondisabled groups is sometimes virtually identical (Larsen, Rogers, & Sowell, 1976).

Vellutino and his colleagues (Vellutino, Smith, Steger, & Kaman, 1975; Vellutino, Steger, & Kandel, 1972), argue that perceptual functioning is not at issue in defining differences between good and poor readers. "Disabled readers can perceive letter and word symbols accurately, but mislabel them in oral reading because of a basic difficulty in associating symbols with their verbal counterparts" (Vellutino, Steger, Moyer, Harding, & Niles, 1977, p. 378).

Similarly, studies have shown that directional confusion may be a *result* and not a *cause* of reading disability and that good and poor readers have identical scanning tendencies in visual recall (Vellutino, Pruzek, Steger, & Meshoulam, 1973; Vellutino, Steger, DeSetto, & Phillips, 1975; Vellutino, Steger, Kaman, & DeSetto, 1975). Vellutino (1977) concluded that when visual perception is investigated as a causative agent in reading disabilities, research fails to substantiate a causal relation. Rather, he suggests that reading disabilities be viewed as verbal deficits. More will be said of this in the section dealing with auditory perception and in Chapter 13 on reading.

There is a small body of literature dealing with the perceptual abilities of children with brain injury of both the soft- and hard-sign varieties. Brain-injured children have been noted to perform more poorly than normal children on tasks of spatial orientation (in which they are asked to find a route by means of a visual map) (Rudel & Teuber, 1971; Rudel, Teuber, & Twitchell, 1974), body scheme (Rudel, Teuber, & Twitchell, 1974), and mixed or hidden figures (Cobrinik, 1959; Teuber & Rudel, 1962). Others have noted that visual confusion is often present during rapid, automatized naming of visually presented pictures (Denckla & Rudel, 1976). A host of concomitant perceptual disorders (Bortner, 1971; Ingram, 1969; Mattis, French, & Rapin, 1975) have been noted including directional confusion (Hermann, 1959), figure-ground difficulties (Bender, 1967; Birch, 1962), inadequate visual synthesis and analysis (Birch, 1962), visual-motor difficulties (Cruickshank, 1967; Frostig & Maslow, 1973; Kephart, 1960), and visual-memory deficits (Guthrie & Goldberg, 1972; Chalfant & Scheffelin, 1969).

In sum there seems to be little doubt that learning disabled children, brain-injured children, and poor readers exhibit poor performances on various types of perceptual tasks. It is the *nature* of the relation between perceptual and academic success that is unclear. Correlational studies indicate only that they tend to co-occur.

Auditory Perception

Research interest eventually shifted to the area of auditory perception, but the results parallel those of the visual perception research. There exists a small but significant body of literature that investigated the relation of auditory perception to brain injury and reading disabilities. Significant correlations were found between forward and backward digit span and brain damage (McFie, 1969; Rudel & Denckla, 1974), discrimination of speech sounds and poor reading (Johnson & Myklebust, 1967; Wepman, 1960), and auditory sequencing problems and reading deficits (Senf, 1969).

The relation of auditory processing variables to academic achievement has been widely researched. The literature is not as large, however, as that pertaining to visual perception. The most comprehensive review to date is the one conducted by Hammill and Larsen (1974) in which thirty-three studies referencing over 300 individual correlation coefficients are reported. The authors concluded that the traditional auditory perceptual tasks utilized in special education are not substantially (and certainly not causally) related to adequate reading ability. The tasks upon which these correlations were based included auditory-visual integration, sound blending, auditory memory, phonemic sound discrimination, and nonphonemic discrimination. In a recent review Lyon (1977) reached a similar conclusion: "The relationship of auditory-perceptual skills to reading ability does not support the view that the intact auditory-perceptual skills are necessary for the adequate development of reading ability" (p. 570).

In sum, the work on the relation of auditory perceptual ability to academic skills suggests that, as tested, auditory perceptual abilities have little to do with academic success. There appear, however, to be other auditory phenomenon which may have some significant relation to reading (see the discussion of linguistic awareness in Chapter 13).

Sensory Integration

The view that an individual must be able to "integrate" information across modalities led to an interest in the relations of various intersensory abilities in academic skills.[3] The seminal work in this area was done by Birch and Belmont (1964). Their concern was with auditory to visual, match-to-sample processing. Children listened to taped patterns and were asked to select visual patterns which matched. In a series of studies employing retarded readers (Birch & Belmont, I., 1964, 1965b; Muehl & Kremenak, 1966) and brain-damaged individuals (Aten & Davis, 1968; Birch & Belmont, 1964; Birch & Belmont, 1965a), the deficit populations performed less well than the normal control populations. Expanding the basic paradigm, others have documented crossmodal difficulties with the use of haptic and visual forms in brain-damaged persons (Connors & Barta, 1967; Rudel & Teuber, 1971).

The crossmodal ability research came under attack from two positions. First, in a series of articles the methodology was questioned regarding specific details of presentation, feedback, and reward systems (Beery, 1967; Bryden, 1972; DeLeon, Raskin, & Gruen, 1970; Ford, 1967; Goodnow, 1971; Kahn & Birch, 1968; Milner & Bryant, 1970; Muehl & Kremenak, 1966; Rudnick, Sterritt, & Flax, 1967; Sterritt & Rudnick, 1966.) As pointed out by Freides (1974), however, none of the procedural changes disconfirmed the findings that handicapped subjects performed less well than normal subjects on tasks of intersensory processing.

Further attack on the position that intersensory processing was at the heart of the disabilities came not in the form of methodological problems but from the finding that "Retarded readers, brain-damaged and middle-class and impoverished children were impaired intramodally as well as crossmodally" (Freides, 1974, p. 286). Studies confirming these findings were done by Muehl and Kremenak (1966), McGrady and Olson (1970), Zurif and Carson (1970), Rudel

---

[3]Freides' (1974) review of the intersensory research is the most complete and the most thorough analysis available. It was used as the basis for this report.

and Teuber (1971), Sterritt, Martin, and Rudnick (1971), Bryden (1972), Kuhlman and Wolking (1972), Rudnick, Martin, and Sterritt (1972), and Vande Voort, Senf, and Benton (1972). Freides noted that "Birch and his associates indicated that the auditory-visual integrative task was sensitive to just about any form of disorder, including youth" (1974, p. 303). With the deficits noted in both intra- and intermodality processing, it appears that what researchers were noting was a generalized processing deficit, and not a unique or specific disability related to crossmodal processing.

Modality Preferences

One of the major goals in the evaluation of learning disabled children became, during the 1960s, the differentiation of strong and deficient modalities. Basic to this goal was the belief that not only could preferred modalities be identified, but that once identified, instructional strategies could be developed to correspond to these references. This belief has had very little empirical justification.[4]

Of the available research, the studies by Newcomer and Goodman (1975) and Ringler and Smith (1973) are illustrative. Neither of the studies found any significant results indicating that matching modality preference to instructional technique was of benefit. Later Newcomer and Hammill (1976) and Salvia and Ysseldyke (1978) in their reviews of research on the ITPA determined that *modality preference could not be established with accuracy.* Furthermore, there is evidence (cited in Freides, 1974) to suggest that people use the *most efficient mode* for processing and not necessarily the mode of presentation. There is a fallacy, therefore, in the task-analytic assumption that teachers can control the way a child operates on a problem by controlling the modes of input or output.

MOTOR DISABILITIES

Research concerning motor impairment in learning disabled children is not so extensive as that on perception. There is evidence that motor impairments frequently exist in the population of learning disabled children. These reports are primarily concerned with the clinical reports of clumsiness, lack of body awareness, poor directionality, lack of gross and fine motor coordination, and general unorganized behavior. (See for example the works of Clements, 1966; Chalfant & Scheiffelin, 1969; Kephart, 1960, 1963, 1968.)

The importance that early perceptual-motor theorists accorded motor functioning was noted earlier in this chapter. The sequence of development was thought to be from motor understanding to perception to cognition. A disability at the motor level was thought to impair the development of abilities at higher levels. This position has not, of course, been substantiated. Work by Rosner (1973), Cratty (1970), Hallahan and Cruickshank (1973), and Masland (1969) attests to the lack of correlation between motor impairment and academic success.

[4]The reader is referred to Bracht (1974) for a review of ATI research in education.

TRAINING OF PERCEPTUAL AND PERCEPTUAL-MOTOR FUNCTIONING AND THEIR RELATION TO ACADEMIC ACHIEVEMENT

The logical extension of the belief that motor and perceptual functioning underlie adequate academic achievement is that intervention should be directed toward improving them when deficits are found. Two questions arise regarding this approach: (a) Can we train perceptual and motor functions? (b) Is there any carryover into academic skills?

Research on Training Visual-Perceptual Processes

Research in the training of visual perception has provided little positive encouragement for its proponents. The cumulative results of several reviews (Hallahan & Cruickshank, 1973; Hammill, 1972; Hammill & Wiederholt, 1973; Larsen & Hammill, 1975; Myers & Hammill, 1976) indicate that extensive, serious methodological errors (such as inadequate length of time in training, inappropriate control groups, lack of control for Hawthorne effect, inadequate numbers of subjects, inappropriate training materials, and inadequate data analysis) eliminate over half of the available studies from serious consideration. Of those that remain, the results are generally negative. In addition, as the experimental procedures become more stringent, the tendency is to find increasingly negative results (Myers & Hammill, 1976).

The work by Myers and Hammill is illustrative of the findings in general. They note that when the Frostig approach is used as the intervention strategy, over half of the available studies indicate no benefits to visual-motor areas, while over two-thirds of the studies using the approaches of Kephart, Getman, Cratty, and Barsch report negative results. Hallahan and Cruickshank (1973) noted that the *one* adequate study which they identified dealing with the Frostig program (Alley, 1968) found no positive effects of the program. The Larsen and Hammill (1975) work looking at the effect of training on the areas of visual discrimination, spatial relations, memory, and auditory-visual integration indicated only minimal relations of these variables to academic achievement. The effects of training to improve sensory-motor functioning appear also to be generally lacking. In sum, although there are those who offer testimonial that one or another of the perceptual-motor programs has worked with a given child, the controlled research argues against the continued use of such programs.

Research Related to Perceptual and Perceptual-Motor Functioning and Increased Academic Skills

The question "Does training in perceptual and perceptual-motor abilities result in increased academic, cognitive, or language abilities?" has been answered with a resounding no. The studies reviewed by Hallahan and Cruickshank (1973) and those of Myers and Hammill (1976) clearly indicate that *academic gains cannot be expected* from the use of perceptual and perceptual-motor training programs. The Myers and Hammill review suggested that over 70 percent of the studies reviewed indicate no positive effects of training programs on academic, cognitive, or language abilities, while at least another 8 percent show equivocal results *regardless of the training procedures implemented.*

Summary

The research evidence leads us to these conclusions: perceptual and perceptual-motor training are ineffective for (1) improving the perceptual-motor abilities themselves and (2) for promoting increases in academic achievement.

IMPLICATIONS FOR INSTRUCTION

We suggest only one approach for teachers of children with perceptual difficulties: teach the children to read, write, and do arithmetic! If, for example, a child is reversing letters, it does no good to instruct him in a perceptual program and hope for the reversals to eliminate themselves. Rather, the teacher should deal with the reversed letters directly. That most often means helping children become aware of the similarities and differences between letters and in focusing on their using syntactic and semantic cues as decoding aids. Children who understand what they are reading seldom confuse *was* for *saw* in a sentence. The crux of the matter is that if perception is information extraction, then training on static perceptual tasks will never lead to academic gains. We must engage instead in helping the child develop appropriate learning strategies for extracting meaning.

SUMMARY AND CONCLUSIONS

Perception has been an overriding concern in the field of learning disabilities. Indeed, the popular view of the child with a learning disability is that he or she reads letters backwards, almost in mirror-fashion.

Perception was viewed for a long time as the basis for later cognitive development. Early workers in the field (Kephart, Frostig, Barsch, Getman, Doman, and Delacato) advocated that perceptual problems be treated directly and that they be treated before academic interventions were attempted. More modern conceptions of perception recognize that perception and cognition are interactive and have mutually influencing effects at all developmental levels.

Poor performances on perceptual, perceptual-motor, and sensory integration tasks are characteristic of learning disabled children. Although these deficits have been identified, their significance is unclear and their value as the basis for intervention programs lacks validation. The only recommendation that can be made to teachers who work with children who exhibit such deficits is that they concentrate on teaching the curriculum. Teaching perceptual tasks does not foster academic gains, neither does it prepare children for careers and/or advanced schooling. Furthermore, crosscultural research (cited in Gallagher & Reid, in press) has indicated that near-point perception improves as a function of instruction in reading.

SUGGESTED READINGS

Anderson, R. C., Spiro, R. J., & Montague, W. E. (Eds.). *Schooling and the acquisition of knowledge.* Hillsdale, N. J.: Lawrence Erlbaum Associates, 1977.

Forgus, R. H., & Melamed, L. E. *Perception: A cognitive-stage approach.* New York: McGraw-Hill, 1976.

Freides, D. Human information processing and sensory modality: Cross-modal functions, information complexity, memory, and deficit. *Psychological Bulletin,* 1974, **81,** 284–310.

Newcomer, P. L., & Hammill, D. D. *Psycholinguistics in the schools.* Columbus, Ohio: Charles E. Merrill, 1976.

Pick, H. L., & Saltzman, E. *Modes of perceiving and processing information.* Hillsdale, N. J.: Lawrence Erlbaum Associates, 1978.

Chapter 6

Attention and Vigilance

INTRODUCTION

Attention and the related term *vigilance* mean more things to more people than perhaps any word other than *perception*. For William James, the definition of attention was obvious:

> Everyone knows what attention is. It is the taking possession by the mind, in clear and vivid form, of one out of what seem several simultaneously possible objects or trains of thought. Focalization, concentration, of consciousness are of its essence. It implies withdrawal from some things in order to deal effectively with others (James, 1890, p. 403–404).

Attention has been examined as a part of perceptual processing, has itself been defined as a psychological process, has been defined as both a transient state and a developed ability, and has been related to mental age, school achievement, and cognitive style. Attention also has been related to cognitive span and cognitive process, to physiological states, and not least of all, to learning disabilities. As Norman suggests (1976), perhaps the notion of what attention is and does was clear to James, but since his time, the clarity has been lost in a sea of competing theories, models, terminology, and research evidence. It conjures up nothing less than visions of the elephant examined by blind men.

A DEFINITION OF ATTENTION AND VIGILANCE

The definitions employed in this chapter will reflect a cognitive, information processing viewpoint. Attention is defined as an activity of cognitive perform-ance (Blumenthal, 1977). We may think of attention as the capacity to focus our awareness. This focusing may be to specific external stimuli, the meaning of a conversation, or to internal states that have no external referents. Focusing our awareness upon internal or external stimuli allows us to impose an order upon both our thoughts and information.

Vigilance may be defined as a type of cognitive control (Blumenthal, 1977) whereby our awareness of a stimulus, event, or thought is maintained in focus over some time period. Blumenthal notes in his discussion of cognitive controls (in which vigilance is included) "cognitive control maintains the interacting components of cognition on one train of action, recycling one set of perceptions, memories, or motor activities, and cognitive control maintains coherence of thought during acts of making choices and pursuing goals" (p. 151).

Any theory of attention presupposes some orientation with regard to what is perceived by the individual, and with regard to the level at which the attentive process takes place. Attention can be viewed as the selective aspect of both one's perception and response (Forgus & Melamed, 1976). First, it implies that a given characteristic of the stimulus "catches" our awareness, and, second that internal decisions also control that awareness (recall Bjork's model in Chapter 4).

Models of Attention

Three models that have dominated ideas of attention for a number of years are those referred to as *(A)* single-channel, limited-capacity, *(B)* multichannel, limited-capacity attentional, and *(C)* parallel, unlimited-capacity nonattention-al. (See Figure 6-1.)

The first model of attention was designed by Broadbent (1958) and reflected the belief that (1) attention is switched rapidly between competing sources of information and (2) that information is processed from only one source at a time. It is a model of what might be called *early selective attention*, which essentially means that the stimulus to be attended to is selected in the very beginning of the information processing event. The model predicts that pertinent stimuli will be selected primarily on the basis of physical traits (tone, frequency, hue, density, etc.). In addition, the model suggests not only that capacity is limited, but that information must be attended to serially. In 1964, Treisman elaborated upon the difficulties of the Broadbent model by showing that more than one stimulus could be attended to at one time, and that a consideration of stimulus relevance was necessary to determine the level of processing which would (or would not) occur.

In the multichannel model, the capacity of the individual to attend to sources of information is still limited, but an individual may attend to a number of sources of information (at the superordinate and subordinate levels) provided that the channel capacity is available. This model is reflected in the work of

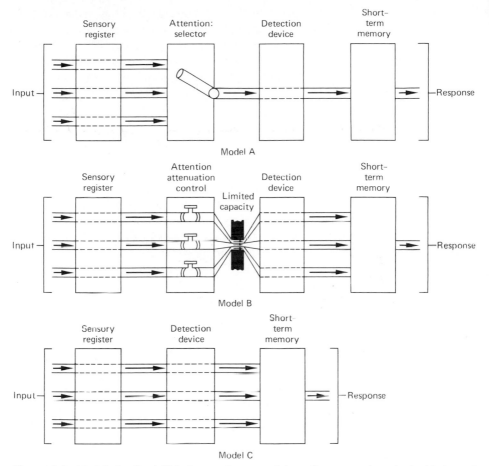

Figure 6-1 Models for the initial stages of sensory information processing. *A,* single-channel, limited-capacity attentional model; *B,* multichannel, limited-capacity attentional model; *C,* parallel, unlimited-capacity non-attentional model. *(From R. M. Shiffrin & W. S. Geisler, Visual recognition in a theory of information processing. In R. L. Solso (Ed.),* Contemporary issues in cognitive psychology: The Loyola Symposium. *Washington, D. C.: V. H. Winston & Sons, 1973, p. 63.)*

Norman and Rumelhart (1970), Neisser (1967), and Norman and Bobrow (1975).

The first two models are conceptualized as two-stage models. In order that the reader have a better understanding of what is meant by a two-stage model, let us consider Neisser's (1967) model. It is both representative and widely used in the research pertaining to learning disabled (and other special) populations. Neisser's conceptualization of what happens during attention is predicated upon the belief that in order to focus upon a specific object or stimulus, we must first differentiate that object from its environmental background. Neisser therefore proposed a preattentive stage which is characterized by a rather global analysis of the entire object. When this first stage is completed, we are able to proceed to a more analytic stage, called the focal attention phase. During this second phase, the figure is analyzed into its specific informational aspects. Thus, we move from a more peripheral to a more central type of vision—from identification to a decision about the next eye movement (Forgus & Melamed, 1976). Does the two-stage model "work" as a model of attention? As with many other areas of research pertinent to understanding the learning disabled, the evidence is unclear. Two-stage models employing some type of movement from global attending to specific attending appear valid for understanding only some of the data.

The third model (parallel, unlimited-capacity nonattentional) assumes "no attention and in some cases no limitations on capacity during perceptual processing. All attentional effects are due to characteristics of short-term store following perceptual processing" (Shiffrin & Geisler, 1973, p. 63; also see the discussion of Anderson's 1975 model in Chapter 3.). Perhaps the most novel of the models is the third, because it attempts to do away with the whole notion of attention. It places what is attended to within the realm of *short-term memory* and the cognitive processes utilized within that system.

> As soon as we are forced to use the meaning of signals to aid us in our selection, the problem becomes very complex. The meaning of the peculiar sound waveform that comprises a word cannot be determined without extensive analysis of the signal, an analysis that must use information stored in memory. At this point, the whole purpose of attention seems to disappear, for if we need to extract the meaning of all incoming signals to determine what to attend to, how does the idea of selectivity help us? (Norman, 1976, p. 30).

Perhaps the answer is that selectivity does not help at all, at least this was the position taken by Schiffrin and Geisler (1973) who suggested that: (1) all information undergoes processing; (2) every source is at least processed into short-term memory; and (3) it is during the employment of cognitive strategies utilized in short-term memory that selective mechanisms are introduced. In short, they suggested a model of *late selective attention*.

Do early selection mechanisms or late selection mechanisms govern processing? To what degree is attention and focusing of attention cognitively controlled? Is attention serial (one thing at a time processed) or parallel (with simultaneous mechanisms for analysis)? At present, research findings can be interpreted as support for both models. More of the research, however, is in support of the Shiffrin and Geisler model (Corteen & Wood, 1972; McKay, 1973; Shiffrin & Geisler, 1973; Von Wright, Anderson, & Stenman, 1975).[1]

Summary

An approach to attention which emphasizes the cognitive process involved in the child's manipulation of information allows the analysis of what is actually

---

[1]The model referred to here as the Shiffrin and Geisler model is, in actuality, the culmination of work by a number of individuals including Deutsch and Deutsch (1963), Deutsch, Deutsch, and Lindsay (1967), Shiffrin and Gardner (1972), Shiffrin, Gardner, and Allmeyer (1972) and Shiffrin, Craig, and Cohen (1972).

happening. It provides not only a description of the behavior, but also an explanation of what is occurring. Because the research to date is inconclusive, we will assume that those models which treat attention as a preanalysis function and those which treat it as a late analysis function are both useful in discussing different types of problems.

THE DEVELOPMENT OF ATTENTION

Attentional behavior and cognitive development are exceedingly difficult to separate (Blumenthal, 1977; Piaget, 1976). First, attention is a cognitive process whose existence depends upon other cognitive processes. Every child in infancy (if not before) is engaged in organizing experiences. This organizational propensity allows children to begin to impose order upon the world, which in turn enables information to be extracted and meanings to be developed. Humans select stimuli which have consistency, importance, and relevance, perceived as a function of current ideas about the world (Smith, 1977). This is not to suggest that we attend only to what is already known. We also attend to those things that provoke us and necessitate changes in our cognitive abilities. Except in instances in which the intensity of the stimuli causes an involuntary response, attention and cognition become almost inseparable.

That children develop facility in attentional behavior even during infancy has been well documented. Young infants focus in response to such varied stimuli as voice versus nonvoice noise, the smell of mother, and their mother's voice. Although some authors still tend to view these behaviors as orientating reflexes or the orientation of receptor organs, that view denies the now recognized intentionality of these infant behaviors (McFarlane, 1978; Schiff, 1980). Two types of attention may be useful in analyzing infant behavior (Lewis, 1975). The first type is the infant's perception of stimuli on the basis of intensity: an involuntary response to a loud noise or a flash of light. The second type is voluntary and depends on such factors as effective attachment, motivation, or previous knowledge. This second type of attention is dependent upon the organism's already developing cognitive structures.

The continued development of what might be called intentional attention has been documented in a number of studies (Maccoby, 1967, 1969; Mackworth & Bruner, 1966; Vurpillot, 1968). Kagan (1967, 1970) suggested, for example, that the fixations which the infant engages in are the beginnings and expansions of internal representations. Indices such as smiling and cardiac deceleration during the infant's fixations on a face reflect more than the development of coding cell patterns. Very early in the infant's life, the differentiation of schemata could become a cognitive control process, focusing the child's behavior. Internal representations may then account for the preferences of children to different types of patterns later in life.

Much of the evidence which supports a developmental perspective is derived from studies in which the correlates of attention have been measured (for a review see Krupski, 1980). During the organism's attention to a task, there are physiological changes that occur related to respiration (Lacey, 1959,

1967), heart rate (Sroufe, 1975; Sroufe, Sonies, West, & Wright, 1973), skin conductivity (Kahneman, Tursky, Shapiro, & Crider, 1969), and brain wave features (both electroencephalograph and evoked potention) (Adrian & Mathews, 1934; Ross & Ross, 1976; Fuller, 1978; Glass, 1959, 1960, 1964; Kooi, 1971; Mulholland, 1969). In every case evidence suggests that the ability to attend improves and increases in duration with age. Attentive ability may be impaired by limitations in (1) the amount of data available to work with, (2) the capacity of the system, (3) the ability to organize the material, and (4) the ability to relate new material to past experience.

In sum attention is a cognitive process governed by the *meaningfulness* of stimuli. It is often measured by the use of physiological correlates. Attention is not a passive perceptual function. It is an *active, dynamic state* that improves throughout childhood (Forgus & Melamed, 1976; Schiff, 1980).

Selective Attention Deficits in the Learning Disabled

There is considerable evidence that attentional deficits exist within the learning disabled population when tasks requiring voluntary attention, either sustained (Krupski, 1980) or short-term (Hallahan & Reeve, 1980) are employed. Research has been carried out to examine the effects of proximal distractors (Tarver & Hallahan, 1974), field-independence/dependence (Keogh & Donlon, 1972), color word reversal (having *red* printed in green and *green* in red) (Mondani & Tutko, 1969), presence of irrelevant stimuli (Atkinson & Seunath, 1973), embedded figures (Sabatino & Ysseldyke, 1972), and neurological damage (Clements & Peters, 1962; Chalfant & Scheiffelin, 1969; Ounsted, 1955). Although the existence of attention-related deficits among children who are learning disabled has been well documented, explanations as to why they occur and their impact are still lacking.

A cognitive approach to the study of attention calls into question the rather popular view that a deficit in early selective attention may cause the learning difficulties of many children. This view has been advanced primarily by Ross (1976) and Hallahan and his colleagues (Hallahan, 1975; Hallahan, Gajar, Cohen, & Tarver, 1978; Hallahan, Kauffman, & Ball, 1973; Hallahan, Kauffman, & Ball, 1974; Hallahan, Tarver, Kauffman, & Graybeal, 1979; Tarver, Hallahan, Cohen, & Kaufmann, 1977; Tarver, Hallahan, Kauffman, & Ball, 1976). They argue that the learning disabled child is ineffective in attending to relevant rather than irrelevant stimuli, and that it is this basic lack of selective attention which produces the learning disability.

The selective attention research was based on Broadbent's (1958) model, in which he described attention as a single-channel process. For more than one stimulus to be processed, the individual was thought to need to "switch" back and forth between the stimuli. Maccoby and Hagen (1965) and Hagen (1967) constructed a task designed to analyze selective attention as a developing process in children.

This task consists of a series of cards (seven in all) with two pictures on each card. On top is a picture of an animal and on the bottom a picture of an object.

Each child is instructed to pay attention to the animals only. The cards are shown, one at a time to the child, at the rate of one item every two seconds. The cards are placed face down in front of the child and the child is shown a probe card and asked to turn over the card identical to the probe card. Next, the child is presented with a large card showing the seven animals and is asked to match the animals with the objects shown during the testing phase. The first phase (in which the animals are the objects of the questions) is referred to as the central learning task. The second phase is referred to as the incidental learning task, incidental because the child is at no time instructed to focus upon the objects or to associate animals to objects. The use of the task is well documented in the investigation of the development of selective attention in normal populations between the first and seventh grades (Hagen & Kail, 1975). The results of these studies have affirmed that as age increases, the scores on the central learning task increase. The incidental scores, however, have been found to remain the same or to decline (though the decline in scores is not the usual finding).

Since the central learning/incidental learning paradigm is supposedly sensitive to selective attention fluctuations, the task was employed by Hallahan and his colleagues in an attempt to ascertain whether differences between normal and learning disabled children could be identified. The results of their studies (listed above) supported the contention that the learning disabled performed differently. This line of research was potentially important for the field of learning disabilities. First, it was an attempt to describe developmentally the attentional performance of learning disabled children. Second, these investigations advanced beyond the perceptual differentiation problems which previously dominated explanations of learning problems. Third, the research may lead to an understanding of a more pervasive type of disability than has previously been considered.

A comparison of the incidental and central learning scores of the learning disabled children, however, indicated that they *were* selectively attending to the task. In every case, the mean scores on the central task exceeded the mean scores for the incidental task. The fact that the learning disabled did not score as highly as the normal children (that the proportion of central to incidental scores was low) is probably indicative of inefficient processing and not inattention. This interpretation is substantiated by the fact that the incidental scores of the learning disabled did not significantly differ from the scores of the normal children. To employ the construct of selective attention is to place the processing limitations of the learning disabled too early in the sequence.

Employing an alternative model such as that of Shiffrin and Geisler could be useful in reinterpreting the findings. In the Shiffrin and Geisler model, the process of "selection" occurs in short-term memory. What is selected is organized, coded and, in short, "worked out" by the individual. What Hallahan et al. described in their work may be the effect of inefficient cognitive processing on a learning task. Indeed this selective attention deficit may easily be described as a problem in selective *recall*. Although Tarver et al. (1977) later suggested that verbal rehearsal may be the cause of such a deficit, it would be important to recognize that rehearsal is also only one of many strategies available to the individual. Hypotheses related to other strategies would need to be investigated as well.

INTERVENTION STRATEGIES FOR CHILDREN WITH ATTENTIONAL DEFICITS

Children who, for whatever hypothesized reason, are having difficulty attending in learning situations are at a considerable disadvantage. How does the teacher intervene to enhance the child's capabilities? Both strategies for modifying the child's behavior and strategies for modifying the learning experience can be used.

Strategies for Modifying Child Behavior

Since the lack of attention is often viewed as a characteristic of the hyperactive syndrome, it is no surprise that the methods of treatment advocated for the hyperactive are the same ones often suggested for the child with attentional deficits. Two interventions often used with both the hyperactive and children with attentional deficits are drug therapy and diet control. Both of these techniques rest upon the assumption that the attentional deficit is related to the physiological or neurophysiological characteristics of the child. The effects of these therapeutic techniques appear to have the effect (when successful) of allowing a better integrated response. They do not in and of themselves result in any greater degree of learning, but they do lead to sustained attention (Hallahan & Cruickshank, 1973).

The use of verbal rehearsal strategies is a third way of modifying the attentional behavior of the child. Rehearsal encourages active processing of the material and thereby enhances attention. It is closely related to verbal labeling. Labeling is, in effect, a coding strategy which facilitates the processing and storage of material (see Chapter 4). Wheeler and Dusek (1973) found that induced verbal labeling had a facilitating effect for young children, while for older children the labeling appeared to be a hindrance. In discussing the application of labeling to the learning disabled population, Ross (1976) raised an important point. He noted that it may be totally inappropriate and possibly harmful to a child if an elementary strategy is imposed at an inappropriate level. As with any technique utilized with learning disabled children, verbal labeling should be introduced judiciously. Not all children respond to instructional techniques in the same manner. Labeling may prove beneficial to some children, while proving to be an ineffective strategy for others. As noted earlier, however, induced labeling may eliminate performance differences between learning disabled and normally achieving children on a recall task (Torgesen & Goldman, 1977).

The technique of having a child engage in reflection prior to action constitutes another type of child-oriented modification. This technique ("look before you leap") rests upon the belief that individuals will perform better if they reflect on what it is that they are to accomplish. This is, in effect, a method of requiring the child to organize through reflection prior to action. This technique has been found to be useful in helping hyperactive children to focus attention (Douglas, 1972; Ross & Ross, 1976). By actively engaging in thinking through a task, children alert themselves to the requirements of the task. They are, in effect, making sure that the necessary processing capacity will be available. This mustering of resources appears to have the effect of intensifying the level of concentration and thereby increasing processing efficiency.

Self-Monitoring Strategies

Currently, considerable attention is being given to children's self-monitoring and self-control of both task-oriented and social behaviors. Cognitive behavior modification (CBM) is an approach that attempts to modify behavior and emotion by influencing or changing the individual's pattern of thought. CBM focuses on cognitive change. CBM includes numerous self-treatment techniques, among them, self-guidance, self-verbalization, self-instruction, self-monitoring, self-recording, self-reinforcement, self-rehearsal, and self-talk (Lloyd, 1980). As some have noted (Keogh & Glover, 1980), many treatments and interventions fit under the CBM rubric with the difference among them being where along the behavioral/cognitive continuum they appear to fit. Whatever the term chosen, there are a number of principles that appear to be relatively stable (Pressley, 1979). First, the focus is on cognitive change as the active ingredient in successful treatment. Second, for intervention to be successful, the individual must understand, to some degree, the process involved. Third, the emphasis is on self-treatment to the extent that individuals ultimately monitor, instruct and record their own behavior. The intent is to ensure that the individual will be able to apply the intervention when needed without, or with minimal, help. Fourth, the goal of the therapy is to inculcate more adequate strategies for interaction with the environment (Lloyd, 1980; Mahoney, 1977; Mahoney & Kazdin, 1979; Meichenbaum, 1977; Meichenbaum, 1979). Though some of these techniques are not new (i.e., verbal rehearsal, behavior modification, etc.), their use to affect change in cognitive strategies is relatively recent. The potential power of CBM may hold promise for the learning disabled, since many suffer from problems related to the deployment of attention/vigilance, strategizing, etc.

The basic CBM technique employed in many situations is self-instruction (Meichenbaum & Goodman, 1971). This technique requires: (1) modeling of a task (behavior) by an instructor who simultaneously describes what he or she is doing, (2) performance of the task (behavior) by the individual while the instructor verbalizes it, (3) performance of the task (behavior) by the individual while he or she verbalizes it, (4) performance of the task (behavior) while the individual whispers the verbalized task, and (5) finally, simultaneous covert self-instruction and task (behavior) performance. A second technique, self-monitoring, requires that the individual check performance by asking such questions as "Am I doing what I am supposed to be doing?" A third technique, self-evaluation, requires that the individual ask such questions as "How well am I doing?" Clearly, the effective use of these techniques demands that the individual know the questions that need to be asked, and when something is right or wrong, appropriate or inappropriate.

CBM has been used with impulsive and attention-disordered children and children with social problems to improve both their modes of functioning and academic skills. *Self-instruction* has proved effective in modifying handwriting behavior (Kosiewicz, Hallahan, Lloyd, & Graves, 1979). *Self-recording* improves performances in academic content areas (Hallahan, Lloyd, Kosiewicz, & Kneedler, 1979). Instruction in *self-scanning* strategies is effective in modifying reading vocabulary and comprehension (Egeland, 1975). Some researchers report generalization of these self-monitoring techniques to other academic skills (Camp, Blom, Hebert, & van Doorninck, 1977; Douglas, Parry, Marton, & Garson, 1976).

In the area of social behavior (i.e., disruptive behavior), self-instruction, self-evaluation, and self-recording have all proved effective modifiers (Broden, Hall, & Mitts, 1971; Moletsky, 1974; Snyder & White, 1979). But CBM may be at best equivocal when compared to external instruction and reinforcement (Bolstad & Johnson, 1972; Kaufman & O'Leary, 1972; Santogrossi, O'Leary, Romanczyk, & Kaufman, 1973; Turkewitz, O'Leary, & Ironsmith, 1975). The CBM paradigm appears to be quite amenable to influencing impulsive behavior. Numerous investigators have documented decreases in impulsivity when using such dependent measures as the Matching Familair Figures Test or the Porteus Maze (McKinney & Haskins, 1980; Messer, 1976; Nelson, 1976; Nelson & Birkimer, 1978; Palkes, Stewart, & Kahana, 1968).

Although research on the application of CBM to the learning disabled and other exceptional populations continues (see *Exceptional Education*, Vol. 1, No. 1, 1980), conclusions that can be drawn from this research are at best tentative. Serious questions have arisen as to the generalizability of the techniques (Bender, 1976; Guralnick, 1976), the feasibility of using the techniques with groups, and the situations or conditions to which the techniques appear most adaptable. Though opinions differ, CBM techniques do not appear to generalize very well to situations that are not pencil and paper oriented (Lloyd, 1980) and when there is similarity but not direct one-to-one correspondence of training materials and criterion measures (Bender, 1976; Guralnick, 1976). As noted by Keogh and Glover (1980), even though some generalization to similar cognitive training tasks has been evidenced, other studies indicate no transfer from tasks to classroom measures (Meichenbaum & Goodman, 1971; Moore & Cole, 1978). In those studies that have shown concomitant changes in classroom behavior (Bornstein & Quevillon, 1976; Kendall & Finch, 1978), the design of the studies prohibited evaluating whether the CBM technique or simultaneous operant reinforcement contributed to the noted changes. In one training program in which the training was directly focused upon social problem solving (Ross & Ross, 1976), no generalization to real-life problem situations or of stability over time was evidenced.

Clearly, much more information is needed before conclusions concerning applicability can be made with any assurance. First, the effects of individual differences upon the different cognitive training techniques need to be explored. The high verbal requirements may be inappropriate for linguistically immature children (Keogh & Glover, 1980). Similarly, verbal rehearsal may be inappropriate for different age groups (Kendler, Kendler, & Carrick, 1966; Meichenbaum & Goodman, 1969; Ridberg, Parke, & Hetherington, 1971). Second, research must be undertaken that will be able to differentiate the effects of cognitive training and other often simultaneously used techniques. Third, it is important to be aware that for cognitive training to be effective, the training *must* lead to the development of a strategy, which implies that knowledge of what, when, and how to apply the strategy must be assured in the training. If the training results in rote learning without knowledge of applicability, then the effect of the training will be negligible. Finally, research must be undertaken to define and to refine what is meant by CBM and what training techniques are most appropriate for given situations, individuals, and goals. The wholesale acceptance of the validity of the techniques would be highly inappropriate at this time. Research on the development of interventions for modifying cognitive strategies, however, may prove to be of utmost importance for helping individuals achieve a degree of personal control (Brown & Campione, 1978).

Strategies for Modifying the Learning Environment

Although we are lacking research which specifically tests means of fostering attentional behaviors in learning disabled children through manipulation of the environment, there are some research findings which suggest potentially effective educational approaches. Berlyne (cited in Ross, 1976) pointed out conditions under which the presentation of a stimulus results in heightened attention: under conditions of novelty, complexity, uncertainty, surprise, conflict, and change (p. 42). Each of these conditions helps to clarify ways in which greater attention can be fostered by the way lessons are structured.

Consider, for example, the use of novelty and change in instruction. Very often, especially with children who need a great deal of practice, teachers devise repetitive drills and exercises. Certainly practice must be given once a skill is learned, but practice need not be dependent on repetitiousness. Any skill or concept can be presented in a variety of ways. When a novel mode of presentation is used, children are more likely to attend. Learning rhymes, for example, need not be confined to poems, games, songs, riddles, and stories. Children can be asked to recall television jingles and to write their own jingles to advertise academic "objects," such as the letter *A*, the number *7*, the concept *over*, etc. These "commercials" have, of course, been a very effective part of "Sesame Street." One might think about combining the commercials with a show. Lessons can be conducted by puppets or by having the children stand inside a box with the "TV screen" cut out and perform. Children can have quiz shows and game shows. Creative dramatics activities can be used. Given enough variety and inventiveness, perhaps someday the workbook and the ditto sheet may be novel, rather than the modus operandi! When the format and presentation of activities cannot be changed, sometimes the materials can.

Children will often become very attentive when new materials are introduced, even if they are to be used to perform an old, familiar activity. Children will approach a modeling task with new vigor, for example, when the modeling clay is put away and cookie dough or papier mâché is introduced.

Complexity is a factor which is almost never manipulated in classrooms. We have come, it seems, to the collective conclusion that we must always begin with the easiest task and build on and on to increasingly more complex ones. Children surely cannot profit from tasks that are beyond their comprehension, but often they respond quite well to tasks that appeal simply because they are complex—and, therefore, challenging. Children are much happier, for example, using the word *prestidigitation* rather than *magic,* and a whole generation of children loved *supercalifragilisticexpialidocious!* We are not suggesting that children be reared on complexity, but rather that teachers consider complexity a variable that can be manipulated.

The Genevans (cf. Inhelder, Sinclair, & Bovet, 1974) make considerable use of the manipulation of complexity in their learning experiments. Pascual-Leone (1976) described their technique as "graded learning loops." The Genevans generally devise a variety of tasks of varying complexity. They begin by presenting the most difficult (A_4). Most children will be unable to answer that difficult question or to solve that very difficult task. The Genevans, therefore, present a task that is somewhat easier (A_3). For children who still cannot perform, they revert to simpler (A_2) and still simpler (A_1) tasks. Finally, they present a task which is so very easy that the children answer it spontaneously (A_0). Once the easiest task (A_0) is answered, the Genevans begin working back up the ladder of complexity (A_1, A_2, A_3, etc.). The children are encouraged to compare the more difficult tasks to the easier ones and to build on their answers to the easy tasks to answer those which are more complex. Not only does this strategy enable children to develop more and more complex modes of reasoning, it also generally stirs feelings of satisfaction and self-pride. Those of us who have pursued advanced studies remember that nothing was more satisfying than the successful completion of the course (e.g., statistics or neurology) which from the outset appeared to be the most impossible.

Perhaps one of the most compelling strategies for use in teaching is the failure to resolve uncertainty. Consider the following experiment. Figure 6-2 represents a hollow, soft rubber tube to which two balloons, one inflated and one noninflated, are attached. The clasp across the tube prevents the air from flowing through it. What would happen if the clasp were removed? (Hint: the balloons would not inflate equally.)

Communicating the response and the reason ends the thought that children are likely to give such a puzzle. Leaving the question unresolved, however, encourages them to ponder. Many of us probably recall reading "The Lady and the Tiger" in high school. Of all the stories read during those four years, this is probably one of the best remembered. And what we remember best about it is that we never learned the man's fate. The depth of processing theorists (Chapter 4) as well as Piaget (1976) argue that by telling the answer, we in a sense

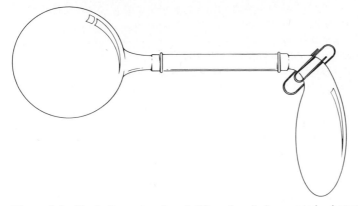

Figure 6-2 The balloon experiment. When the clip is removed, what will happen?

"short-circuit" children's reasoning. So long as they continue to think and to work on problem solutions, children will generate new questions and new goals for themselves. When we stipulate all the goals and make certain that they lead to adequate solutions, we narrow the field of children's thinking. A caution is due. We are not suggesting that children be left uncertain as to the structure of a lesson or task, or their class schedule, or their responsibilities. Suspense about outcomes and problem solutions, however, is highly motivating and often extends the limits of curiosity.

Related to both novelty and uncertainty, but still sufficiently distinct to warrant separate comment, is the use of surprise to focus attention. There have certainly been enough surprises in history (the stock market crash, Waterloo, Pearl Harbor, etc.) to capitalize on in teaching. Creating a situation in students' minds rather akin to the one that actually occurred ensures that surprises will follow automatically.

Children also appear to enjoy probability tasks (Wachs & Furth, 1974) in which answers always incorporate some surprises. In one game, for example, children are given a bag of marbles—perhaps ten yellow marbles and two blue ones. Children are then asked to predict what color marble will most likely come out if they choose just one. (Nearly all children will predict a yellow marble on the first try, but after that marble has been replaced and the game is repeated, they will predict that a blue marble will be chosen on the second try!) Even simple matching tasks or matrix tasks can be carried out by using a "bag of tricks." When red and blue circles, squares, and triangles are contained in a pouch and a matrix with yellow shapes in place is shown to the children, they will have great fun in predicting what shape and color piece will be drawn next from the bag. As more and more pieces are drawn, there are fewer and fewer surprises, but then the joy of having figured out just which pieces are left supplants surprise. Using surprise to modify instructional interventions requires only a little thought.

The Genevans seem to have been the major group to stress conflict. They see conflict not only as a vehicle for sustaining attention, but also as a catalyst for learning. For them, it is the major mechanism of change. The Genevans (cf., Inhelder et al., 1974) examined conflict between predictions and outcomes as well as between subsystems. As an example of the Genevan work, children were shown roads made of matchsticks. A house was pasted onto each matchstick. Matchsticks of equal length were used in two roads, one assigned to the child and one assigned to the examiner. The child, for purposes of discussion Lisa, was asked whether she or the examiner had a greater distance to walk (it was clear from the configuration that the roads were of equal length). The child was also asked to count the number of houses and to determine whether she and the examiner would pass the same number of houses or whether one of them would pass more. After Lisa had answered correctly, the configuration was modified so that the roads were in zigzag patterns, with one extending beyond the other. The number of matches had not been changed, only the configuration. Lisa was then asked whether she would get just as tired walking on her road as the examiner would get walking on his. Lisa (age five) answered that the examiner would become more tired, since his road went further. The examiner asked Lisa whether they would pass the same number of houses. Lisa answered yes and counted the houses (five for the examiner and five for her). At this point, Lisa began to notice that her answers conflicted. What she knew from her knowledge of length suggested that the examiner had further to go, but what she knew about numbers told her that the roads were the same. The examiner continued to alternate questions of number and length and Lisa eventually resolved her conflict. In doing so, however, she gained new insights and reached a higher level of reasoning which integrated her knowledge of numbers with her knowledge of length.

SUMMARY AND CONCLUSIONS

In this chapter we have reviewed models of attention. The older models which viewed attention and selective attention as separate (or separable) processes have been supplanted by more explanatory models which view all attention as selective. A reinterpretation of the selective attention studies with learning disabled children has suggested that their demonstrated deficits may be better thought of as problems in efficiency of processing after information has reached short-term memory. It is necessary to remark that our recommendations are not designed as techniques for making the deployment and maintenance of attention a curricular goal.

SUGGESTED READINGS

For additional readings see the sources listed at the end of Chapters 3, 4, and 5.

Chapter 7

Social and Emotional Considerations with the Learning Disabled

INTRODUCTION

"Few cases of learning disorders are without emotional difficulties" (Bryant, 1966, p. 271). The ramifications of this statement are overwhelming. Surely, there exist thousands of learning disabled children and adolescents whose emotional and social needs have not been and are not being met. The intent of this chapter is to provide information in three areas: (1) ways in which learning problems coexist with emotional and social development, (2) research findings on the emotional and social characteristics of learning disabled persons, and (3) the possibilities for intervention which are within the teacher's purview. We are not suggesting that the teacher assume the role of primary therapist. We do, however, agree with Abrams and Kaslow (1977) that the learning disabled have needs which extend beyond the academic that teachers must address.

RELATION BETWEEN LEARNING DISABILITIES AND EMOTIONAL PROBLEMS

Although learning disorders and emotional difficulties are related, this relation needs clarification. There does not appear to be any simple one-to-one relation between learning disabilities and emotional and/or social problems. As noted earlier, the most widely used definition of learning disabilities eliminates those persons whose primary problem is emotional disturbance. If the emotional disturbance is the *cause* of the learning problem, eliminating the emotional disturbance would ameliorate the learning problem. In the case of learning disabilities, however, this does not happen (Connolly, 1971). Although the child may become more accessible, therapeutic intervention is not expected to rectify the learning problem. Yet, the coexistence of emotional and social problems within the learning disabled population has been recognized, and many argue that when they do occur together, differential diagnosis is often impossible.

The genesis of social and emotional problems is open to speculation. The debilitating effects of a handicap may result less from the disability than from the way persons in the society react to the handicapped individual (Bartel & Guskin, 1968). Children are, for example, labeled learning disabled, because they fail to meet the society's needs for literacy, the demands of an educational system, and the requirement to be able to succeed in school. When the child who cannot read is labeled, the negative characteristics are emphasized, while the positive achievements of the individual are often overlooked (Wright, 1974). Perhaps it is one residual effect of the Protestant ethic (Bartel & Guskin, 1968) which colors perceptions of those who are unable to succeed and/or be contributing members of society. It is little wonder that children with learning disabilities, often described as "bad students," develop mechanisms of coping which affect their emotional and social development. There can be no denying that we all strive to some degree to fulfill what we perceive as others' expectations. Poor treatment by others often leads to evasiveness, underactivity, and silence (Kronich, 1976).

The past few years have seen a rise in the concern over *ecological* factors. It is important to recognize that both the *context* in which the behavior is observed and *who* is doing the observing weigh heavily on whether a behavior is viewed as appropriate or acceptable, deviant or debilitating. Behavior, therefore, is expected to vary a great deal depending on the situation and the companions. A child's behavior in the classroom, for example, is expected to be quite different from his or her behavior on the playground or at home. Thus, society, embodied in the context and the perceiver, may be the determiner of what will become socially or emotionally frustrating situations. The existence of a problem may very well be the result of the reactions of others (Algozzine, 1977).

The effects of societal expectations, though focused on the learning disabled individual, also affect significant others in the child's environment and these persons, in turn, affect the child. Determination of the worth of a child by the larger society necessarily affects the functioning of the family unit (parents, siblings, and often more distant relatives), causing them to question not only their child, but also their own abilities and worth. When Dorothy takes all the top honors at the graduation exercises, mother and father are generally proud of the fine job they did in bringing up their daughter. Conversely, when John has difficulty with school tasks or when he becomes a behavior problem, his parents are likely to ask themselves how they went wrong. More successful siblings wonder "Why me? Why did I have to have a handicapped brother?"

Factors that interfere with adequate emotional and social development may also be learned. In some cases, the learning disabled child may be placed with other learning disabled children who have severe behavior disorders. It is possible that the learning disabled child might adopt their style of behavior, especially if it is seen as effective behavior. In integrated classes where there is a wide variety of models to choose from, copying negative behavior would seem to be less likely.

There can be no naïve assumption that societal events occur in isolation. The complex *interaction* of child and society must be recognized as the source of handicapping emotional problems. Often some thwarted needs in the growing child's emotional life will manifest themselves in undesirable behaviors, because the child attempts to accommodate to the demands of the situation while still maintaining psychological integrity.

The effect of a damaged sense of self on the development of many disabled children has become of increasing concern (Blanck & Blanck, 1974; Buchholz, 1978; Giffen, 1968). Once a child learns that he or she has limited ability to initiate actions successfully, that child may become unable to act, may compensate by becoming aggressive, or may try to mask his or her inability by overcompensation (Rawson, 1973). If we gain notions of competence through recognition of what we *can* do, then the effect of conventional educational programs, focusing on the weakness of the child, may sorely impede the achievement of feelings of competence. It is not surprising that reports of severe anxiety and the need for support (Bender, 1967), as well as feelings of being unloved, permeate the literature on learning disabilities (Wender, 1971).

The functioning of any individual is a function of interpersonal interactions and societal prescriptions (Siller, 1976). Placed in situations which are too complex, many learning disabled children revert to infantile patterns which were once successful (Eisenberg, 1967). Helplessness and dependency, useful at one stage of life, become tools and strategies of coping. Passivity, dependency, aggression, compensation, withdrawal, coping, shame, and guilt are all possible reactions to the realization that one is handicapped (Siller, 1976). Of these, perhaps the last two are the ones *least* frequently explored. Placed in a situation where failure equals "stupid," "disappointing," or "bad," the learning disabled child is constantly reminded of his or her less than adequate performance. Stress from guilt (for being inadequate) and shame (for not fulfilling expectations) may take a considerable toll. Stress and tension often raise the frequency of ineffective behavior and add to a cycle of disapproval, thoughts of inadequacy, and subsequently, more aberrant behavior (Pohl, 1976).

One area of emotional development that is just beginning to be investigated is the study of temperament. Temperament is a very difficult entity to define adequately. It refers to "within-child stylistic characteristics which affect the relationships of the child and his family, and which determine, in part, his response to the environmental and experiential demands of socialization" (Keogh & Pullis, 1980, p. 240). More simply put, temperament concerns the way an individual behaves (Thomas & Chess, 1977). It refers to the biological or constitutional characteristics the child brings to his or her interaction with others in the environment. Even very young infants may be viewed as possessing predispositions affecting interactions with others. These unique individual differences also affect what will be extracted from the social environment. The course of the predispositions is determined by complex interactions with the environment, but the environment in turn is also affected (Buss & Plomin, 1975). Analysis of temperament characteristics may prove valuable for understanding and predicting emotional and social development. Some researchers have identified characteristics (such as approach or withdrawal, adaptability, threshold of responsiveness, intensity of reaction, quality of mood, distractibility, attention span, and persistence) which have been used to cluster children into groups of easy, difficult, and slow-to-warm children (Thomas & Chess, 1977). These groups have proved relatively stable, and in the case of the difficult child, have shown some correlation with later behavior problems. Though research has been done with at-risk populations (Lambert & Windmiller, 1977), mentally retarded populations (Chess & Korn, 1970), and preschool populations (Lewis, 1977), no studies have been undertaken with learning disabled children. The questions surrounding temperament are far from settled. As noted by Keogh and Pullis (1980), while the interactionist focus of the temperament concept is appealing, questions remain regarding definition, underlying traits, the organization of traits and changes in organization, the effect of various parental variables, the type of data to be collected in studies, and the concept of its basis—biological or constitutional.

In sum, many of the emotional and/or social problems of learning disabled children are likely to result from the interaction of the child and society. A child who cannot read or calculate is not a problem in a society in which such skills are not valued. Furthermore, even in a relatively accepting environment a difficult child will tend over time to reduce the support which was once forthcoming. It is extremely difficult, therefore, to argue that the problems we deal with as special educators are "in the child." Particularly when, as we shall see shortly, the prognosis for achievement and adult well-being is often dependent on a loving, supportive early environment.

RESEARCH ON EMOTIONAL AND SOCIAL DEVELOPMENT IN THE LEARNING DISABLED

The research on emotional and social development can be separated into several specific areas: (1) teacher/child interactions, (2) self-concept and academic achievement, (3) juvenile delinquency, (4) human figure drawings, (5) nonverbal skills and social perception, and (6) parent and family concerns. Each will be examined in turn.

Teacher/Child Interactions

Teachers may have a great deal to do with fostering negative self-regard in the learning disabled. Bryan (1974b) found that learning disabled children had as many interactions with peers and teachers as nonlearning disabled children. Yet, for the learning disabled, over one-half of the teacher interactions revolved around work-related issues, while, for the nonlearning disabled, only one-quarter of the interactions did so. With respect to the reinforcing quality of the interactions, Bryan found more negative reinforcement in the interactions between teachers and learning disabled children than between teachers and nonlearning disabled children.

With regard to teacher expectations, it appears that teachers form negative *preexpectations* of learning disabled children even before instruction takes place (Foster, 1976; Foster, Schmidt, & Sabatino, 1976). Not only were teachers' expectations negatively biased toward children they were told were learning disabled, but these negative expectations continued even after evidence to the contrary was provided (Jacobs, 1976, 1978). Others (Sutherland & Algozzine, 1979) have also noted that simply labeling a child as learning disabled resulted in differential treatment. The performance of labeled females was significantly lower than the performance of children labeled normal, though both groups were in fact normal fourth grade girls. The implication is *not* that teachers are purposefully biased, or even that all teachers are negatively biased. Teachers as a group, however, tend to be unaware of the effects labeling has on their interactions with children.

Siller (1977) raised an important issue which has rarely been discussed by special education personnel—the feelings of teachers regarding their own worth while working with children whose progress is limited. Teachers are generally achievement oriented. They find themselves frustrated when children in their classes do not succeed. How the teacher's feelings of anger, frustration, and guilt affect the child and his or her perceptions of him/herself are still unknown. Perhaps the clear understanding that not all children accomplish tasks at the same rate and in the same manner would do much to alleviate the often self-induced pressures of accountability and do much to alleviate consequent feelings of frustration.

The feelings of teachers toward the learning disabled represent only one source of information regarding the social and emotional well-being of this population. Bryan (1974a, 1976) evaluated the learning disabled child with respect to sociometric ratings. Both the amount of acceptance and the amount of rejection by peers were analyzed. In the early study dealing with children in the third, fourth, and fifth grades, Bryan found less acceptance and more rejection of learning disabled children. After a 1976 follow-up, Bryan concluded that the negative social status of the children remained the same even though the comparison population had changed. In an attempt to ascertain whether the social behavior of the learning disabled, in and of itself, was enough to cause the learning disabled child to be recognized as "different," Bryan and Perlmutter (1979) had female undergraduate students evaluate children in videotapes, without knowing whether they were learning disabled or not. Their results indicated that learning disabled children could be identified *without any prior information*. Similarly, Bryan (1974b) had undergraduate education majors view videotapes without prior knowledge of who was learning disabled. These students also correctly identified the learning disabled children. Of the ratings, speech, language, likely academic achievement, and attractiveness were the factors of importance.

In a further analysis of interactions among learning disabled children and their teachers and peers, Bryan, Wheeler, Felcan, and Henek (1978) found important qualitative differences in the type of language used and the types of interaction. For instance, the learning disabled children made considerably more competitive statements than the control group. The control-group children were the initiators of many more statements. In addition, there were trends indicating that the learning disabled both gave and received more statements of rejection and were asked fewer questions. The finding of more competitive responses in the Bryan et al. study is consonant with the results of a study by Sabatino, Naiman, and Foster (1976). They found that the learning disabled child's penchant for competition mitigated against acceptance by nonlearning disabled peers. Among the highest cluster of reward preferences of the learning disabled children was peer approval—a dilemma.

It appears, then, that the learning disabled are viewed as socially and/or emotionally different by both teachers *and* peers, that they are less likely to be chosen by others as friends and more likely to be rejected, that teachers see them in a negative light, and that their aggressiveness works against them.

Underachievement and Self-concept

Siperstein, Bobb, and Bak (1978) suggested the relation of self-concept and academic achievement is influenced by factors other than purely social ones. They assessed the social status of the learning disabled by looking at academic ability, athletic ability, and physical appearance. Their findings indicated a very complex situation. Though the nonlearning disabled group was more popular, they were proportionately represented among the isolates. Furthermore, although the nonlearning disabled group had most of the "stars," there were no differences between the groups on the measures of physical appearance and athletic ability. Siperstein et al. concluded that "The reasons behind a child's diagnosis as learning disabled and also the label learning disabled do not bring about automatic social isolation" (p. 101). There is then a process of desocialization that the learning disabled child becomes part of. What factors could account for such findings?

One possible factor is underachievement. Positive correlations among academic achievement, self-concept, and intelligence have been established (Gorlow, Butler, & Guthrie, 1961). Zeitz (1976) concluded that as academic achievement disintegrates, estimates of self-concept decline. This effect of lower estimates of self-concept as a function of academic achievement has been recognized by those working with the learning disabled. Black (1974), for example, found learning disabled children to be generally lower in self-concept than peers, and that the estimate of self-concept was directly related to the amount of underachievement (that is, the lower the level of achievement, the lower the level of self-concept). Knaus and McKeever (1977) confirmed the findings of Black, and concluded that effective intervention should focus not only on academic remediation, but also consider the social and emotional needs of the child. It should be noted that socioeconomic status mediates the relationship between self-concept and underachievement such that the higher the socioeconomic level of the child, the more devastating the effects of underachievement on self-regard.

The problem certainly is not simply one of being labeled. Learning disabled children placed in self-contained classes, for example, did not differ in self-concept scores from regular-class children who were never referred (Coleman, in press). Self-concept appears to suffer in situations in which the learning disabled child uses highly achieving or normally achieving children as the standard by which to judge his or her own worth. This comparison is most likely to occur when the learning disabled child is placed in resource-room programs, mainstreamed settings, or regular classrooms (Coleman, in press; Rogers, Smith, & Coleman, 1978). Such placements, therefore, appear to be more damaging to feelings of self-worth than placements in self-contained classes (Strang, Smith, & Rogers, 1978).

One variable seldom taken into account in deciding on appropriate placements for learning disabled children is the effect of the placement on their feelings of self-worth. Why they may react negatively to being integrated with normally achieving children is unclear. The evidence offered here suggests that it may stem from negative interactions with their peers, "strictly business" relations with their teachers, and/or unfavorable comparisons with peers that lead to declining feelings of self-worth. Perhaps these findings should at least be considered when decisions are made about placements in the least restrictive environment.

Juvenile Delinquency and the Learning Disabled

There is a trend towards examining the relation between juvenile delinquency and learning disabilities. It has been recognized often that juvenile delinquents generally have less than adequate achievement levels. Berman (1975) reported that a vast majority of juvenile delinquents are learning disabled in at least one aspect of academics. Wright (1974) suggested that over one-half of the males referred to educational evaluation clinics are so referred because of conduct disorders. Hresko (1977), however, noted that the evaluation of learning problems in the juvenile delinquent population must take into account the effects that high rates of truancy and absenteeism, external social pressures, and less than adequate home environments may have on achievement. There exists a wide variety of environmental conditions that give rise to learning problems which are not, by definition, learning disabilities (see Chapter 1). To label any deficit as a learning disability confuses the issue. Hastily drawing conclusions about juvenile delinquency and learning disabilities may give rise unnecessarily to negative connotations. After all, it has not been demonstrated that most learning disabled children are delinquent.

Research has failed to substantiate a causal link between learning disabilities and juvenile delinquency. Learning disabled children are not more susceptible to becoming juvenile delinquents, nor does school failure lead to delinquency. In a longitudinal study to be completed in late 1980, Keilitz, Zaremba, and Broder (preliminary report, 1979) noted two important findings. First, in a large sample of juvenile delinquents (ages 12 to 15) 32 percent were found to be learning disabled. In contrast, among nonjuvenile delinquents only 16 percent were labeled learning disabled by their criteria (that figure is unusually high). Second, they found that learning disabled and nonlearning disabled youth engaged in the same delinquent behaviors. They argued, consequently, that "somewhere in the juvenile justice system, learning disabled children are treated differently from nonlearning disabled children" (p. 9). Getting good grades in school may well appear to judges as a redeeming quality.

Well-designed and long-term research efforts are needed to disentangle learning problems and juvenile delinquency. The existence of learning problems within the juvenile delinquent population is not at issue: they surely exist. What is in question is whether it is better to recognize these as academic difficulties or to speculate that they are *learning disabilities*. We must, however, guard against the assumption that learning disabled children are likely to become delinquents. This is one conclusion current data do *not* permit.

Human Figure Drawing

Since human figure drawing has been equated with both the perception of body image and social-emotional intactness, a number of studies have attempted to investigate the drawings of learning disabled persons. Some have found no significant differences between learning disabled and control groups on human figure drawings (Follansbee, 1978; Gounard, 1975). Others have found differences. Bachara (1975–76) discovered emotional indicators of insecurity, lack of confidence, and feelings of helplessness. Epstein (1978) found many more shrunken or distorted limbs, excessive trunk detail, vacant faces, exaggerated body parts, poor organization, lack of activity of the figures, intense anxiety, attitudes of helplessness and dependence, lack of self-esteem, and intellectual inadequacy. Different findings may have resulted from the use of different scoring systems and differences in the populations sampled, especially age differences. All that can be said with certainty is that the figure drawings of some learning disabled children are different from those of some normally achieving children. Whether one can infer inadequacy, a lack of security, a lack of confidence, etc. from figure drawings is open to question.

Nonverbal Communication and Social Perception

Two problems which seem to be gaining attention are nonverbal and social perception difficulties among the learning disabled. For the purposes of this discussion, nonverbal communication consists of hand and arm gestures, facial expression, posture, and position and movement of legs and feet. Social perception is the decoding of the expressions of others, the emotional content of the voice, or the interpretation of information within a given context. We have chosen to include the areas of social perception and nonverbal communication under the section on social and emotional considerations for a number of reasons. First, either may affect the person's functioning in a social setting. Second, disabilities in either area affect the perceptions of competence others may have of the learning disabled.

Although social perception or misperception and the unskilled use of nonverbal cues were hypothesized a number of years ago to be problems for the learning disabled (Johnson & Myklebust, 1967), they have received little research attention. Most studies relate to the decoding of social information and only a few to encoding problems (Bryan, 1978). Bryan and Conners (1978) assessed learning disabled children's ability to modify their use of language based on situational demands. When compared to normally achieving age-mates, the learning disabled failed to modify their instructions in accordance with listener needs, when explaining the rules of a game. Bryan (1977) also used a series of scenarios to assess the ability of the learning disabled to interpret the nonverbal aspects of communication. In all cases, the learning disabled were less effective in interpreting nonverbal cues.

This lack of facility was also noted by Wiig and Harris (1974) with respect to the interpretation of emotions expressed nonverbally. The six emotions assessed included anger, fear, embarrassment, frustration, joy, and love. When compared to a control group, the learning disabled were less accurate in identifying these emotions. Similarly, Rosenthal, Archer, DiMatteo, Hill and Rogers (1977), using scenarios, found that learning disabled children were less accurate in comprehending nonverbal communications than nondisabled children, even when audio descriptions accompanied the film presentation. Finally, a study by Emery (1975) compared the abilities of learning disabled and normally achieving children in judging simple social events. Learning disabled children were much less able to describe scenes they had just seen. In addition, judgments of facial expressions were below expectations. Learning disabled children also failed to engage in nonverbal behaviors that facilitate and maintain interactions. When interacting with nonlearning disabled children, their eye contact was short (often consisting of furtive glances) both when listening and speaking, and they smiled less (Bryan, Sherman, & Fisher, 1980).

The implications of these studies are that the learning disabled may be less capable of extracting the meaning and communicating during social situations. Consequently, the learning disabled may have much less opportunity for normal peer and teacher relations than had been thought. Chances for success in academic as well as social areas may, consequently, be decreased.

Parent and Family Concerns

One aspect of learning disabilities that has, until recently, been rather neglected is the effect a child's classification has on the family. Labeling necessarily brings about changes in the relationship between the family and the community (Farber, 1968). Often aware that something is amiss with their child *before* the school contacts them, the parents of the learning disabled must ascertain not only that the appropriate educational services are received, but that decisions arrived at appear to be the best, that the diagnosis is complete, and that they understand and can communicate with professionals. At the same time, they must effectively provide for the other children in the family and maintain their own personal well-being.

Beginning with the diagnosis, parents are confronted with professionals who may not be adept at explaining their findings. Diagnostic reports may be written for other professionals, rather than parents. Especially when children are mildly impaired, family members are often uncertain about which aspects of the child are disabled and which are intact (Kronick, 1974). The term *learning disabilities* is confusing even for professionals. Informing parents about what it is *not* probably helps little in their understanding of what it is.

The most immediate reaction of the parents may be one of guilt, based on the suspicion that they did something wrong. Mothers often believe that they are somehow responsible—that *they* did not produce a healthy child, *they* did something wrong during pregnancy, it was *their* body which did not function adequately (Siller, 1977). Often, these feelings are compounded by blame on the part of the father. Parents can often be helped by good listening and good information. Parents have both a right and a need to know the nature of the problem and the services available. Many times, lack of clarity leads parents to seek more acceptable diagnoses, often at both great financial and psychological expense (Wolfensberger, 1967). Professionals must remember that an informed parent is not only of benefit to the child, but is also the mandate of the law.

Guilt is not the only reaction of parents. Usually, there are also fear, shame, denial, and feelings of helplessness (Begab, 1968). Anger is also usually present (Thompson, 1975). These emotions often prepare the way for successful coping and readjustment. Anger, for example, is not an inappropriate response. When anger reaches the point that it interferes with the functioning of the family unit, when it leads to continued stress and tension, and when it threatens the unity of the family, however, it is debilitating, rather than facilitating. Such emotional reactions may help to explain why parents have a tendency to respond in less affectionate ways to their learning disabled children (Owen, Adams, Forest, Stoltz & Fisher, 1971).

When the effects of learning disabilities are discussed with regard to family dynamics, consideration must be given to siblings. Just as the presence of a learning disabled child places stress on the parents, it does so on the other children. The focus of the family often shifts to meeting the needs of the learning disabled child, sometimes at the expense of other children. Often academic and social needs of the learning disabled child take precedence over the needs of other family members. In school, the brother or sister of a learning disabled child may be placed in the uncomfortable position of being responsible for the sibling. Sometimes the additional burdens lead to resentment and frustration, which in turn lead to guilt and perhaps shame. In short, the emotional well-being of the entire family may be affected.

Learning disabilities is a complex phenomenon. The learning disabled child affects the family. The family, in turn, plays a central role in determining whether the child effectively deals with the problem, or if the problem will prove debilitating for both the family and the child (Abrams, 1970). There is no one simple answer for coping with the needs of the parents, siblings, and the learning disabled person. The learning disabled child should not become the focal point of the family to the exclusion of the needs of others. Neither should the learning disabled child be permitted to become the family scapegoat (Vogel & Bell, 1977). These problems are not at all easy to resolve. Yet, perhaps through appropriate counseling and educational intervention, some improvements can be made. In the following section, we will consider some ideas for intervention in the social and emotional development of *both* child and family.

INTERVENTION

Since the learning disabled child represents a *whole* person, including a psychological self which is as important as the child's academic self, any program which attempts to deal with only the educational aspect is inadequate. Because of the importance of family dynamics, the family milieu must be considered when providing treatment. Teachers should not assume the role of therapists. Their job is to teach the children to read, write, and do arithmetic. They must, however, work in conjunction with therapists to provide environments supportive to growth.

The traditional psychiatric model is probably not appropriate for intervention with the learning disabled (Connolly, 1971). The traditional model assumes that the child has a choice of whether or not to be cured. The implication is that the child could decide not to have a learning disability if so desired. It neglects factors not under the control of the child. A second assumption of the traditional psychiatric model is that once the emotional factor is removed (that is, treatment is successful), the concomitant learning problems will also be resolved. The model does not recognize that the emotional problems may, in fact, be resolved while the basic learning disability will remain.

Perhaps the most common of the treatments for social and emotional problems in learning disabilities is one known as the "crisis" model. This model does not emphasize preventive measures. Rather, one waits until a problem or crisis occurs and then intervenes. Little is resolved except the problem of the moment. Usually, there is little follow-up and intervention ceases until the next episode. A more effective method might be to use the crisis to begin systematic intervention, so that future problems might be diminished in severity or possibly even eliminated.

Frequently when ongoing support is offered, it amounts to a teacher's controlling interactions between children to ensure that they remain on an acceptable level. While this control model is effective in the classroom (at times with a considerable expenditure of energy), the model does not recognize that a world exists outside the classroom. That world is not under the control of an adult. The approach is consequently of little value in establishing continuous, effective behavior.

For many children with social and emotional problems, a supportive services model provides intervention outside of the classroom. This intervention might take the form of individual or group therapy, with the goals of the program adjusted for each child. While this type of intervention is not needed for every learning disabled child, it should be considered for some children. Many times, parents and teachers cooperate in designing appropriate programs to be carried out both at home and in school, using the principles of behavior modification (see Chapter 16). Sometimes a therapist is also included in the evaluation and planning process.

Perhaps the most effective intervention is one in which, within the regular environment, the child is provided with an appreciating, respecting teacher whose goal is the realization of the potential of all children, and where acceptance and not condoning is the method of interaction. Given a sensitive and perceptive teacher, the educational environment can be arranged to the maximum benefit. (For an extended discussion, see Chapter 16.)

Learning disabled children must also be provided with opportunities, such as participation in youth organizations, to interact with others outside of the school situation. Parents and concerned others should make sure that such options are open to them. The inclusion of learning disabled children into nonacademic school programs (clubs, interest groups, and athletic programs) is also important. Too often we have neglected the nonacademic talents of the learning disabled, prevented them from having normal social/athletic experiences, and then criticized them for not developing adequate social skills. As some have noted (Wallbrown, Fremont, Nelson, Wilson, & Fischer, 1979), teachers need to be aware of signs indicating that children are having difficulty in social situations and need assistance. These signs include withdrawal, aggression, crying, despondency, and lack of motivation. Alternative ways of learning socialization skills should be provided. These may be fostered through such activities as role playing (Wallbrown, Fremont, Nelson, Wilson, & Fischer, 1979) or contingent observation (Porterfield, Jackson, & Risley, 1976).

Families, too, need to be included in programs for social and emotional development. Before a family reaches the point at which its stability is threatened, it should have the opportunity to seek counseling and therapy (McDowell, 1976). The focus of such counseling should allow the parents to see that they are not alone with their problems, to put them in touch with others who are also providing for learning disabled children, and to allow them to see that a normal family existence, with self-fulfillment for them, is a potential reality. In addition, other family members, brothers and sisters, need to be made aware that they, too, have a right to self-fulfillment and that the focus of their lives need not be the learning disabled brother or sister.

Emotional and social growth and stability are as necessary for the learning disabled child as for anyone else. Considering the negative views of soceity, their attainment of this right to self-fulfillment is much more of a task than it is for others. Yet, it is not an impossibility, if we recognize that these children and adolescents are capable, productive individuals, with contributions to be made to society. Siller (1976) says it succinctly, when noting: "Truly beautiful things can occur when atmospheres are created where the human worth of everyone, disabled and nondisabled alike, is promoted and the growth of all is facilitated by appreciating and respecting individual differences" (p. 479).

SUMMARY AND CONCLUSIONS

This chapter has documented that a rather high correlation between learning disabilities and emotional problems exists. Research on the emotional and social problems of learning disabled children has revealed a number of potential problems. The relationship teachers build with their learning disabled pupils tends to differ qualitatively from the relationships they build with their normally achieving pupils. Lowered teacher expectations and thwarted teacher achievement may contribute to that more negative relationship. Additional problems may include emotional effects of the child's underachievement, problems in social perception, and disturbed family relationships. Finally, a significant correlation between learning disabilities and juvenile delinquency was observed when groups of delinquent youth were studied. Although delinquency and learning problems do coexist, there is no clear indication of a causal relation between them. It is still unclear whether many of the academic difficulties demonstrated by delinquents stem from prolonged absences from school, lack of interest in academic achievement, etc.—problems of motivation rather than learning disability.

Four types of models have dominated intervention strategies with learning disabled children who display concomitant emotional problems: the traditional psychiatric model, the crises model, the control model, and support-services model. The traditional psychiatric model has proven minimally useful in dealing with the problems of learning disabled children and youth. Perhaps that is because the model is founded upon inapplicable assumptions. The crises model is useful for dealing with problems as they arise, but does nothing to prevent future episodes. The control model is really a default model in which it is assumed that a good teacher will control his or her class and, therefore, prevent instances of disruptive behavior. This model does not, of course, take the needs of children into account in helping them to develop personal controls. Perhaps the most useful, effective model is the support-services model. Few teachers are equipped to become therapists and indeed their responsibilities for instruction preclude their ability to use a considerable amount of time for nonacademic interventions. Parents (often through the use of behavior modification programs) and agency or school guidance personnel need to work cooperatively with the teacher in developing child and family support systems.

SUGGESTED READINGS

Gazda, G. M., Asbury, F. R., Balzer, F. L., Childers, W. C., & Walters, R. P. *Human relations development.* (2d ed.). Boston: Allyn and Bacon, 1977.

Gordon, T. *Teacher effectiveness training.* New York: David McKay Co., Inc., 1974.

Gordon, T. *Parent effectiveness training.* New York: Times Mirror, 1975.

Yamamoto, K. (Ed.). *The child and his image.* Palo Alto, Calif.: Houghton Mifflin Co., 1972.

Part Three

With the passage of PL 94-142 came a renewed interest in assessment practices, because the congressional hearings that preceded passage of the law as well as the increase in class action suits made clear that many unfair and discriminatory practices were common. This section of the text, therefore, provides a comprehensive approach to assessment which draws data from a wide variety of sources and models. Both screening and diagnostic tests that are frequently used with learning disabled children are described and reviewed for their technical and theoretical merits. A continuous measurement system is recommended for those whose responsibility it is to do instructional planning. An individualized educational program (IEP) should be devised for each child to establish tentative initial and annual goals. As children progress and teachers learn more about their knowledge and abilities, new information must be incorporated into the instructional plan. The final pages of this section examine a variety of systems for providing services to learning disabled children and make some speculations about new roles that may be carved out for learning disabilities professionals in the future.

Photo on facing page: Ongoing Observation of Child Behavior.

Chapter 8

Purposes and Considerations of Assessment

INTRODUCTION

The passage of PL 94-142 initiated a resurgence of interest in the use and development of more accurate, economical, and fair assessment procedures for children who are being considered for special education services and for those who need regular reevaluation. The efficacy and efficiency of both Child Find and placement decisions are dependent on our ability to select and develop appropriate tests and to use them in ways which maximize the chances for accuracy of description and prediction. A knowledge of the purposes of testing and the considerations necessary for the selection of tests and development of test batteries is needed by all who participate in the referral process. Because the law stipulates that no single test or evaluation procedure shall constitute the basis for diagnostic or placement decisions, most testing is carried out by interdisciplinary teams. The variety of professionals involved depends upon the problems and needs of the individual child. A core of professionals, however, evaluates every child. For example, most diagnostic teams include a school psychologist, an educational evaluator (hopefully a learning disabilities special-ist), and a physician. When problems related to areas of specific expertise arise, speech pathologists and other specialists may be called in. Although a good deal of what occurs in evaluation centers around tests and testing, assessment considerations go far beyond the limited information derived from tests.

What is testing? A test is simply "a set of tasks or questions intended to elicit particular types of behaviors . . . under standardized conditions and to yield scores . . ." (American Psychological Association, American Educational Research Association, and the National Council on Measurement in Education, 1974, p. 2). The assumptions that underlie testing are that: (1) a continuum of traits and/or functions exists and can be defined, (2) groups or individuals can be given a series of tasks or questions which will lead to differential responses, (3) the presentation of these tasks and responses occurs under controlled circumstances, and (4) a quantitative characterization of that group or that person's place on the continuum is appropriate (Newland, 1973). Examples of quantitative observations often measured by tests include:

Bryan's score on the *Huntley Test of Androgeny* is 115.
Bridget's score on Mr. O'Malley's science test is 88.
Carol's social quotient on the *Bernie/Douglas Social Maturity Scale* is 95.
Jim's *WISC-R* IQ is 125.
Kellie can run 1 mile in 8 minutes.
Nancy's score on the *Grahm Reading Achievement Test* is 75.

Assessment, however, leads to no such quantification. *Assessment is a process of putting test scores into perspective by relating them to the child tested rather than to the test used.* An assessment evaluates a total child as an organism interacting with his or her environment and examines as many variables as possible that may influence both the test scores and the interplay of the variables themselves. Some considerations in assessment might be the child's state of health, physical or sensory limitations, attitudes, interests, motivation, family constellation, acculturation, social maturity, appraisal of self-worth, etc. Rather than scores, an assessment seeks to determine what a child is doing, in what areas he or she is not performing, and some indication of what the child might be able to do.

Topics to be covered in this chapter include purposes and models of assessment and factors which influence test selection—cultural, theoretical, and statistical.

PURPOSES OF ASSESSMENT

Assessments are used for a variety of purposes. Some of these include screening, diagnosis for classification, placement or teaching, planning cither for individuals or groups, and appraisals of past performance for individuals or groups.

Screening is most often carried out when large numbers of persons are to be surveyed to determine whether they fit into a particular category. Screening is a first step in a more substantial evaluation process and so is frequently imprecise and leads to the identification of more persons than are to be categorized ultimately. For example, if a school develops a new service or program (or perhaps would like to demonstrate the need for services and programs), the school staff needs to identify those children who are eligible. The entire school population may be surveyed, usually in groups and using paper and pencil tests.

The final selection of students is then carried out using more accurate and more thorough (and necessarily more costly) testing techniques.

The diagnostic process is considerably more precise and is usually conducted individually. Higher standards are held for the tests being used and administration of the instruments is more carefully controlled. When diagnostic evaluations are carried out for purposes of placement, interviews and tests covering a wide variety of domains (e.g., IQ, aptitudes, attitudes, personality variables, achievement) are generally used to determine what type of child is being dealt with and the most appropriate procedures and setting for the child's learning needs. Most often, however, considerations beyond those which label a child learning disabled, emotionally disturbed, or retarded and which determine the severity of the problem are needed in order to plan an educational program (Jenkins & Pany, 1978). Diagnostic testing for teaching cannot be carried out using only tests (even those focused on academic achievement). Observations, teacher and parent reports, and an ongoing evaluation process known as diagnostic teaching must also be used.

A third purpose of assessment is for planning. Screening procedures are often used to determine whether groups need to be formed, whether services need to be offered, and to which groups particular children should be assigned. Results of annual achievement tests are often used for this purpose, but other types of measures, physical fitness tests, for example, may be used as well.

Finally, assessment can be used to investigate the effectiveness of past procedures and programs. This type of testing usually involves screening procedures, rather than diagnostic ones, and is usually conducted in groups. When the success of various intervention approaches is being measured or when teacher performance is being evaluated, group tests are sufficient. Individual scores are not reported, because revealing individual differences or characteristics is not a goal. Requirements set for the selection of instruments are generally less stringent than for either screening or diagnostic purposes.

Of course, there has been a great deal of abuse of testing. At least three-fourths of the public schools and a greater number of private schools have regular testing programs. Samuda (1975, p. 9) lists some of the more harmful consequences of testing:

> (1) permanent classification of individuals; (2) invasion of privacy; (3) lack of confidentiality of test scores; (4) limited conceptualizations of intelligence and ability; (5) domination by the testers; (6) too much testing; and cultural bias.

Although the provisions of PL 94-142 may help to eliminate some of these problems, many will continue to constitute abuses and misuses of the results and purposes of testing.

MODELS OF ASSESSMENT

Mercer and Ysseldyke (1977) have identified five conceptual models used in assessment procedures: the medical model, the social deviance model, the psychoeducational process model, the task analytic model, and the pluralistic model. Each of these is based on a different set of assumptions, data collection techniques and procedures, and definitions of normality.

The Medical Model

The medical model seeks to discover overt symptoms of some underlying pathology. Normality is defined as the lack of such symptoms. Unless personal characteristics (such as age, race, intelligence, socioeconomic standing, etc.) are known to be related to symptomatology, they are irrelevant to the model (sociocultural characteristics do not influence procedures used in an appendectomy). Measures tend to focus on the number and intensity of pathological symptoms. Because they reflect underlying organic conditions, the following types of evaluative procedures are used: developmental and health histories, behavioral and neurological assessment scales, and screening and classifications for sensory and physical handicaps.

This model has been widely applied in education: Normal children are those who do not present any symptoms of academic failure. When failure does occur, the assessment often focuses on the isolation of underlying causes. In the field of learning disabilities, this has often meant a search for neurological, perceptual, and linquistic factors to explain learning problems. In its extreme, it has resulted in the psychoeducational process (or underlying abilities) model described below.

The Social Deviance Model

This model assumes that behaviors are learned and that they are related to particular roles and systems, such as the school, home, community, peer group, etc. The definition of normalcy, therefore, depends upon the particular context. There are multiple definitions of what constitutes normal behavior and a child may be judged to be normal in one situation and abnormal in another. This model is very frequently employed in educational settings. The in-school and out-of-school behaviors of most children are judged separately and are often found to be at variance. When aptitude and achievement tests are given in schools, they relate specifically to a particular system. Failure may be attributed to a variety of sources, including lack of opportunity to learn, lack of motivation to learn, etc.

Ecological strategies (see Hobbs, 1975) constitute a type of social deviancy model. Ecological strategies involve the assessment of a child's assets and liabilities within particular settings, i.e., at home, at school, in Mrs. Slaton's class, etc. Intervention often involves the manipulations of some aspect of the child's environment.

The Psychoeducational Process Model

The psychoeducational model has also been called the "underlying abilities" model[1] because it attempts to identify prerequisite abilities, or more appropri-

---

[1]See chapters 3, 5, and 12, especially discussions related to the *ITPA*.

ately, *disabilities* that *cause* learning difficulties. Its adherents compare the scores of children on test-named processes (1) to the scores obtained by other children through the use of norms and (2) to their own scores on other tests. Most often, however, even when the overall tests appear to be valid and reliable, the subtests seldom are. It is the *subtest* scores, however, that are used for plotting intraindividual performance on profiles and as the basis for interventions. The value of such training for academic progress has been widely challenged, but still, the model flourishes (Jenkins & Pany, 1978).

There are six important characteristics of the model (Mercer & Ysseldyke, 1977, pp. 77–78): (1) It is a continuous model in that it attempts to measure the extent to which a child deviates from the norm. (The norm is determined psychometrically.) (2) It is an evaluative model which views adequate psychoeducational development as good, and poor development as bad. (3) It is a deficit model, because children are labeled in terms of their inabilities rather than their strengths. (4) Because children are exposed to approximately the same kinds of educational settings, the problem is viewed as existing *within* the child. (5) Deficits can be difficult to recognize and can be mistaken for disturbance or stupidity. (6) The model is completely culture bound, because it evaluates the child on his or her ability to acquire those skills which are determined by schools. Schools are notorious (or famous, depending on one's point of view) for their reflection of white, middle-class attitudes and values. Many of the characteristics associated with the psychoeducational process model are clearly suspect.

The Task Analysis Model

Since the task analysis model does not compare children against each other, there is no distinction made between normal and abnormal. Adherents measure the extent to which a child has mastered enabling behaviors necessary to the completion of a task, and the characteristics of the task as well. The goal of remediation is to take children from where they are vis-à-vis a certain skill and to move them to where the teacher (or significant others) wants them to be. It is a reductionist model in that it analyzes complex terminal behaviors into component skills, teaches those skills, and then attempts to integrate the component skills into a terminal behavior. Although proponents of the model recognize that there is no one skill hierarchy to be taught and that children may take alternate routes in achieving a terminal behavior, little or no provision is made for diversity of learning styles. There is no attempt in this model to identify causes, because the children are described in terms of their achievements, not their problems. This is the model embraced by the behaviorists (see Chapter 3).

The Pluralistic Model

The pluralistic model assumes that differences in test performances among racial and ethnic groups are due to test biases. Proponents, therefore, argue that many conceptions of normal are needed and that tests need to be culture-related in order to enable children of minority groups to demonstrate their capacities. Three major approaches have been taken: First, some advocate the creation of culture-specific tests. Second, others suggest that children be tested, taught relevant skills, and retested, so that the ability to profit from teaching can be measured. Finally, local norms are used. (Local norms will be discussed more fully in the section on statistical considerations.) The development of multiple normative frameworks allows the comparison of a child's performance to his or her same-group peers. The problem, of course, is that those who would use minority status in a prejudicial way can continue to point to racial and ethnic inferiority just because special norms are needed.

TEST SELECTION

All too often, tests are used because they are known and available, or because they are closely associated with a particular discipline rather than because they have been carefully chosen for use in a specific case or situation. Although that may appear as harsh criticism, many examiners do in fact have a standard battery of tests they use, regardless of the presenting problems of the child. Certainly a good evaluation depends on the flexibility of the examiner as well as his or her skill in test administration and interpretation. How, then, are tests located and what considerations should control their use?

The best source for locating a test is the series of *Mental Measurements Yearbooks* (edited by O. K. Buros) which is available in the reference section of most libraries. Not only does Buros list many of the most widely used tests, but he also includes evaluations of them. One problem with Buros' work, however, is that newer tests (because of publication lag) are not included. Other sources, particularly for newer tests, include: *Journal of Educational Research, Perceptual and Motor Skills, Personnel and Guidance Journal, The Reading Teacher, Journal of Educational Measurement, School Review, Elementary School Journal, Learning Disabilities Quarterly,* and *Topics in Learning and Learning Disabilities.*

Cultural Considerations

One overriding consideration in the selection of tests is the cultural background of the child. There are two crucial issues between which a delicate balance must be achieved. First, many tests discriminate against minority group children. Second, many minority group children do not receive adequate services, because their cultural difference masks their learning problems (Sandler, Jamison, Deliser, Cohen, Emkey, & Keith, 1970).

Test Discrimination   Many of the followup studies (cf. Fleming & Attonen, 1970; Gozali & Meyer, 1970; Haberman, 1970; Jose & Cody, 1971) failed to confirm the findings of Rosenthal and Jacobson (1968) that children behave the way they are *expected* to behave and that the perceptions and attitudes of the teacher influence their interactions with their pupils so that self-fulfilling prophecies arise and are perpetuated. There is increasing evidence, however, to indicate that teachers' perceptions of social stereotypes may be more closely related to the placement of children into reading groups than were the ability levels of the children (Rist, 1970). Other research supporting the self-fulfilling prophecy is discussed in Chapters 7 and 9.

In 1968, the Black Psychological Association requested a moratorium on testing in the schools. Although the moratorium was never instituted, the issue of discrimination against minority pupils was brought to professional and public awareness and a considerable amount of reevaluation of testing philosophy and practice was begun. The misuse of test scores included the support of genetic causation theories by test data related to race, nationality, sex, and region (Cleary, Humphreys, Kendrick, & Wesman, 1975). Alternative problems which could explain low IQ and achievement scores among minority groups have been reviewed and discussed by Avila and Havassy (1974), Cleary et al. (1975), Gay and Abrahams (1973), Samuda (1975), and Sarason (1973). These include: nutrition, self-concept, motivation, anxiety, testing environment, language and dialect differences, and different cultural dynamics. (Different cultural dynamics might include attitudes toward whites and others of the dominant culture, systems of time allocation, expressions of identity, and the effects of poverty.) It cannot be assumed, however, that IQ scores simply reflect middle-class learning and achievement. The IQs of parents and their children are correlated only .50 (Cleary et al., 1975). Children of fathers whose IQs are near 140 have an average IQ of about 120, that is, they have regressed half-way to the population mean. In addition, the spread of their scores about their own mean of 120 is almost as large as the spread of IQs among children in general. IQ and other achievement and mastery tests can be used effectively with minority children so long as they are used and interpreted properly. The value of such tests lies in their ability to predict future learning in education and, perhaps, to some extent, vocation. These types of tests "have predicted future learning for all segments of our society with modest but significant validity and generalizability" (Cleary et al., 1975, p. 24).

What steps can be taken to ensure fair testing? Tests can be restricted to use with those for whom they were intended. For example, persons with impairments as well as different language environments should be excluded, unless the tests were normed on such groups. It must be kept in mind that tests measure more than what they are designed to test, especially with respect to socialization and specific learning. Only tests with clear, well-written manuals should be used. Examiners must be well-trained and must adhere to all instructions and guidelines during test administration. A variety of tests should be used and data reviewed in light of alternative assessments. Alternative means for assessing children's school achievement might include pluralistic models, translations, and culture-fair tests. Avila and Havassy have suggested that the use of Piagetian measures rather than IQ tests may prove useful. Since, however, there is considerable evidence from cross-cultural research that Piagetian measures are sensitive to sociocultural influences (Gallagher & Reid, 1981), that recommendation is doubtful.

Masked Learning Problems   The problem of having real learning problems masked is a thorny one, especially in regard to children whose language is not

Standard English. Testing should certainly be in the child's primary language, if one can be established. Proficiency not only in language skills, per se, but in academic areas, must be tested in both languages. Samuda (1975, pp. 177–204) has compiled a list of tests which are advertised as appropriate for use with minority adolescents and adults. Lapp and Flood have developed a similar list of informal and formal measures for use with younger (kindergarten through grade four) minority children (Lapp & Flood, 1978, pp. 513–514). Once nondiscriminatory testing has been carried out and proficiency of the child in language or dialect has been determined, sorting learning deficits from experiential factors becomes easier. Of course, task analytic systems which seek to determine what children know (rather than to compare them) can be helpful in deciding upon intervention strategies, especially since:

> It has not even been demonstrated that the level of problem-solving behavior in *nontest* situations is highly correlated with the level of similar types of problem-solving processes in the standardized test situations (Sarason, 1973, p. 971).

Theoretical Considerations

One of the most important theoretical considerations which can guide test selection is often overlooked: the appropriateness of the underlying model. It is sometimes argued that this consideration is irrelevant. People point to the IQ test and claim that although there is no underlying model, IQ tests have been quite accurate in determining future learning ability. Perhaps that argument would be more valid if the results of testing were used impartially and atheoretically. They are not. Although perceptual tests, for example, are by and large based on inaccurate and/or antiquated models, although performance on these tests is not related or is only marginally related to academic performance, and although the abilities measured by such tests represent fragmentations of a single perceptual process, some argue for their continued use in special education. Why? Special educators have agreed for some time now that an IQ score is not very useful for teachers, because it is difficult to plan instructional programs based on the knowledge that the child's IQ is 110. It is equally difficult to plan instructional programs on the basis of a child's having a low score on a test of visual closure. What does that information contribute to the teaching of reading, spelling, or arithmetic? It is rather analogous to Baker's suggestion (cited in Ricks, 1971) that miles are becoming less and less meaningful as units of measurement in these days of jet travel and monumental traffic jams. Baker advocated the use of *agomins*. Agomins (or minutes of agony) are more meaningful than "two miles to work" when one spends thirty minutes each day in a traffic jam two blocks from the door! The point, of course, is that just because we have a unit of measurement available and we are familiar with it, does not mean that that measurement system is useful.

A second consideration in test selection is how well the test suits one's purpose. For example, should the test be formal or informal? Group or individual? Does it yield diagnostic or survey information? Does its content match precisely those abilities in which the examiner is interested? Does it yield the types of data that are needed? Should one select a standardized test that measures relative standing, such as percentile ranks or age equivalents, or a criterion-referenced test which indicates what a child can and cannot do vis-à-vis a given task or domain?

Another consideration is how well the test suits the characteristics of the children to be tested. Is it appropriate for a given age level? How long will children be asked to sit? What are the demands of the test which may render it unfair for minority, bilingual, or specific groups of handicapped children? Is it of an appropriate level of difficulty? Was the test standardized on similar children? This latter question is one which is frequently overlooked in the field of special education. Many of the tests in popular use have few or no handicapped children in their norming sample, nor have they established diagnostic validity.

Consideration also needs to be given to the facility with which the test can be administered and scored. Is the format familiar to the children to be tested? Is it appropriate (e.g., Does it require preschoolers to use paper and pencil?)? Does it take special training to be able to administer and score the test? Is the manual clear and easy to use? Are scores easily interpreted? (It should be remembered that the more difficult a test is to administer, score, and interpret, the greater the margin for examiner error.) Does administration require a special physical setting? Special materials? Special personnel?

Finally, one must compare the costs of the tests. How much does the test itself cost? Are test materials reuseable or consummable? Must the test be administered, scored and/or interpreted by high-salaried personnel? What is the ratio of examiners to children? How much is the commitment in time? How frequently must retesting be done?

Statistical Considerations

Statistical considerations include the adequacy of the norming sample, the tests' validity, reliability (including subtest reliability), and predictive ability. The type of scores a test yields is also an important consideration.

Norming Sample   When a test is standardized, it is administered to a large number of people so that norms (or averages) can be obtained. The types of norms vary. Some tests report age norms, some grade norms, some mental age norms, etc. Some offer a combination. The important thing is that the norming sample be representative of the group with whom the test will be used. Standardized tests are usually normed nationally so that the sample of people whose scores are included approximates that of their representation in the population at large (e.g., percentage of rural, urban, suburban). Informal (or nonstandardized) tests usually have no norms. Whether one is using standardized or informal tests, however, it is often useful to develop local norms.

Local norms ensure that a child who is tested can be compared to an appropriate group. Local norms are generally useful under two circumstances:

when looking back, and for administrative purposes (Ricks, 1971). When looking back, it is quite appropriate to compare a child's past performance to the local group of which he or she was a part. For example, if a child attended an inner-city school in which the overall level of performance was lower than the national norm, it would be appropriate to ask the question of how well this child did in relation to other children in that school. When planning for that child's future, however, it would be unreasonable to suppose that the child would always remain a member of that group. Hence, the use of national norms would be more beneficial. When administrative questions are at issue, one is usually concerned only with the local group, so that reference to national standards is irrelevant.

Local norms can be developed simply by calculating the average score and standard deviation of the children taking the test. For example, one might take the average of all the 1980 first graders (plus or minus one standard deviation) as the norming group for the same school's 1981 first graders. Remember that norms vary by age group and so should be calculated separately by age or grade. The average of all children from the first to sixth grades, for example, is meaningless.

Finally, it is imperative that the norms of standardized tests be checked to make sure that the norming sample is representative of the group being tested. Even many of the most widely used tests in special education have been normed on "normal" children. Many tests claim to be based on a nationally representative sample, but minority and socioeconomic groups often do not appear in the norming sample with the same frequency that they appear in the general population. Sometimes a norming sample will include something like 2 percent blacks and 1 percent or 2 percent of other minorities. Although such a test may claim to be representative, it is, in fact, still normed on white, middle-class children. When the published norms are not appropriate for the children being tested, local norms may be preferable, depending on one's purposes.

Reliability   Once it has been established that a representative norming sample is available or that local norms are appropriate, a test should be checked for its reliability. A test is reliable if it yields approximately the same results under varying conditions. Hence, reliability is a measure of consistency. Essentially, reliability raises the question of how sensitive the test is to irrelevant variations, such as how the person was feeling, what time of day the test was given, what the temperature was like that day, etc. Reliability is not affected by systematic changes in score, for example, those due to learning and growth. It is, however, affected by unsystematic variations that cause testing error. Reliability tells us the extent to which we can be satisfied that approximately the same test score would be obtained if the child were given the test again, and again, and again. Reliability is expressed as a positive decimal ranging from .00 to 1.00, where 1.00 represents perfect reliability. Salvia and Ysseldyke (1978, p. 92) suggest the following reliability standards for standardized tests: For group data a minimum of .60. For testing that will be used to make inferences about the behavior of an individual child, they recommend a minimum reliability of .90 and, for screening instruments, a .80 minimum standard. These figures are quite similar to those recommended by many other authors.

Several forms of reliability are often reported in test manuals: test-retest reliability, parallel forms reliability, and internal consistency reliability. Test-retest reliability measures the stability of the test across two or more administrations. The longer the period of time between testings, the lower the coefficient is expected to be. Parallel forms reliability is obtained by comparing the results of one set of questions with a second set administered to the same group. Internal consistency is a measure of how well various items on the test measure the same thing. It is often calculated by comparing an individual's score on the odd numbered items with the same individual's score on the even numbered items and is referred to as split-half reliability.

One extremely important consideration with regard to reliability for special educators is the reliability of subtests. When tests, either underlying abilities tests or achievement tests, are used for diagnostic purposes, the important information is often derived from the subtests rather than from the total score. In fact, remediation is most often planned on the basis of subtest results. Additionally, an examiner seldom has as much time to test a child as he or she would like to have. Since time is at a premium, most examiners use a battery of subtests, rather than administering any test in toto. In each case, the overall reliability reported for a test is immaterial. What must be checked are the reliability coefficients for the specific subtests which will be used. Reliabilities for subtests are frequently disappointing and often fall far below the standards recommended above. Most people who use them seem to be unaware that if they were to administer the same test to the same child at a different time, even the next day, very different results could be obtained on the subtests. How can one plan remedial strategies when there is no certainty that the results reflect the abilities of the child rather than measurement problems inherent in the subtest?

Standard Error of Measurement Before test validity is discussed, the value of using the standard error of measurement to establish confidence intervals will be examined. *Confidence interval* is a term which refers to an estimate of the range in which a child's true score lies. According to theory (Aiken, 1976, p. 64) "68 percent of a group of examinees having the same observed score will have true scores falling within plus or minus one standard error of measurement of that observed score." Ninety-five percent will have true scores falling within plus or minus two standard errors of measurement. If a child's score on a test is 100 and if the standard error of measurement is 3.16, we may assume with some confidence that the child's true score lies between 96.84 and 103.16.

This is not to be confused with the use of the standard deviation of the test to establish the severity of problems. Let's suppose a child's score on a test is 100. The mean for the appropriate norming sample is 120 and the standard deviation is 12.16. Does the child who scored 100 have a problem? One way to answer that question is to say that the test mean for the appropriate norming sample plus or minus one standard deviation represents the range of normal scores, i.e., 107.84 to 132.16. Any score below 107.84 would consistute reason for concern. A score two or more standard deviations below would be an indication of a severe deficiency. Likewise, a score two standard deviations above the mean of the norming sample would indicate superior performance. One cannot interpret the severity of the problem in terms of the standard deviation alone. Decisions must always be made taking the standard error of measurement into account. Unfortunately, even among widely used educational tests, the standard error of measurement often approaches the size of the standard deviation. In such a case, what might look like a serious problem may in fact be due to the error of the test.

Validity Another concern in test selection is validity. Validity measures help us to understand what a test is measuring, so that scores can be adequately interpreted. Unlike reliability, validity is subject to variations in both systematic and unsystematic errors. Since a reliability coefficient measures consistency versus error, a test can be reliable without being valid, but a *test or subtest cannot be valid unless it is reliable*. Five types of validity will be discussed: content validity, criterion-related validity, construct validity, concurrent validity, and predictive validity.

Content validity is often referred to as face validity, that is, whether the test appears to measure what it says it does. It also refers, however, to whether a test samples from all the areas it should. The content validity of an achievement test may be judged by determining the degree to which the items of the test sample the objectives of instruction. Subject matter experts usually make this decision. No numerical value is, therefore, associated with content validity.

Criterion-related validity is established by comparing the results of the test under consideration with results on a criterion test, i.e., if one test is known to be an adequate measure of socialization skills, for example, a new test will be measured against the standard. When the results of the criterion are available at the time of the testing, the comparison becomes a measure of concurrent validity.

Construct validity is established by determining how well related test scores—presumed to be a measure of some construct—are to measures of behavior in situations where that construct is thought to be an important variable. Construct validity is generally established indirectly by testing various hypotheses regarding the definition of the construct, the theory from which the construct is derived, and experimental studies. To have construct validity, a test must have both content and concurrent validity.

Finally, predictive validity is an especially important variable for special educators to consider in test selection. Seldom is a test used to determine what a child can or cannot do at any given moment. We usually want to know how well that test predicts what the child will be able to do in the future. Of what value is a reading test, for example, if it doesn't have any relation to subsequent instruction? If a reading test has reliability and if children's scores on that test correlate highly with later reading ability (measured either against a test or some other measure of ability, such as a teacher's grade or reading level), then the test has predictive validity and may be useful. The careful examiner who searches through the manuals of tests frequently used in special education will find that few of them report anything about their predictive validity. Unless examiners are prepared to measure the test's predictiveness in their own local sample, a test which reports more adequate data on predictive validity would be a wiser choice. One must still, however, guard against the temptation to regard a score on a highly correlated or enabling variable as *causal*. A low score on a phonics test, for example, even if it had predictive validity to later phonics performance would not necessarily mean that a lack of phonics knowledge was the cause of a reading problem.

Types of Scores Yielded   One final consideration in test selection that is related to measurement characteristics is the types of scores yielded. Most tests provide norming tables that offer the user a selection from among a variety of possibilities. A single test, for example, might offer percentile rankings, age equivalents, and grade equivalents. Often there may be scores which allow the child's performance to be placed within a particular subset of scores, such as the upper fourth (quartiles) or the upper ninth (stanines). It is important to note that the purpose of standardized tests is to indicate where on a particular continuum (e.g., mathematics achievement) a child's score lies. To do that, the test must necessarily compare that child's score to those obtained by other children the same age. The most appropriate score, therefore, is probably the percentile rank, because it most clearly reflects the placement of the child's score in relation to the scores of the other children in the comparison group.

Although the use of age and grade equivalent scores is very popular, they are misleading and tend to create confusion. Both parents and professionals tend to interpret equivalence scores as indications of the child's proper placement or level of functioning. A third-grade child who scores at the fourth-grade level has not mastered the material taught in the first four grades. That child has learned more of the material taught in the third grade than did others in the standardization sample. Since that child would have more raw score points than the average third grader, he or she would obtain a higher grade (or age) equivalent score. It does not matter how these raw score points were accumulated. The child might have answered consecutive questions or might have given a sporadic performance missing early questions but answering later ones. The score then reflects only that the child performed better than the average third grader.

Even when scores are interpreted correctly there still exists a very widespread problem in relation to the interpretation of the entire test battery. Frequently, testers or test consumers equate scores on one test (or set of tests) with scores obtained from a different test (or set of tests) to determine whether the child is performing up to capacity or whether a discrepancy between potential and achievement exists. Since the tests were normed on different populations one would not expect a percentile rank on one test to be the same as a percentile rank on a second test (Salvia & Ysseldyke, 1978).[2] Furthermore, since perfect correlations do not exist between two achievement tests or between an achievement test and an intelligence test, there are bound to be discrepancies even for children who are performing up to expected standards. Errors of measurement that are inherent to all tests also make direct score comparisons impossible. Finally, one would anticipate that any score on one test (e.g., an intelligence test) would be related to a *distribution* of scores on another test (e.g., an achievement test): no one would expect *all* persons with a 120 IQ to achieve at the 85th percentile on a reading test. There are too many other factors mediating performance.

Many formulas have been developed for comparing scores across tests, but to date none has been devised which escapes serious criticisms. A number of test publishers also provide expectancy tables that assist in decisions related to underachievement and performance discrepancy. These tables suggest, for example, score expectations for a child in comparison to others of the same grade and IQ. Even these tables, however, must be interpreted subjectively. All information about the child that is available must be taken into account before a decision about evenness of performance or underachievement can be made. Also recall that scores should always be discussed not in terms of a specific number, but in terms of the likely range of scores.

Bayesian Identification   With increasing disenchantment with traditional methods of identification, other methods of making classification and placement decisions have been sought. One such alternative, the use of Bayesian procedures, is proving viable. The technique essentially entails the calculation for each individual of the probability that he or she is correctly classified as learning disabled. The calculation of probability is dependent upon the student's being evaluated according to a number of weighted variables. These are behaviors associated, in expert opinion, with being learning disabled. Weighting takes into account the existence of the characteristic in both the population of learning disabled children and the population of normally achieving students. Alley, Deshler, and Warner (1979) indicated that the Bayesian procedure consists of a series of decisions based upon probability. First, students are evaluated by the classroom teacher according to a checklist of behaviors. The results are subjected to Bayesian analysis and the probability that the child is learning disabled is calculated. If the probability is high enough, then the second step is begun. A test battery consisting of a limited number of tests or subtests tapping the particular areas suggested in step one is administered to the student. Again, the scores are transformed into probabilities. The Bayesian theorem is employed to determine the probability that a child is learning disabled given (1)

[2]Percentile scores, however, are often the best type of score to use to report testing results to parents and teachers. They avoid the misinterpretations so often associated with age and grade equivalence, while they clearly state the findings of standardized tests—a child's standing in relation to his or her peers.

the performance of the individual, (2) the weights assigned to the subtests (how likely this trait is to appear in the learning disabled and normally achieving populations), and (3) the percentage of children classified learning disabled by a given school district. At this point, a probability is computed that reflects the "degree of belief" or "best bet" (Alley, Deshler, & Warner, 1979, p. 78) that a given child is learning disabled.

The Bayesian approach, an attempt to improve the decision-making process, has been widely employed in such fields as business, economics, and medicine where definitive statistics have not operated satisfactorily. At present, the Bayesian approach is new to educational decision making. The technique has been used with elementary school children (DeRuiter, Ferrell, & Kass, 1975; Wissink, Kass, & Ferrell, 1975) and adolescents (Alley, Deshler, & Warner, 1979). The technique is not, however, either widely known or employed at this time. Since the field of learning disabilities is in disagreement over the concept and construction of discrepancy formulas, the Bayesian approach may prove to be a useful alternative.

SUMMARY AND CONCLUSIONS

In this chapter, we have examined the difference between testing and assessment, the purposes of assessment, and several models which constitute a framework within which testing and assessment take place. We very briefly addressed the issue of nondiscriminatory testing. For a more complete treatment of this subject, see Oakland (1977) and/or Samuda (1975). Theoretical and statistical considerations in test selection were also briefly reviewed and some of the most common oversights pointed out. Most important among these is the necessity of checking subtest reliability and predictive validity as well as avoiding direct comparisons between scores. For a more complete and more statistically oriented treatment of considerations in testing selection, the reader is referred to Nunnally (1967).

SUGGESTED READINGS

Aiken, L. R. *Psychological testing and assessment.* Boston: Allyn and Bacon, 1976.

Bureau of Education for the Handicapped. *Developing criteria for the evaluation of protection in evaluation procedures provisions.* Washington, D. C.: The United States Office of Education, Bureau of Education for the Handicapped, Division of Innovation and Development, State Program Studies Branch, 1978.

Nunnally, J. C. *Psychometric theory.* New York: McGraw-Hill, 1967.

Oakland, T. *Psychological and educational assessment of minority children.* New York: Brunner/Mazel, 1977.

Salvia, J., & Ysseldyke, J. E. *Assessment in special and remedial education.* Boston: Houghton Mifflin, 1978.

Samuda, R. *Psychological testing of American minorities.* New York: Dodd, Mead, 1975.

Wallace, G., & Larsen, S. C. *Educational assessment of learning problems: Testing for teaching.* Boston: Allyn and Bacon, 1978.

Chapter 9

Screening and Early Identification

INTRODUCTION

In recent years, there has been a great expenditure of energy directed toward the early identification and treatment of children with learning disabilities. Most American school systems have screening programs at the kindergarten and first-grade levels. A national survey indicated that those which do not pointed to the following: (1) they lacked staff and funds, (2) they had a school philosophy (or state law) that prohibited the exclusion of children from regular classroom activities, (3) they were unable to find valid screening instruments, (4) they used kindergarten, itself, as a screening program, and (5) mandatory entrance examinations conducted by physicians provided some screening (Maitland, Nadeau, & Nadeau, 1974). Most schools, however, which conduct screening tests for hearing and vision, also include testing for school readiness.

Since 1970 when the inclusion of handicapped preschoolers was mandated for Head Start programs, there has also been considerable effort exerted to identify potential problem children at the preschool level. The mandate raised questions that had not previously been addressed. For example, what were the signs of learning problems which could be observed in preschoolers? Although children with severe deficits can be identified, how are those with subtle learning problems to be detected? What kind of program could be offered children who were identified? Were there aspects of special education practices that would need to be incorporated into preschool curriculums? What were the advantages and disadvantages of early identification?

Although there is considerable overlap between screening practices at the kindergarten and preschool levels, these two areas will be treated separately in this discussion. Children at the preschool level have not yet had the opportunity to demonstrate that they are failing at school tasks, the minimum requirement for a diagnosis of learning disabilities, although PL 94-142 allows a diagnosis based on abilities thought to be correlated with school performance.

SCREENING

Screening consists of surveying rather large groups to determine where people stand vis-à-vis a variable of interest. Screening is the first part of a two-part process. First, rather imprecise instruments are used to survey the population in question. For example, screening may be carried out to determine which children have hearing difficulties. The second step of the process is diagnosis, i.e., the step in which one asks questions about the *nature* and *severity* of the problems identified in screening. (This second step will be discussed in the next chapter.) To be effective, screening must have the following characteristics: (1) it must be followed by diagnosis, (2) the problems identified in the screening procedure must be critical to successful school performance, (3) the behaviors sampled by the screening instrument must be representative of the total activity, and (4) finally, a treatment which ameliorates the problem must be instituted.

Screening is particularly difficult when one is searching for a learning disabled population. First, there is no general agreement as to what should constitute the content of such an investigation. What behaviors should be measured? Should the ability to perform tasks that are necessary to the successful completion of kindergarten and first grade be measured? Should maturational correlates of learning such as perception be measured? Both direct and indirect (correlational) measures have been used with moderate success. The problem is, of course, that these measures identify children who are "at risk" or "vulnerable," and not specifically children with learning disabilities. Many of the children identified by such instruments are from poverty cultures, many are disturbed, many are retarded. In fact, a perusal of the validity data from a variety of screening tests indicated that most of them are quite accurate in predicting problems among very severely impaired populations and in predicting the successes of superior children. What they are least accurate in predicting is the future performance of children who do not have pervasive problems. They are, therefore, effective in predicting failure for children who are moderately to severely mentally retarded or severely emotionally disturbed, but are least effective in predicting failure among children who will later be labeled "learning disabled," regardless of the later persistence of the child's reading and/or other problems.

It is the *specific disability* that is most difficult to isolate. Critchley (1975) stated that specific developmental dyslexia, for example, can seldom be diagnosed even by a careful, complete clinical battery prior to the age of seven.

Furthermore, learning disability is defined as a discrepancy between achievement and potential. Both IQ and achievement tests, however, whether used in a screening situation or as part of a diagnostic battery, measure experiential factors. Determining the child's potential, particularly before instruction has been given, is extremely difficult. In screening programs, tests designed to measure intelligence or achievement variables are generally written. Since most learning disabled children have significant problems in reading (and sometimes writing and spelling), their knowledge and skills will probably not be discovered by such tests.

Cautions and Considerations

A number of serious problems related to the use of screening devices have been identified: classification attempts which produce pathology, the issue of selection criteria, Pygmalion effects, subtest reliability, measures of predictive validity, the accuracy of teacher judgments, the need to set cutoff scores, the relevance of abilities measured in correlational tests, the failure of the test to identify truly deviant children, the failure of the examiners to follow screening with diagnostic procedures and, finally, the lack of a validated intervention program.

Arbitrary Standards   Arbitrary determinants of what constitutes abnormality are often used in educational screening (Salvia & Ysseldyke, 1978). Many test constructors, for example, began by observing that approximately 25 percent to 40 percent of children in early elementary grades were having difficulties in first, second, and third grade. They then set about constructing a test that would identify children who would later be in the lower third of their third-grade classes. This use of *relative deviancy* as a criterion established in advance that approximately a third of the children would be considered failing in the third grade. That kind of expectation is a result of the kind of teaching system we use in this country. Classes are conducted so that the teacher teaches to the mean, i.e., the average student. It necessarily follows that 50 percent of the class will be performing at or below the mean. To designate the lowest third as deviant is to construct an arbitrary definition of what deviancy means. When the American Association on Mental Deficiency lowered the cutoff for subaverage intellectual functioning from one to two standard deviations below the mean, it effectively reduced the incidence of mental retardation in the schools.

When screening tests, in effect, stipulate that 33 percent of the children in a given class will be labeled as deviant, that does not mean that the lowest third of the class is learning disabled. Even if we accept the necessity for arbitrary standards, a complete diagnostic battery is still needed to determine who is learning disabled and who suffers from other types of problems.

Selection Criteria   What criteria are to be used to test the effectiveness of a screening instrument? Many test batteries have been devised and recent years have seen a proliferation of screening tests. It would be easy to suggest that screening tests could be considered adequate if they had compatible norms, good reliability, and demonstrated validity. The issue, however, is somewhat more complex. First, there is the question of what content is sampled and how relevant and representative it is. Next is the question of how performance in the later grades is to be measured. Are the same behaviors still pertinent? Should the teacher's judgment of the child's rank in his or her class be used? Should grades constitute the criterion? Should tests be used? What tests are appropriate? Some screening batteries (cf. Eaves, Kendall, & Crichton, 1974) predict future performance differentially, e.g., they are more accurate in predicting future word analysis and listening skills rather than reading per se. In addition, some criterion tests may be better able to discriminate among children's performances at lower levels (Feshbach, Adelman, & Fuller, 1974).

Pygmalion Effects   Pygmalion effects are also reason for caution in the use of screening devices. (See also Chapters 7 and 8.) A high degree of predictability in the use of screening instruments may be derived from reinforced or reduced parent and teacher expectations (Forness & Esveldt, 1975).

> When children are identified as high risk, a set of expectancies, anxieties, and differential treatment patterns may develop. Effects may be particularly insidious in that preschool or kindergarten children have not yet developed the deficit conditions for which they were identified . . . persons dealing with high risk children are, in fact, not identifying; rather, they are hypothesizing about future development from present behavior. Thus, the act of predicting learning problems may . . . have a built-in expectancy phenomenon (Keogh & Becker, 1973, p. 8).

Subtest Reliability   Subtest reliability in many of the most widely used screening devices is unacceptable. A review of tests, especially those measuring correlates of learning, showed that a majority of subtest reliability coefficients fall far below the .80 standard usually recommended. Subtest scores are not crucial, however, if the test is to be used simply to identify high-risk children. Many of these screening devices, however, have manuals that recommend that children's profiles be developed from the test data. Once this step is undertaken, subtest reliability is of utmost importance. Many of these screening programs go even further and advocate differential remedial instruction to match the deficit areas designated by the profile. When subtests are unreliable, these types of recommendations are completely unjustified.

Validity   Measures of predictive validity, of course, depend to a great extent on the reliability of overall test scores and of subtests. There are, however, other questions associated with validity. First, many of the test instruments used to screen for learning disabilities were developed to diagnose specific types of problems, such as reading deficits, perceptual processes, psycholinguistic delays, mental retardation, etc. (Beatty, 1975). In one instance, when a battery of readiness, perceptual, and intelligence tests was used, many children who were noted as potential failures in kindergarten scored within normal limits on the *Metropolitan Achievement Tests* at the end of first grade (Badian & Serwer, 1975). Traditional correlates may, therefore, be unsuited to the task of predicting later failure. Quite importantly also the tests that are being used tend to overidentify minority children and children of lower socioeconomic status (Sims & Bastian, 1976) even when efforts to eliminate the effects of discrimination are made. There are conditions related to the testing environment itself which prejudice test results (Mackler & Holman, 1976). Many minority children are intimidated by the testing situation which is so foreign to their experiential backgrounds. Keogh and Becker (1973, p. 7) noted a methodological paradox that further hinders estimates of predictive validity:

> If early identification and diagnosis were insightful and remedial implementation successful, the preschool or kindergarten high risk child would receive the kind of attention and help which results in successful school performance. In essence, he would no longer be high risk and would, instead, be a successful achiever. Predictive validity of the identification instruments would, therefore, be low. In such a case, success with the child would negate accuracy of prediction. Research of development of predictive tools is thus limited by ethical considerations. Having identified a child as high risk, the researcher is obligated to intervene, thus limiting examination of the long term predictive validity of the instruments. *

Unvalidated screening programs are, however, detrimental to both those children who are, and those children who are not identified (Monteith, 1976). Accuracy is clearly an essential characteristic of an early identification program.

Teacher Reports   What seems to be as accurate as any known test or test battery is teacher observation. Whether checklists, observation forms, or rating scales are used, teacher reports seem to be quite accurate. Furthermore, when test results and teacher judgments disagree, most school districts view teacher judgments as more important (Maitland, Nadeau, & Nadeau, 1974). Many predictive instruments have used teacher judgments to validate their own effectiveness. Early test results correlate between .40 and .60 with later criteria (Eaves, Kendall, & Crichton, 1974). These results are only moderately useful and are certainly not sufficiently precise for use with individual cases. Feshbach, Adelman, and Fuller compared the results of using the Jansky-de Hirsch (1973) battery and a teacher rating scale. Although both scales were approximately 75 percent accurate in their predictions, the test battery produced nearly twice as many false positives. At any rate, a kindergarten teacher's rating predicted first-grade reading achievement as well as the psychometric battery. It would be easy to conclude from such findings that one should simply rely on teacher judgments and save the time and money associated with psychometric screening. Again, however, the issue is not so simple.

Many studies have indicated that disruptive behavior, sometimes euphemistically called "active participatory" behavior, is the critical factor in determining teachers' perceptions of children's classroom functioning (cf. Forness & Esveldt, 1975; Spivak, Swift, & Prewitt, 1971).

*Reprinted from *Exceptional Children,* by B. Keogh and L. D. Becker by permission of The Council for Exceptional Children. © 1973 by the Council for Exceptional Children.

While it is evident that teachers rate these high 'participators' as high risk children, it is not clear whether such an evaluation is due to actual learning problems in this group or to the interruptive effect which their behavior has on classroom routine and the inordinate amount of time which needs to be spent with them . . . teacher ratings may have, in part, reflected lack of adherence to some idealized model of classroom conformity (Forness, Guthries, & Nihira, 1975, pp. 267–268).

What is significant about these comments is that teacher judgments provide rather accurate indices of future school performance. One of the major screening tests, the *Slingerland Screening Tests for Identifying Children with Specific Language Disability,* that is supposed to measure written language, also measures behaviors (e.g., copying, dictation) which are much more closely related to classroom demands than they are to any estimate of language functioning. Perhaps implicit in the definition of "good student" is the assumption that classroom formalities will be adhered to. Indeed, Doyle's (1979) work has shown that most decisions made in classrooms are directed toward optimizing management rather than learning!

Correlated Behaviors   A very serious question that has been raised in other chapters of this book, but is especially important in a discussion of screening instruments is whether correlated behaviors are tapping relevant abilities. Since no causal (or *prerequisite*) connection has ever been established between, for example, perceptual functioning and academic abilities and since the cross-cultural research indicates the opposite (that schooling improves perceptual functioning), it is difficult to justify the use of measures of correlated behaviors as the foundation upon which training sequences should be introduced. Since perceptual functions and school performance are related, there may be a defensible argument for their use in prediction (even though the correlations tend to be low). Controlled studies have not, however, demonstrated that the training of such functions improves reading, mathematics, or spelling performance. It appears also that the determination of perceptual functioning is important only for the youngest children and even among them, not all children with perceptual deficits will have difficulties in school. It is widely believed that most youngsters achieve some minimal threshhold of perceptual functioning which enables them to perform academic tasks, even if they do not perform so well as their peers. Evidence that this assumption is viable comes from the performances of visually impaired children who (with a minimum of visual information) function quite adequately in reading and other academic tasks. There appears to be no reason then that instructional goals should be based on the improvement of perceptual functioning. Emphasis on traditional school tasks such as reading and arithmetic should yield perceptual advances as a byproduct. Since learning disabled children need more rather than less instruction in school-related tasks, it is imperative that instructional time be spent in teaching toward goals which will enable the person to function in society. Producing "good perceivers" is not a goal of schooling, nor does it permit students to compete for places in advanced schools and in the job market. There is no substitute for learning to read and to calculate.

Cutoff Scores   When screening tests are given, four outcomes for each child are possible. As noted in Table 9-1, a child who is truly deviant may be identified or not identified. Similarly, a child who is *not* truly deviant may or may not be identified. How well children who are deviant (i.e., who will eventually fail) are identified is the major concern of a screening program. When cutoff scores (if a high score indicates competence) are shifted, high cutoff scores err in the direction of including more false positives, but they will usually pick up a high percentage of the truly deviant children. When cutoff scores are lowered, on the other hand, fewer children are falsely labeled as deviant, but many of the truly deviant children are missed. It is preferable, of course, to identify too many children rather than miss children who will need help. Unfortunately, few screening tests report their accuracy with hits and misses.

Nearly all psychometric batteries establish cutoff scores. When determining who shall and who shall not be considered potential problem learners, it is not possible to establish a single score. Jansky and de Hirsch (1973), for example, advocate that cutoff scores be adapted to each school. Their reasoning is that some schools have a preponderance of advanced children while others have a rather high percentage of nonreaders or poor readers. Using flexible cutoff scores ameliorates or at least regulates the problem of imputed pathology mentioned earlier. What it does, however, is to assume that there is some absolute standard that can be used to judge performances within schools. In addition, Jansky and de Hirsch were concerned only with the prediction of reading failures. Reading disability has been used as the defining characteristic of learning disability by those who have based early identification programs on the work of Jansky and de Hirsch (Monteith, 1976). In this case, learning disability is defined by a reading level or test score. Mean reading scores, however, vary widely among tests and the meaning of a reading score is ill-defined. By using reading scores to define a learning disability, we are simply replacing one amorphous term with another.

Emphasis in screening is on identifying as many children as needed to ensure, to the best of one's ability, that all of the children who will need services can be identified. For this reason, it is mandatory that screening be followed up by diagnostic evaluations. By doing in-depth evaluations of the children identified, the examiner will be able to weed out those children who were identified by the screening instrument, but who do not, in fact, require services. The only children who cannot be helped by the follow-up diagnosis are those

Table 9-1   Potentional Outcomes of Screening

	Identified	Not identified
Truly deviant	Positive	False negative
Not truly deviant	False positive	Negative

who were never identified. Unfortunately, what has happened is that many persons who author screening devices advocate remedial interventions based on the results of the screening. None of these instruments has adequate reliability and validity to suggest their use as diagnostic instruments which can be used in the individual case. Certainly, some of the reported success of the intervention programs results from their use with children who were identified, but who did not, in fact, have any difficulties, i.e., the false positives. Since no further evaluation was carried out, the academic successes of these children reflect favorably upon the person who intervenes and receives credit for having remediated deficiencies.

Validated Instructional Programs Finally, once children have been screened, diagnosed, and determined to have problems which need attention, we must begin a validated instructional program. The problem, of course, is that few exist and even fewer have been validated for use with learning disabled children. Even programs that are widely clinically acclaimed are backed by little controlled research data. Those that have been tested have not been demonstrated to be more successful than traditional teaching strategies. Perhaps all that we can say at present is that a sympathetic, consistent approach fosters learning. We have not yet managed to tailor programs to individual children in any predictable way, but teachers appear to be relatively successful in devising individually planned and/or individually administered programs that work, even if they must be designed on a one-by-one basis.

SCREENING TESTS

A few screening tests that are widely used will be discussed in this section. Examples of both direct and indirect (tests which measure correlates) measures will be reviewed. A review of the many tests available is beyond the scope of this book. The reader is referred to Salvia and Ysseldyke (1978) and Wallace and Larsen (1978) for more comprehensive presentations.

Direct Screening Tests

The *Metropolitan Readiness Tests* have been the most widely used in screening programs (Maitland, Nadeau, & Nadeau, 1974). Readiness is a construct that is used to explain why some children succeed in school and others fail. The Metropolitan is a direct test, because its subtests correspond to instructional goals of kindergarten and first-grade curriculums.[1] The test was revised (1976) to conform to content derived from an analysis of the reading process and a review of the research literature (Nurss & McGauvran, 1976). The test is norm-

---

[1]In another sense, the *Metropolitan* may be considered a test of correlated abilities. Auditory memory, visual matching, finding patterns, and sound-letter correspondence, etc. do not constitute reading, although performance on these variables is often highly correlated with successful reading performance. The *Metropolitan* is included here, because many early curricula still stress such readiness skills.

referenced and group administered. Practice tests are given prior to the administration of the battery to teach children to mark their answers correctly and to give them practice in what might be for some of them a very strange situation. Levels of the tests were developed for use with beginning or middle kindergarten children (Level I) and for the end of kindergarten and the beginning of the first grade (Level II). Most of the subtests employ a multiple choice format. Subtests include measures of: (Level I) auditory memory, rhyming, letter recognition, visual matching, school language and listening, and quantitative language. Level II tests measure: beginning consonants, sound-letter correspondence, visual matching, finding patterns, school language, listening, quantitative concepts, and quantitative operations. Salvia and Ysseldyke (1978) evaluated the norming sample and have found it to be both adequate and representative of a national sample. Reliability of the prereading composite scores is acceptable, but subtests in Level I, and area scores in Level II are not. Predictive validity was established by correlating results with scores obtained on the *Metropolitan Achievement Tests*. The authors of the test caution that it does not provide in-depth diagnostic information. Scores should be used as suggestive of strengths and weaknesses that must be verified by other means (Nurss & McGauvran, 1976). Clearly, the *Metropolitan Readiness Tests* are adequate screening devices from a traditional, readiness view.

A higher-level direct screening test is the *Stanford Achievement Test*. We have chosen to review this test, because it was described by Salvia and Ysseldyke as a "model of what adequately developed achievement tests should be" (p.152).[2] It is both a norm-referenced and an "objective referenced" test. Editions of the test are available to measure school skills from kindergarten through community college and special editions are available for use with the blind and deaf. The *Stanford Achievement Tests* sample the following behaviors: vocabulary, reading comprehension, word study skills, language arts, spelling, mathematics concepts, mathematics computation, mathematics applications, science, social science, and listening comprehension (Harcourt Brace Jovanovich, Inc., 1973). Norming sample, reliability, and validity are exemplary. Manuals which accompany the test list test items by instructional objectives and give suggestions for ways to teach those objectives. Since most reliabilities range between .85 and .95, much of the test is useful for individual planning, as well as for screening purposes.

Two new direct tests of reading and language for preschool, kindergarten and first-grade children are the *Test of Early Reading Ability* (*TERA*) and the *Test of Early Language Development* (*TELD*). TERA (Reid, Hresko, & Hammill, 1981) measures three types of early reading behaviors: the child's ability to attribute meaning to print, his or her knowledge of graphophonemic

---

[2]The *Metropolitan Achievement Test* has inadequate norms and reports no data concerning validity. The *California Achievement Test* has a normative sample whose adequacy is difficult to evaluate and similarly reports no data on validity. The *Iowa Tests of Basic Skills* (1974 edition) report no reliability data except a split-half correlation (Salvia & Ysseldyke, 1978).

structure, and his or her knowledge of the conventions of written language. Construct and content validity were demonstrated. Reliabilities for internal consistency ranged from .87 to .96, while test-retest measures ranged from .82 to .94. The test is unique in that it measures reading behaviors directly, rather than correlates of early reading, such as visual and auditory discrimination abilities. *TELD* (Hresko, Reid, & Hammill, 1981) measures the form (phonology, morphology, and syntax) and content (semantics and usage) of children's language, both expressively and receptively. Construct and content validity were found to be adequate. Reliability coefficients for internal consistency ranged from .88 to .92. Reliability coefficients for test-retest data ranged from .72 to .87 over a two-week period.

Indirect Screening Tests

Three tests that measure correlates of school performance will be reviewed here. Unfortunately, only one is normed, but the other two are very widely used, particularly with learning disabled children.

Search   *SEARCH* (Silver & Hagin, 1975, 1976) is a test rather widely used to screen kindergarten and first-grade children for later learning problems. The test measures ten components thought to be related to school achievement: discrimination and matching of asymmetric figures, recall of the orientation of asymmetric figures, copying of designs, verbal rote sequencing, auditory discrimination, articulation, intermodal dictation, directionality, finger schema, and pencil grip. The standardization sample on which the test was normed is limited to eight schools in New York City and twenty-two in North Carolina and does not reflect ethnic or minority groups in the proportion that they are represented in the general population. Although the norms range from ages 63 to 65 to 78 to 80 months, 87 percent of the norming group fell between 66 and 77 months of age. Because of interschool differences, the authors recommend the use of local norms. The ideal cutoff score was set at an arbitrary 30 percent of the sample studied, because clinical examination had found one-third of the original sample vulnerable to learning failure. Although total test score reliability just reached the minimum standard of .80, only one of the subtests did so (p. 34). Tests of predictive validity based on a sample of fifty-two children from a single school indicated that those who scored above the median on the oral reading section of the *Wide Range Achievement Test* at the end of first and the end of second grade were consistently identified by *SEARCH*. The instrument was not so successful in predicting which children would fail to reach the selected criterion score of reading grade 1.7.

Its authors stated that the test results are useful in "determining vulnerability, in analyzing the child's assets and deficits, in determining his need for further diagnosis, and in planning for the remedial procedures specific to his needs" (p. 79). Based on the data presented by Silver and Hagin, their claims are exaggerated. Perhaps the only use of this test for which one can have confidence is to determine the need for further diagnosis. Although it might be useful as a screening device, it can neither be used reliably to delineate individual strengths and weaknesses, nor to plan remedial interventions.

The Slingerland Screening Tests The *Slingerland Screening Tests for Identifying Children with Specific Language Disability* (Slingerland, 1970) are for grades kindergarten through grade five. Because Slingerland believes that each child is individual, she argues against the need for validation procedures (Slingerland, 1974, p. 11):

> For evaluation, it is the belief of this writer that each child must be considered on an individual basis, each one being unique unto himself and not to be included as a numerical figure to be fed into a computer. The variables are so tremendous that they would tend to invalidate the validation procedures.

Neither reliability nor validity data are, therefore, presented. One could, of course, use Slingerland's argument to question the need for giving tests at all! Slingerland suggested the possibility of developing local norms, but also provides "ballpark" figures to suggest disability, i.e., more than fifteen errors. There are eight subtests that can be administered to a group: far point copying, near point copying, visual perception (memory of words, letters, and numbers), visual perception with memory eliminated, visual perception and memory linked with kinesthetic-motor performance, auditory perception and memory linked with visual-kinesthetic-motor association, auditory discrimination of single sounds within the sequence of sounds in whole words, and auditory-visual with kinesthetic-motor eliminated. Individually administered auditory tests are also available for further study. The *Slingerland Tests* are admittedly sensitive to socioeconomic status. Their author recommends that the user take that into consideration when scoring. The test has some limited face validity in that learning disabled children, particularly those with reading problems, often have difficulties with copying, spelling, and handwriting. Certainly, the test may indicate that children will have difficulty if the class in which they are enrolled demands copying, spelling without the aid of a dictionary, etc. It should be remembered, however, that not all children who have such symptoms also have difficulties with academic learning. Furthermore, fifteen errors on the *Slingerland Screening Test* could result from nothing more than haste.

The Specific Language Disability Test An extension of the *Slingerland Screening Tests* was devised for grades six, seven, and eight. The *Specific Language Disability Test* (Malcomesius, 1967) is a group-administered test which includes: far point copying, near point copying, visual discrimination, visual memory, visual memory to motor, auditory discrimination, auditory memory to motor, auditory to visual comprehension (which measures the recall of factual information after an entire paragraph has been read), and spelling. The test is used not only with junior high school children, but also enjoys popularity among high school examiners. It is one of the few instruments available for the screening of learning disabilities at the upper levels. Although the test has neither reliability nor validity data to recommend it, its author advocates the use of the test results for both diagnosis and the planning of appropriate educational interventions.

Summary and Conclusions

Many current practices in screening programs used with learning disabled children appear to be unjustified. It seems that if one is interested in screening, the use of direct tests is the safest route. It is unthinkable that a child be identified for special instructional services, segregated classes, or labeling on the basis of tests that have no demonstrated validity. Even when adequate tests are used, further diagnostic evaluation is required before decisions which affect instructional procedures can be made.

EARLY IDENTIFICATION[3]

The continuing effort to identify handicapped children earlier and earlier and to provide preventive and remedial programs for them prior to their entrance into the elementary schools has led to a concern with learning disabilities among parents and professionals who work with preschool children. It should be clear, however, that unlike blindness, deafness, mental retardation, emotional disturbance, etc., learning disabilities, per se, do not actually exist in the preschool population, because school failure has not yet occurred. The question then becomes one of predicting which children will *later* demonstrate learning disorders. There are several issues which need to be considered in applying the learning disabilities label to preschool children. First, what assumptions underlly early identification and how reasonable are they? Second, what are the observable indications that suggest a developing learning disability and what are their implications for instruction? Third, do the potential benefits outweigh the potential negative effects?

Assumptions Underlying Early Identification

Primary in the assumptions underlying early identification of learning disabled children is that the roots of the later disorder lie in early development. Although this is undoubtedly true to a great extent, it is not always the case. Some children, for example, have normal birth histories, reach developmental milestones within normal age limits, and appear to be progressing quite well throughout early development. It is only when the child is confronted with the task demands of the first-grade curriculum that difficulties begin to be discovered. On the other hand, there are large numbers of children who seem to develop somewhat more slowly than their peers and lack the ability to perform tasks required in preschool and kindergarten. Yet, by the first or second grade,

[3]Adapted from Reid, D. K., 1977.

these children seem to "catch up" and their predicted learning disabilities never seem to materialize.

Another assumption is that identifiable, observable criteria exist which can be used to differentiate the future learning disabled child from his peers. This is not the case. Although there are some specific behaviors (hyperactivity, emotional lability, language problems, and the like) which are often forerunners of a learning disability, they are not always present. Hyperactivity is common, for example, among many two- and three-year-olds and among older, very bright children, as well as among those who will later experience learning problems. Language problems may result from a lack of stimulation in the home and a preschool experience may be sufficient to help the child correct what might have initially appeared as a potential learning disability. It is also often too soon to differentiate the child's primary problems and therefore be certain into which category to place him (e.g., is he emotionally disturbed or learning disabled?). It is for reasons such as these that Hare and Hare (personal communication) in their guide to teaching the preschool handicapped avoid the term learning disabilities altogether. (See Hare & Hare, 1978.)

A third assumption of early identification is that there are suitable instruments which can be used to test and screen such children. As noted earlier, however, the predictive accuracy of such tests is low. It is important also to note that even when children are identified and a preventive or remedial program is carried out, one can never be certain that the child's success is due to the early identification and treatment. Many children who are not treated do not develop a learning disability either.

The final assumption relates to the purpose of early identification: treatment. Those who advocate early identification do so in the hope of intervening successfully. Schaer and Crump (1976) reviewed the results of a number of programs that attempted to intervene with young children suspected of having learning disabilities. They concluded that the results of such programs have been inconclusive. They have offered only limited success in one area, made claims for improvement which were not supported by data, or simply had too few children involved for their effectiveness to be judged.

Observable Indications and Implications for Instruction

Although there is no one telling behavior or set of behaviors that characterize children who are later to become learning disabled, there are a number of "problem areas" that the law requires be evaluated and remediated, if need be. Certainly, evidence of physiological correlates related to learning disability should be sufficient to make the parent or teacher alert to the possibility of other signs. One should also be on the lookout for the bright child who seems to exhibit striking unevenness in his ability to perform a variety of tasks which are all possible for his peers. This discussion will focus, however, on aspects of psychological functioning which, whether they lead to a learning disability or not, bear watching.

Many learning disabled children have a history of perceptual and motor problems. They are often awkward in their movements and unable to perform many simple tasks, such as running or hopping, as well as their peers. These children will also frequently be unable to hold a crayon or pencil. They may be unable to match simple items or designs or to draw a simple circle or copy a square. Some exhibit excessive and apparently unproductive movement, while others seem to languish in their seats. They often appear to be confused about the parts of their bodies, space, direction, and time. Many have particular difficulty remembering rote sequences, such as A, B, C, etc.

Parents and teachers may engage children in a variety of sports, games, and movement activities (such as dance and exercies). Puzzles, drawing, matching, and copying activities will also be helpful. In short, the traditional preschool curriculum appears already to include an emphasis on the very experiences which are needed.

Attention and memory are frequently problem areas for the learning disabled, too. A child who is distractible and is unable to concentrate may have difficulty interpreting information he gains through his senses and storing and later retrieving that information. These children may not know what the important aspects of an object, situation, or event are and, therefore, may have difficulty knowing exactly what to remember or how to remember it. Teachers can help by pointing out important cues, by telling children what they will be expected to remember, and by clearly describing the structure of activities (i.e., first we will . . . , then . . . ,). It is also important to make activities meaningful to children and to help them relate new skills and information to what they already know.

A large number of learning disabled youngsters have problems with language development and usage. Some exhibit language which is immature, while others show signs of defective language. Many have accompanying speech and articulation disorders. Attempts to teach children specific language skills have generally failed, because they have not taken into account the flexible, generative aspects of language and have taken language instruction out of context to teach specific skills in isolation. Children seem to develop language skills by talking about themselves and about things they know. They also benefit from listening to others and from being exposed to a variety of experiences. The child must, after all, have something to talk about.

Finally, the learning disabled are prone to disorders of emotionality. They are easily angered and easily frustrated. Mood shifts are striking and frequent. Outbursts are rather more common than withdrawal, but both may be signs of serious disturbance. Teachers can be supportive, patient, and understanding. They need to help the child cope with his or her feelings of shame and guilt, and to cope with the fear that maybe the other children know or maybe the teacher will find out. Also important for teachers is that they recognize behaviors which are meant to cover up inabilities (e.g., the child who causes a disturbance because that child knows that he or she can't throw the ring on the pole). Finally, it is imperative that teachers be aware of their own feelings and prohibit their own needs for success from interfering with the child's progress.

Benefits versus Negative Effects

Probably the most important aspect of early identification to consider in an evaluation of the benefits versus the problems is the effect of labeling. Once a child has been identified, it is all too easy to set the self-fulfilling prophecy in motion. Among the most compelling evidence we have which relates specifically to children with learning disabilities is a study by Foster, Schmidt, and Sabatino (1976).[4] Those investigators asked two groups of elementary school teachers to view a videotape of a normal, fourth-grade boy engaged in various activities. Half of the teachers were told before viewing the tape that the boy was learning disabled and the other half that he was normal. Those who were told that he was learning disabled later judged him far more negatively than those who were told that he was normal. It appears that the term learning disabled "generates negative expectancies in teachers which affect their objective observations of behavior and may be detrimental to the child's academic progress" (p. 111).

Summary and Conclusions

Clearly, it is important for parents and teachers of preschoolers to be aware of those children who may be at risk. It is probably not beneficial, however, to attempt to label such children. Unfortunately, finding a label for a child is often heralded as something akin to a panacea. We think that if we only knew what the problem was, we could help to reverse it. Knowing that a child is learning disabled, for example, also lifts some of the responsibility for the child's failure from our own shoulders. Yet, our predictions are, at best, only roughly accurate. Our measures are often unreliable and lacking in validity. Most important, no clear evidence exists which suggests that we can successfully remediate these problems that are discovered early.

This rather pessimistic view is not intended as a condemnation. Rather, we must know as much about all children as possible and help each individual to achieve his or her fullest potential. We must continue to seek new and better ways of teaching children. But, we must also have the wisdom to know when our approaches have proven fruitful. Since the very highly structured and specific programs introduced for the preschool, mildly handicapped have not been demonstrated to be effective, there is some speculation that the high-risk preschool child might benefit more "if he were offered a flexible, varied and challenging program early in life; a program in which he could learn and explore under the guidance of an experienced teacher" (Schaer & Crump, 1976, p. 94). That is precisely what traditional, child-centered preschools have always provided. Perhaps it is the child who may later become learning disabled—with perceptual, motor, emotional, and/or language problems—who may particularly benefit from a very cognitively oriented preschool program. Such a program would help children assume an active role in their own learning, compensate for deficiencies in lower-level functions (e.g., perception) by developing and utilizing higher-level functions (e.g., thinking), integrate new learnings with

[4] Also see Chapter 7 in this book.

previous knowledge, and approach tasks holistically. Two such programs developed for normally achieving children but which, from initial field tests, appear to be effective with mildly handicapped preschoolers, have been designed by Kamii and DeVries (1980) and Forman and Hill (1980).

CHAPTER SUMMARY AND CONCLUSIONS

This chapter has presented an overview of screening and early identification procedures. Although screening is meant to be an imprecise process, it is important to be careful about the tools to be used, the predictive value of the variables used, and the nature of the variables, i.e., whether they are causal, correlated, or direct measures. Cautions and considerations of screening programs were suggested. Perhaps the most important of these is to be certain that all children who have or will have learning problems be included among those who are identified. The tradeoff is essentially between overidentification (so that all children who may need help receive it) and the consequences of such identifications to the family, self-concept, teacher expectations, and the like. The view taken here in regard to preschoolers has been that until we can demonstrate both better accuracy in identifying the mildly handicapped child and the effectiveness of intervention programs, the most appropriate procedure is to provide, for children who are suspected of having problems that will lead to learning disability, preschool programs that are as much like the best child-centered programs offered to normally achieving children as possible. These programs tend to provide activities that include literature, language, play, fine and gross motor experiences, and problem solving. Such rich environments may prove more effective for mildly impaired preschoolers than the more sterile, remediation-oriented programs typically associated with preschool classes for the handicapped. This view is, of course, related to the very significant problems related to the identification of *learning disabled* children (Mercer, Algozzine, & Trifiletti, 1979) and may not be appropriate for children with other handicapping conditions.

SUGGESTED READINGS

Forman, G., & Hill, F. *Constructive play: Applying Piaget in the preschool.* Monterey, Calif.: Brooks/Cole Publishing Co., 1980.

Hare, B. A., & Hare, J. M. *Teaching young handicapped children.* New York: Grune & Stratton, Inc., 1977.

Kamii, C., & DeVries, R. *Physical knowledge in preschool education.* Englewood Cliffs, N.J.: Prentice-Hall, Inc., 1978.

Salvia, J., & Ysseldyke, J. D. *Assessment in special and remedial education.* Boston: Houghton Mifflin Company, 1978.

Wallace, G., & Larsen, S. C. *Educational assessment of learning problems: Testing for teaching.* Boston: Allyn and Bacon, 1978.

Chapter 10

Individual Diagnostic Evaluation

INTRODUCTION

When tests were reviewed for their usefulness in screening, they were critiqued with high standards related to reliability and validity in mind. Standards for tests used in diagnosis must be even higher, because decisions that will affect the lives of individual children are to be made on the basis of the test results. When screening, the major tool is the test. Diagnostic evaluation, however, goes well beyond testing and includes a variety of informal reports and measures (e.g., work samples, anecdotal records, self-reports). Exactly what should be included in an assessment battery for learning disabled children is open to debate. Many different types of tests have been advocated, but the optimal combination of tests and the relative importance of each has not yet been established (Beatty, 1977).

Although test scores are required by law to support diagnoses and recommendations for placement, they must not constitute the only evidence. Information from a wide variety of data sources is needed. Designing a diagnostic evaluation is no easy task. It must (1) include a variety of measures to corroborate or disconfirm test findings, (2) survey available data sources, (3) focus on obtaining information that is directly relevant to educational planning, and (4) permit ongoing review. The evaluation must be carried out by a team.

Parents, teachers, the learning disabilities specialist, school administrators, and other professionals (e.g., psychologists, physicians, speech pathologists) have the responsibility to provide data. In its broadest sense, diagnostic evaluation refers to determining if a learning disability exists and collecting information to be used for planning classroom instruction. There are at least eight data sources relevant to a comprehensive assessment: observational data, other available data, information related to language dominance, educational assessment, adaptive behavior, medical and/or developmental data, personality data, and information regarding intellectual functioning (Tucker, 1978, p. 97). Each of these will be considered in our discussion of individual diagnostic evaluation.

OBSERVATIONAL DATA

When a child is referred, as much data as possible should be collected from those who have known that child over a period of time and from those who work with the child daily. Whatever information is amassed should be specific to the child, but it should include such items as anecdotal records and work samples.[1] A number of teacher rating scales have been devised and these are often helpful in guiding input, especially if the child is in a high school or junior high school setting where there may be a number of teachers involved. Interaction analysis might also contribute meaningfully to the diagnostic assessment. Additional forms of observation will be noted in the section on educational assessment.

Rating Scales

Rating scales, like all other observational and measurement devices, may examine the child's behavior, the environment, or the interaction between the child and his or her environment, especially the school environment. Usually, items to be observed are marked as present or absent or are noted to occur never, rarely, occasionally, frequently, or always. Sometimes the rater is simply asked to rate the person on a 5-point scale, with 1 being the lowest, 3 average, and 5 the highest rating. Clearly, rating scales are subjective measures. Many are used as screening devices. They are also helpful, however, as part of a diagnostic battery, because the use of scales allows easy and efficient input from a wide variety of people. Scales have been devised to measure a variety of behaviors, but they are most frequently used when no test exists. Rating scales are popular instruments for screening for delayed development (Frankenburg & Dodds, 1970), for learning disabilities (Myklebust, 1971), hyperactivity (Connors, 1969), and behavior disorders (Quay & Peterson, 1967). Some, on the other hand, focus directly on academic behaviors which are best observed in the classroom and are useful in guiding teachers' input to the diagnostic process (Novack, Bonaventura, & Merenda, 1972; Valett, 1966).

There are important issues regarding the use of scales (Gronlund, 1976, p.

[1]Cogwill, Friedland, and Shapiro (1973), among others, have reported that kindergarten teachers' anecdotal records were quite accurate predictors of later learning problems.

444–445). First, the items on the scale must reflect areas of concern for the diagnostic evaluation and must be related to school performance. Second, the behaviors must be directly observable. Third, both the characteristics to be observed and the points on the scale must be clearly defined. Fourth, three to seven rating positions should be available and the raters should be permitted to rate at intermediate points. Fifth, raters should be instructed to omit ratings whenever they feel unqualified to judge. Sixth, more than one person should rate the child whenever that is possible.

One scale used to identify children in the early elementary grades is the *Rhode Island Pupil Identification Scale* (Novack, Bonaventura, & Merenda, 1972). The scale asks teachers to rate the frequency of occurrence of forty behaviors often associated with learning failure. They are all behaviors which are easily observed in the classroom or in the child's written work. A sample of items would include: difficulty in cutting, breaking the pencil point, crying, avoiding group activity, poor handwriting, letter reversals, difficulty with number concepts, and difficulty completing written work in the time allotted. The reader may have noticed that this rating scale records many of the same activities previously referred to as correlated abilities. For that reason and because it is simply a yes/no check list, it does not meet the criteria specified by Gronlund (1976). It is, however, illustrative of a type of rating scale that is very widely used.

Another rating scale, *The Basic School Skills Inventory (BSSI)* (Goodman & Hammill, 1975), is a criterion-referenced, teacher checklist from which a numerical score can be generated in order to assess a child's ability to perform school tasks successfully. The *BSSI* consists of eighty-four questions developed from an analysis of what teachers thought to be important for educational success. Areas tapped include basic information, self-help skills, handwriting, oral communication, reading readiness, number readiness, and classroom behavior. Test-retest reliability is .96 (Hawthorne & Larsen, 1977), the correlation between the *BSSI* and the *Metropolitan Readiness Test* is .65 (Goodman & Hammill, 1975), and the correlation of the *BSSI* and a teacher rating scale is .74 (Hawthorne & Larsen, 1977). The *BSSI* was normed on approximately 600 four-, five-, and six-year-olds. Its authors reported the composition of the standardization sample to be equal numbers of boys and girls with appropriate demographics. The children were 70 percent white, 22 percent black, and 8 percent Mexican-American. Although it is a checklist rather than a scale, the *BSSI* appears to be an adequate device for use with young children. Like scales, it helps conserve time and money, ensures teacher involvement in the diagnostic process, and enables a more thorough analysis of the child's school-related performance (Bryan & McGrady, 1972).

Interactional Analysis

Several systems have been devised to measure children's relationships with their teachers and their peers. Examples of such systems include the use of sociometric techniques, self-reports, Q-sorts, and observational systems. Sociometric techniques are useful in eliciting information about how people in a group relate to each other (Friou, 1972; Redl & Wattenberg, 1959). Typically, data are collected by asking people to list one, two, or three persons with whom they would most like to do something (e.g., sit next to, have to dinner, be friends). Self-reports are most useful in discovering the child's interests, likes and dislikes, and feelings. Gronlund (1976) suggested the personal interview as the ideal method of conducting a self-report. Q-sorts are used to examine the discrepancy between the child's "true" and "idealized" self. The child sorts a series of statements first according to whether they describe him or her well (most like me) or not so well (most unlike me) and second according to how the child would like to be able to describe herself or himself. Some sample statements which may be sorted include (Kroth, 1973, p. 322): scores high in reading; pays attention to work; rocks in chair; works until the job is finished; and walks around room during study time.

A number of more or less sophisticated observational systems have also been devised to study children's interactional behaviors. One such system is *OSCAR 5* (*Observation Schedule and Record* developed by Medley, Schluck, & Ames, 1968). An observer codes the interaction between the teacher and the child for thirty minutes in five-minute intervals. Interchanges are coded as to what they include and the nature of statements and/or questions. The teacher's response to the child is coded as supportive, approving, criticizing, neutrally rejecting, accepting, or nonevaluative. These types of systems are especially useful in analyzing situations in which problems are occurring. Comparisons of the child's performance in relation to various teachers may also be assessed using interaction analysis systems.

OTHER SOURCES OF AVAILABLE DATA

So long as an investigator complies with legislation which insures parental involvement and confidentiality, many avenues for gathering additional information are generally open. School records quite often contain information related to medical screening and care, developmental history, family history, past subject-matter grades and other information related to school performance, test data from prior assessments and screenings, and copies of letters sent to parents, etc. Release forms may be signed by the parents to enable the assessor to request detailed medical and psychological evidence from physicians and clinics. Not only is valuable information regarding the child's behavior gathered from such records, but important information about the family constellation may be derived from them as well.

INFORMATION CONCERNING LANGUAGE DOMINANCE

One of the most important pieces of information needed for an unbiased assessment is knowledge of the child's language characteristics. (See Chapter 8.) The examiner must know whether the child is bilingual, speaks a nonstandard dialect, speaks two or more languages equally well, or is fluent in only one. No other information can be meaningfully interpreted until the examiner knows whether the child's dominant language is compatible with that used in school, how the child's language facility compares with his or her level of functioning in academic areas, and what language is appropriate for the diagnostic evaluation. Sources for language dominance measures include, among others, Jones and Spolsky (1975), Oakland, DeLuna, and Morgan (1977), and Silverman, Noa, and Russell (1976).

EDUCATIONAL ASSESSMENT

As we have noted repeatedly in this book, no matter what symptoms a child may have that are usually related to learning disabilities, unless there is concomitant academic failure, the learning disabilities label is inappropriate. Two kinds of educational assessment data are gathered: that which comes from tests and that which comes from ongoing evaluation of the child in the classroom. Test data is most often norm-referenced (i.e., the child is compared to his peers), although many criterion-referenced (i.e., the child is evaluated for what he can and cannot do within a subject-matter area, without regard for the performance of his peers) tests have been gaining in popularity. Continuous classroom evaluation, generally referred to as diagnostic teaching, compares the child's performances over time and therefore has the advantage of measuring consistency. Continuous classroom evaluation is valid in the sense that it is directly relevant to classroom performance.[2] Further, diagnostic teaching enables a teacher to determine what task-approach strategies a child uses, how well he or she understands the information tested, precisely what has been learned, and whether students use what they have learned spontaneously (Reid & Hresko, in press). It is important, however, in assessing educational strengths and weaknesses to determine whether the child's performance level reflects a handicapping condition and oftentimes the use of norm-referenced tests help to accomplish that. Tests also enable the examiner to compare the child's classroom performance with his performance on the same or related tasks under controlled conditions. Although these two sources of educational data act as a system of checks and balances, tests are better suited for making classification decisions, while diagnostic teaching contributes more to the teaching plan.

Tests

Two kinds of tests may be used: formal and informal. Formal tests are standardized with regard to the questions asked and the procedures for their administration. Most aim to quantify performance and to provide norms for comparing one child's performance to that of his or her peers. Informal tests are often teacher-made (there are some published tests). They are usually less

---

[2]Oftentimes, the validity of test measures (cf. issues related to perceptual-motor testing) is less clear.

comprehensive, have fewer items, and have more questionable reliability and validity, since they depend on the level of the individual teacher's expertise. They can, nevertheless, contribute important specific information to the educational assessment.

The sheer numbers of tests available for the assessment of educational performance prohibit a thorough examination of them here. Our goal is simply to present a variety of tests which are illustrative of the *kinds* of measures which are used in the evaluation of learning disabled children. The interested reader is referred to Wallace and Larsen (1978) for a comprehensive overview. Since there is seldom enough testing time to give a series of complete tests, and since a concern in educational testing is the establishment of profiles of strengths and weaknesses which can lead to corrective and/or remedial interventions, particular care will be given to the evaluation of subtest reliabilities. Tests in the following areas will be described: oral language, reading, spelling, writing, and mathematics. Tests related to other curriculum areas (e.g., social studies, economics) are frequently used in schools as part of their annual testing and screening programs, but they are not usually part of the diagnostic evaluation.

Language Tests   The results of language tests must be viewed within the context of all other information about the child which is available. These tests are particularly sensitive to cultural and socioeconomic differences. Language tests vary in content with the author's conception of the nature of the language. The *Parson's Language Sample* (Spradlin, 1963), for example, is based on Skinnerian principles. The *Illinois Test of Psycholinguistic Abilities (ITPA)* (Kirk, McCarthy, & Kirk, 1968) is based on an Osgoodian model. A number of other tests have been based on models of language that have grown out of the work of Noam Chomsky (1965). For an account of these models see Chapter 12. Chomsky's psycholinguistic model is certainly the most explanatory model of language acquisition and functioning. Tests based on a psycholinguistic model usually measure aspects of phonology and morphology, syntax, and semantics. Tests most frequently used in oral language assessment include the *Goldman-Fristoe Test of Articulation* (Goldman & Fristoe, 1972), the *Templin-Darley Tests of Articulation* (Templin & Darley, 1960), *Northwest Syntax Screening Test* (Lee, 1969), *Developmental Sentence Analysis* (Lee, 1974), *Carrow Elicited Language Inventory* (Carrow, 1974), *Test for Auditory Comprehension of Language* (Carrow, 1973), the *Peabody Picture Vocabulary Test* (Dunn, 1965), and the *Test of Language Development (TOLD)* (Newcomer & Hammill, 1977). Two of these tests, the *ITPA* and the *TOLD*, will be discussed in detail as illustrations of opposing positions.

The *ITPA* is probably the most widely used test in learning disabilities and is, in some minds, synonymous with assessment and teaching in our field. Chapter 12 contains a description of the subtests and the assumptions underlying their use and notes that research evidence regarding those assumptions has failed to support them. Two other issues, however, need to be raised here: validity and reliability. First, many of the subtests do not measure language, per se. Instead, they measure perceptual and cognitive skills presumed to be correlated with academic functioning. Even this claim has not been substantiated (Newcomer & Hammill, 1976). Salvia and Ysseldyke (p. 357) in their review of the *ITPA* point out: (1) no estimates of validity with other language measures are reported; (2) no evidence of predictive validity is presented; (3) the *ITPA* correlates .96 with chronological age; it is moderately correlated with IQ, and slightly correlated with socioeconomic standing; and (4) finally, the claim (Paraskevopoulous & Kirk, 1969) that greater deviation of the child's scores from his or her mean score indicates a greater likelihood of learning disabilities is substantiated with data from mentally retarded children. Furthermore, the norming sample excluded children who were having school-related problems.

Regarding reliability, the overall psycholinguistic age is a reliable measure (Newcomer & Hammill, 1976), but only two (Auditory Association and Auditory Sequential Memory) subtests exceed .80 (Newcomer & Hammill, 1976). Clearly, using this test for its avowed purpose, defining strengths and weaknesses to be remediated, is risky and unjustified. For these reasons (and because the test takes considerable time both to learn and administer and for each administration) the use of this test in educational assessment is not recommended. It adds little to the information that can be obtained from other, more efficient sources.

TOLD is composed of one measure of receptive and one measure of expressive language in each of the areas of syntax (grammatical understanding, sentence imitation, and grammatical completion), semantics (picture and oral vocabulary), and phonology (word discrimination and word articulation). The five principal tests are those related to syntax and semantics, with the two phonology tests being supplemental. The test is very easily administered and takes approximately thirty to forty-five minutes. It is administered individually and is appropriate for children four to eight. Overall test-retest reliability is .95. For school-aged children, subtest reliabilities are all above .80. The national norming sample included minorities in the same proportions that they are represented in the population. Additionally, the test was found useful with handicapped children (Hammill & Newcomer, 1977; McGee & Newcomer, 1978; Wong, 1979). There is evidence presented in the test manual which indicates satisfactory content, concurrent and diagnostic validity. The only questions regarding construct validity concern the two supplemental tests. Although the subtest reliabilities do not meet the .90 criterion for diagnostic measures, no other test of language reports higher reliabilities (few, in fact, report any). Additionally, no other test measures so many aspects of language development so efficiently. *TOLD* has the potential to contribute meaningful data to the diagnostic evaluation, particularly when classification is the goal.

Reading Tests   There are a number of reading tests. Some measure oral reading (cf. Gilmore & Gilmore, 1968; Gray & Robinson, 1967) and some survey a variety of reading skills (cf. Bond, Balow, & Hoyt, 1970; Durrell, 1955; Gates & McKillop, 1962; Spache, 1963). Some tests (cf. *Diagnosis: An*

Instructional Aid, Shub, Carlin, Friedman, Kaplan, & Katien, 1973 and *Criterion Reading,* Hackett, 1971) are designed to provide data on both assessment and possible interventions. Three standardized tests (*Stanford Diagnostic Reading, Woodcock Reading Mastery Tests,* and *The Test of Reading Comprehension,* because they are widely used in special education, will be discussed in depth. We will also describe two achievement tests (*Peabody Individual Achievement* and *The Wide Range Achievement Tests*) that have reading sections frequently used in educational assessment. Two very popular informal tests (*Informal Reading Inventory* and *Reading Miscue Inventory*) will also be discussed.

The *Stanford Diagnostic Reading Test* (Karlsen, Madden, & Gardner, 1976) is both a norm-referenced and criterion-referenced, group-administered test of reading which measures decoding, vocabulary, comprehension, and rate. Forms of the test span the end of first to the twelfth grades. The test was normed on 31,000 pupils. The stratified-random sample parallels that of the 1970 census in terms of the inclusion of minority and socioeconomic groups. Reliability measures indicate that it is sufficiently reliable for use in diagnostic evaluations. The test's validity, however, must be judged in relation to the reading instruction given in any particular school. The content of reading programs and reading tests vary considerably. For a test to be valid, it must be measuring what the instructional program teaches (Jenkins & Pany, 1978).

The *Woodcock Reading Mastery Test* (Woodcock, 1974) is individually administered to children from kindergarten through grade twelve. The test is contained in an easel kit[3] and takes approximately twenty to thirty minutes to administer. It measures letter and word identification, word attack skills, word comprehension, and passage comprehension (employing a modified cloze procedure). The test was adequately normed, but reliability of subtests is generally weak. The test is widely used in special education because it is easily administered to a wide age group, yields criterion as well as norming informa- tion, and rates students at various levels of proficiency. The results may be used, for example, to describe Dorothy as having mastered 60 percent of fifth-grade and 85 percent of fourth-grade material.

The *Test of Reading Comprehension (TORC)* (Brown, Hammill, & Weider- holt, 1978) is built upon the assumption that reading is an interactive, constructive language process and, as such, focuses on comprehension and silent reading. Eight subtests form the basis of the *TORC.* They are General Vocabulary, Syntactic Similarities, Paragraph Reading, Math Vocabulary, Social Studies Vocabulary, Science Vocabulary, Reading Directions, and Sentence Sequencing. The first three of the subtests are combined to generate a General Reading Comprehension Core. The three content vocabulary subtests and the Reading Directions subtest are used as diagnostic supplements. The

---

[3]An easel kit is a test arrangement in which the stimuli are contained in a binder which can be supported, usually by folding the cover back to form an easel shape. Items are ordered so that one can administer the test simply by turning the pages one at a time to reveal consecutive items. Directions to the examiner are usually on the back of the easel.

final subtest, Sentence Sequencing, is an optional subtest to be used when there is some reason to suspect that the General Reading Comprehension Core is inappropriate. *TORC* is easily administered and scored and is applicable to children first through eighth grades, though its use at first grade is not recommended. The *TORC* was standardized upon a population of 2,400 children. With regard to sex and urban/rural residence, the sample approximates the 1974 United States Census figures. Eighty percent of the reliability coefficients for internal consistency reach or exceed .80, but no other types of reliabilities are reported. The validity of the *TORC* is well-defined for construct, content, and criterion-related validity. *TORC* may be an attractive alternative or addition to the reading tests previously mentioned, because of its focus on comprehension rather than skills.

The *Peabody Individual Achievement Test (PIAT)* (Dunn & Markwardt, 1970) measures mathematics, spelling, and general information, as well as reading recognition and reading comprehension. The test is contained in an easel kit, is administered individually to students from kindergarten through twelfth grade, and yields norm comparisons. Although its standardization is superior to that of most other individually administered tests (Salvia & Ysseldyke, 1978), subtest reliabilities are weak. Many, however, meet the .80 criterion for screening.

The *Wide Range Achievement Test (WRAT)* (Jastak & Jastak, 1965) is an individually administered paper and pencil test which measures reading (word and letter recognition), spelling, and arithmetic. There are two levels of the test. One is for use with children twelve years and younger and the other for persons over twelve. No attempt was made to obtain a representative sample for norming purposes and no handicapped children were included. Although split-half reliabilities all exceed .90, no test-retest measures are reported. The manual recommends the test for use in the diagnosis of reading, spelling, and arithmetic, but too few questions investigating an area too limited in scope are used for the test to have much validity as a diagnostic instrument. The test's popularity rests on the ease and rapidity with which it can be administered and on its use by clinicians whose interest in educational variables is minimal at best. The *WRAT*, however, is widely viewed as overestimating reading scores (Torgesen, 1979).

Informal Reading Inventories (IRI) (Johnson & Kress, 1965) permit the establishment of reading levels (independent, frustration, and instructional for reading as well as listening comprehension) and a careful analysis of the child's strengths and weaknesses. Since they are to be used as informal tools, no norming or reliability and validity measures are available. *IRIs* can be group or individually administered and include such elements of reading as word recognition (timed and untimed), comprehension (oral and silent), and some-times reading rate. They consist of having the student read passages orally, while the examiner notes errors, and silently. The child is asked several questions, often involving re-reading (e.g., "re-read the line that says that . . ."). *IRIs* can be constructed by the teacher so that precise information can be gained as to how the child is performing within the reading series being used in class. Careful analyses of *IRIs* can provide important diagnostic data, if the child's perform- ance is compared to what the teacher knows about his or her typical reading behavior.

Finally, another informal measure of reading performance which is based on the psycholinguistic conception of reading described in Chapter 13 is the *Reading Miscue Inventory (RMI)* (Goodman & Burke, 1972). The *RMI* examines the discrepancy between what the reader believes is on the written page and what is actually there, i.e., the reader's miscues. A series of questions guides the analysis of the child's protocol and provides information related to the child's reading strategies, strengths, and weaknesses. These, in turn, are used as the basis for instructional planning. The child's oral reading is usually taped to permit later reevaluation. When he or she is finished reading, the child is asked to retell the story. The teacher needs to acquire some skill in probing without asking leading questions so that as many details of the plot, characters, etc. as the child can remember may be included in the retelling. Emphasis in this type of analysis is on the child's ability to use linguistic cues and background information rather than on sound-letter correspondences and other phonic skills. Although there has been some controversy surrounding the *RMI*, it provides an attractive alternative to more skills-oriented reading tests. (See *RMI* questions in Table 10-1.)

Spelling Tests Few formal spelling tests are available, though several are contained as part of achievement tests (cf. the *Stanford Achievement Test*), diagnostic reading tests (cf. *Gates-McKillop Reading Diagnostic Tests*), or as an integral part of a basal spelling program. One standardized test that measures spelling ability when words are dictated is the *Test of Written Spelling (TWS)* (Larsen & Hammill, 1976). The test measures children's knowledge of both regular and irregular spellings of words used in at least ten widely used spelling series. It is one of the best normed and most reliable spelling tests available.

Table 10-1   Questions in the Reading Miscue Inventory

1   DIALECT: Is a dialect variation involved in the miscue?
2   INTONATION: Is a shift in intonation involved in the miscue?
3   GRAPHIC SIMILARITY: How much does the miscue look like what was expected?
4   SOUND SIMILARITY: How much does the miscue sound like what was expected?
5   GRAMMATICAL FUNCTION: Is the grammatical function of the miscue the same as the grammatical function of the word in the text?
6   CORRECTION: Is the miscue corrected?
7   GRAMMATICAL ACCEPTABILITY: Does the miscue occur in a structure which is grammat- ically acceptable?
8   SEMANTIC ACCEPTABILITY: Does the miscue occur in a structure which is semantically acceptable?
9   MEANING CHANGE: Does the miscue result in a change of meaning?

Source: From Goodman, Y.M. & Burke, C.I. *Reading miscue inventory: Manual procedure for diagnosis and remediation,* New York: Macmillan, 1972, pp. 126–127.

Teacher-made spelling tests can be easily constructed by following the steps listed in Table 10-2. For those individuals who are not interested in developing their own informal spelling inventory or who do not wish to use a norm-referenced assessment, one alternative is to use one of the criterion-referenced tests usually furnished with basal spelling series. One such criterion-referenced device, the *Diagnostic Spelling Test*, was developed by Kottmeyer (1970). It allows the teacher to evaluate a child's performance according to specific criteria to be transferred into educational goals.

Writing Tests   A number of achievement tests include estimates of written expression (cf. *California Achievement Tests, Stanford Achievement Tests,* and the *Metropolitan Achievement Tests*), but they are typically unreliable and assess writing skills without recourse to the child's compositions. There are two diagnostic tests, the *Picture Story Language Test* (Myklebust, 1965), and the *Sequential Test of Educational Progress* (Educators Testing Service, 1958), but the reliability and validity of the first is questionable (Hammill, 1975) and the second suffers from the same problem as the achievement subtests. A third measure, the *Test of Written Language (TOWL)* (Hammill & Larsen, 1978) is designed to evaluate written expression in terms of handwriting, thought units, spelling, style, word usage, vocabulary, and thematic maturity. *TOWL* can be administered in approximately forty minutes in either an individual or group setting. Scoring is facilitated by numerous examples and guides. The norming sample is comparable to the 1970 United States Census with respect to sex and urban/rural residence. The test has both validity (criterion, construct and content) and reliability (internal consistency, test-retest, and inter-rater) coefficients which, in most cases, range from .80 upward. Of the standardized tests available to measure expressive written language, the *TOWL* is the most preferable.

An alternative technique to use in evaluating the child's written language is to use one of the child's original compositions as the basis for a qualitative analysis. Considerations to be used in judging such a composition should include knowledge of the child's dominant language, the amount of experience that child

Table 10-2   Steps in Developing a Spelling Inventory

Devising the inventory
Select 15 words from the basal spelling book. (Words are selected by dividing the number of words included in the basal's word list by 15 and then incorporating every *n*th word into the spelling inventory. If there are 45 words introduced in the basal, then every third word would be used. Select 20 words at every additional level, using the same procedure. Words selected at each level become the spelling list for that grade.
Administering the test. At each level:
Say the word. Use it in a sentence. Say the word again. Have the children write the word.
Scoring:
A child who misses 7 of the words at any given level has reached his spelling level. Only children who succeed at lower levels should be tested.

Source: Adapted from Mann and Suiter, 1974, pp. 17–18.

has had in writing compositions, and the quality of instruction in the mechanics of writing, such as handwriting, punctuation, etc. The last two of these considerations may be best evaluated by comparing the child's work to that of his or her peers. In addition, the composition should be judged on the following bases: adequacy of content and organization, inventiveness, grammatical structure, use of writing conventions, and vocabulary (see also Chapter 14).

Tests of Mathematics   Nearly all achievement tests include measures of mathematics. Perhaps the most useful of these is the subtest of the *Stanford Diagnostic Achievement Test*, because of the high quality of the test and its flexibility with regard to norm and criterion referencing. The *Stanford Diagnostic Arithmetic Test* is also extremely useful for analyzing mathematics performance for all of the same reasons (i.e., norm and criterion referencing, adequate norming sample, reliability, etc.). The *PIAT* and *WRAT* (see Reading Tests above) also have arithmetic sections, but their disadvantages have already been mentioned.

The Key Math Diagnostic Arithmetic Test (Connolly, Nachtman, & Pritchett, 1971) includes a number of subtests (numeration, fractions, geometry and symbols, addition, subtraction, multiplication, division, mental computation, numerical reasoning, word problems, missing elements, money, time, and measurement) which are administered individually using an easel format. It takes approximately thirty minutes to administer and no formal training is needed for the examiner. Although the normative statistics for *Key Math* are weak, the test can be very useful as a criterion-referenced device. The authors have grouped each of the test items into possible instructional clusters, so that diagnostic teaching is facilitated.

Diagnostic Teaching

Diagnostic teaching is a process of continuous evaluation, teaching, and reevaluation prior to further teaching. It is roughly equivalent to the instructional cycle described by Bartel, Bryen, and Bartel (1975) in the flow chart in Figure 10-1.

First, the teacher, with knowledge of the student and the curriculum content, appraises the abilities of the student, formulates hypotheses regarding the child's abilities, and, on that basis, sets instructional goals. Methods, materials, instructional setting, and procedures are chosen for their potential in meeting that goal. Once the educational intervention has been carried out, a reevaluation of the child's knowledge ensues and new instructional goals are formulated. Traditionally, this process has focused on rather large teaching segments, but it is more useful as a tool to monitor the achievement of short-term objectives. What is unique about diagnostic teaching is that it is based not on class performance, but on individual performance and it is therefore an indispensible tool for modifying *IEPs*. One method through which diagnostic teaching may be carried out is called applied behavioral analysis.

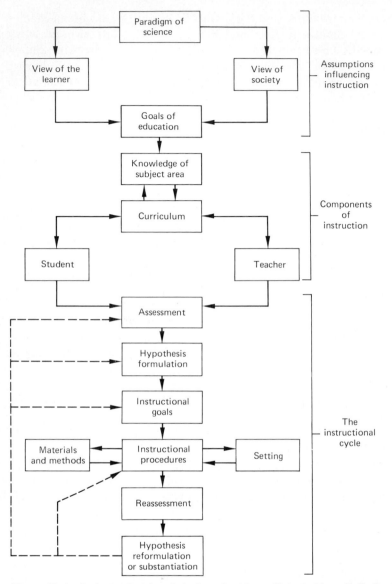

Figure 10-1 An instructional cycle in flow chart form. *(Adapted from N. R. Bartel, D. N. Bryen, & H. W. Bartel, Approaches for alternative programming. In E. L. Meyen, G. A. Vergason, & R. J. Whelan (Eds.), Alternatives for teaching exceptional children, 1975.)*

Applied Behavioral Analysis   Applied behavioral analysis is the application of operant techniques and research methods to the study of ongoing classroom behaviors. Lovitt (1967) suggests the following diagnostic procedure: (1) collection of baseline data; (2) the assessment of behavioral components which maintain and modify behavior; (3) an analysis of the programming skills of the referring adult, and (4) explanation of the diagnostic findings in ways which directly suggest interventions.

When a child is referred by his or her teacher or parent for learning and/or behavior problems, the first step in the diagnostic process should be specifying precisely which behavior or behaviors are troublesome. Once the behavior is defined, its frequency must be established. For purposes of discussion, let us assume that Vera is referred because she is "doing poorly in reading." The first job of the examiner is to discuss with the referring agent, in this case, the teacher, Mr. Lawson, just what is meant by "doing poorly." After careful analysis, it is determined that Vera makes errors in decoding when she is reading orally. Errors in letter-sound correspondence in oral reading are easily observed and counted, so the collection of baseline data can begin.

Axelrod (1977) noted that there are two types of measurements: lasting products and observational recording and that there are four types of observational recording: frequency, duration, interval, and time-sampling. The measurement of lasting products refers to measuring the student's work output. It corresponds with marking papers, i.e., measuring the amount completed and correct in children's workbooks, exercises, homework, etc. Observation recording is used when behaviors are transitory. Since Vera's problem is demonstrated in oral reading, observation recording would be appropriate in her case. How should this observational data be collected? Frequency data may be collected in which the number of errors made by Vera in a specified period of time are recorded. Mr. Lawson, her teacher, need only tally the number of errors Vera makes while reading. For some behaviors, for example, being out of one's seat, measures of duration may be more appropriate. In this case, the teacher would measure the amount of time that the child was out of his or her seat. This kind of measurement is not functional in Vera's case. Interval data provide some indications of both the frequency and duration of behaviors. A recorder would observe a child for five- or ten-second intervals and note whether the child was out of his or her seat for any of that time. Time-sampling is a simpler technique in that the teacher would not have to observe the child for a full interval. Instead, the teacher could divide the time into convenient intervals, let's say, fifteen-minute segments, and observe the child's behavior only at the end of that time. Because Vera's behavior of interest, her "target" behavior, is discreet and is not continuous over time, frequency recording would be chosen for collecting baseline data.

Now, let us suppose that Vera reads aloud each morning for three five-minute periods. Mr. Lawson would count the number of errors that Vera made, calculate the percentage of words Vera read correctly, and record them on a graph such as the one in Figure 10-2. The percentage of words read correctly would be plotted each day until an estimate of a functional range of Vera's decoding behaviors was established. While baseline behaviors are being recorded, Mr. Lawson may wish to employ a reliability check by having a second observer record the frequency of Vera's decoding errors and comparing that person's tally with his own. Baseline data provide a clear indication of Vera's

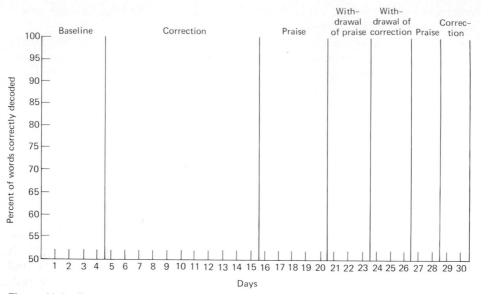

Figure 10-2 Record of student behavior.

day-to-day consistency—a reliable estimate of her performance in a form which is easily communicated to others.

The next step in the assessment of Vera's reading problem would be to examine the behavioral components that maintain her behavior: the antecedents, her responses, and the contingency system and its consequences. The antecedents are stimulus events that occur prior to the behavior. These may include instructions, requests, prompts, questions, gestures, etc. Vera's response to these antecedents is what was measured during baseline. The contingency system includes whatever reinforcement (or lack of it) Vera receives after her reading. For example, perhaps Mr. Lawson nods his head as Vera reads correctly or perhaps he frowns when she errs. The consequences may be some tangible reward that Vera receives for satisfactory performance or perhaps a note to her mother or a good grade on her report card.

Let us suppose that in Vera's case, what precedes her making an error is the direction to read words that contain short vowel sounds. Because Vera's behavior always occurs in response to Mr. Lawson's direction for her to read and his behaviors become the stimuli for hers, an analysis of the stimulus-response chains or the pattern of interaction between them must also be analyzed. In this case, it was found that Mr. Lawson responded to Vera only after she had erred and that this response generally consisted of a frown.

Finally, the diagnostic findings must be translated into intervention strategies. In this case the recommendations might be twofold: first, to have Mr. Lawson correct Vera's reading by saying the mispronounced work correctly, but softly. Second, Mr. Lawson might praise Vera by saying "good" or "very good" each time she completed a full sentence without making any errors. After several days of baseline data had been collected, the first of these interventions would be instituted. The incidence of Vera's reading errors would be expected to decrease. After several additional days, when her behavior had stabilized, the second intervention would be begun. The number of decoding errors Vera made would be expected to decrease dramatically. As a check on the efficiency of these interventions, the second and then the first interventions could be stopped. A rise in the number of errors Vera made in oral reading would be expected. The interventions would then be introduced once again in reverse order.

Applied behavioral analysis has several advantages over the use of standardized tests. First, the measurement is continuous. Second, the teacher is directly involved in the diagnostic process. Third, the areas to be assessed are directly related to the child's performance. The validity of the diagnosis is, therefore, ensured. Fourth, the diagnostic process leads directly to the establishment of intervention strategies. Fifth, the effectiveness of intervention strategies is measured from their inception, so that adjustments may be made if they are not appropriate. Finally, labeling is not needed. For more comprehensive descriptions of applied behavioral analysis, the reader is referred to Axelrod (1977) and to Haring and Bateman (1977).

There are, of course, some significant difficulties associated with the use of behavioral analysis. Only overt behaviors can be considered in diagnoses. Constructs such as capacity, potential, and intelligence are inappropriate. Only *specific* behaviors can be studied. Complex processes, such as reading and oral language usage, whose nature is changed when they are reduced to their elements, are not amenable to such analyses. The model assumes that the responsible adult is always able to determine the most appropriate target behavior. Information about etiology is not useful. Learning is viewed as the sum of discrete and linearly related acquisitions. Finally, applied behavioral analysis techniques are often misused. The transition from concrete to social reinforcement and generalizability of the target behaviors, for examples, is frequently not planned.

ADAPTIVE BEHAVIOR SCALES

Two scales are most often used to assess adaptive behavior. They are the *Vineland Social Maturity Scale* (Doll, 1953) and the *AAMD Adaptive Behavior Scale:* Public School Version (1974 revision) (Lambert, Windmiller, Cole & Figueroa, 1975).[4] A new scale is the *Behavior Rating Profile.*

The *Vineland Social Maturity Scale* is used to guide a personal interview in which the examiner interviews a person (often a parent) who knows the child under study. The purpose of the scale is to determine whether the child habitually performs the behaviors in question. The scale is not used to determine whether the child *can* perform the behaviors. The measure can be used to evaluate social competence from birth through age thirty. It assesses self-help

---

[4]AAMD is the acronym for the American Association on Mental Deficiency.

skills, the ability to eat and dress without assistance, mobility, occupation, communication skills, self-direction, and socialization. Since the standardization procedures were carried out over twenty-five years ago, the scale is in need of updating (Salvia & Ysseldyke, 1978).

The *AAMD Adaptive Behavior Scale* was adapted from a larger scale (Nihira, Foster, Shellhaas, & Leland, 1969): items that were not relevant to school behavior were eliminated. The scale surveys independent functioning, physical development, economic activity, language development, numbers and time, domestic activity, vocational activity, self-direction, responsibility, socialization, violent and destructive behavior, antisocial behavior, rebellious behavior, untrustworthy behavior, withdrawal, stereotyped behavior, inappropriate interpersonal manners, unacceptable vocal habits, hyperactive tendencies, psychological disturbances, and the use of medication. The scale was designed for use with retarded, disturbed, and developmentally disabled persons, but since it is one of few adaptive scales available, it is sometimes used with learning disabled children as well. The norms appear to be representative of children in California where the test was normed, but reliability and validity measures are too low to enable the use of this instrument alone for placement decisions.

Another behavior assessment device is the *Behavior Rating Profile (BRP)* (Brown & Hammill, 1978). Using an ecological approach, the *BRP* is designed to give a profile of abilities by combining information from a variety of settings and persons. Subtests include Student Rating Scales: Home, School, and Peer; Teacher Rating Scales; Parent Rating Scales; and a Sociogram. The *BRP*, designed for use with children aged six years, five months through thirteen years, six months, is easily administered and scored. The authors report statistical information indicating that internal consistency, concurrent validity, construct validity, and diagnostic validity are acceptable. The strength of the *BRP* is in the use of independent measures combined to yield an ecological profile, that is, one that takes into account the child's functioning in a number of settings and judged by a number of persons. The test authors caution that the *BRP*, like the other adaptive behavior rating scales, should not be considered representative of all behaviors, nor should the *BRP* be used to define or to apply the label of emotional disturbance to any individual.

MEDICAL AND DEVELOPMENTAL DATA

It is important in the assessment process to rule out the possibility that medical causes underlie the learning problem. Only after everything possible has been done to treat the medical problem should the child be considered for special educational services. Correction might enable the child to profit from a traditional instruction program.

There are many reasons why a physician should be consulted when a diagnosis of learning disabilities is suspected. Since learning disabilities are often accompanied by other symptoms (e.g., otitis media, obesity, allergies), these should be identified and treated. Only a physician has the ability to determine when pharmacotherapy is indicated. Pediatric neurologists or pediatricians with special neurological training are also relatively helpful in screening for learning disabilities. A screening program used by a pediatrician may include the following types of evaluations: medical history, physical examination, evaluation for minor neurological dysfunction, parent and teacher reports of hyperactivity, figure drawings, and a word recognition test (Keele, Keele, Huizinga, Bray, Estes, & Holland, 1975). Also, a thorough neuropsychological examination may be extremely important in the formulation of a prognosis for the child. The difficulty of working with physicians, however, is that they tend to value their own contribution to the diagnostic process above that of other professionals, whom they often view as minimally competent (cf. Rourke, 1976).

Developmental and readiness measures are frequently used by medical personnel as well as school officials. Two that are important to this discussion because of their popularity are the *Denver Developmental Screening Test* (Frankenburg, Dodds, & Fandal, 1970) and the *Boehm Test of Basic Concepts* (Boehm, 1971). The *Denver Developmental* is a screening device which is norm-referenced and individually administered. When given in toto, the test takes only about twenty minutes, which includes the time for scoring and interpretation. The test is useful for children from birth through six and is often used to keep track of developing children by pediatricians. Clinicians, for example, might ask a few age-appropriate questions concerning items on the test each time the child makes a visit to the clinic or doctor's office. The purpose of the test is *not* to determine the child's level of development, but to check for developmental delays. Items survey four areas of behavior: personal-social, fine motor, gross motor, and language. Since not all children are good "performers" in a physician's office and since visits are usually brief, parents are frequently asked to report whether or not their child can and/or does perform certain acts (e.g., whether their infant lifts his head, rolls over, smiles, etc.). The scoring sheet is designed so that the examiner can tell at a glance whether the child's functioning in any given area is comparable to the performance of the norming group. The response sheet lists all skills and is marked to indicate the age at which 25 percent, 50 percent, 75 percent, and 90 percent of the norming sample passed the item. A child is considered delayed if he fails an item passed by 90 percent of younger children. An abnormal result is indicated by two delays in two separate sections or two delays in one section, one delay in another and failure to pass any item at age level. The norming sample consisted of 1,036 children and tended to overrepresent children whose fathers had higher-level occupations. Reliability is adequate for a screening device, but no evidence of validity is presented.

The *Boehm Test of Basic Concepts* is designed as a group-administered instrument, but it is often administered individually in diagnostic and clinical settings. The test takes about fifteen to twenty minutes to measure abstract, school-related concepts in the following areas: space, quantity, time, and miscellaneous (e.g., like, different). The testing format includes the presentation of a picture in a test booklet. The examiner reads a statement that is true of one of the pictures and the child is asked to mark the appropriate one. Norms are inadequate and reliabilities are marginal (Salvia & Ysseldyke, 1978), but the test can be useful as a corroborative device in the diagnostic assessment.

PERSONALITY AND INTELLECTUAL ASSESSMENT

In most states, the administration of personality and intelligence tests is restricted to licensed psychologists or psychiatrists. Personality testing includes the use of projective techniques, rating scales (some were mentioned in the sections on rating and adaptive behavior scales in this chapter), self-report measures, situational measures, and observational techniques (Walker, 1973). Both the psychological and psychiatric evaluations examine the "intrapsychic and psychosocial status of the child and the systems dynamics of the family" (Silver, 1976, p. 240). With the learning disabled population, these evaluations may also attempt to differentiate the child whose emotional problems cause academic problems from the child whose learning problem is at the root of his or her emotional difficulties. Of course, making this distinction is not always possible.

The most commonly used test of intelligence employed with learning disabled children both in school psychology and in clinics (Anastasi, 1976; Tarver & Hallahan, 1974) is the *Wechsler Intelligence Scale for Children—Revised, 1974 (WISC—R)* (Wechsler, 1974). The test contains verbal subtests which include information (a survey of learned factual information), comprehension (of verbal directions and customs and mores), similarities (between verbal stimuli), arithmetic, vocabulary, and digit span. The performance tests are picture completion, picture arrangement (in a sequence to produce a logical story), block design, object assembly (from disjointed puzzle pieces), coding (of symbols and copying them), and mazes. Norming, reliability, and validity have been rather well-documented. Although some of the subtests fail to meet the standard for individual diagnosis at some age levels, the full-scale, verbal, and performance IQs are clearly reliable. Most subtests for most age groups at least approach acceptable standards.

There has been a great deal of research attempting to discover profiles of intellectual strengths and weakness among disabled readers by comparing performances on *WISC* subtests. In their review of this literature, Lequerica and Weiner (1977) reported that in about 60 percent of disabled readers, performance IQs are higher than verbal IQs, but that a variety of patterns are found. Ackerman, Peters, & Dykman (1971, p. 48) made the following statement:

1   While verbal ability makes a more important contribution to school success than nonverbal ability, adequate Verbal IQs did not assure school success.
2   While discordance between *WISC* Verbal and Performance IQs (15 points or greater) was somewhat more frequent in the LD sample, and more commonly in favor of Performance IQ, the significance generally attributed to this discrepancy should be tempered by a consideration of the absolute level of functioning on the

two scales separately. . . . Where the performance score was moderate to high and the verbal score low, the child was likely to be a poor reader. Both scores contribute in that the child needs integrity in both domains, but the verbal score appears more important for predicting reading success.

Several other tests are often used to estimate intellectual functioning. The *Peabody Picture Vocabulary Test (PPVT)* (Dunn, 1965) is often used because its author suggests that it provides a measure of verbal intelligence. Although the test is well standardized, its utility is frequently overestimated. The *PPVT* measures *only* receptive vocabulary. Correlations with *Stanford-Binet* and *WISC IQs* range from .30 to .92.

The *Slosson Intelligence Test* (Slosson, 1971) is an individually administered test that is often used for screening purposes. In some states it is permitted as evidence for placement decisions or for follow-up testing. Salvia and Ysseldyke (1978) report that the test was normed on an unspecified population and gives limited information about its technical adequacy. Although scores on the *Slosson* are correlated very highly (.90 to .98) with scores on the *Stanford-Binet*, the two tests cannot be used interchangeably because the means and standard deviations of the *Slosson* vary so greatly at different age levels.

One test battery used primarily with adolescents (since so few tests or rating instruments that can be administered by persons without psychological certification are available for testing children at this level) is the *Detroit Tests of Learning Aptitude* (Baker & Leland, 1935), consisting of nineteen tests covering a wide variety of psychological characteristics. The *Detroit* includes tests of pictorial and verbal absurdities, pictorial and verbal opposites, motor speed and precision, auditory attention span for related and unrelated words, oral commissions and oral directions, social adjustment (two subtests), visual attention span for objects and letters, orientation, free association, designs, number ability, broken or disarranged pictures, and likenesses and differences. The examiner is free to choose any or all of these subtests for a given child. J. Hunt (1972) criticized the test on the following grounds: it measures primarily verbal functions (the ratio of verbal to performance subtests is 3 to 1); test items are dated; the choice to use a large number of subtests could require an extensive testing period; statistical data are inadequate for norming, reliabilities, etc.; the validity of the test rests in part with the examiner who must design his or her own battery. The test's strengths are that it is useful for adolescents, its makeup is flexible in that whatever subtests the examiner deems appropriate can be selected for administration, and it provides clinical evidence to corroborate or disconfirm other findings. Many school systems which use the *ITPA* to diagnose younger children use the *Detroit* to assess older ones, because they are interested in assessing modality functions. It should be noted that the *Detroit* suffers from nearly all of the problems raised in regard to the *ITPA:* it is inadequate with respect to norms, reliability, and of course, validity. Furthermore, the use of measures of modality functioning has received even less support for adolescents than it has for younger children.

Because it also can be administered by persons who do not hold a license in psychology, the *Woodcock-Johnson Psycho-Educational Battery* (Woodcock & Johnson, 1977) is rapidly growing in popularity. The test is designed to assess abilities in three general areas: cognitive ability, achievement, and interests. It is appropriate for ages three to eighty years and older. The three general areas are divided into twenty-seven component tests. A complete listing is given in Table 10-3. The sampling of areas is complete and extensive. The administration of the battery is uncomplicated and can be done by a variety of personnel, including trained paraprofessionals (Woodcock, 1978). The administrator can choose appropriate subtests based upon current needs. Norms were developed to reflect the population as indicated by the 1970 United States Census. Regarding reliability, the split-half reliability coefficients for the subtests vary according to age. Though one subtest is quite low (.46) and others nearly so (.60 to .70), most are within the .80 to .90 range. Across ages, the subtest reliability coefficients are generally quite high. Reported internal reliability for cluster scores ranges from .78 to .95. The battery appears to have well-established content, construct, and

Table 10-3   Subtests of the Woodcock-Johnson Psycho-Educational Battery

Tests of cognitive ability:
  Picture vocabulary
  Spatial relations
  Memory for sentences
  Visual-auditory learning
  Blending
  Quantitative concepts
  Visual matching
  Antonyms—synonyms
  Analysis—synthesis
  Numbers reversed
  Concept formation
  Analogies
Tests of achievement:
  Letter-word identification
  Work attack
  Passage comprehension
  Calculation
  Applied problems
  Dictation
  Proofing
  Science
  Social studies
  Humanities
Tests of interest level:
  Reading interest
  Mathematics interest
  Language interest
  Physical interest
  Social interest

criterion-related validity. In one study of the concurrent validity of the battery (Reeve, Hall, & Zakreski, 1979), evidence was found that the battery holds up well when compared to the *WISC—R,* but some questions arise as to its use with learning disabled children. These children, as a group, score within mildly retarded range when their scores on the *WISC—R* indicate average intellectual potential. This finding raises serious questions about how learning disabilities can be differentiated from mild retardation with any certainty.

Summary and Conclusions

We have reviewed eight of the data sources for gathering diagnostic information that were identified by Tucker. These have included information from parents, teachers, tests, rating scales, and a host of professionals. Once this information is gathered, it must be integrated and decisions concerning the child's placement and educational program must be made by an interdisciplinary team. Although the exact composition of the team has been left to the discretion of the individual states, such a team usually includes some combination of the following: the child, his or her parents, a teacher and/or learning disabilities specialist, the school psychologist, a school administrator, a social worker, and a physician. One person, usually the school psychologist or the learning disabilities specialist, must write a report that integrates the test findings and relates those findings to educational programming.

MAKING SENSE OF THE DATA

The diagnostic process is never the same in any two cases, so precise rules for conducting evaluations cannot be given. There are, however, some procedures for dealing with data that facilitate its integration. It is wise to obtain as much information as possible about the child prior to testing so that test selection can be guided by working hypotheses. Tests should be carefully selected and overtesting should be avoided. The selection of appropriate and reliable subtests is often more efficient than the use of whole tests. A shotgun approach to testing is inefficient and usually raises more questions that it answers. Furthermore, without having obtained and read existing records, avoidance of test duplication becomes impossible.

The first step after assembling the information is to begin looking at the most pervasive and fundamental data: age, sex, school placement, language usage, family circumstances, etc. Initial working hypotheses about the kinds of behaviors, approaches to learning, and academic performances should then be derived. As strengths and weaknesses in academic functioning are identified through testing, that data can be used to confirm or disconfirm the initial assumptions. A similar procedure is useful in making sense of behavior. The evaluation of Samuel, whose sample report is included in the Appendix at the end of this chapter is illustrative.

In the case of Samuel's evaluation, information obtained prior to testing included previous medical and school records and an interview with his mother.

The extensive City Hospital evaluation included reports of personality and intelligence testing. Since there were no indications of the use of a nonstandard dialect either in the records or during the interview with the mother, a decision was made to omit tests of language dominance, unless Samuel's speech seemed to indicate the necessity of administering one. It did not. The evaluation focused exclusively on tests of academic functioning, including aptitude measures. Because the purpose of testing was to provide data that would enable areas of strengths and weaknesses to be identified, so that initial direction for diagnostic teaching could be established, considerable attention was given to the assessment of written language and mathematics performances. Following testing, it was decided that insufficient information was available about Samuel's allegedly hyperactive behavior in the fourth-grade class, so a rating scale and classroom observation were added.

Initial working hypotheses, therefore, included the possibility of a nonstandard dialect. This hypothesis was not borne out by the data. A second hypothesis formulated early was that Samuel's performance, affected by both organic problems and emotional difficulties, would be erratic. Again, this hypothesis was not supported by data. Except for oral language, Samuel's performance was remarkably consistent and was essentially characterized by avoidance of what appeared to be overwhelming frustration at his inability to succeed at school tasks. Since he had given up trying, Samuel was no longer making progress and so his deficit was cumulative. His behavior during testing suggested to the examiner that Samuel had indeed acquired sophisticated social knowledge and used it to charm his way through difficult experiences. Failing that, the old avoidance behaviors (acting out, regression, and irritability) reemerged.

The report of the evaluation should contain a number of sections. Those listed in the sample report at the end of this chapter are usually sufficient. Information is needed to contact the child. His or her parents should be listed at the top. Other topics should include the reason for the referral, background information, tests administered, behavior during testing, results of testing, other data gathered, conclusions (which may include prognosis), and the delineation of treatments or interventions. The sample report was designed as the stepping-off point for individual educational planning.

A few additional comments about the construction of such a report are in order. First the writing must be precise and nonevaluative. Instances of behavior should be described, but the use of labels should be avoided. A positive attitude should dominate the writing. Educational reports should be written in the third person: the use of "I" should be avoided. Whatever judgments are made should be very carefully supported by data. Findings should not be reported test-by-test, but results should be integrated across tests. Isolated behaviors are not important, but patterns of behavior should be detected and described. Test results should be reviewed and *integrated* with all other information available about the child, including background information, behavior during testing, etc. All test findings should be explained with reference to a standard that is easily identified, preferably percentile rank. One caution about the presentation of test data is that it is not sufficient to name subtests and to give scores on them. First, naming the subtest assumes that the persons reading the report are as familiar with the test's content as the person writing it. Few teachers, parents, or children have such expertise. Second, the reporting of scores can be quite misleading. Few of the tests or subtests have been standardized on special populations, so it is often difficult to know just what a given score may mean for a learning disabled child. In addition, reporting scores often short-circuits the reader's attention. Many readers will skim through the material for an overview of test scores.

Recommendations for instruction should include provisions for large and small-group (or one-to-one) instruction. Recommendations must be feasible and efficient. It would be foolhearty to suggest procedures that require sustained, individual attention for a teacher who is to have the child in a class of thirty. On the other hand, it would be equally wasteful to recommend large-group instructional techniques in instances where individual teaching is possible.

SUMMARY AND CONCLUSIONS

Diagnosis, a second step in the evaluation process, differs from screening in that it proceeds at a more intense level, with the goal being to determine whether a learning disability exists, to define specific educational capabilities and disabilities, or both. Diagnosis goes beyond testing, and considers information from a variety of sources. The eight sources of data relevant to a comprehensive assessment considered here were observational data, other available data, information related to language dominance, educational assessment, adaptive behavior, medical and/or developmental data, social and emotional data, and information regarding intellectual functioning. With respect to observational data, information is usually gained through teacher or parent rating scales, and/or interactional analysis such as sociometric techniques or observational systems. Other available data include school achievement records, prior test data, and medical records. Information is available only with parental consent. Information concerning language dominance is important in view of recent legislation mandating testing and assessment in the child's primary language. Educational assessment refers to evaluation of the child's ability in academic areas. Data are usually gathered from both evaluation of the child in the classroom and test data, either norm-referenced or criterion-referenced. The tests used generally fall into two categories, formal and informal. Each contributes different kinds of information. Assessments mentioned in this chapter were in the areas of language tests, reading tests, spelling tests, written language tests, and tests of mathematics. Tests described here were chosen because of their representativeness, high rate of use, or perceived excellence.

Diagnostic teaching is a method of continuous evaluation and teaching. It sometimes incorporates such techniques as applied behavioral analysis. Its advantages lie in observing the child's performance across a variety of real situations. Medical and developmental data play an important part in the assessment of some children whose learning problems may have a physiological component amenable to treatment. In addition, use of developmental scales allows medical personnel to monitor continually the growth of children so that deviations can be identified early. The areas of social and emotional development and intellectual assessment were reviewed together since, in most states, the use of a majority of personality and intelligence tests is restricted to licensed psychologists or psychiatrists. Personality tests usually are of an inventory format, rating-scale format, or employ a projective technique. Intellectual assessments range from highly individualized lengthy tests, to shorter individual tests, and group tests. Although a number of vocabulary tests are being employed as measures of verbal intelligence, criticism has been raised concerning their continued use for that purpose.

The chapter concluded by indicating that gathering data is but one step in the educational evaluation. A major part of the work is in integrating that data and in developing a written report which synthesizes information and presents it in such a way that *IEPs* can be developed without further extensive testing. A number of issues regarding format and style were addressed. All reports should be concise, clear, positive, based upon data gathered, and should include recommendations for instruction.

SUGGESTED READINGS

Aiken, L. R. *Psychological testing and assessment.* Boston: Allyn and Bacon, 1976.

Oakland, T. *Psychological and educational assessment of minority children.* New York: Brunner/Mazel, 1977.

Salvia, J., & Ysseldyke, J. E. *Assessment in special and remedial education.* Boston: Houghton Mifflin Company, 1978.

Wallace, G., & Larsen, S. C. *Educational assessment of learning problems: Testing for teaching.* Boston: Allyn and Bacon, 1978.

APPENDIX

EDUCATIONAL EVALUATION

Name: Samuel Brown   Birthdate: 9/9/69
Address: 127 East Avenue   Sex: Male
         Brookdale, New Hampshire   Telephone: None
         10101

Reason for Referral:

In December, 1978, City Hospital diagnosed Samuel as an organically impaired boy with Specific Learning Disability. The Hospital recommended an educational evaluation, referral to the Placement Center of the Board of Education for special class placement, and individual counseling for him and his mother.

Background Information:

Samuel, aged 10, is the second of three children in a middle-income black family. At City Hospital, Mrs. B. expressed concerns about Samuel's learning difficulties and fear that he may have inherited them from his father, an employed machinist she described as "forgetful." Mrs. B. acknowledged that despite a good relationship with her children, she had been rough and punitive with them. Once in anger, she threw a brush at Samuel resulting in a head injury that required stitches. She said Samuel had been a difficult child, high strung and having temper tantrums to which she had given in. She thought he demanded a lot of attention, wanted to remain a baby, and ate too much. According to his mother, she tried to prevent Samuel's brothers from teasing him and him from teasing them. She said her husband was more patient with the children and that he spent a lot of time with Samuel.

Mrs. B. indicated Samuel had had behavior problems in school since kindergarten. Teachers reported he wanted to play a lot. In first grade he stood on his desk. In the second grade, he was transferred to a special class where his behavior improved, but the class was discontinued. He spent two years in a regular third-grade class. His current fourth-grade teacher noted that he deals with his learning difficulties by walking out of class and being disruptive. He appears overwhelmed by frustration when unable to do assignments and, although motivated to work, can do so only on a one-to-one basis. He has been rude and sassy to teachers, but gets along fairly well with peers, despite occasional fights.

The report from City Hospital indicated a Verbal IQ in the low-average range, a Performance IQ in the borderline retarded range, and a Full Scale IQ in the dull-normal range on the WISC—R. He earned a superior score on a test tapping knowledge of social expectations, was average on a vocabulary subtest, and below average on a test of general information. The Hospital suggested that Samuel was extremely upset over his failure to learn, and showed reactive, irritable, and regressive behaviors. They noted that he felt inadequate in his interactions with others, ambivalent toward his family, and in need of emotional nurturance.

Tests Administered:	Examination Dates:
Key Math Diagnostic Arithmetic Test	4/19/79
Woodcock-Johnson Psycho-Educational Battery (Part 1)	4/19/79
Test of Written Language	4/19/79
Test of Language Development	4/20/79
Behavior Rating Profile	4/20/79
Woodcock Reading Mastery Tests	4/20/79
Informal Reading Inventory	4/23/79
Classroom Observation	4/25/79

Behavior During Testing:

Samuel is of average height and build. He was immaculately groomed for the testing session. Although he was guarded at first, he quickly relaxed. He was polite, cooperative, seemed well-motivated, and eager to show what he could do, despite his repeated questions about how much longer testing would take. When confused, Samuel became figity, lost concentration, and for ensuing questions answered quickly without reflection. He responded positively to praise and individual attention. On occasions when he "gave up," he continued to work when given praise by the examiner reflecting on his good work, but was unable to utilize queries and prompts. He showed some playfulness and a capacity for self-assertion. On leaving, he shook the examiner's hand and thanked her for a wonderful time.

Test Results:

General Cognitive Ability   Samuel's performance on a test of cognitive ability indicated that his overall mental age is approximately eight years—that is in keeping with previous findings that he was performing in the borderline retarded to dull-normal range. He scored at the 55th percentile for children of his chronological age on verbal aptitude tests (e.g., verbal analogies, antonyms, synonyms, etc.) He scored at the 35th percentile on tests of mathematical aptitude. He encountered serious problems on tests of oral vocabulary (16th percentile) and concept learning (20th percentile). Samuel showed difficulties throughout the testing with questions related to temporal concepts. He was unable to tell the examiner any part of his birth date. He could recite the names of the days of the week, knew the name of the day on which he was tested, but did not know the month or the year. He did, however, know that Christmas is in the winter, the season when school started, etc.

Oral Language   Samuel's receptive language abilities vary considerably. He has little difficulty carrying out directions given orally or with memory for sentences (70th percentile). His receptive vocabulary is comparatively weak (35th percentile) but he shows relative strength in tasks tapping syntactic understanding (50th percentile).

With the exception of his poor performance on the test of oral vocabulary, Samuel performed within expectations for his mental age on all expressive language measures (e.g., paraphrase, grammatic closure). The examiner observed no deviations from standard pronunciation or standard English syntax.

Written Language   Samuel's instructional reading level was grade one (15th percentile). Word recognition skills were at a mid-first-grade level. His rate of processing was slow and he could not identify words when they were exposed for 30 seconds. With unfamiliar primer words he substituted ones that began with the same consonant or consonant blend, and were roughly the same length or configuration. He also showed inversion, reversal, and sequencing problems, as well as additions and omissions of letters. He was often able to correct himself when given more time. When reading paragraphs he did not make use of context cues in decoding unfamiliar words, but tended either to omit them or substitute.

Analysis of Samuel's reading miscues revealed that most could be classified as having a high degree of either graphic or sound similarity. Most of the grammatical and semantic miscues were acceptable. In some instances, however, there was a change of meaning. There was no noticeable tendency for Samuel to self-correct.

His listening comprehension was on a high second- to low third-grade level, and so corresponded with expectations for his mental age. He was generally able to answer factual questions and simple inferential ones about a story being read to him.

Samuel's instructional level in spelling corresponded roughly to his instructional level in reading: grade one. He was able to give the letter names of all the consonant sounds, but only of the short vowel *a*. Spelling errors were marked by letter reversals and by a clear tendency to start an unfamiliar word with the last sound heard. Story composition was severely limited by the energy he needed to devote to spelling and letter formation. Sentences were short, repetitive, and syntactically immature. He seemed unaware of story elements, such as the need for a setting, plot, characters, etc.

Samuel's handwriting is a definite area of concern. Comparison to standard models placed his handwriting at approximately a five-year-old level. His handwriting was characterized by poor spacing and letter formation, failure to attend to the spatial orientation of letters and words, poor organization of the material on the page, difficulty in planning and controlling the direction of his pencil, fluctuation in attention and control, letter inversions and reversals, lack of alignment, and inconsistent slant. His handwriting is extremely difficult to decipher. At times, he has difficulty in explaining what it is he has written. His handwriting is a blend of manuscript and cursive. With respect to letters with tails, he showed special difficulty in knowing where to begin and generally terminated the tail on the line rather than below it.

Mathematics and Arithmetic   Samuel was able to do simple addition and subtraction of numbers below 10, by counting on his fingers. Although he has apparently been taught how to add 2 place numbers with regrouping, he was unable to do them independently. He needed assistance in the form of visual and verbal prompts (e.g., a line drawn between the columns, a reminder to start with the right side column and to "put down the ____" and "carry the ____"). When writing down a column of dictated digits for additition, he failed to line them up correctly. He could count by 10's to 100, by 5's to 100, by 2's to 14, by 3's to 6, and by 4's to 8. He could only do one-step mental addition and subtraction of single digits, and one-step word problems involving the same processes. He was unable to solve any problems presented in equation form, where he had to supply the missing sum or addend in an empty box. He was unfamiliar with fractions.

He knew the names and values of coins and could add at least one quarter, dime, nickel, and penny together. He was familiar with the ruler, but could measure by whole inches only. He was familiar with the vocabulary of inches, feet, and yards, but not with their symbols. He could tell time by the hour, and with much greater difficulty, by the half-hour. He showed familiarity with the calendar, and could read from it the number of days in the month and identify the calendar day associated with a specific number. He functioned at the 55th percentile on a logical task calling for the recognition of what information was needed to solve a problem.

Classroom Behavior   Samuel was observed in his classroom because his teacher reported that he was hyperactive. During the two-hour observation, Samuel did not exhibit any sustained inappropriate or nongoal directed behavior that was not a clear response to his inability to answer a question. What appeared to be periods of considerable movement were immediately preceded by the presentation of a question to which Samuel did not know the answer. These situations took place most often in group settings. Following the teacher's indication of an incorrect answer (e.g., "No. Does anyone know the right answer?), Samuel became distracted from the task, began to fiddle with pencils, books, and papers, occasionally got up from his desk, and usually remained in this mode of functioning for 10 to 15 minutes or until the activity changed. Teacher reprimand did not alleviate the situation. His behavior was disruptive and distracting to both other children and to the teacher. More importantly, it interfered with Samuel's learning. More formal teacher, parental, and self-ratings of Samuel's school behavior indicated that both teachers and parents rated his behavior as a problem. Most importantly, Samuel viewed his own behavior—in school and at home—extremely negatively.

Summary and Conclusions:

Samuel appears to be functioning academically approximately two years below the average performance expected of children of his mental age. He is a willing student who is eager to show what he can do. He seems to become easily frustrated, however, when he cannot perform adequately and copes with that frustration by avoiding his lessons and/or by acting out. Although impulsive behavior is frequent, it nearly always follows situations in which he is asked to respond to a question to which he does not know the answer. Samuel needs sympathetic and consistent instruction in all academic areas. It is important that he be asked to perform tasks that he is capable of accomplishing and that he be given some assistance on an individualized basis, such as resource room instruction or peer tutoring, to help him stay abreast of class assignments. Some support should be sought for the family, so that Mrs. B. especially can be helped to deal more effectively with her responses to her son's problems.

Recommendations for Intervention:

Group reading   Since Samuel is functioning approximately at first-grade level, there will be a number of reading assignments in his fourth-grade placement that will be too difficult for him. Samuel should be given assistance in reading in the content areas. A peer tutor would be helpful, so that the teacher could be free to do other things. A tutor might tape reading assignments so that Samuel, as well as other children with reading problems, could listen to the tapes as they read through their assignments. If the mother is literate, having his mother read one of the assignments for the next day might be a good way to begin to get the family involved in Samuel's education. Reading to him would not be likely to lead to punitive and high-pressure situations. It would, however help Samuel to be prepared to respond in class when the teacher calls on him and it would help him to make guesses about the words that he has difficulty reading when he does read the material by himself. The parents should also be encouraged to read newspaper accounts, stories, etc. to Samuel. Although Samuel should be encouraged to answer questions voluntarily in class, it might be prudent for the teacher to resist calling on him. If the teacher is comfortable with that recommendation, the children in the class might be paired so that each has recourse to "a friend" when he or she does not know the answer. In that way, Samuel could ask for assistance without feeling that he has failed. Of course, if the teacher is sensitive to the information Samuel can give, he or she can ask Samuel questions that he can answer.

<u>Individualized Instruction in Reading</u> Since Samuel is ten years old, it would be appropriate to use either experience stories or high-interest, low-vocabulary readers for his instruction. Since he appears able to make reasonable guesses about what the words he is to read might be on the basis of their initial consonants and general length and configuration, he should be instructed to check his reading by asking himself if what he is reading makes sense and if it sounds like English (he scored well on tests requiring him to judge syntactical adequacy and appears to have adequate listening comprehension skills for a child with his mental age). He should be instructed to read to find out about a topic. He should have access to a "buddy" who can tell him words that he does not know. Phonics instruction should be given as it is needed rather than by rules or exercises. If experience stories are to be used for part of Samuel's instruction, care should be given to making certain that his problems with spelling and letter formation do not interfere with his writing. In short, his stories can be dictated and transcribed by the teacher or another pupil. Instruction and practice in handwriting seem in order. Once Samuel has acquired the ability to write automatically, he can record his own stories, letters, etc. If spelling instruction is given, it would probably be most important to help Samuel learn to check his writing for errors as he makes them and to use the dictionary.

<u>Individualized and Small-Group Math Instruction</u> Samuel needs a better conceptual understanding of the processes underlying addition and subtraction, as well as a knowledge of number facts. He needs to understand place value, and the spatial arrangements and steps involved in addition and subtraction of 2 place numbers. One initial strategy that can be used is to have him prepare a number chart from 0 to 99, which can be laminated. He can then use a wax crayon on it. The concepts of 1 more, 2 more (or less), etc. can be taught on the chart, with Samuel moving his crayon forward or backward the appropriate number of spaces. Once a particular "game" has been established, such as the game of "plus 4," he can be asked to predict what the number will be, and he can also translate these games into equations or into standard computation form. The chart might also enable him to participate in some class activities.

Samuel could become the official chart-maker for the class. Everything that can be graphed or charted (the temperature, contributions to charity, etc.) should be converted into a graphic display that is easy for him to construct, demonstrate, and explain to the other children in the class. Charts could be used to help him keep track of and plan his time.

Marge Nemeth
Examiner

Chapter 11

Individualized Educational Programming

INTRODUCTION

This chapter is designed to address topics related to PL 94-142. First, the chapter considers individual educational plans (IEPs). Second, the implications of the law for preschool and secondary education are examined. Third, the concept of least restrictive environment and service delivery models are reviewed. Fourth, due process is explained. The chapter concludes with consideration of possible changes in the roles and training of learning disabilities teachers.

INDIVIDUALIZED EDUCATIONAL PROGRAMMING

PL 94-142 requires than an IEP be prepared for each handicapped child. The IEP must (1) be written; (2) state the child's present level of educational attainment; (3) include annual instructional goals; (4) include short-term instructional objectives; (5) specify the specific educational services to be provided and the extent to which the child shall be included in regular education programs; (6) contain the projected dates for the initiation and duration of the program; and (7) specify criteria and evaluation procedures which will be used to determine whether annual instructional objectives have been achieved *(Federal Register,* 1977). See Figure 1 for an example of an IEP.

The IEP serves a dual function, i.e., as an evaluation and as a teaching plan (Margolis, Hill, Reid, West, & Hresko, 1978). The IEP functions as a kind of report card in the sense that its preparation must begin with an assessment of the pupil's level of functioning—the delineation of the things he or she can and

Date

| | Mo. | Day | Yr. |

INDIVIDUALIZED EDUCATIONAL PROGRAM

Student _____ DOB _____
       Last   First   Middle   Mo.   Day   Yr.

School_____

PRESENT LEVEL OF PERFORMANCE

_____

_____

GOALS (OBJECTIVES) LONG TERM — PRIORITIZED

_____

_____

_____

_____

_____

_____

PLACEMENT RECOMMENDATIONS AND JUSTIFICATION:

_____

_____

_____

Portion of Time in Regular Classrooms:

Individualized Educational Planners (signature)	Relationship to Student	Date	Individualized Educational Planners (signature)	Relationship to Student	Date

Figure 11-1 A sample individualized educational program format. *(Adapted from the Individualized Educational Program form of the Dallas Independent School District, Dallas, Texas.)*

Page 2

Date

_____ _____ _____
Mo. Day Yr.

INDIVIDUALIZED EDUCATIONAL PROGRAM

Student _____
         Last   First   Middle

Address _____

Teacher _____

School _____

Short Term Objectives	Specific Educational and/or Support Services	Persons Responsible	Significant Dates		
			Begin	End	Review

Recommendations for Specific Procedures/Techniques, Materials, etc.

Evaluation Criteria for Goals and Objectives

Figure 11-1 *(Continued)*

cannot do. The areas of evaluation will vary from student to student and with the nature and/or severity of the student's particular disability. The IEP for a person who has a specific learning disability might focus on academic areas such as reading, mathematics, social studies, and science, as well as receptive and expressive language, social adaptation, physical education, speech skills, and career-vocational skills (McNutt & Heller, 1978).

Most often, diagnostic teaching (including criterion-referenced tests and parent-teacher observations) provides the best source of data regarding the child's level of functioning. For many areas that need to be assessed, standardized tests simply have not been developed. For other areas, tests that do exist often suffer from poor subtest reliability. Even when the overall test score is reliable, it is often too global a measure to be useful in the identification of the student's specific strengths and weaknesses. Furthermore, standardized tests include only items that discriminate among students. They, therefore, do not cover the full range of any content children are expected to know. Clearly, standardized tests are more useful in estimating levels of group performance than in individual educational planning. PL 94-142 requires their use for classification and placement purposes, but *not* for the specification of instructional plans.

The second function of an IEP is to establish a teaching plan to which both parents and school officials can agree. The plan includes a statement of long-range and short-range goals, the setting and personnel to provide specific services, and the final level of performance anticipated.

The IEP should be developed by those who are to implement it. People who teach children are able to make contributions that the analysis of test results cannot make. An IEP should be considered as a *guide*. One common interpretation of the IEP is that it is both binding and unchangeable. Turnbull, Strickland, and Brantley (1978), however, stress that it is "not a legally binding document which constitutes a guarantee or promise . . . that a handicapped child will accomplish a specified number of goals and objectives within a particular time period" (p. 7). Factors such as accident, absence, sickness, unexpected rapid advances, and new levels of achievement may all necessitate revision of an IEP. An IEP should evolve as the teacher interacts with and comes to know the child. Major revisions in the IEP, however, require parental consent.

The development of the content of an IEP necessitates that both during the initial assessment and during the planning stage the personnel involved have a good working knowledge of the curriculum that is to be considered. This does not mean the curriculum of a particular school, or district, or state, but rather knowledge of content. Some have raised concern over whether even teachers have an adequate knowledge of the content areas they teach (Poplin, 1979). Though some (Turnbull, Strickland, & Brantley, 1978) have suggested that teachers use established scope and sequence materials, Larsen and Poplin (1980) believe that the remedy is teacher development of curriculum. Using the concept of curricular maps (see Figure 11-2 for an example), they suggest that by

Academics - - Written Expression Curriculum - - Capitalization

General Objective: Capitalizing first word in a sentence

Short-Term Instructional Objectives:

Criteria: 90% over 6-week period (measured 6 times)

Behavior	With verbal cues	Independently
1. Identifies capital letters	AC	MS 3-78
2. Recognizes first word of sentences	AC	MS 3-78
3. Identifies errors in capitalizing first word of sentences	AC	MS 4-78
4. Corrects errors in capitalizing first word of sentences	AC MS IN ORIGINAL COMP 5-78	SC 9-79
5. In original composition, capitalizes first word in sentence	SC 10-79	*

*indicates mastery

Figure 11-2   Short-term instructional objectives for "capitalizing first word in a sentence." *(From Poplin, M. S., The science of curriculum development applied to special education and the IEP. Focus on Exceptional Children, 1979, 12(3), 1-16. © 1979 by The Love Publishing Company.)*

determining the constructs (written expression), goals (capitalization), general objectives for major concepts, and short-term instructional objectives, teachers will become more expert about the content areas they must teach.

Long- and short-range goals are frequently stated as behavioral objectives. Teachers must be careful, however, *not* to stress specific behaviors rather than the development of competence. One is reminded of the preschool classes in which handicapped children were given instruction to prepare them for kindergarten. The performance objectives established in these preschool classes included such items as recitation of the ABCs, discrimination of colors, counting, etc. Even handicapped children who succeeded in accomplishing these specific objectives failed to thrive in their kindergarten classes, perhaps because they had not had the more general experiences they needed in language, concept, and psychomotor development to gain from kindergarten instruction (Reid, 1978). Furthermore, the use of strict behavioral objectives may affect teacher expectancy. Teaching by objectives cues the teacher into looking for achievement related to only those goals, in the time sequence allotted, to the mastery level indicated. The child who "goes beyond" by achieving knowledge not specified, by reaching completion of goals in less than the allotted time, or who is simply unable to reach the specified mastery level may be unfairly penalized. What the teacher "expects" the child to do most definitely will determine what the teacher acknowledges as growth. We often forget that a child can demonstrate knowledge by a wide variety of performances. Why, then, should only one specific predetermined behavior be used as a determinant?

The IEP, however, is more than a set of objectives and goals. It is an attempt to implement a process leading to consideration of each child as an individual learner. The IEP process begins with children being referred for consideration as exceptional learners. Although PL 94-142 contains certain requirements regarding referral and subsequent evaluations (see Figure 11-3), the implementation of the law along with the terminology used to discuss the various personnel varies considerably from one state to another.

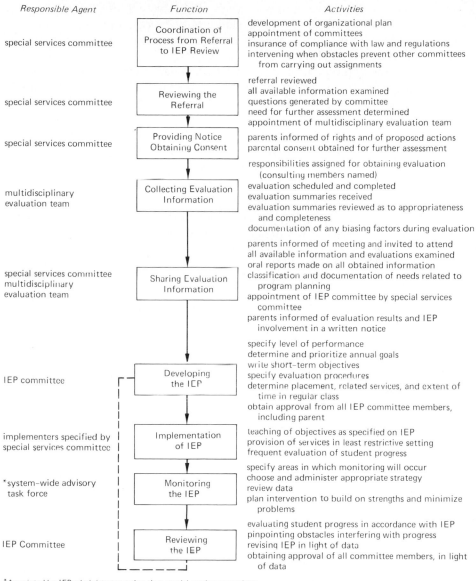

Responsible Agent	Function	Activities
special services committee	Coordination of Process from Referral to IEP Review	development of organizational plan appointment of committees insurance of compliance with law and regulations intervening when obstacles prevent other committees from carrying out assignments
special services committee	Reviewing the Referral	referral reviewed all available information examined questions generated by committee need for further assessment determined appointment of multidisciplinary evaluation team
special services committee	Providing Notice Obtaining Consent	parents informed of rights and of proposed actions parental consent obtained for further assessment
multidisciplinary evaluation team	Collecting Evaluation Information	responsibilities assigned for obtaining evaluation (consulting members named) evaluation scheduled and completed evaluation summaries received evaluation summaries reviewed as to appropriateness and completeness documentation of any biasing factors during evaluation
special services committee multidisciplinary evaluation team	Sharing Evaluation Information	parents informed of meeting and invited to attend all available information and evaluations examined oral reports made on all obtained information classification and documentation of needs related to program planning appointment of IEP committee by special services committee parents informed of evaluation results and IEP involvement in a written notice
IEP committee	Developing the IEP	specify level of performance determine and prioritize annual goals write short-term objectives specify evaluation procedures determine placement, related services, and extent of time in regular class obtain approval from all IEP committee members, including parent
implementers specified by special services committee	Implementation of IEP	teaching of objectives as specified on IEP provision of services in least restrictive setting frequent evaluation of student progress
*system-wide advisory task force	Monitoring the IEP	specify areas in which monitoring will occur choose and administer appropriate strategy review data plan intervention to build on strengths and minimize problems
IEP Committee	Reviewing the IEP	evaluating student progress in accordance with IEP pinpointing obstacles interfering with progress revising IEP in light of data obtaining approval of all committee members, in light of data

*Appointed by IEP administrator rather than special services committee

Figure 11-3 Sequence and functions of committee activities. *(From Turnbull, A. P., Strickland, B. B., & Brantley J. C.,* Developing and implementing individualized education programs. *Columbus, Ohio: Charles E. Merrill, 1978, p. 38. © 1978 by Bell and Howell Company.)*

The setting(s) and person(s) to provide specific instructional experiences for the child must be stipulated in the IEP. How can health and medical personnel contribute to a child's growth and development? What can the parent do to participate in his or her child's education? Should instruction be provided by a speech therapist, a reading teacher, or a resource room specialist? What can be accomplished in the large group setting? How can pervasive functions and activities, such as language and social skills, be encouraged on the playground, at lunch, and in the school bus? These considerations (among others) are important when developing the IEP.

Finally, the determination of the ultimate level of mastery anticipated for each instructional area allows parents and teachers to evaluate the pupil's progress and to revise the IEP appropriately. What, for example, should constitute mastery in spelling? Must a child learn to spell correctly 100 percent of the words attempted? Eighty percent? Perhaps there is some better way of measuring spelling competence, such as the student's application of morphophonemic rules or his or her ability to use a dictionary.

The IEP not only functions as a report card and a teaching plan but, in addition, serves as the basis of an agreement between the parent and school. It is the IEP that often provides the content for due process hearings (see below) in which services to be provided to a particular student or group of students are contested. The IEP is, in that respect, the cornerstone of the legislation.

The development of the IEP is the responsibility of the local school district. Most often, district officials delegate the responsibility for the IEP to those who will deliver the services, but district officials are ultimately still responsible and should be involved in seeing that the IEP is appropriate and that the services can be delivered.

Implications for Preschool and Secondary Education

Handicapped children between the ages of three and five and eighteen to twenty-one have received a flawed mandate (Cohen, Semmes, & Guralnick, 1979). As written, PL 94-142 does *not* mandate education for all preschool or postsecondary handicapped children:

> . . . with respect to handicapped children aged three to five and aged eighteen to twenty-one, inclusive, the requirements of this class shall not be applied in any State if the application of such requirements would be inconsistent with State law or practice, or the order of any court, respecting the public education within such age groups in the State [Public Law 94-142, 1975, Section 612(2) (b)].

Although interest in developing programs for the preschool handicapped has been encouraged by incentive grants, only about half of the states have taken advantage of them. Interest, however, remains high. For the reasons discussed in Chapter 9, however, such programs appear better suited to children with handicapping conditions other than learning disability (see also Mercer, Algozzine, & Trifiletti, 1979).

Cegelka and Phillips (1978) reviewed the implications of the legislation for secondary students. They argued that the most important outcome of the new legislation will be the inclusion of handicapped students in vocational training programs that will ensure at least entry-level skills. Programs can no longer be concerned only with future academic planning. High school programs, especially since education for the handicapped may continue until they are aged twenty-one, must be concerned with the child's total life adjustment. Wiederholt and McEntire (in press) note that three program options are quite common: self-contained classes, resource programs, and vocational training. They note, however, that these options are in fact quite dissimilar from school to school, district to district.

Some students may not have the skills to succeed in regular classes and some of the objectives of regular class programs may not be compatible with the needs of the handicapped students. Flexible programming in which the mildly handicapped student can participate in whatever way may prove most beneficial is needed.

Some Criticisms of PL 94-142

Although not opposed to the tenor of the law, which is, of course, to protect the rights of handicapped children, Reid (1978) has criticized PL 94-142 on the following counts:

> **1** The federal government has legislated a behavioral approach to special education without adequate research data to substantiate such a position (Goodman, 1977).
> **2** Those who advocate educational procedures based on the attainment of behavioral objectives view knowledge as finite, well-defined, and as acquired through social transmission. They fail to recognize that knowledge is acquired only when it can be integrated into existing knowledge.
> **3** Predicting future performance from test data is to confuse correlation with causation and to assume that what is tested is relevant to life adjustment.
> **4** Precisely what achievement is to be measured is never stipulated by the law. Much of what is frequently measured in learning disabled children is of questionable validity.

Both Hammill (1979) and Reynolds (1978) have also expressed skepticism. They fear that some communities will go through the motions of developing IEPs and fulfilling other requirements of the law without substantially improving the educational program of handicapped youngsters. Parents may be directed toward "signing off" on the IEPs without having had any real involvement in their planning. Surface progress may mask a lack of real achievement. Measurement systems will have to be devised that assess the domains set out individually for each child. Reynolds cautions that complying with the legislation requires accountability to handicapped pupils, their parents, the public, and to a host of other professionals.

Criticism of PL 94-142 has not been confined to the field of special education. Regular educators are also concerned with the impact of the law. Their needs are real and justified and must be addressed in order that the regular class and special class teacher be able to carry on meaningful dialogue. The concerns of the regular class teacher are many and include: (1) the need for accurate information regarding concepts, such as least restrictive environment and mainstreaming, (2) the need for in-service training in order to alleviate fears of being unprepared to teach exceptional children, (3) the lack of support from administrative personnel in implementation of IEPs, (4) the seeming lack of concern on the part of administration with regard to increased time commitments, (5) the lack of being included in the development of IEPs for the children they will teach, and (6) a concern for the historically poor relationship between special education and regular education and the fear that this will interfere with implementation (Ryor, 1978).

Still another criticism of PL 94-142 concerns finances. While we firmly believe that the right to free and appropriate education transcends financial concerns, local school districts must balance the books. The law gives little help. Funding procedures have been carefully explained (Ballard & Zettel, 1978). By 1982, 40 percent funding will be technically available from the federal government. What the law mandates, however, are upper limits. Whether any money becomes available is up to the budget allocations of Congress.

SERVICE DELIVERY SYSTEMS AND THE LEAST RESTRICTIVE ENVIRONMENT

The implementation of PL 49-142 has forced the public to become aware of the need to develop an appropriate and efficient system of providing services for each learning disabled child. But changes in the manner in which special educators provide services began undergoing change long before PL 94-142 became a reality. Questions concerning the efficacy of special class placement were being raised during the 1930s, and became more intense during the late 1960s and early 1970s. What was the effect of labeling? Was self-concept affected by educational segregation? Could handicapped children achieve in regular class settings? All these questions were raised prior to PL 94-142. To facilitate discussion of these issues, we will consider different types of educational settings, their feasibility, how they relate to the concept of mainstreaming, and the factors that have led to a reevaluation of approaches to the education of the learning disabled.[1]

Educational Settings

Children can be served in any one of a number of varying educational settings. Which one is selected depends upon the learning disabled child's needs, the needs of the other children who are in the class, and the needs, behaviors, and capabilities of the teacher with whom the child is placed (Heron, 1978).

Availability of a variety of educational possibilities is necessary to the notion of *least restrictive environment*. Least restrictive environment implies a continuum of services from very restrictive (removed from traditional educational settings) to nonrestrictive (the normal educational setting). Children should be placed in as normal an educational environment as possible, so that

---

[1]The literature pertaining to legislation and court action has been reviewed elsewhere. The interested reader is referred to Cohen and DeYoung (1973), Kirp, (1973) and Kirp, Buss, and Kuriloff (1974).

they may benefit to their maximum potential. Unfortunately, the term has become synonomous with *mainstreaming*. Mainstreaming refers to the placement of learning disabled children into regular education settings for all or part of the day. PL 94-142, however, does *not* equate least restrictive environment with mainstreaming. Rather it stresses the need to find an *optimal* placement for each handicapped child. One of the most widely used models for conceptualizing educational placements is shown in Figure 11-4. Deno's (1971) cascade model portrays educational services as a continuum ranging from the most to the least restrictive. It reflects the fact that it is not only the physical plant that should be considered in determining least restrictive environment. The exceptional child must also be more regularly included among groups of his or her normal peers and with other handicapped children. In addition, as one moves along through Deno's system, the administrators are *not* educational personnel, but rather individuals involved either with health-related or economic offices. Not until the child moves into the school/class setting do educational personnel

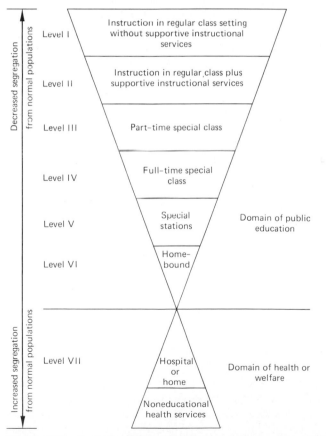

Figure 11-4 Cascade model of special education service. *(Adapted from Deno, E., Special education as developmental capital. Exceptional Children, 1970, 37, pp. 229–237. Reprinted by permission of The Council for Exceptional Children. © 1970 by The Council for Exceptional Children.)*

become involved. The following are components of the Deno cascade model.

Noneducational Services   At the most restrictive level is the noneducational setting reflecting a concern with either the physical or mental health and well-being of the child. The educational needs of the child are secondary. Placement in this type of setting is usually of short duration.

Instruction in Hospital or Domicile Settings   In this setting, the child, although outside of the regular educational environment, is receiving educational services. Classmates are also the individuals with whom he or she lives. For some children, hospital stay may be required, with classroom instruction taking place within the hospital. Chronic health conditions, injury, or temporary disease may be causative factors. For other children, the nature of their disabilities may require staying in a residential setting. Few learning disabled children, however, are so severely disabled that maintenance in a twenty-four hour residential setting is necessary. Occasionally children classified as learning disabled, however, do need intense, comprehensive intervention. The setting is far from ideal, however, because peer identification is only with similarly handicapped children. The potential for interaction with less handicapped and normal children is lacking.

Homebound Instruction   Homebound instruction refers to instruction which takes place within the confines of the child's home. The reason the child is at home may be the result of any number of events. The child may be convalescing after hospitalization for disease or injury, or the child may be recovering from illness or fractures. For some children, homebound instruction provides much needed instruction that otherwise would be unobtainable. For other children, homebound instruction is exile from the school setting.

Some school districts have used the concept of homebound instruction in order to educate children who do not fit into existing educational services, who are disruptive, or who would require extensive modifications of existing programs or structures. These reasons are not valid, morally or legally. Under PL 94-142, each child has the right to a *free and appropriate education.* Financial or management concerns are insufficient reasons for not providing appropriate educational services.

Special Stations   Special stations are, in effect, special schools segregated from the rest of the educational system. They are in operation during the regular school day. These special schools may be of two types, either public or private. Since children are in classes with children who have similar handicapping conditions, their exposure to normal peers will be limited to what family can provide in the afternoons and evenings, on weekends, and during vacation periods. These facilities usually are moderately large in terms of numbers of children attending, but not in terms of the teacher/student ratio. Many of the public facilities of this type are contractual, that is, they contract with surrounding school districts (perhaps on a county basis) to provide services to children for a given period. At the end of the two-year cycle, the child is evaluated and either returns to the school district for placement or is reassigned to the special school. Special schools are the first stage in the model where educational considerations govern the placement of the child.

Full-Time Special Class   The full-time special class is the traditional model for the education of the learning disabled child. The child is placed in a special class, within a regular school for the entire day. Contact with nonhandicapped children may be on the bus before and after school, during recess, possibly on the playground, in outside organizations, and during vacations. Some full-time special classes are partially integrated into regular education classes. There is one-way movement—children from the special classes may participate in some regular school activities (gym, lunch, art, etc.), but children from the regular classes are not participants in the special classes. Considerable controversy has arisen over the effectiveness of this type of classroom.

Part-Time Special Classes   The part-time special class allows the child to be placed in the regular educational setting for a substantial part of the day, but to return to the special class for basic skill development. While it is true that the child spends an extended period of time during the day with peers, the subtle stigma of the special class often remains. The benefit of such an arrangement is that the child receives as much education in the mainstream as possible, but still has access to extensive individualized attention on a daily basis. The success of the child in such a program depends not only upon the productivity of the student, but also upon the cooperation of the teachers and the acceptance of the student by children in regular classes.

Regular Class Attendance Plus Supplementary Instructional Services   This category encompasses numerous models and consists of the child leaving the regular class setting for supplemental instruction in a specialized setting. The services provided may be comprehensive or less intensive. They may take place on less than a daily schedule. The instruction may be in small groups or individually administered. To implement this model, the resource room is quite attractive, especially financially.[2] More children can be served by fewer teachers than under the contained-class models.

Regular Class Placement, Minimal Supportive Services   At the far end of the least restrictive continuum lies regular class placement. The most normal of the educational settings, it allows for maximum interaction of handicapped and normal children. Supplementary services are minimal and may not result in direct intervention with children. One possible organization under this model is

---

[2]For an extensive treatment of the concept of the resource room and its implementation, the reader is referred to Wiederholt, Hammill, and Brown (1978) and Hammill and Wiederholt (1972).

the use of the *consultant-teacher* to provide direction where necessary to the regular class teacher. Alpert (in press) suggests that the school psychologist may serve as the change agent in such a setting. The primary responsibility for the student, however, remains with the regular classroom teacher.

SUMMARY

More and more school systems seem to be finding the teacher-consultant model helpful. While resource rooms enable the special educator to focus on the development of basic skills, providing an integrated program is often difficult. Using special educators as a support system for regular teachers can help to bridge the gap between regular and special educators. But special educators must be better trained in interpersonal skills than they are at present if such a system is to be effective. It is often quite difficult for the special educator to listen to the needs of the regular educator, to be able to *hear* that the teacher has fears about working with handicapped children, that that person has his or her own self-concept on the line. Teachers do, after all, judge their own effectiveness by the gains their students make. Crises can easily develop if special educators come in with plans that require one-to-one teaching, elaborate preparation, and the like.

On the other hand, the special educator often feels that he or she is supposed to be the "expert" and, therefore, has an investment in seeing that the instructional strategies advocated are effective. What is needed is honest and frank communication between the classroom teacher and the teacher-consultant. Each must be able to express feelings, reservations, and fears of failure. The teacher and the teacher-consultant must admit that no one has the answer to teaching all children and as many alternatives as possible must be considered. The relationship must be seen as one in which two educated persons are making their best guesses about the types of learning experiences that may help a child. Those experiences need to be viewed from the start as tentative. They need to be evaluated, and the freedom to change to a different strategy without having to admit failure must be guaranteed.

MAINSTREAMING

Throughout the discussion of the models, the concept of mainstreaming was alluded to. Exactly what mainstreaming is varies with who defines it. Nyquist (1975) has suggested that "mainstreaming is a commitment to integrating people who are exceptional into our society rather than excluding them" (p. 2). The Council for Exceptional Children (1975) has presented one of the most complete and varied listings of what mainstreaming is:

•Providing the most appropriate education for each child in the least restrictive environment.

•Looking at the educational needs of children instead of clinical or diagnostic labels such as mentally handicapped, learning disabled, physically handicapped, hearing impaired or gifted.

•Looking for and creating alternatives that will help general educators serve children with learning or adjustment problems in the regular setting. Some approaches being used to help achieve this are consulting teachers, methods and materials specialists, itinerant teachers, and resource room teachers.

•Uniting the skills of general education and special education so all children may have equal educational opportunity.

Mainstreaming is not:

•Wholesale return of all exceptional children in special classes to regular classes.

•Permitting children with special needs to remain in regular classrooms without the support services that they need.

•Ignoring the need of some children for a more specialized program than can be provided in the general education program.

•Less costly than serving children in special self-contained classrooms. (Cited in Paul, Turnbull, & Cruickshank, 1977, p. vii–viii.)

Earlier, we alluded to the fact that self-examination had been going on in the field of special education for a number of years. Research has demonstrated segregating and socially stigmatizing effects of special classes and labeling (Dunn, 1968; Jones, 1972; Kirp, 1974; Ross et al., 1971). Others have noted that the special classes appeared to be serving functions other than educational ones, such as removing and isolating those who were "different" (Christopolos & Renz, 1969; Dunn, 1968; Jones, 1972; Hammons, 1972; Willower, 1970). Further, some have criticized the lack of curriculum in the special classes (Garrison & Hammill, 1971; Hammons, 1972; Iano, 1972). The result of such self-analysis was the seeking of alternatives to traditional programs. The range of suggestions includes multilevel alternatives, contractual agreements, and a "zero-reject" model. The zero-reject model (Lilly, 1971) is based upon the belief that, "Removal from the mainstream educational program must be an administrative impossibility" (p. 745–746).

Attempts at mainstreaming have met with varying degrees of success. Some positive effects of mainstreaming appear to be increased social behavior and positive attitudes (Gottlieb, Gampel, & Budoff, 1975), increased academic competence (Haring & Krug, 1975), less rejection (Goodman, Gottlieb, & Harrison, 1972), and increased positive attitudes on the parts of teachers, administrative personnel, and exceptional students (Fine, Deutsch, & Garland, 1977). Inclusion in regular classrooms does not ensure better self-acceptance (Coleman, in press) or acceptance by regular class peers (Iano, Ayers, Heller, McGettigan, & Walker, 1974; Monroe & Howe, 1971). What appears to be of prime import in determining the success or failure of a given mainstreaming program is a function of the type of individual program utilized and the degree to which integration takes place (Guerin & Szatlocky, 1974; Richmond & Dalton,

1973). Whether a program succeeds or fails also rests upon the dedication of the school principal to the concept of mainstreaming (Fine, Deutsch, & Garland, 1977).

Keogh and Levin (1976) reviewed the results of several years of study at UCLA dealing with the mainstreaming of exceptional children in California. They concluded their article with several important statements concerning the effectiveness of mainstreaming programs:

>   1   Mere physical placement in the regular classroom is not enough to ensure either academic achievement or social acceptance. Mainstreaming is not just a function of time and space.
>   2   The impact of labeling as an explanation for educational failure or behavioral deviance is seemingly overestimated.
>   3   Despite recognition that mainstream education places major, perhaps prime, responsibility of education of exceptional pupils on regular educators, it is clear that few regular class teachers feel competent to take on this task.
>   4   Effective individual instructional programs require appropriate analysis of pupils' educational abilities and styles (p. 9).

Perhaps in the next round of planning, we will be able to avoid the current weaknesses of most program development and institute effective change (Gallagher, 1976). We would be remiss if we did not call for additional research into the alternatives for educating the learning disabled. As of now, our understanding of alternative service models and the ramifications of such models is minimal. Philosophical commitments to mainstreaming have outraced its research support (Gickling & Theobald, 1975).

DUE PROCESS

PL 94-142 includes procedural safeguards under the term "due process" requiring, in effect, a series of checks and balances to ensure proper educational placement of a child. The concept of due process encompasses a number of separate elements. Regarding identification, placement, evaluations, or IEPs, either the parents or a public agency may request a hearing for an impartial examination and discussion of what is in question. During a hearing, it is permissible to obtain expert witnesses, introduce evidence (provided to all parties), seek counsel, question witnesses, and obtain written copy of the proceedings. If there is no settlement, or if the parties involved do not agree with the findings of the impartial hearing, then the case is brought to the state education agency. The findings of the state agency are binding unless civil action is pursued. During this entire process, the child must be maintained within the public education system.

A second point to be made is that parents have the right to more than one opinion before making a decision. If the parents do not agree with the evaluation of the public education agency, they have the right to an independent educational evaluation, unless the public agency has moved for an impartial hearing to present their case.

A third very important point is that parents must be informed of any proposed actions from beginning to end. This includes, but is not limited to, initial actions, rationale for decisions, information regarding tests, and any other pertinent information. This information is to be presented to the parent in such a manner that the parent understands the content and intent of the actions or decisions.

Finally, the parent (or surrogate parent where the parent is unable to participate) must give consent for actions to be taken through the preplacement process which ends with the development of the IEP. From that point on parental permission need not be obtained, though parents must be informed of all proposed actions.

The rights of the child are protected through these due process procedures. Parents remain informed and are given the opportunity to challenge the decisions made concerning their children. As Keogh and Levin (1976) point out, however, although the placement procedures are well-defined and guard against improper placement, there is no guarantee that after the child has been placed, the education administered will be adequate.

THE CHANGING IMAGE OF THE LEARNING DISABILITIES TEACHER OR SPECIALIST

It appears that there are at least three major changes in the role of the special educator as we now know it. First, fewer and fewer learning disabilities teachers and specialists will have self-contained classes. Second, learning disabilities teachers will need to become more sophisticated parent educators. Third, learning disabilities personnel will have to become adept at conference/ counseling skills.

Role Shifts

Since schools are able to afford fewer specialists and since self-contained classes will be a last resort for learning disabled children, teachers and specialists in the field of learning disabilities will increasingly act as teacher-consultants (Ozer, 1978), diagnosticians, or resource room specialists. They will seldom have opportunity to work daily with groups of children they can think of as "my class." They will have to service large numbers of children, either directly or through the intermediary of the classroom teacher. A wide variety of diagnostic, intervention, and interpersonal skills will be needed.

Parent Education

Since parents have a great deal to say about the educational programs designed for their children, it behooves us to make certain that parents are educated concerning the programs and possibilities that are available for their children

(Kroth, 1978). They can then participate more fully and more effectively in the design and evaluation of programs, and also contribute at home to their child's education. Many instructional programs, for example, can be implemented with a minimum of training. Parents need to be viewed as partners in the educational process. In order to more effectively educate parents, teachers need to be aware of a number of factors (Kroth, 1978). First, parents do not represent a homogeneous group. They differ in terms of the amount of educational experience they have, their learning skills, and their personalities. Second, parent groups which are small have a tendency to be more meaningful than parent groups which are large. Large groups "end up being lectures with a one way flow of information" (Kroth, 1978, p. 90). Finally, parent groups appear to work best when the time is structured. Goals should be explicit, the number of sessions should be set, and the length of time should be clearly indicated. The teacher also needs to be aware of other factors that lead to successful parent education. These include preparing a conducive environment, becoming an effective listener and recorder, and learning to adhere to preestablished time limits (Barten & Barten, 1973).

Conferencing Skills

Conference skills are required not only for the transmission of knowledge from professional to professional, but also for the transmission of knowledge from professional to parent (an ability most professionals find difficult to acquire). Being able to convey information in a meaningful manner, while continually monitoring the parents involved is a difficult operation (Rockowitz & Davidson, 1979). For many professionals, the parent conference is approached with the intention of transmitting information, almost in the form of proclamations or announcements. Few teachers are schooled to approach such a meeting as a process of *interpersonal* communication. The communication process, however, consists not only of giving information, but also of eliciting and valuing the other person's feelings, reactions, and understandings.

The parent conference can be enhanced if consideration is given to the needs of the parents. First, upon entering the conference environment, parents should be introduced to everyone in attendance. The evaluation procedures utilized should be reviewed. The parents should be encouraged to discuss their perceptions of their child's functioning. The person leading the conference should be sensitive and skilled enough to understand and restate the parental concerns before proceeding. Second, the findings of the evaluations should be shared with the parents. Detailed presentations should be introduced with overview statements. Time should be allowed for parents to react to the information they have received. Only after the information has been shared with the parents (and child if present), and they have reacted, should recommendations be made. Parental and child recommendations and priorities should be taken into consideration. When all the recommendations have been made and monitored, the parents should be provided with a summation and be allowed to react again. Finally, at the closing of the conference, time must be allowed for future planning. If this sequence can be followed, then the chances for a meaningful parent-teacher conference will be increased.

SUMMARY AND CONCLUSIONS

The IEP is one of the cornerstones of the new federal legislation. It could help to improve services for both normal and handicapped youngsters, but it also has the potential for covering up inadequate programming. For the most part, IEPs have been interpreted to necessitate the spelling out of specific behavioral objectives—both long- and short-term. Too often, these objectives are content-centered, rather than child-centered, are based on the results of standardized testing, and allow only a narrow definition of both curriculum and competence. It is unquestionably true that teachers must elucidate goals for children and that they must have some means planned for accomplishing these goals. The use of a diagnostic teaching model, however, is probably more effective in making certain that children achieve commensurate with their ability than is the delineation of restricted performance criteria.

A variety of service delivery systems exist that range from segregation to integration. The selection of a delivery system must depend on the child's abilities and not on labels or categorizations of disability. In many instances, one would anticipate the need for using a variety of service models to provide an appropriate education. Too often, the answer to placement selection has been mainstreaming into regular classes with little in-service instruction or ongoing support for teachers. The resource room and teacher-consultant models seem to be two effective methods for bridging that gap. Mainstreaming should not, however, be viewed as the answer for all learning disabled children. The complete array of alternatives should be considered. Finally, the roles of special educators appear to be changing. Learning disabilities teachers need to develop diagnostic skills, to become parent educators, and to learn conferencing/consulting techniques. Learning disabilities specialists will have to work in an increasingly wider variety of roles and settings.

SUGGESTED READINGS

Bureau of Education for the Handicapped. *Developing criteria for the evaluation of due process procedural safeguards provisions.* Washington, D.C.: The United States Office of Education, Bureau of Education for the Handicapped, Division of Innovation and Development, State Program Studies Branch, 1978.

Bureau of Education for the Handicapped. *Developing criteria for the evaluation of individualized education program provisions.* Washington, D.C.: The United States Office of Education, Bureau of Education for the Handicapped, Division of Innovation and Development, State Program Studies Branch, 1978.

Bureau of Education for the Handicapped. *Developing criteria for the evaluation of least restrictive environment provision.* Washington, D.C.: The United States Office of Education, Bureau of Education for the Handicapped, Division of Innovation and Development, State Program Studies Branch, 1978.

Chinn, P. C., Winn, J., & Walters, R. H. *Two-way talking with parents of special children: A process of positive communication.* St. Louis, Mo.: The C. V. Mosby Company, 1978.

Hammill, D. D., & Wiederholt, J. L. *The resource room: Rationale and implementation.* New York: Grune & Stratton, Buttonwood Farms Division, 1972.

Losen, S. M., & Diament, B. *Parent conferences in the schools: Procedures for developing effective partnership.* Boston: Allyn and Bacon, Inc., 1978.

Paul, J. L., Turnbull, A. P., & Cruickshank, W. M. *Mainstreaming: A practical guide.* Syracuse, New York: Syracuse University Press, 1977.

Wiederholt, J. L., Hammill, D. D., & Brown, V. *The resource teacher: A guide to effective practices.* Boston: Allyn and Bacon, 1978.

Part Four

This section of the book is concerned with curriculum content and gives both an evaluation of traditional approaches to language, reading, writing, and mathematics, and intervention strategies that take into consideration the executive functions of the persons being taught. Because we view teaching as a problem-solving activity in which the characteristics of the learner, the nature of the content or ability to be learned, and the materials and instructional strategies available must all be taken into consideration, the chapters in this section discuss not only educational interventions and informal assessments, but also the nature of the discipline to be learned. There are, for example, discussions of what language is, what reading is, what writing is, and how what we think about the nature of these disciplines influences our selection of intervention strategies. Chapter 12 is devoted to oral language acquisition and use. Chapter 13 examines the effectiveness of methods for teaching reading, the nature of dyslexia, and new emphases in the teaching of reading that are currently evolving. Chapter 14 focuses on written language, specifically handwriting, spelling, and composition. Chapter 15 is devoted to mathematics, because we believe that the understanding emphasized by this discipline is very important to all persons. We have been distressed that programs for learning disabled children that focus on the remediation of deficits often subordinate mathematics to reading instruction. The final chapter in this section is devoted to two contrasting approaches to classroom management. Although the humanistic approach is clearly more consonant with the cognitive approach to teaching that we have been advocating, we recognize the need for teachers of learning disabled children to be familiar with behavior modification techniques as well.

Photo on facing page: From Testing to Teaching

Chapter 12

Oral Language

INTRODUCTION

Oral language is a major area of concern in learning disabilities. Articles concerned with verbal abilities are becoming more common (cf. Bryan, 1978; Hresko, 1979; Hresko & Reid, 1978; Magee & Newcomer, 1978; Wallach & Goldsmith, 1977; Vellutino et al., 1977) and it appears that this trend will continue for some time. Concern for the communication abilities of the learning disabled is *not,* however, a new phenomenon. As early as 1967, Myklebust and Johnson were convinced that language impairments were widespread among the learning disabled. In fact, if you will recall the definition offered in Chapter 1, learning disabilities are defined as problems in oral and written language. Preoccupation with perceptual-motor deficits, however, eclipsed the importance of communication. Our treatment of language will be divided into two sections: the associationist and cognitive views of language. Within each we will examine acquisition and development of language, and the characteristics of the language of the learning disabled, and language intervention approaches. The discussion of the nature of language will follow an historical focus rather than a philosophical one.

THE NATURE OF LANGUAGE AND ITS ACQUISITION: THE ASSOCIATIONIST VIEW

The predominant view of language in learning disabilities (and all special education for that matter) has been the one that originated from behavioral psychology. Early in the associationists' attempts to elaborate upon language acquisition and functioning (Skinner, 1957), questions arose concerning the viability of the model (Chomsky, 1959) with such ferocity that the Skinnerian explanation of language was dropped from serious consideration quite rapidly. Other associationist explanations of language, however, gained acceptance. Osgood (1953), working from a Hullian orientation, proposed a model for the communication process. Osgood's model has also come under fire. Currently, behaviorists have tended to recognize some of their problems in explaining language and are diligently at work researching such topics as the development of meaning and the acquisition of syntax in hopes of uniting learning and cognitive theory into *neopsycholinguistics* (Staats, 1974).

Associationism is best described as a strong reductionist theory. The view of language places it within the same context as other observable behaviors. Since the associationists hold that language like all behavior is learned, it follows that language can be taught. Language behavior can be thought of as either one-stage ($S \rightarrow R$) or two-stage mediated ($S_r \rightarrow {}_s R$) learning. Focusing on the individual word and the meaning attached to that word, the associationists have all but ignored the developmental aspects of syntax. For them, the presence of a given verbal behavior, in the presence of an appropriate stimulus, is sufficient to ensure the continued use of that utterance. Important to note is the absence, in the associationist model, of any type of innate mechanism for the acquisition of language. Associationism sees no need to call into play internal, genetically transmitted devices for language behavior. Language (or verbal behavior) corresponds to the established rules of learning theory.

Associationists approach the effects of neurological impairment on language from two perspectives. First, they consider neurological impairment as deterring necessary physical responses. If the speech mechanism were impaired, for example, the ability of the individual to respond verbally would be limited. Second, related performance variables, such as perception and memory, might be impaired. In either case the assessment of the impact of the impairment would be a psychometric, quantitative analysis based on the frequency of errors. Implementation of appropriate learning techniques (e.g., variations in mode of presentation, rate, reinforcement schedule, etc.) or direct remedial training in the specific abilities impaired should result in improved functioning.

From the associationist viewpoint, maturational lag would be interpreted as indicative of inadequately formed associations. Any idea of critical periods of language acquisition (Lenneberg, 1967) would be unacceptable. When an individual's language was seen as defective, the behaviorist would interpret the problem in terms of the specific difficulty impairing the language learning rather than as delayed maturation.

Osgood's Model

Of primary importance in understanding the view of language that dominated special education is the work of Charles Osgood. It was Osgood's mediational model of communication that generated the most research in learning disabilities. Osgood's intent was to apply mediated stimulus response theory to communicative behavior. He generated a three-stage, two-dimensional model of the process of communication; a model that underwent refinement through the collaborative work of Osgood and Miron. This model attempted to incorporate the understanding of meaning, a task omitted in previous models.

Osgood's model is termed a *mediated* model, because it employs the Hullian notion of an intervening (mediating) step between the stimulus and response. It is a behavioral model in the sense that the development of meaning is explained as the development of *associations* between various internal states and observables. The model supposes a sequence of events that relates an external stimulus (S) to an internal response (r). A resultant internal stimulus (s) leads, in turn, to a final external response (R): $S_r \rightarrow_s R$. It is commonly referred to as an *underlying abilities* model, because:

> it indicates the several sensory, cognitive, and motor systems necessary for normal linguistic performance. . . . These prerequisite systems can be called "subsymbolic" in that they are required for normal symbolic behavior though, in and of themselves, they are not symbolic (Taylor & Swinney, 1972, p. 49).

The model is presented in Figure 12-1. It seeks to explain behavior on three levels: the projective level, the integrational level, and the representational level. Each of these three levels of neural organization concern different functions. At the projective level, responses are of a general involuntary nature, for example, a child's withdrawal from pain or startled reaction to a loud noise. At the integrational level the child's responses are automatic in nature, but the response is the result of some type of association rather than a reflexive reaction. Predictive mechanisms, for example, direct the child's responses to certain sequential grammatical structures. Most children will respond to a given noun phrase such as "Jack and Jill . . . " with an associated verb phrase. At the representational level conscious consideration of meaning occurs. Associations between representations are the *outcome* of actions at this level. Mediation is stressed and becomes the essential element in the development of meaning.

In addition to his three stages, Osgood postulated three levels of language functioning: decoding, association, and encoding. Decoding is synonymous with the more familiar term, reception. Encoding corresponds to expression. Association refers to the mediating process.

The Wepman Model

At the same time, Joseph Wepman and his colleagues were also engaged in developing a model of communication, primarily from clinical work with aphasic

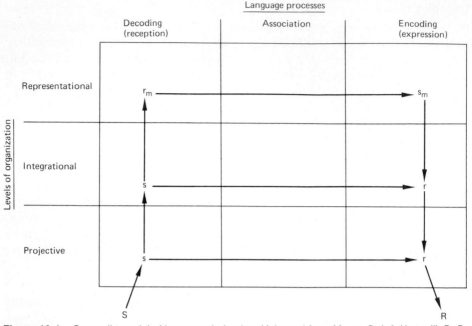

Figure 12-1   Osgood's model of language behavior. *(Adapted from Myers, P. I. & Hammill, D. D.* Methods for learning disorders. *New York: Wiley, 1976.)*

patients. Wepman's model contributed to the understanding of communication through the inclusion of a feedback mechanism, a memory component, and the defining of modalities of transmission (auditory and visual modes of input and vocal and motor modes of output). Both Wepman's model and Osgood's model, however, remained essentially similar.

The *ITPA*

Building upon the early work of Seiver who attempted to synthesize the Osgood and Wepman models of communication, Kirk, McCarthy, and Kirk (1963) developed a test that was to dominate both language assessment and intervention programs in the schools, especially in learning disabilities. The test was called *The Illinois Test of Psycholinguistic Abilities,* but is generally known by its initials, the *ITPA.* The model is displayed in Figure 12-2. The subtests of the *ITPA* can be related to the representational and integrational (automatic) levels of Osgood's model. At the representational level, the six subtests are:

  1   Auditory Reception: In this subtest, the child's ability to differentiate meaningful from nonmeaningful sentences is measured. The child is required to answer "yes" or "no" to questions such as "Do porpoises precipitate?"
  2   Visual Reception: In this subtest, the child is presented with a visual stimulus and is then required to choose (by pointing) a conceptually similar one from among four alternatives.

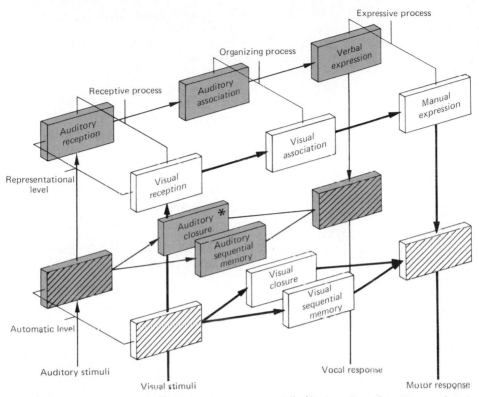

Figure 12-2 The model of the Illinois Test of Psycholinguistic Abilities. *(From Paraskevopoulos, J. N. & Kirk, S. A. The development and psychometric characteristics of the Revised Illinois Test of Psycholinguistic Abilities. Urbana, Illinois: University of Illinois Press, 1969, p. 14. © 1969 by the Board of Trustees of the University of Illinois.)*

3 Auditory Association: This subtest, designed to evaluate the development of semiautonomic systems in the child, requires that the child respond to a series of verbal analogies by completing the second half of an analogy, such as "Sugar is white; grass is————."

4 Visual Association: Children are asked in this subtest to associate concepts. The stimulus consists of a picture to which the children respond by pointing to one of four choices. They are asked "What goes with this?"

5 Verbal Expression: Here the child is asked to describe a series of objects presented one by one. The child is evaluated with respect to his ability to verbalize about the color, size, shape, function, etc. of the object in question.

6 Manual Expression: The last subtest of the representational portion of the *ITPA* is that of manual expression. A series of pictures is shown to the child with the requirement that the child pantomime the use to which the object is put.

At the automatic level six additional subtests are included that assess functions thought to be automatic in nature, although highly organized and integrated. These six subtests are:

1 Grammatic Closure: This subtest attempts to assess the child's understanding of English syntax. It is a completion task in which the child is presented with pictures and a stimulus sentence with part omitted. For example, the child may be shown pictures: one with a dog and one with two dogs. The examiner would say, "Here is a dog. Here are two ———."

2 Auditory Closure (optional): This subtest assesses the ability to generate a whole word when only parts of the word are presented. An example would be the oral presentation of "–ovie –tar," with the child expected to reply "movie star."

3 Visual Closure: This subtest assesses the child's ability to identify an object when only part is shown, for example, to identify a *shoe* when only a *heel* is visible in the drawing.

4 Sound Blending (optional): This subtest requires the child to synthesize a series of separate phonemes presented orally into a word.

5 Auditory Sequential Memory: Essentially a test of digit span, the goal of this test is to ascertain the child's short-term memory ability.

6 Visual Sequential Memory: A visual test of short-term memory, this test asks the child to reconstruct from memory a sequence of nonmeaningful geometric designs.

These twelve subtests (ten mandatory and two optional) form the body of the *ITPA*. The extensive use of the *ITPA* qualifies it as the basis of an entire test-related approach to learning disabilities. In fact, for a number of years, the *ITPA* was to the learning disabilities specialist what IQ tests were to the psychologist: the major tool of the trade. As we shall see in the section dealing with intervention, numerous techniques and teaching devices have been based upon the *ITPA*. Because it had such a profound impact on the direction the field of learning disabilities was to take, we will review the *ITPA* model in detail.

Assumptions Underlying the *ITPA* and Related Programs   The *ITPA* is based on a number of assumptions. First, the model assumes that an appropriate frame of reference for analyzing the language of children is that of adult communication. Variations in language use between adult and child, therefore, are viewed as important only from a quantitative perspective. The model also assumes that language acquisition can be understood in terms of the principles of learning theory, and therefore does not attempt to elucidate sequences of acquisition of specific language structures. Furthermore, the model regards the factors identified as discrete and isolatable. Functioning, for example, at the auditory representational level is viewed as separate and distinct from functioning at the auditory association level. Each of the discrete elements described by the model is assumed to be *essential* for adequate language functioning. Should any be at deficit, school achievement and language functioning would be expected to be adversely affected. Finally, the model assumes that once a problem has been identified, intervention can be instituted that will not only improve the underlying abilities, but also language and academic functioning.

ITPA-**Related Interventions**   Since the *ITPA* has been the main source of assessment of psycholinguistic abilities over the past two decades, remediation techniques based on the *ITPA* model have formed the basis of a number of intervention programs. The MWM Program for Developing Language Abilities (Minskoff, Wiseman, & Minskoff, 1972), the GOAL program (Karnes, 1972), and Aids to Psycholinguistic Teaching (Bush & Giles, 1977) are three representative programs. Each consists of remedial activities based upon the ability areas specified by the *ITPA*. Although each program is unique in terms of the activities suggested for remediation, all rest upon the same assumptions: the abilities are discrete; the abilities are necessary for language and academic achievement; the abilities are trainable.

Some examples of activities from these programs should suffice to indicate the nature of instruction. The Bush and Giles material suggests that for training visual association, appropriate activities would be picture dominoes, or interpreting abstract art work. For auditory sequential memory, appropriate activities would be verbatim repetition of sentences, related words, or unrelated words. For manual expression, activities that include charades or pantomime would be advocated. Minskoff, Wiseman, and Minskoff suggest that for training of auditory discrimination (a sub-area of auditory reception) an appropriate activity would differentiate among various environmental sounds, beginning with the concept of same and different, and ending with the specific identification of the sound. For the GOAL program auditory sequential memory is remediated through teaching the child to respond to sequences of tapping sounds made by the teacher. This last activity is similar to the suggestion by Kirk and Kirk (1971) that for children with deficits in auditory sequential memory "Help direct attention to details, using motor cues, by: (a) when presenting a series to be repeated by the child . . . , tapping or making some dramatic gesture with each element of the series; (b) asking the child to make some motor response, such as tapping or clapping each time an item is given" (p. 160).

Another Osgood-oriented language training program is the Peabody Language Development Kits (PLDK). The PLDK (Dunn & Smith, 1968) is perhaps the most widely used of the language intervention programs in classrooms. The kits were developed using a synthesis of Osgood's model and the work of Guilford. See Figure 12-3. The focus of the kits is on the training of global language ability, as opposed to the specific abilities approach of the other models reviewed. The authors noted that an attempt was made to focus on the development of "an automatic level of sentence structure, reflecting basic syntactic rules" (1968, p. xxi). An attempt was made during the development of the kits to adhere as much as possible to the behavior modification principles of Skinner. Unfortunately, the PLDK suffers from the same faulty assumptions regarding language as do other programs developed from an Osgoodian tradition.

> Like the *ITPA*, it is based upon a model of psycholinguistic processes that has been demonstrated time and time again to be *empirically* and *in principle* incapable of

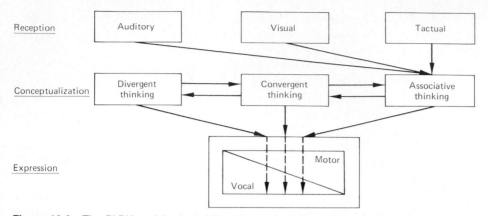

Figure 12-3 The PLDK model adapted from the work of Osgood and Guilford. *(Adapted from Dunn, L. M. & Smith, J. O.* The Peabody Language Development Kits. *Circle Pines, Minnesota, 1968.)*

characterizing human language functioning (especially the knowledge that underlies linguistic performance) as we know it (Rosenberg, 1970, p. 212).

It appears that the only redeeming feature of the PLDK is that it generally stimulates children to become more communicative, although the level of language ability is not changed (Hammill & Wiederholt, 1973).

Examination of the Assumptions Underlying the *ITPA*   Two of the assumptions underlying the specific abilities model (those dealing with adult-based concepts of language processing and the lack of interest regarding the sequence of acquisition in the development of language) are to be considered more philosophical in nature than the other four. These two assumptions are more difficult to test than the others. Since both address the same area, they will be dealt with together. Some of the most compelling reasons for questioning these assumptions are found in the literature dealing with the acquisition of language and the current research mapping linguistic strategies onto emerging cognitive abilities. Research from the fields of cognitive and developmental psychology leave little doubt that a child's cognitive abilities evolve in such a way as to indicate differential abilities at different developmental periods, with each level being qualitatively distinct from the preceding and succeeding ones (Bloom & Lahey, 1978; Gallagher & Reid, in press; Sinclair-de Zwart, 1973). Language has a strong symbiotic relationship to cognitive development (Bloom & Lahey, 1978; Braine, 1965, 1971, 1979; Palermo & Molfese, 1972; Verhave, 1972).

It is, for example, possible to assume that there are inherent schema (principles of organization or cognitive structures) and that these structures are crucial in determining the form of output (Verhave, 1972, p. 192).

This interactionist position argues that since adult and child cognitive structures differ, adult and child language differ. Miller and Yoder (1972) have cogently argued that a developmental approach to the assessment and intervention of child language difficulties *must* be utilized, regardless of the theoretical framework in which the intervention or assessment takes place (that is, whether the program is based on principles of behavioral or cognitive psychology). The *ITPA*, of course, does not do that.

The third assumption regarding the discrete nature of the abilities measured will be examined using the research pertaining to the *ITPA*. This assumption consists of two parts: (1) the specific subtests are discrete, and (2) the dimensions of the model (levels of neural organization, processes, and modalities) are discrete. A number of excellent reviews have addressed these issues: Sedlak and Weener (1973); Proger, Cross, and Burger (1973); Newcomer and Hammill (1976).

What we are asking, in effect, by looking at this assumption, is whether the *ITPA* has construct validity. One major method of establishing the construct validity of a device is to factor analyze it, expecting that the emergent factor structure will replicate the theoretical model. One would expect that, if the model hypothesized the existence of a visual channel and an auditory channel, the factor structure would emerge with a factor representing the visual tasks, and one representing the auditory tasks. The studies that have employed only the subtests of the *ITPA* in the factor analyses (without any criterion tests) offer scant support for the channel-level-process model on which the *ITPA* is based (Sedlak & Weener, 1973, p. 124). Proger, Cross, and Berger (1973), on the other hand, concluded that some consistent results are evidenced: a general psycholinguistic factor often emerges and channel abilities emerge with frequency. Their main criticisms of the factor studies are that any given factor structure can change with the population being studied, and that the use of subtests to define emerging structures is questionable. Sedlak and Weener, however, raise the most critical question: given the *ITPA* model (in which three dimensions—organization, channels, and processes—are postulated), what would be the appropriate factor structure to hypothesize, since the emergence of one dimension would of necessity violate another? "Factors which would honor channel distinctions would violate level and process distinctions; factors which would honor process distinctions would cut across channels and levels, and so forth" (Sedlak & Weener, 1973, p. 125). Newcomer and Hammill (1976) dismiss the importance of these studies altogether for lack of appropriate criterion tests. When criterion tests are left out, the result is "a treatment which maximized their intercorrelations and resulted in multiple subtest loadings on large general factors" (p. 36).

If factor studies are reviewed which do use criterion measures, the situation becomes more clear. Two studies (Hare, Hammill, & Bartel, 1973; Newcomer, Hare, Hammill, & McGettigan, 1975) in which the *ITPA* was factor analyzed along with criterion measures designed to tap each of the *ITPA* subtest areas confirmed the structure of the *ITPA* at least for the dimensions of organization and process. "Any weakness regarding the construct validity of the ITPA subtest appears primarily due to the modality dimension" (Newcomer & Hammill, 1976, p. 37).[1]

The differences between the results of studies using criterion measures and those which do not employ such measures are significant. While studies using only the subtests of the *ITPA* indicated that the channels of communication often emerged, those using the criterion measures found no evidence whatsoever for the existence of such channels. This finding is important, since one very extensive use to which the *ITPA* has been put is determining the modality preferences of children. Newcomer and Hammill (1976) suggested that:

> While certain groups of individuals may produce characteristic patterns of modality strengths and weaknesses, this information has no empirically demonstrated relevance for academic instruction (p. 62).

Similarly, Proger, Cross, and Burger (1973) concluded that:

> While one would *like* to believe that individualizing instruction on the basis of modality strengths leads to more efficient progress, the research reviewed . . . does not support this view (p. 175).

The fourth assumption concerning the *ITPA* is that the abilities identified are, in fact, related to language and should any or all of these abilities be at deficit, language functioning will be adversely affected. Of course, the assumption here is that the abilities, in fact, measure language. First, from an analysis of what appears to be current thinking regarding what is language, the *ITPA* is, *at best,* a model of communication. Yet, even as a measure of communication, the model is inadequate as judged by its developer (Osgood, 1975). Language *can be viewed as communication, as a code, or as information processing, but not* as a composite of discrete abilities. Except for studies examining the relation of the *ITPA* to the Parsons Language Sample, there is, as pointed out by Newcomer and Hammill (1976), a noticeable lack of research attempting to relate the *ITPA* to recognized measures of language. As a result, the belief that the *ITPA* is a measure of language rests more on faith than evidence.

The next two assumptions, regarding the ability to improve deficit functions and their relation to academic achievement, are of extreme importance. These underlie the uses to which the *ITPA* has been put. The research on the "trainability" of the *ITPA* abilities has been negative. Numerous methods of intervention have been employed in attempts to "train" the abilities identified

---

[1]Since it is frequently argued (cf. Hall, 1980) that many of the problems in demonstrating the strengths of the specific abilities tests (both in language and perceptual-motor skills) and their applications to instruction have resulted from sample hereogeneity which results from poorly operationalized definitions of learning disability, it should be noted that these studies were carried out on normal fourth-grade children.

by the *ITPA* as deficient. Among these are included (but by no means restricted to) activities and programs developed by Kirk and Kirk (1971), Bush and Giles (1969), Karnes (1972), and Minskoff, Wiseman, and Minskoff (1972). In addition, others have attempted to analyze the training programs with reference to the length of time in training, the types of subjects, the materials used, the number of subjects, and the measures used in assessing performance (Hammill & Larson, 1974; Newcomer & Hammill, 1976; Proger, Cross, & Burger, 1973; Sedlak & Weener, 1973). The most significant finding of these reviews is the lack of consistent, replicable results. A simple reporting of the number of studies involved in attempts at training psycholinguistic processes is astounding. Newcomer and Hammill (1976) report that over 281 studies were conducted between the years of 1962 to 1973. In spite of the vast number of studies, the results are unclear.

Newcomer and Hammill (1976) reported their review of the training studies by discussing the findings according to the populations studied. For example, with the retarded population, they conclude that "there was not a single subtest for which a majority of the researchers reported that training was beneficial" (p. 73). Considering the disadvantaged, they found evidence of positive effects of training only for those subtests related to association skills and verbal expression. At the preschool level, positive effects of training were noted at the associational level. For the elementary school-aged child, the verbal expression area and subtests of general language ability appear to be open to remediation. When all studies are reviewed, only two subtests appear consistently amenable to intervention, the Auditory Association subtest and the Verbal Expression subtest. Most unlikely to respond to intervention are the Visual Sequential Memory subtest and the Visual Closure subtest. Comparable results were found by Logan and Colarusso (1978) for the GOAL and MWM programs. Findings such as these are extremely disconcerting when one considers the extensive use of both the *ITPA* and *ITPA*-related training systems in our schools. The major conclusion to be drawn is that the efficacy of training psycholinguistic functioning has not been demonstrated.

Effects on Academic Gains   Referring to the relation of the abilities to academic achievement, Newcomer (1975) stated that for all intents and purposes, there exists an "insignificant and partially useless relationship between most *ITPA* subtests and measures of academic achievement" (p. 403). Sedlak and Weener concluded:

> The crucial question, therefore, appears to be to what extent remediation programs directed at psycholinguistic deficits will affect measures of school achievement. The results thus far indicate that programs directed solely at psycholinguistic deficits have little, if any, effect on school achievement (p. 142).

Despite research findings and the major changes in theoretically accepted positions in the fields of psychology and psycholinguistics, the controversy over the *ITPA* and related training programs continues. In the absence of new data to support the position, defenders (cf. Lund, Foster, & McCall-Perez, 1978) continue to challenge the conclusions reached by opponents (Hammill & Larsen, 1974, 1978). Unfortunately, the continued defense of what appears to be a highly untenable position neither clarifies the issues nor furthers the state of the art.

The last assumption, that abilities measured by the *ITPA* are necessary for academic success, also fairs poorly. The reviews of Sedlak and Weener, Hammill and Larsen, and Newcomer and Hammill are exceedingly consistent in their findings for the areas of reading, spelling, and arithmetic: *when IQ is controlled, no subtest is significantly correlated.* Inability to confirm the model's assumptions plus the knowledge that the test itself is not valid, reliable, or adequately normed (see Chapter 10) has led us to conclude that use of the *ITPA* for educational diagnosis and/or intervention can be neither recommended nor supported.

Behavioral Models and Programs

Thus far, the impression has been given that the Osgoodian model is the only associationist model in learning disabilities. This is not so. Other models more current and in many ways more influential are available.

The common thread among the programs to be described is that the principles of learning theory constitute the instructional techniques. What differentiates the programs is their content and whether they focus on language directly (syntax, semantics, and phonology) or on related behaviors. Braine's (1963, 1965) early theory of contextual generalization, for example, postulated that a segment of a sentence, because it has been experienced within the contexts and constraints of other components of a sentence, would recur within the same sentential position. Braine's more recent work (1979) has focused on the learnability of language, and he has proposed a model for the analysis of language by means of a language scanner which, rather than creating hypotheses about what rules are good to learn, holds the rules in a center that allows for comparison to other sentences, past experience, and nonrule sentences.

Interesting though the theories of such neobehaviorists may be, they have not been translated into intervention strategies or techniques and, therefore, have little direct usefulness. Other approaches have had a more direct effect. They comprise two program groups. The first group is characterized by the work of Dever (1978) and Gray and Ryan (1973). Their program goals were derived from developmental psycholinguists, but their orientation to instruction and the sequencing of language structures is clearly behavioral. A second group, of which the DISTAR Language Program (Englemann & Osborn, 1972) is illustrative, defines both its goals and interventions in accordance with behavioral principles.

Teaching the American Language to Kids (TALK)   The TALK program (Dever, 1978b) is based on hierarchical task analysis, that is, an analysis that begins at the goal and works backward through what appear to be logically sequenced behaviors. (See Figure 12-4 for an example.) One potential problem of hierarchical task analysis is that the sequence identified for instructional purposes may not reflect the sequence of spontaneous development. Though originally developed for use with mentally retarded individuals, the program has application to less severely impaired children and may prove useful with some learning disabled children. The newness of the TALK program precludes a discussion of the full extent of its effectiveness.

Monterey Language Program: Programmed Conditioning for Language (PCL)   The PCL differs from TALK in that it attempts to teach a broader spectrum of language skills, focuses on oral response, and is highly developed in terms of program sequence (Gray & Ryan, 1972). The PCL was originally based upon developmental sequences in child language acquisition, but the sequence was revised to accomodate the technology employed. The PCL's success rests upon its exceedingly well-designed program. The program utilizes basic behavioral programming technology and principles. Though some research evidence has been obtained that attests to the usefulness of the program and transference from one setting to another (Gray & Ryan, 1973), it is tentative, and further research with this method is necessary.

Both of the above mentioned programs are quite different from the Osgoodian approach to language intervention. They are, in a sense, a hybrid of developmental language information and behavioral technology. One problem with these approaches is the emphasis on language structures, rather than on the communicative use of the language. These programs are not the only ones that attempt to combine behavioral technology with developmental psycholinguistics. The Bricker and Bricker program (1974) attempts to combine behavioral technology with developmental psycholinguistics and Piagetian theory, while others (Miller & Yoder, 1974) follow more closely the tradition of Dever and Gray and Ryan.

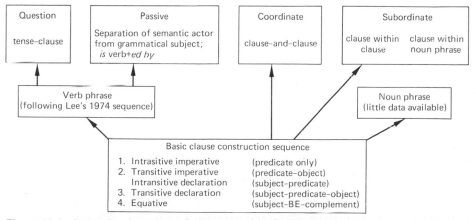

Figure 12-4   Instructional sequence *(bottom to top)* for English question, passive, coordinate, and subordinate construction. *(From Dever, R. B. Language assessment through specification of goals and objectives.* Exceptional Children, *1978, 45, pp. 124-129.)* Reprinted by permission of The Council for Exceptional Children. © 1978 by The Council for Exceptional Children.

DISTAR: Language The last program to be discussed is DISTAR. Developed to be used as a classroom teaching device, the program is meticulously sequenced and contains explicit directions to the instructor. The material contained in the program is taken directly from the language of the classroom and is thought to be necessary for children to succeed in school. It is based upon concept analysis that teaches the child the set of characteristics that define the concept, the set of nonexamples of the concept, and the set of irrelevant instances. The material included does not follow any accepted theory of language development. As Englemann and Osborn noted (1969, p. 6), "They must have mastered the language of instruction, which encompasses all the basic descriptions used by the teacher to discuss examples of a concept." The contents of the three DISTAR language programs are presented in Table 12-1. A perusal indicates that the content of the language programs is, indeed, the language of the traditional classroom. Two questions arise. First, how well does success in the program correlate with accepted language measures? Second, what is the relationship of this learning to nonclassroom language (language in the broader world)? At this time, there is not enough information to answer these questions.

Summary

This section has dealt with the influence of associationism on educational strategies in language. Three types of programs have been described: (1)

Table 12-1   Sample Content from DISTAR I, II, and III: Language

DISTAR I
    Descriptions of objects
    Actions
    Instructional words
    Classification
    Information
    Applications
DISTAR II
    Definitions
    Descriptions
    Questioning
    Analogies
    Synonyms
    Opposites
    Verb tenses
DISTAR III
    Sentence discrimination
    Identification of subject, predicate, verb
    Subject-verb agreement
    Punctuation
    Identification of adjectives and adverbs
    Discrimination of questions, statements, commands

Source: Englemann & Osborn, 1971, 1972, 1976.

ITPA-related programs derived from the models of Osgood and Wepman, (2) the programs that use developmental sequences combined with behavioral intervention, and (3) programs that are more purely behavioral. Because each is rather unique in its contribution, it is difficult to critique them as a group. Problems with the *ITPA*-oriented materials have already been discussed. The programs of Dever and Gray and Ryan run the risk of other behavioral programs, i.e., transference. If learning can be shown to transfer effects, and if the gains are long-lasting and related to methods of language assessment which acknowledge distinctions between adult and child language, then they are potentially useful to teachers of the learning disabled. Without additional research, little can be added about their effectiveness.

With respect to the DISTAR program, two objections arise. First, the program is more accurately described as concept-learning, rather than a language-learning, experience. Language is simply a tool. Second, whether the content of the DISTAR Language Program is valid is unanswered. There is not enough research to assess its effectiveness at any level.

One common thread among these programs is that they assume that children learn language according to the principles of learning theory. Yet, there is no indication that this is true. From what is known about language development and acquisition, children develop language to achieve communication and a degree of control over the environment. Intervention that stresses communication and use is of primary interest when dealing with the child for whom there is the possibility of achieving normal language capabilities, and who comes to school already with language. For extremely disabled children, whose functioning is essentially nonverbal, behavioral intervention might be desirable. For the mildly handicapped child, such intervention would seem inappropriate.

THE NATURE OF LANGUAGE: THE COGNITIVE-DEVELOPMENTAL APPROACH

There exists a group of psycholinguists who view language as a code of communication (Bloom & Lahey, 1978), as the function or use of that communication in an interaction between or among people (Halliday, 1978), and as the processing of linguistic information (Bever, 1970). For these individuals, language is inextricably bound to the cognitive development of the child, or to the development of specific linguistic structures.

Chomsky's seminal theorizing in transformational generative grammar (1959, 1965) was most probably the greatest impetus for developmental psycholinguistics.[2] In the 1960s linguistics and psychology were becoming more and more closely aligned. Information processing theorists were seeing the necessity for studying child language. Psycholinguists were beginning to consider

[2]The contributions of others such as Slobin (1971), McNeill (1966), Brown (1958), Menyuk (1964), and Berko (1958), to mention a few, and the ofttimes forgotten European theorists of the Piagetian tradition (especially Sinclair-de Zwart, 1973) must also be recognized for the impact on the study of child language.

the study of cognition a field within psycholinguistics, one that Miller (1965) referred to as cognitive psycholinguistics. This new strain of psycholinguistics would, in Miller's words:

> . . . be forced to accept a more cognitive approach . . . , to talk about hypothesis testing instead of discrimination learning, about the evaluation of hypotheses instead of the reinforcement of responses, about rules instead of habits, about productivity instead of generalizations, about innate and universal human capabilities instead of special methods of teaching vocal responses, about symbols instead of conditioned stimuli, about sentences instead of words or vocal noises, about linguistic structure instead of chains of responses—in short, about language instead of learning theory (p. 20).

Evolving from a tradition which is nativistic or rationalistic in orientation (although this emphasis varies, as will be seen), this group of cognitive psycholinguists viewed language as acquired *by the active child* in the absence of direct language teaching. Language then becomes an actively constructed system developed by each individual from his or her personal experience with objects and persons:

> That is, language is not learned in the sense of the direct acquisition of knowledge from experience but rather as the induction of rules and categories across many instances. Meaning, for example, derives not from associations, but from a dynamic creative process of the child as he or she interacts with and draws from the environment (Hresko & Reid, 1978, p. 6).

Differences between the associationist tradition and the cognitive psycholinguistic model are profound. First, the cognitive psycholinguists believe that language is acquired without direct instruction. Language, therefore, cannot be remediated by direct, structured imparting of knowledge. Second, the psycholinguistic model assumes that there are differences in the structure of adult and child language. Third, the model assumes that the focus of language research should be on the semantic, syntactic, and phonological capabilities of the child. Finally, the model assumes that since education usually takes place within the context of a social setting, poor language *usage* may seriously limit the child who demonstrates competent language *abilities*. Before addressing each of these assumptions with respect to their research findings, let us look at the meaning of acquisition and how the model handles problems in acquisition.

Language Acquisition

From a cognitive psycholinguistic perspective, there are two important views of how a child acquires language. First, as proposed by Chomsky (1965) and McNeill (1966), the child is endowed with universal language structures, a natural ability or propensity to acquire language. This model proposes the existence of a language acquisition device (LAD). While useful in explaining the occurrence of linguistic universals, the LAD tells us little of the nature of the acquisition, or the relation of the emergence of language to other emerging systems. The other view of language acquisition (Bloom, 1970; Bloom & Lahey, 1978; Sinclair-de Zwart, 1973) suggests that what comes into play in the acquisition of language are more general cognitive structures, and that the cognitive and linguistic systems are inextricably bound in development. Language then depends not on unique language acquisition devices, but on the same organizing and structuring propensity that more general cognitive development depends upon. The child then employs this structuring propensity to extract from interactions with the environment (that is, objects, people, and actions), the information necessary to construct an exemplar of the linguistic code, subject to the social constraints of his or her surroundings. Thus, the child learns (in the broad sense) the system (or code), how to function with the code, and how to express various meanings (to others) with the code. The child is *not* a passive individual who simply absorbs what others provide; rather, he or she actively sorts and chooses the information to attend to, tries various combinations to see their effect, and thence constructs language. There is no evidence whatsoever to suggest that the child classified as learning disabled acquires language in a different way.

Research

First, the cognitive psycholinguistic model, as noted, does not ascribe to the position that language can be taught, since it is not "learned." Evidence relevant to this assumption comes from a number of different sources (de Villiers & de Villiers, 1978). For instance, it has been noted that if language were learned through methods of association, the infinite number of sentences and words to which one would have to be exposed would be astronomical. Second, children learn correct usage even when the models to which they are exposed are inadequate. Third, children during language acquisition are observed to make errors in usage, as if attempting to develop a rule by generalizing an instance. For example, children say "goed" or "comed" when first learning the rule for forming the past tense of irregular words even though previously they had been observed to use "went" and "came." In addition, cognitive psycholinguists recognize that although operant techniques appear useful in teaching some specific language structures, the programs are less than successful when generalization to novel situations is necessary.

Early diary studies, and more recently, studies by Brown (1973), Bloom (1970), and Bloom, Lightbown, and Hood (1975) regarding adult/child language differences have supported evidence that language structures appear across children in a given sequence, and that this sequence is relatively invariant (Bloom & Lahey, 1978). Differences in the well-formedness of the language have been noted along with differences in apparent processing ability. Even when the utterances between child and adult appear the same, Bloom and Lahey (1978) maintain that:

> . . . although adult and child utterances may be identical in their surface form, there are almost certainly important differences between their underlying cognitive and linguistic representations (p. 253).

The difference between the associationists and the cognitive psycholinguists rests on their beliefs of what language is and how one intervenes. Language when viewed as a communication code can be seen to have little use for postulated underlying abilities or labels and sentence patterns. Therefore, the proper focus of research is on the form of language, the content expressed, and the use to which the child puts language.

The focus of the associationist model is on performance variables that affect the ability to attend to information in the environment. Several points must be noted. First, the psychological variables that affect information processing are *not,* in and of themselves, language. Second, most individuals with underlying ability deficits learn language in spite of their deficits and after language is attained, *still have their specific deficits.* Bloom & Lahey (1978) have even shown that specific, underlying deficits may, in fact, be compensated for through the use of language.

In regard to the assumption that even children with adequate, measured *language ability* may have problems with *language usage,* research with the learning disabled is highly relevant. Bryan (1978) reviewed the work on social abilities of the learning disabled, and concluded that they perform less adequately than their peers in social settings requiring language. Similarly, Bloom (1977) found that one aspect of the learning disabled child's language problem is in the communicative aspect of language. The learning disabled fail to respond adequately to listeners' reactions to what has been said. The abilities to monitor and to modify language to meet demands of the situation are often impaired.

The cognitive psycholinguists are at variance with a number of the positions taken by the proponents of the specific abilities and behavioral orientations. Perhaps the most important is what constitutes the basis for studying language. For them (and for us) the proper study of language is language, not processing variables related to language, especially if the goal of the program is to intervene in the child's language development. Intervention, however, must recognize in a way the behaviorists fail to do that it is the child who must construct language. The learning of particular content, therefore, is viewed as an inappropriate instructional goal. Language learning is instead viewed as having to be flexible and creative, both syntactically and semantically.

A comparison of the Osgoodian and cognitive psycholinguistic approaches indicates disagreement at the most fundamental level—the theories simply do not interact. Perhaps *the* point of agreement of the conventional and alternative approaches is that both believe adequate function of the components of their respective theories is necessary for school success. Fundamental differences, however, as to what constitutes language, whether language can be taught, and the methods of intervention provide significant obstacles to any synthesis of the models.

Cognitive Psycholinguistics and the Learning Disabled

Since we are probably dealing with a population whose characteristics include neurological involvement, the question of how the theory handles neurological impairment is important. The literature has shown that neurological impairment might affect a child's acquisition of language in a number of ways: (1) by limiting the child's ability to extract information from the environment and hence structure linguistic material, and (2) by limiting the child's ability during certain critical stages of language development. Researchers have only begun to investigate questions of *how* neurological impairment might affect language acquisition. Most of the efforts of the psycholinguists have centered on determining the sequence and strategies employed in language acquisition.

With more of the biological nature of the child being recognized in the cognitive psycholinguistic approach, the theory is able to absorb ideas of critical periods of language development. In Lenneberg's now classic work (1967), he presented the idea that during the child's neurobiological growth, there exist certain time spans that are critical for the acquisition of language. Among the evidence cited is the finding that depending on the age at onset, the condition known as aphasia (problems with oral language ability) has differential prognoses. The younger, the better chances are for the remission of symptoms. Others have analyzed the mylination of the nervous system, relating that phenomenon to language acquisition. The cognitive psycholinguistic model has no difficulty in incorporating these findings. They reflect an understanding of the interaction of the organism with the environment, an interaction that is, to a large extent, a function of the intactness of the organism.

Of critical import is the manner in which the concept of maturational lag is handled. The psycholinguists recognize that individuals acquire language (and other abilities) at differing rates. For some children, the process appears to move at an average rate, for others, the sequence is more rapid, and for some, the sequence is normal but the rate is delayed. If the child is maturing neurologically at a delayed pace, the development of structures dependent on neurological functioning would also be expected to be delayed. Regarding the question of defective language (in that the language is inferior or intrinsically disturbed), the cognitive psycholinguists recognize that distortions may occur in the child's acquisition of language or in the manner in which the language is employed (Bloom & Lahey, 1978).

The syntax of the learning disabled has been studied by a number of researchers, employing both experimental tasks and established language assessment devices. Hresko (1979), employing an experimental sentence repetition task based on the work of Clay (1971), found that five- and six-year-old learning disabled children were much poorer in the development of syntactic ability than normal children of the same age group. They evidenced difficulty with sentences exemplifying unfamiliar declarative constructions, preposed clauses and phrases, and relative clauses. In addition, the use of function words was inferior. Similar sentence repetition studies of the learning disabled have revealed difficulties with other constructions: contractions, conjunctions, noun-pronoun reference, number agreement, and the use of the verb "to be" (McCoulskey, 1971; Rosenthal, 1970; Young, 1971).

Wiig, Semel, and Crouse (1973) and Hresko, Rosenberg, and Buchanan (1977) found differences in morphological ability between normal and learning disabled children. Their results led them to conclude that the learning disabled children were delayed in the acquisition and development of morphological rules.

Using the *Northwestern Syntax Screening Test (NSST),* Wiig and Semel (1975) found differences between learning disabled children and normal children in both the expressive and receptive domains. On the expressive portion of the test, 62 percent of the learning disabled scored below the 25th percentile. Concerned with the abilities of the learning disabled child through adolescence, Wiig and Semel (1975) assessed productive capabilities in a task requiring the adolescent to include a stimulus word in a self-produced sentence. Wiig and Semel indicated that the learning disabled adolescent was more likely to produce either an ungrammatical sentence or an incomplete sentence than normal children.

As can be seen, the cognitive psycholinguistic approach has been successful in establishing some syntactic characteristics of the learning disabled, at both elementary school-age and during adolescence. The small number of studies reviewed here are illustrative of an increasingly large body of literature. For a more comprehensive treatment the reader is referred to reviews by Bryan (1978) and Wiig and Semel (1980).

As the general field of cognitive psycholinguistics has moved from an isolated consideration of syntax to interest in the semantic aspects of language, so have those interested in the learning disabled included in their research evaluations of the semantic capabilities of the learning disabled. In the study of Hresko, Rosenberg, and Buchanan cited earlier, learning disabled children were found to have vocabulary deficits, evidenced by lack of facility with nouns, adjectives, verbs, and adverbs. This finding is at variance with that of Wiig and Semel (1976) who report no difficulty on the part of the learning disabled with respect to vocabulary. Their finding, however, is restricted to nouns and not the other classes noted by Hresko, Rosenberg, and Buchanan. Wiig and Semel (1975) assessed the abilities of learning disabled adolescents to picture name (Visual Confrontation subtest of the *Boston VA Aphasia Test,* Goodglass & Kaplan, 1972) and to retrieve and name antonyms (Verbal Opposites subtest of the *Detroit Tests of Learning Aptitude,* Baker & Leland, 1959). In the results of both tasks, the learning disabled adolescents made more errors and took longer to respond than normal adolescents. Hresko's 1979 sentence repetition study indicated that learning disabled children had more of a tendency to change the semantic elements of the sentence when imitating than did normal children. In analyzing the results of studies dealing with learning disabled children and adolescents with regard to semantics, Wiig and Semel (1976) concluded that:

> The consistent observation across age levels of anomia and verbal paraphasia as an aspect of dyslexia and learning disabilities . . . strengthens the position that the convergent language production deficits in learning disabilities reflect subtle aphasia (p. 216).[3]

[3]For a discussion regarding the inference of aphasia, refer to Chapter 13.

The above studies appear to justify the conclusion that learning disabled children evidence language difficulties. Whether they are best described as aphasic is open to discussion.

The area of phonological development is a sorely neglected one. Although some information exists regarding the discrimination of speech sounds by learning disabled children, descriptions of the articulation ability of these children is lacking. As Turton (1975) pointed out, the relation between auditory discrimination ability and articulation disorders has been advanced by numerous authors (Carrell & Pendergast, 1954; Cohen & Diehl, 1963; Kronvall & Diehl, 1954; Reid, 1947a, 1947b; Templin, 1957). More recent research suggests that any relation between articulation disorders and auditory discrimination problems must be viewed cautiously. Marquardt and Saxman (1972) suggested that any relation is, at best, tenuous. Aram and Nation (1975) indicated that language deficits appear hierarchically ordered in that *problems in semantics subsume problems in syntax and phonology, while problems in syntax subsume only phonology, with problems in phonology standing alone.*[4]

In evaluating research concerning the characteristics of the learning disabled from a framework of syntax, semantics, and phonology, it becomes readily apparent that cognitive psycholinguistics has provided a useful model for studying and explaining language problems of the learning disabled.

Intervention in Language Development: The Cognitive/Developmental Approach

In opposition to the associationist approaches predominant in learning disabilities, this alternative emphasizes the child's abilities in semantics, and secondarily in syntax and phonology. The child's ability to *use* language is also examined, for it is ultimately usage that will be of prime importance. As Rosenberg (1970) stated:

> A language training program should reflect the likelihood that experience is related more to transformational and semantic development than to deep syntactic and phonological development (p. 214).

Very few individuals in the field of learning disabilities have begun to employ the cognitive-psycholinguistic approach in teaching the learning disabled child with language disabilities, and perhaps the main reason is the lack of prepackaged materials and programs. As Cazden (1971) pointed out, interven-

---

[4]Related to this area are the findings concerning inner ear problems with the learning disabled. Both Katz and Illmer (1972) and Wunderlich (1970) have noted the high percentage of learning disabled children who suffer upper respiratory illness and inner ear problems. They note that such disabilities are often related to fluctuating hearing loss. *Otitis media* may also result in hearing loss or difficulty in evaluation (Northern, 1976; Northern & Downs, 1974; Masters & Marsh, 1978). *Otitis media,* a peripheral middle ear deficit, is often misdiagnosed as a central processing deficit and as a result, children suffering from middle ear infections are often misdiagnosed as learning disabled (Miller, 1978). Some caution should be exercised, however, about inferring language impairment on the basis of middle ear pathology (Masters & Marsh, 1978).

tion programs utilizing associationist approaches are much more easily packaged for distribution and, therefore, are much more likely to be popular.

The beginnings of scholastic interest in language development grew out of a belief that facility with language was essential both to thought and to educability (Cazden, 1971). Although the truth of this statement is accepted by many in the field of learning disabilities, there is no clear evidence that the problems of the learning disabled are, in fact, *caused* by language deficits. The discussion to be developed here, therefore, will focus on intervention in language development for the sake of *improved language function,* and not with improvement of academic skills as a goal. Although it is popular to talk of language *facilitation* (Bloom & Lahey, 1978), we believe that the term *stimulation* is better. This should not be construed as indicating disagreement with the basic notions proposed by Bloom & Lahey, for we believe, as they, that:

> The rules of language cannot be written out, described, or otherwise given to the language learner. . . . The rules of language must be induced by the learner from tangible experiences with objects and events, linguistic forms, and interpersonal interactions (p. 57).

We do believe, however, as outlined elsewhere (Hresko & Reid, 1979), that the person who intervenes in language development with learning disabled persons must take a more active role than the term *facilitator* suggests. The growth of language depends on the intensity and quality of the *interaction* between the person guiding the intervention and the child. The person who intervenes must direct, develop, and monitor the interaction, maintaining its focus and direction while incorporating those aspects of language to be stressed for the particular child. For these reasons, the term *stimulator,* is preferred. The cognitive-psycholinguistic view of language assumes that language cannot be taught in a didactic manner, but rather that language intervention depends upon the development of opportunities for the child to discover and internalize appropriate adult forms of language. In a variety of settings (both at home and in the school), the child is expected to *extract* the appropriate language structures.

Context-Based Child-Centered Intervention Through guided interaction with other language speakers and experiences, the child will construct appropriate adult language forms and functions. Because of the self-constructive nature of the interaction, the intervention takes place in various situations, with content becoming dependent upon the given context. The *general stimulation* approach is most often employed where a child's language is generally delayed or where the function of the intervention is to replicate the natural process of language acquisition. Emphasizing the semantic aspects of the language development (with syntax and phonology as secondary considerations), the language stimulator attempts to function as a promoter and a responder. The stimulator establishes the setting, the reason for talking, and then engages the child. The *specific stimulation* strategy differs from the general strategy described only in that its focus is on stimulating development of *specific* areas of deficit. This type of strategy is useful in situations in which a child is in the process of acquiring a new structure or is in need of correcting a misuse. These methods differ from the behavioral strategies in that they emphasize the self-generated language of the child in either natural settings or contrived contexts. The strategies of specific and general stimulation are in widespread use in preschools and clinics, but are noticeably absent from school programs for the learning disabled. They depend upon teachers' knowledge of language acquisition and development and teachers' ability to foster meaningful learning interactions in naturally occurring settings. Existing programs, in which materials and methodology are outlined and adherence to a given structure is mandatory, have been much more popular in schools. Yet, time and time again, the argument that they lack empirical and theoretical validity has been raised against such programs (Rosenberg, 1970).

Halliday's Functions Halliday's (1975) description of seven functions of language provides a framework from which the language stimulator can monitor the interactions of the child with others and still focus the interaction when necessary (Hresko & Reid, 1979). Halliday's seven functions include: (1) instrumental function: obtaining self-satisfactory goods and material, (2) regulatory function: control or influence others, (3) interactional function: establishing and maintaining contact, (4) personal function: asserting oneself, (5) heuristic function: exploring and learning about the world and creating personal environments, (6) imaginative: making believe and using language playfully, (7) information function: developing interaction with others. The first four of these appear rather early in the child's development, with heuristic and imaginative functions appearing later, and the informative function being the last to appear. Each of these functions is utilized singularly in the beginning. They are combined only after other aspects of language (such as grammar, vocabulary, and dialogue) have been mastered. As described by Halliday, these seven functions eventually come to distinguish two aspects of meaning: (1) the representation of experience, and (2) the connotative and social aspects of an interaction. As the child develops language that is more closely aligned to that of the adult, the functions are combined so that one utterance accomplishes more than one function and every utterance has both ideational and interpersonal aspects. These functions are useful in defining the social contexts. They are not presented to suggest that the language stimulator should "teach" them. Rather, they constitute a method of defining contexts for general and specific stimulation.

Intervention techniques include those observed in mother-child interactions: (1) repeating, (2) rephrasing, (3) elaborating, (4) prompting, (5) prodding, and (6) answering one's own questions (Snow, 1972). In addition to these, four techniques from learning theory can be applied to the language stimulation setting. These include (1) modification of rate, (2) modification of prosody, (3) reinforcement, and (4) modeling. These techniques are very similar to those found in operation in naturalistic settings. Both modification of rate and prosody are often used by parents during repetitions (when they may slow their speech) and emphasize particular aspects of a word or phrase by changing the intonation or stress. As Ferster points out (1972), the use of natural reinforcers may prove useful.

Both cognitive psycholinguists and behaviorists would agree that the technique of modeling (perhaps the most widely used of the language intervention techniques) is successful but for different reasons. The behaviorist would argue that it is important because imitation occurs. The cognitive psycholinguists would argue that modeling is important, because the child is given the opportunity to have examples of language from which to induce the rules and usages of language.

The Bloom and Lahey Model   A similar approach is that proposed by Bloom and Lahey (1978). This approach rests upon the belief that engineering intervention rests upon three factors: (1) the linguistic needs of the child as determined by evaluating the child's language performance, (2) language development does not consist only of the development of form (words and syntactic structures), but depends also on the development of knowledge of

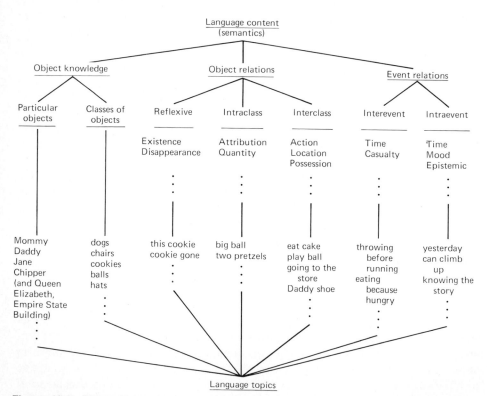

Figure 12-5   The content and topics of language. *(From Bloom, L. & Lahey, M.* Language development and language disorders. *New York: Wiley, 1978, p. 12.)*

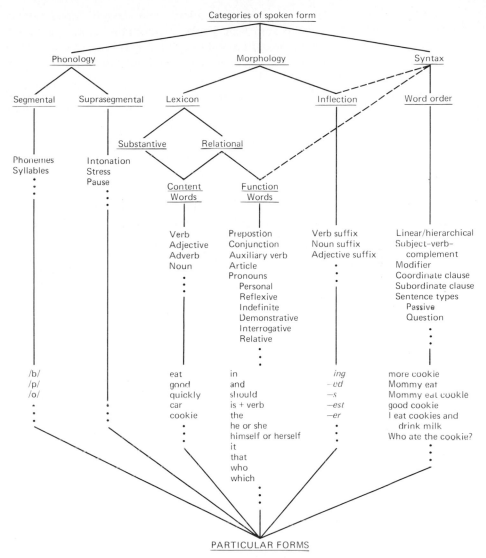

Figure 12-6   The categories of spoken form and particular forms. *(From Bloom, L. & Lahey, M. Language development and lanugage disorders. New York: Wiley, 1978, p. 16.)*

differing contents, and employing language for differing uses, and (3) the most accurate basis upon which to develop language intervention is through the use of knowledge of normal language development. Clearly, Bloom and Lahey pursue a cognitive-developmental psycholinguistic orientation. Figures 12-5, 12-6, and 12-7 have been provided to show the phases of development considered by Bloom and Lahey. There are interactions between content and form, and between content, form, and use. Working upon the premise that language intervention is a unique entity for every child, there are no lesson plans available for the teacher who chooses this approach. Rather, Bloom and Lahey present in their text *Language Development and Language Disorders* (1978) an encompassing view of what language is and how one might go about intervening.

Interactive Language Teaching   An example of the more structured approaches to intervention is the Interactive Language Development Teaching (ILDT) program of Lee, Koenigsknecht, and Mulhern (1975). ILDT is an interactive language development program in that teaching is done through conversational interchange. Of particular importance is that the sequence of language structures designed to be taught has been based upon the theory that normal language development leads to mature adult language. The authors of the program report that clinical research over lengthy periods of time has indicated definite gains on a number of language measures, both of receptive and expressive modes.

The ILDT presents material to be learned in story form, and uses questioning to elicit desired responses. The clinician then helps the child elaborate upon the answer. Clinicians are encouraged to ask questions beyond the lesson to stimulate creative thinking. Table 12-2 presents the interchange techniques suggested by the authors. All of the interchange techniques occur *after* the child has responded, thus allowing the clinician to work with the child's product.

Summary

The differences between the cognitive and associationist persuasions are more than simply differences in instructional methodology. Cognitive approaches view

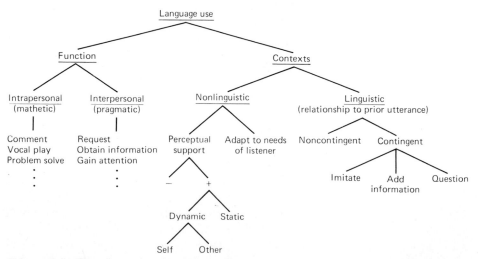

Figure 12-7   The uses of language. *(From Bloom, L. & Lahey, M. Language development and language disorders. New York: Wiley, 1978, p. 19.)*

the child as active, as an initiator of interaction who is sustained by the need to gain more and more knowledge about the various aspects of the world in which he or she lives. Children are not little adults with respect to language. They are developing organisms, whose cognitive and linguistic systems are not only different from adults', but whose growth at any given level is different from that which preceded it and that which is to come. Educators must take these differences into account in their language intervention. Interventions must stress the child's need *to develop,* rather than *to be developed.*

SUMMARY AND CONCLUSIONS

This chapter reviewed the approaches to language that have predominated in the field of learning disabilities and suggested a new direction. The two positions that were described were the associationist and the cognitive—developmental

Table 12-2 Language Interchange Techniques

Technique	Sample Interchange
1 Complete model	Child: That dog.
	Stimulator: That is a dog.
	Child: That is a dog.
2 Reduced model	Child: That dog.
	Stimulator: Is a.
	Child: That is a dog.
3 Expansion request	Child: John painting.
	Stimulator: Tell me all of it.
	Child: John is painting.
	Stimulator: Tell me more.
	Child: John is painting a picture.
4 Repetition request	Child: He eated skedies.
	Stimulator: What did you say?
	Child: He ate skedies.
	Stimulator: Again.
	Child: He ate skedies.
5 Repetition of error	Child: He ate skedies.
	Stimulator: He ate skedies?
	Child: He ate spaghettis.
6 Self-correction request	Child: Mary went, don't she?
	Stimulator: Is that right?
	Child: Mary went, didn't she?
	Stimulator: Is it right now?
	Child: Yes.
7 Rephrased question	Child: Pia sleeped all day.
	Stimulator: Slept.
	Child: Pia slept all day.
	Stimulator: Did Pia sleep all day?
	Child: Yes, Pia slept all day.

Source: Adapted from Lee, L., Koenigsknecht, R. A., & Mulhern, S. T. *Interactive language development teaching.* Evanston, Ill.: Northwestern University Press, 1975.

psycholinguistic. The associationist position is exemplified by the work of Osgood, whose model formed the basis for the *ITPA* and related training programs, as well as models employing behavioral principles for intervention. Serious questions arose concerning the adequacy of the associationist conceptions of language and the interventions advocated.

The cognitive approaches were presented as viewing the child as an active constructor of language. Language was not viewed as the sum of discrete abilities, but rather as a complex code, whose development is intrinsically related to cognitive development. In addition, this approach views child language as essentially different from adult language in the form it takes, the use to which it is put, and the content it describes. Furthermore, differences are noted in the processing of language by both child and adult. The model was presented as more capable of incorporating ideas of maturational lag, neurological impairment, and the idea of critical stages of development.

Intervention from the cognitive view was presented as one of stimulation. Active intervention was stressed. The need for natural language settings to promote growth and the need to develop self-generated language were stressed. Halliday's seven functions of language were presented as one way to contrive context. The Bloom and Lahey work focusing on form, content, and use (rather than phonology, syntax, and semantics) was also advocated. A more structured language intervention program, which has apparently enjoyed some measure of success, was also described.

SUGGESTED READINGS

Bloom, L., & Lahey, M. *Language development and language disorders.* New York: John Wiley & Sons, 1978.

de Villiers, J. G., & de Villiers, P. A. *Language acquisition.* Cambridge, Mass.: Harvard University Press, 1978.

Newcomer, P. L., & Hammill, D. D. *Psycholinguistics in the schools.* Columbus, Ohio: Charles E. Merrill, 1976.

Reading

INTRODUCTION

One of the most critical problems facing a significant number of learning disabled children is their difficulty with reading. No one area of academic difficulty has received more attention in the press, in discussions among teachers, at parent meetings and parent-teacher conferences, in universities and research laboratories, and in legislative assemblies across the country and throughout the world. In a world preoccupied with literacy, the inability of some children (particularly those living in industrialized nations) to read or to read well causes great consternation. In this chapter aspects of reading problems that are relevant to the field of learning disabilities and conventional and innovative approaches to reading and reading instruction will be reviewed in an attempt to determine the wisdom of current practices and to make recommendations for the future.

READING PROBLEMS

Reading problems are referred to by a variety of names, most of them more confusing than helpful. Often children with reading problems are labeled *dyslexic,* for example. Although the term is in widespread use, it means very different things to different people. All too often it is used as if it represents a clearly defined syndrome or, worse yet, a disease. *Dyslexia,* however, is simply a word derived from the Greek that means a difficulty with reading. It is no more suggestive of a disease or a syndrome than the word *headache.* The use of such fancy terms is understandable but unfortunate. When a child is described as having difficulties with reading, that does not seem to imply an explanation. Saying that a child is dyslexic, however, often gives teachers and parents the idea that they now understand *why* the child cannot read! We will use the term dyslexia in the present discussion, because of its current popularity, but we do so advisedly. In this section, we will define the populations to whom this term applies, consider its relation to learning disabilities, describe the characteristics of dyslexics, discuss alternative explanations, subsyndromes and correlates, and finally, suggest possible prognoses.

Definitions of Dyslexia

As Critchley (1970, p. 11) pointed out, the Research Group on Developmental Dyslexia of the World Federation of Neurology recommended the acceptance of two definitions of dyslexia:

> A disorder in children who, despite conventional classroom experience, fail to attain the language skills of reading, writing and spelling commensurate with their intellectual abilities.

> A disorder manifested by difficulty in learning to read despite conventional instruction, adequate intelligence, and sociocultural opportunity. It is dependent upon fundamental cognitive disabilities which are frequently of constitutional origin.

The first definition is clearly more general than the second and describes a wide variety of reading disorders. The definition includes reading problems related to poverty, bilingualism, emotional disturbance, etc. It may be thought of as *secondary dyslexia,* because many of these problems with reading appear to stem from a more pervasive, primary difficulty. The definition has only two restrictions: that the children have conventional classroom experience and that they be unable to read at a level commensurate with their intellectual abilities. These restrictions eliminate children who, for example, fail to learn to read because of prolonged absence from school, poor instruction, or mental retardation. (It should be noted that such children are generally included when terms such as *reading problems* and *retarded readers* are used.)

The second definition refers to specific developmental dyslexia, which may be thought of as *primary dyslexia,* because it is not necessarily related to larger problems. When it is, the relation is only incidental (Critchley, 1970). Children included within this category exhibit difficulties in learning to read despite apparently adequate intelligence, emotional stability, and an instructional program that has proven effective for most of their classmates (HEW National Advisory Committee on Dyslexia and Related Reading Disorders, 1969).

Specific developmental dyslexia is considered to be genetically determined (Brewer, 1973; Critchley, 1970, 1975; Critchley & Critchley, 1978; Hallgren, 1950; Miles & Miles, 1977), because of its frequent occurrence in more than one member of a family and its predominance in boys.

Estimates of the incidence of dyslexia range from 5 percent to 15 percent (Gomez, 1972). Critchley (1975) suggested that the figure for all backward readers is probably around 10 percent of English-speaking children (the problem, by the way, is worldwide) with about one-fifth of the boys and one-twentieth of the girls falling into the category of specific developmental dyslexia. Duane (1974) noted that incidence rates vary with the criteria used to define the handicap:

> Arbitrary determinations of the percentage of children at a given age who fall more than two years behind the norm on a given task provide only that information, and do not tell us how many children actually possess specific reading or language disability. (p. 32)

The identification of specific developmental dyslexics from among the population of poor readers is often extremely difficult. There is no single clinical factor accepted as pathognomic (Critchley, 1970), nor is there a clear-cut syndrome characterized by signs of brain damage or perceptual deficit. These children, however, represent the lower end of the continuum of reading disabilities. Their problems are particularly severe and persistent. Much of the research that examines reading problems fails to discriminate between types of disabilities and often includes children who, for any reason, are reading two years below grade level.

Learning Disabilities and Dyslexia

What is the relation between learning disabilities and reading problems? Reading problems encompass all of the problems cited above related to the general definition of dyslexia. In contrast, learning disabilities by definition exclude children whose primary difficulty is emotional disturbance, poverty, sensory impairment, etc. Learning disabilities also may refer to problems with oral language, mathematics, motor performance, social interactions, and a host of other difficulties that have little or nothing to do with reading problems. The relation is represented in Figure 13-1. The shaded area in the diagram represents those reading problems that are due to a disorder in one or more of the basic psychological processes, including problems that stem from brain injury and perceptual deficits. It does not include problems that are due primarily to visual, auditory, or motor handicaps, mental retardation, emotional disturbance, or environmental disadvantage. It, therefore, includes all children with specific developmental dyslexia and some of the group whose dyslexia is secondary. It does not, however, encompass all remedial reading problems any more than reading problems constitute the parameters of learning disabilities. It should be noted, however, that because Americans place such a great emphasis on

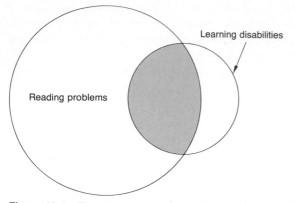

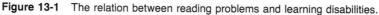

Figure 13-1   The relation between reading problems and learning disabilities.

ιeading, most children who are identified as having learning disabilities suffer from problems associated with learning to read and often constitute the most recalcitrant reading problems.

Although definitions can be used to define the overlap and distinction between reading and learning disabilities, their separation in the real world is somewhat more difficult. As mentioned in the introduction to this section, dyslexia does not constitute a clearly defined syndrome, and it is sometimes difficult to determine the cause of reading failure. Furthermore, with financial exigencies causing a reduction of specialized personnel on school staffs, there is often competition between remedial reading personnel and special education personnel for the same jobs. McCarthy (1978) pointed out in *The Reading Teacher* that reading is a field rather more narrow in scope than special education. Certainly within a continuum-of-services model interdisciplinary cooperation is necessary. Reading and learning disabilities personnel would profit more from examining ways they might interrelate rather than building defenses to protect territorial boundaries.

Characteristics of Dyslexics

Characteristics of dyslexic children vary somewhat according to the nature of the problem. Since our interest here is in that portion of delayed readers who fall within the learning disabled population, only characteristics of that population will be discussed.[1] Saunders (1962) described the characteristics of dyslexic children as follows: slow, choppy, word-by-word oral reading, frequent reversal of letters and words, transposition of letters within a word, confusion of words

---

[1]Many of these characteristics may be shared by other categories of disabled readers. Low socioeconomic status, for example, is often associated with motor, sequencing, and oral language difficulties. Some problems, however, are rather specific to the group under consideration. Reversals, for example, account for only a small portion of the reading errors exhibited by the general group of delayed readers (Shankweiler & Liberman, 1972). As Guthrie and Tyler (1978) point out, however, we have no means by which to divide poor readers into subgroups for differential instruction.

with only slightly different configurations (e.g., quit, quiet, quite), and frequent guesses and repetition of words and phrases. These errors in oral reading are often accompanied by deviant speech: articulation defects, stammering and stuttering, and concept reversals, such as confusion of *over* and *under* and *yesterday* and *tomorrow*. Fairly typical patterns of spelling and writing errors are also characteristic of these children. These include poorly formed and often nearly illegible penmanship, reversals, substitutions, omissions, transpositions, and other misspellings. These children manifest difficulties when copying as well as in spontaneous writing and exhibit a larger number of symptomatic errors when under pressure. (It should be noted that writing, spelling, and oral language problems often co-occur with reading problems, but should not be used to diagnose reading problems.) Another way to conceptualize the problems of intermediate readers is to classify them as difficulties in decoding accuracy, orthographic regularity, segmenting, and construction of semantic representations (Guthrie & Tyler, 1978). Learning disabled readers exhibit all of these problems.

Explanations for Dyslexia

There are a number of alternative explanations that have been offered in regard to specific developmental dyslexia. (The causes of reading disorders related to brain injury and/or perceptual deficits are self-explanatory.) Although educators have frequently argued that causative factors are not helpful in determining teaching strategies, many of the diagnostic and intervention techniques currently used by educators stem from conceptualizations dependent on models that subscribe to particular causal inferences. Some of these have been discussed in the chapters on perception, attention, and language. An understanding of what may or may not cause reading retardation is essential if parents and teachers are to understand the nature of a child's problems, the preferred strategy for their remediation, and routes available for compensatory interventions. More important, awareness should help to eliminate future trips down blind alleys. A number of explanations will be discussed and evaluated below. Some of them are so speculative that they are of historical interest only, but, in some cases, they have gained such popular acceptance that we would be remiss in omitting them.

Critchley (1970) reported that suggestions that specific developmental dyslexia stems from minimal brain damage are largely unconvincing. He argued that no brain pathology has ever actually been demonstrated in a case of specific dyslexia and that inheritance appears to be a more plausible factor than damage. Furthermore, in the case of early, minimal brain damage, the nervous system would be expected to compensate for the loss. Dyslexia, however, is a condition that covers the entire life span.

Critchley (1970) also noted that some writers view specific developmental dyslexia as one form of a more pervasive language disorder, i.e., a form of congenital aphasia. He argued against such a consideration. Comparisons have been made by studying adults with functional losses and then using the similarity of symptoms in children without known disease entities as the basis for inferring similar causes. (See a parallel argument in the chapter on hyperactivity.) Critchley stated that there are:

> profound psychological, linguistic, and philosophical differences . . . between the problem of a developmental dyslexic, and that of an adult who has long ago acquired language in the usual way, and then lost it. (p. 104)

Although Critchley's arguments with regard to congenital aphasia may be well-founded, more and more evidence is mounting that suggests that reading problems are very closely related to language functioning. Some of the language problems of learning disabled children and especially poor readers have been noted in Chapter 12. Others will be discussed below.

Orton (1937) noticed that many of the poor readers he studied preferred a crossed pattern of eye, hand, and foot use, e.g., the right hand, left foot, and right eye. He speculated that these overt physical signs indicated "mixed dominance" or incomplete lateralization for language and that this problem was in turn related to reading difficulties. Dominance refers to that half of the brain which controls language functioning and is thought to develop over a period of years. One would expect, since each hemisphere normally controls the opposite side of the body, that right handers would be left dominant and left handers right dominant. Brown and Simonson (1957) have shown that 98 percent of right handers are left dominant, as would be expected. What runs counter to Orton's theory, however, is that 75 percent of left handers are also left dominant. Furthermore, studies of dichotic listening and brain plasticity following the surgical removal of the left hemisphere in children before ages eight or ten raise questions as to whether brain lateralization is in fact closely related to eye, hand, or foot preference (Duane, 1974). Kinsbourne (1975) has even uncovered some evidence that suggests that children are lateralized for language from birth. Duane argued that it is not surprising that studies examining children with mixed laterality often find no higher incidence of reading problems than in the general population. Attempts to improve reading by changing handedness, footedness, or eyedness are not justified.

For some time now special educators have regarded perceptual problems as paramount in reading failure. Considerable evidence, however, has been amassed against such a theory.[2] In their reviews of the literature both Benton (1975) and Vellutino (1977) have argued that visual-perceptual deficits do not appear to characterize children with reading disabilities. The visual demands of reading are actually rather minimal, the discrimination of only twenty-six letters, and most retarded readers can make those discriminations with little effort. Furthermore, children suspected of having difficulties discriminating among letters do not appear to have difficulties discriminating other forms of visual presentations, such as pictures. A number of researchers have suggested that the difficulty lies not in visual processing, but rather in *naming* the correctly

[2]Also see Chapter 5 on Perception.

preceived letter (*b* and *d* also sound alike!). Rudel (1977; Denckla & Rudel, 1976a; Denckla & Rudel, 1976b) described dyslexics as showing impairment in the ability to make rapid verbal responses to visual stimuli and to retrieve the exact names for those stimuli. Reid, Hresko, and Margolis (1978) found that even when the visual stimuli were familiar and easily identified, poor readers took longer than a group of controls to process a match between a picture and a graphically presented sentence. The difference between good and poor readers is almost certainly cognitive/linguistic (Gupta, Ceci, & Slater, 1978). Training on visual-perceptual tasks, therefore, appears not to be warranted (Denckla, 1972; Smith & Marx, 1972; Zach & Kaufman, 1972).

Another facet of what was considered visual-perceptual problems was the issue of ocular imbalance. Goldberg (1968, cited in Critchley, 1970, p. 59) concluded that:

> Defective vision and muscle imbalance do not have a significant role in the etiology of a condition that is influenced by cognitive learning. . . . Muscle imbalance and strabismus do not affect the interpretation of symbols by the brain.

Many early writers thought that auditory discrimination played a significant role in reading. Clearly the problems are more complex than was originally thought (Rees, 1973). Elkonin (1973), Klima (1972), Liberman (1971), Mattingly (1972), and Shankweiler and Liberman (1972), for example, have all argued that "reading requires of the child an awareness of the structure of his language, an awareness that must be more explicit than is ever demanded in the ordinary course of listening and responding to speech" (Liberman, 1973, p. 2). Linguistic awareness predicts early reading achievement, especially when tasks tap the relation between the oral and written codes (Evans, Taylor, & Blum, 1979). Children with severe problems in reading appear to have great difficulty in making the phonological structure of their language explicit. These children have difficulties with rhyming and in speaking pig latin (Savin, 1972): two skills that require the segmentation of phonemic structure in spoken language.

Liberman (1973) and her colleagues have shown that we hear syllables (phonemes encoded into unitary sounds) in spoken language rather than individual phonemes and that the ability to segment language into phonemes is not well-developed in children who have difficulty learning to read. She further suggested that although problems with phonemic segmentation can account for difficulties with consonant identification, they cannot explain the greater difficulty children have reading vowels (vowels stand out in the syllables of which children are apparently aware and the vowel is acoustically marked by a burst of sound whenever it appears). Vowels, she hypothesized, are more difficult for children because of the orthographic complexities of the spelling-to-sound correspondence and because vowel sounds are so fluid that they tend to be indefinite as phonological entities. Training in auditory discrimination skills are, therefore, of dubious value.

Theories of sensory integration present a more complex picture. A number of studies have been done (cf. Birch & Belmont, 1964, 1965) in which children were asked to match rhythmic patterns with visual presentations. Although delayed readers typically do more poorly than good readers, the reasons why they do more poorly are not clear. Vellutino and his colleagues (Steger, Vellutino, & Meshoulam, 1972; Vellutino, Steger, Harding, & Phillips, 1975; Vellutino, Steger, & Pruzak, 1973) suggested that the results were due to the confounding of memory and attention factors. Friedes (1974) and Blank (Blank & Bridger, 1966; Blank, Weider, & Bridger, 1968) raised other issues, such as the possibility that poor readers are unable to use verbal mnemonics to aid recall. Although further research might prove fruitful, it is probably fair to say that most serious researchers discount the theory of sensory integration as an important causal factor in dyslexia. There is even some question as to whether problems with sensory integration are the cause of poor reading performance or the result of it (Benton, 1975). (See Chapter 5 for additional discussion.)

Probably the most widely accepted explanation of specific developmental dyslexia is cerebral immaturity or maturational lag. Kinsbourne (1973a) suggested that since the performance of dyslcxic children on neurological examinations and on reading tasks approximated that of younger children, their problems might be due to a lag in the maturation of the central nervous system.

> Such developmental lag could be the result of unusual delay in the establishment of neuronal interconnections or of neurochemical transmitter formation, or in the myelination process. The etiology could be acquired, i.e., nutritional, or secondary to putative injury, or genetic. However, the last has more commonly been invoked. From a descriptive standpoint, this view is not without merit. It is additionally supported by the male preponderance of reading retardation regardless of socioeconomic background, and it is generally accepted that the rate of maturation in the female exceeds that of the young male (Duane, 1974, p. 22).

Important contributions of this hypothesis are: (1) the suggestion that no structural defect, deficiency, or loss has occurred in dyslexic children (Kinsbourne, 1973a), (2) that dyscalculia, apraxia, and perhaps even the lack of a musical ear are analogous problems (Critchley, 1970), (3) that pharmacological treatment may some day be possible (Critchley, 1977), and (4) that specific developmental dyslexia may be viewed as an extreme variation on a continuum of reading behaviors (Duane, 1974).[3]

Subsyndromes and Correlates of Dyslexia

Writers have not only postulated a variety of explanations for dyslexia, but have also formulated hypotheses regarding specific subsyndromes. Boder (1973), Johnson and Myklebust (1967), Myklebust (1965), and Vernon (1971) delineated two dyslexic subtypes: auditory linguistic and visual spatial. Kinsbourne and Warrington (1966) similarly identified two subgroups of backward readers: the

---

[3]For more comprehensive discussions of dyslexia the reader is referred to Benton (1975), Critchley (1970), Critchley and Critchley (1978), Duane (1974), and Vellutino (1977).

group retarded in language and a second with lower performance IQs and difficulties with finger differentiation and arithmetic facts. Bannatyne (1966) and Smith (1970) separated dyslexics into genetic and minimal neurological dysfunction groups. Bateman (1968) identified three subgroups using the *ITPA*: auditory memory problems, visual memory problems, and problems in both. Ingram, Mason, and Blackburn (1970) identified two subgroups by analyzing reading errors: audiophonic and visuospatial, with the errors of most children being mixed. Mattis, French, and Rapin (1973) isolated three syndromes in dyslexics: language disorders, articulatory and graphomotor dyscoordination, and visual-perceptual disorders.

Although the identification of subsyndromes might enable educators to individualize instruction when a diagnosis of dyslexia is made, these studies generally suffer from a number of methodological problems that render their results equivocal: in many instances no distinction was made between secondary dyslexics and developmental dyslexics; many of the children were from clinic populations that drew from a wide variety of socioeconomic levels; ages ranged over as much as ten years; and the numbers of children studied were generally quite small. It is likely that all of these subtypes (genetic, brain damaged, auditory, visual, linguistic and perceptive, articulatory and graphomotor) appear among the group of disabled readers, but whether these constitute subsyndromes of developmental dyslexia is still at issue. Furthermore, it is unlikely that all of the characteristics—regardless of how pervasive—that identify any group of children would be relevant to their reading performance. It would be equally unlikely that many children would not exhibit a variety of problems that cut across syndromes.

In his review of the literature examining types of reading problems, Vernon (1977) identified four main points at which the reading process can break down: (1) in the analysis of complex, sequential visual and/or auditory-linguistic structures, (2) in the linking of visual and auditory-linguistic structures, (3) in the establishment of regularities in phoneme-grapheme correspondences (perhaps the most frequent problem), and (4) in the grouping of words (which *can* be read) into phrases. Perhaps it would prove more fruitful for teachers to examine the reading performances of all children for indications of their competence (or lack of it) in regard to the process of reading itself, than to plan instructional strategies around subtype diagnoses.

Special educators all too often have spent and continue to spend valuable classroom time "remediating" auditory, visual, and other sensory processes thought to be prerequisite to reading, rather than focusing instruction on reading itself. Mammoth efforts have been expended in trying to improve perceptual functions, when the preponderance of research on the process of reading indicates that higher-level cognitive functions are generally more crucial. Finally, as far as most of the correlates of reading are concerned, whether they are the cause or the result or simply the accomplice of reading failure has yet to be determined. Correlates have included a wide variety of behaviors, some more seductive than others, because they appear to be more closely related to the process of reading itself. Special educators have trained children in perceptual functions, in oral language, handwriting and spelling skills, in Piagetian tasks, in phonics and word drills and close tasks. Children are often so busy doing exercises and drills that little time is left for reading.

Prognosis

Although the last decade has witnessed a proliferation of interest and research on dyslexia, little is known about the prognosis for such children. It is generally agreed that most dyslexics can be taught to read, even though the ultimate level reached by many might be halting and slow. Making judgments about prognoses is particularly difficult, because so little is known about the incidence of dyslexia in the adult population. We have made no appreciable progress in teaching methodology or follow-up studies since Critchley (1970) wrote:

> There is no justification for anything less than optimism provided only that dyslexics are correctly diagnosed at an early age, and are granted without delay the services of special remedial teaching at the hands of sympathetic experts (p. 121).

Indeed, Rawson (1968) found that of twenty dyslexic boys who had been so diagnosed and so instructed, an impressive number had become professionals (medical doctors, lawyers, and even academics) and successful businessmen.

It is unfortunate, however, that many dyslexic children do not enjoy such opportunity. The results of a follow-up study by Frauenheim (1978) indicated that dyslexic children continued to have severe, residual learning problems in adulthood. PL 94-142 has given impetus to the inclusion of handicapped children in preschools, but because reliable techniques for predicting school failure among mildly impaired young children have not yet been developed, these children are often not helped until they enter kindergarten and first grade and then actually begin to fail in school tasks. Ansara (1969) lamented that many children were not identified and serviced until after the third grade, because many principals and teachers think that the children are simply "late bloomers." Although Ansara does not address the issue of false positives (see section on early identification), she decried, and rightfully so, the prolongation of frustrations and self-doubts that accompany school failure.

The method of financial support for schools that is currently used in this country is partially at fault. Parents and teachers are typically reluctant to label a child in his or her early years, because of the suspected deleterious effects of labeling. Funding for schools, however, is dependent on the numbers of children who have been classified. Schools cannot generally provide the kind of individualized, sympathetic instruction needed by dyslexics unless such funding is provided. It is not surprising, therefore, that many children receive no remedial help until the third grade. More and more frequently schools are developing resource room and teacher consultant services that would enable children, labeled or not, to receive special instructional services for all or part of the day by their regular teacher or a specialist. Perhaps these kinds of programs will lead to the implementation of instructional programs that will foster better prognoses for dyslexic children as well as others.

Finally, remedial programs may not be enough. Reading has assumed such importance in the minds of most Americans that most parents and teachers focus nearly all their attention on improving reading performance at the expense of the child's other capacities. Compensatory strategies need to be employed by children who cannot read so that they can learn to be knowledgeable, socially adept, and productive citizens. Tape recordings, filmstrips, films, typewriters, talking books, computers, television, listening to others read, and a host of other means for enabling dyslexics to become informed are readily available in most homes and schools, but are seldom used in other than incidental ways. People are not treated as somewhat defective if they are not musicians or athletes or mechanics, but the inability to read or even delayed reading seems to constitute a reason for shame in this society. We must overcome this implicit notion that a student's worth is related to his or her reading ability and begin to supplement remedial reading instruction with the teaching of compensatory strategies that will help to minimize both the stigma and the accumulated deficit.

CONVENTIONAL APPROACHES TO READING INSTRUCTION

There is a wide variety of programs that have been used to teach learning disabled children. Some are more popular than others; some are used almost exclusively with learning disabled children, but none appears to produce greater results than others. No attempt has been made to present an exhaustive compilation. We wish only to provide an illustrative survey of the most prominent and/or promising approaches. It should be noted that the categories are not necessarily mutually exclusive.

Basal Readers Series

Basal readers are developed in series, usually representing reading levels rather than grades per se. They are typically used with groups of children. They consist of a collection of stories in which vocabulary is controlled for meaning frequency. Emphasis from the start is on meaning and appreciation. Sight words are taught initially; only gradually are phonics and other word-analysis skills introduced. The series are often quite expensive, because they contain a large number of pictures, often colored. Over the past ten years there has been a shift in basal reader programs from the white, middle-class family on the farm and in suburban settings to multiethnic, urban settings. In addition to the readers themselves, the basal series include teachers' manuals, workbooks, placement and achievement tests, and sometimes even audiovisual and spirit duplicating materials.

One format for teaching usually associated with the basal series is the Directed Reading Activity (DRA). The DRA usually consists of six parts (Kaluger & Kolson, 1969): First, through preparatory experiences such as pictures, audiovisual materials, questions, discussion, etc. the teacher attempts to engender a lively interest for the story to be read. The strategies used during the motivation/previewing segment of the lesson are usually aimed at helping children relate their past experience to the content of the new story. The second step is preparing the children for the particular concepts and vocabulary to be used in the story. New words are often written on the blackboard and are used in a variety of exercises, games, and drills in order to ensure that the children will recognize the words when they meet them in the story and to make certain that they know the meaning of the words as they are used in that particular context. Next, a part of the story is read, usually silently, in response to some direction from the teacher designed to guide the children's reading, i.e., to give them a purpose to read, a question to answer. For example, the teacher might say, "Read the next paragraph to find out who saw Bob come home." When most of the children have found the answer, someone is asked to tell the class and often the paragraph is read aloud. The reading is usually followed by skill activity designed to reinforce the new words and concepts presented in the story or perhaps some word-analysis skill. Workbooks or ditto sheets are often used for this purpose. The fifth step in the DRA is application. The children are asked to use whatever skills or knowledge they have gained from the story in a new way. Sometimes dramatizations are used. Sometimes children are asked to write or draw, or to read similar stories. Sometimes discussions or classroom games are used. Very often the step that is meant to encourage application becomes the basis for homework. Finally, the teacher must evaluate the effectiveness of the lesson. Children may be tested either formally or informally and the general conduct of the lesson itself reviewed. The evaluation provides the basis for the preparation of the next day's lesson.

Since Chall's (1967) landmark study comparing the effectiveness of reading methods, basal readers have lost popularity. Chall's study showed that approaches that emphasized decoding appeared to be superior, especially for poor readers. Basal readers are seldom used with children known to be learning disabled, because of the widely held belief that decoding problems are severe among these children: reversals, transpositions, grapheme-phoneme correspondences, and difficulties with short-term memory (Kinsbourne, 1973; Rudel, 1977). Furthermore, many writers assume that because learning disabled children are of normal intelligence, they do not have difficulties with comprehension. There is some evidence, however, that this is not the case (Wallach and Goldsmith, 1977; Weaver, 1978).

Phonics Programs

Reading programs that emphasize phonics can be obtained as supplemental materials or as entire reading systems including readers, workbooks, and teachers' guides. They differ from the basal reading series in that they teach phonics from the beginning and in a more direct and concentrated fashion. Most often, however, stories to be read for meaning, as in the basal series, are also recommended. Some are *synthetic* in that they begin with letters and sounds that are blended to form words. Others depend on the *analysis* of some basic sight words that were previously learned. Phonics systems also vary with respect to the numbers of rules and phonic elements to be learned, whether they begin with the introduction of consonants, long vowels, or short vowels, and whether they incorporate spelling and writing.

Phonics methods have quite often been recommended for learning disabled children. In part, these recommendations have stemmed from the notion that learning disabled children have difficulty with visual and auditory perception: emphasis on phonics depends on the development of readiness skills related to letter and sound discrimination. As we have noted earlier, however, it appears that these hypotheses concerning the causes of reading failure in learning disabled children are no longer tenable. Indeed Kershner (1975) has shown that poor readers tend to persist in the use of perceptual strategies long after successful readers have shifted to more cognitive, linguistic strategies.

Another hypothesis has been that learning disabled children suffer from a selective attention deficit (see Chapter 6) and therefore need systematic aid in attending to relevant features such as shape and position of graphemes (cf. Hallahan & Kaufman, 1976; Ross, 1976). Batemen (1976) as well as others has argued that deficits in selective attention render phonics the teaching method of choice. The assumption here that may not be valid is that attention can be selectively deployed in reading without regard to meaning. It has been demonstrated repeatedly in studies of eye fixation in reading that attention is directed by cognitive-linguistic determinants (see Wanat, 1976 for a review of the relevant literature), that is, the range of fixation is determined by phrase and clause structure. As Gallagher (1976) so aptly put it, reading is not eye-to-mind, but rather mind-to-eye. The discrimination of words and letters is in fact aided by meaning (Goodman, 1965).

Although phonics are often advocated as a means of reducing the memory load for children who have exhibited short-term memory deficits, they learn the system with great difficulty and some evidence suggests children may not spontaneously apply phonics rules while reading (Spache, 1976, p. 219). Smith (1973) has argued that too many rules would be needed to enable children to sound out words. Such huge numbers of rules would have the effect of straining memory capacity. In addition, Chomsky and Halle (1968), as well as C. Chomsky (1970), have shown that English orthography is more closely related to morphology than the sound system. Words that have similar meanings are spelled similarly rather than words with similar sounds. *Nation* and *national,* for example, are spelled the same but *him* and *hymn* are not. Furthermore, as Wallach and Goldsmith (1977) pointed out, the word *painted* is not simply a string of seven letters to be sounded out in sequence. It has two meaning parts: *paint* and *past.* Finally, many words cannot be read until their meaning is known. Consider the following sentence paraphrased from Smith: Permit me to read the minute print on my permit. The pronunciation of *permit, read,* and *minute* are dependent on an understanding of the grammar and meaning of the sentence rather than on purely phonological rules.

There are, however, significant and cogent arguments that have been offered in support of a phonics approach, especially in regard to beginning reading. A number of explanations of the reading process[4] view reading in English, because it is alphabetic, as a mapping of written into oral language that may occur orally or subvocally. Evidence exists in abundance that suggests that all readers subvocalize to some extent (cf. McGuigan, 1970). Since subvocalization may be more characteristic of good rather than poor readers (Klapp, Anderson, & Berrian, 1973), phonics and oral reading strategies that make use of the child's knowledge of oral language are recommended by some authors for beginning reading instruction. Indeed, reading is viewed as a secondary language process that consists of this "translation." Comprehension and higher-level functions occur *after* the conversion to oral language has taken place. As the reader becomes more and more adept, decoding becomes increasingly more automatic and the conscious mind is freed to focus on meaning (LaBerge & Samuels, 1974).

Linguistic Readers

Instructional systems that use the linguistic model are based on the work of a great American linguist, Leonard Bloomfield. Bloomfield (1942) argued that meaning should not be emphasized in beginning reading. Rather, he argued, the child should be taught elements of the graphic code which correspond to the acoustic signals of oral language, that is, syllables. Bloomfield was opposed to phonics instruction: Words should *not* be sounded out letter by letter, but should be read as wholes. New words should be spelled, but never sounded out. Bloomfield argued that the initial words learned by the child should be very carefully controlled so that only words with regular spellings and one sound per letter would be introduced at first. Bloomfield viewed reading as the mapping of sound to print which should capitalize on the linguistic knowledge with which the child came to school. Linguistic readers frequently have few pictures.

Although the present authors were unable to find research on the use of linguistic systems with learning disabled children, their use has an intuitive appeal: first, because they capitalize on the child's knowledge of language, and second, because, as noted above, disabled readers tend to have considerable difficulties segmenting phonemes. For children who have difficulty making language elements explicit, linguistic methods may facilitate the understanding of correspondences between speech and print.

Unusual Graphic Representations

The most prominent among the systems that use altered orthography is the Initial Teaching Alphabet (ITA). ITA uses forty-four characters, most of which are familiar as letters of the alphabet, but which represent only a single sound. Only lower-case letters are used and are simply enlarged to represent capitals. ITA can be used with either basal or phonics instructional systems. Once the

---

[4]See Singer and Ruddell (1976) for a fairly comprehensive account of these and competing information processing and psycholinguistic models.

altered alphabet has been mastered, children must shift to conventional orthography. The ability to read conventional books seems to present no problems for most children, but the shift from writing in ITA to conventional spellings seems to present more problems (Ruddell, 1974). ITA is, of course, limited to beginning reading. ITA was developed by Pitman (1963).

Another means of altering the graphic representation is UNIFON (Malone, 1963), which is an altered spelling system for teaching English and other European languages quite similar in detail to ITA. Other programs use special color codings to indicate distinct sounds. Over thirty colors are used, so fine color discriminations are required. Words in Color (Gattegno, 1962) is a synthetic phonics program in which children are taught the sounds of letters rather than letter names. Readers are printed in black and white, so children use a variety of wall charts to help them make the correspondence between the sound and the letter or letters which represent it in traditional orthography. The few studies which have examined the effectiveness of the system report that it is no more effective than more traditional approaches to reading instruction (Heilman, 1965; Hill, 1967; Lockmiller & DiNello, 1970). Ideographs have also been used with children who have had considerable difficulty learning to read alphabetic representations (Rosin, Poritsky, & Sotsky, 1971) and have been found to be quite successful. These programs are experimental, however, and have not received widespread use. Carroll (1972) suggested that differences in reading ideographic versus alphabetic writing may be more apparent than real.

Finally, Woodcock (1967) in an effort to overcome the problems of conventional orthography devised the Peabody Rebus Program, using *rebuses* or *picture words*. The rationale behind such a program is that children can learn about the nature of the reading process by decoding easily identified pictures. This program is, of course, only for beginning readers and is designed to provide a bridge between oral and written language. Transition to traditional reading using conventional orthography is accomplished by substituting increasingly more, carefully controlled words for rebuses. The format for much of the system is programmed. Children check an answer by wetting the space underneath it. If the space turns green, the answer is correct. If it turns red, the answer is wrong. Two readers accompany the programmed texts. Children who complete the Rebus Program develop a substantial beginning reading vocabulary. No evidence has accumulated that would enable judgments to be made about the effectiveness of such a system for learning disabled children.

Programmed Texts

Programmed texts are based on behavioral principles of immediate feedback and reinforcement. Reading skills are very carefully sequenced and such small steps are taken between items that children are strongly guided to give correct answers. Information as to whether a response is correct or incorrect is readily available, sometimes in the next item and sometimes on an answer sheet or answer column. Children work individually, but it would be misleading to suggest that the instruction is individualized. All children, in fact, go through the same program in the same sequence (Spache, 1976). Because answers must be determined before the workbook is printed, only questions that have a single correct response can be included. The focus of most texts is on phonics skills. Often the semantic and syntactic elements of the text are repetitious and dull. Programmed instruction has the advantage of enabling the child to work at his or her own pace and without the constant assistance or supervision of a teacher. It has been the experience of the present authors, however, that learning disabled children are often able to complete the frames correctly, but fail dismally on the test. (Most systems provide for periodic testing.) What precisely is being learned during a programmed sequence, therefore, is often difficult to apprehend (Erlwanger, cited in Gallagher & Reid, in press). Programmed texts also tend to teach skills in isolation rather than in context, so whether any skills acquired will generalize to new situations is dubious. Learning disabled children often need large numbers of repetitions when learning a new skill. Programmed texts would appear to provide one vehicle for repetition which still leaves the teacher free for other activities.

There is danger, however, in expecting programmed texts to provide the total or even primary basis of reading instruction. Behaviorists, including the writers of programmed texts, function on the premise that higher-order, complex skills, such as reading, can be fragmented into component parts. In addition, they assume that the teaching of the component parts will lead to the acquisition of the skill. Piaget (1978), however, points out that the "reduction" of the higher- to lower-order skills is, in fact, only apparent, because the lower-order concept must sooner or later become enriched by the higher-order conceptualization. The text makes no provision for the application of higher-order skills: it is left to chance. One would expect that children who are able readers can make the application themselves. There is no reason to suspect that that is true of learning disabled children.

One variant of programmed reading instruction, the Direct Instruction Model designed by the University of Oregon and published as DISTAR (Englemann & Bruner, 1969), has gained considerable national visibility. In the Follow Through evaluations that compared teaching programs it was found to be unusually successful (Abt Associates, 1977). The authors of DISTAR have argued that the cause of reading problems is unimportant to teachers. Englemann (1969, p. 38) stated: "Specific statements of what the child has not been taught represent a sufficient diagnosis in the educational setting." He argued that since diagnoses such as *brain injured* or *perceptually disordered* do not indicate teaching strategies, etiology is of no concern to teachers. As Haring and Bateman (1977) have so aptly pointed out, it is commonly held that children who do not learn have learning disabilities. Once it has been established that the child is learning disabled, the label is used to describe the reasons *why* the child cannot learn. Englemann's stance is an attempt to reduce the incidence of such circular reasoning. Few professionals would disagree with him. The question which is at issue is how this should be done. Professionals of a psychoeducational persuasion argue that differential diagnoses may help establish appropriate, differential teaching strategies (cf. Bannatyne, 1973). The proponents of DISTAR argue, however, that knowledge of the child's functioning is unimportant; one need only understand the task (Haring & Bateman, 1977).

DISTAR is based on the behavioral principles of teaching sequences of skill hierarchies designed to minimize error, providing ample practice and opportunity to respond, and using immediate feedback and positive reinforcement. Children are taught in small groups with the teacher leading them as if they were a choir. Signals are used by teachers to cue children in responding. The pace is prescribed and rapid. Biweekly continuous progress tests enable the teacher to regroup the children. Those who fail the test repeat the previous sequence of lessons. Those who pass, go on to a new series of lessons. What lessons are taught, for how long, and when is carefully controlled. For example, "Symbol-Action Games" begin on the first day and continue through seventeen lessons. "Blending, Say It Fast" also begins on the first day, but continues through forty lessons. Lessons are one-half hour in duration. The teacher is provided with a script for each lesson. The intention is clearly to make the system "teacher proof."

How valuable DISTAR is as a teaching program for learning disabled children is unknown. Englemann would most assuredly argue that, since etiology is unimportant, a program successful with disadvantaged children would work equally well for the learning disabled. Whether or not DISTAR was really so successful, however, is open to controversy (see *Harvard Educational Review,* 1978, *48,* 125–192 for an account of the controversy). House, Glass, McLean, and Walker (1978) formed an independent panel to evaluate the Follow Through evaluation. They noted that one cannot say with any assurance that DISTAR or any of the other "back to basics" programs were superior to other, more child-centered approaches. First, the effectiveness of the teaching approaches varied greatly from one school to the next. Models were misclassified, measurements of the results were inadequate, and the statistical analyses were found to be flawed. In addition, House et al. noted that quite early in the Follow Through experiment sponsors from other programs complained that a reduction in the number of variables to be measured favored the behaviorists. Unfortunately, the popular press has heralded the Follow Through findings as pointing to the need for a back-to-basics movement in this country, and the federal government has endorsed such an educational platform.

Language Experience Approach

The language experience approach usually consists of having individual children write or dictate stories about their personal experiences, wishes, dreams, etc. Occasionally, groups compose a single story with each child offering a part. Sometimes the teacher and sometimes other children record the story on the chalkboard or large chart. Stories are frequently edited before being copied in final form on a wall chart or a notebook. The language experience approach has a number of distinct advantages for learning disabled children: it capitalizes on the child's unique experience and interests; it helps to clarify the significance of written language; children control their own vocabulary and language structure; interest is virtually guaranteed; and finally, reading and seeing or sharing their own stories may be a boost to the morale of children whose previous reading experiences had been fraught with failure.

Language experience places early emphasis on the learning of the code (Chall, 1967). The editing step provides ample opportunity for the teacher to emphasize letter-sound correspondences, structural analysis, etc. Language experience stories frequently include a variety of graphic, syntactic, and semantic structures that can also be used to advantage in instruction. Words are read in context, so that semantic and syntactic cues can create constraints and expectancies that can aid identification (Goodman, 1976a).

Allen and Allen (1970) recommend a broader conception of language experience. They suggested that a systematic attempt be made by the teacher to help the children become more precise and more varied in their verbal expression as well as more aware of the structure of their language. Children must be encouraged to listen to, tell, write, and discuss stories on a wide range of topics. A variety of resources other than the children's stories should also be used in reading instruction: objects and activities that are part of the classroom, home, or community environment, class books on a variety of subjects, and library books. Allen and Allen further stress learning to research and report on a particular topic by using a variety of self-selected materials, by summarizing, outlining, editing, and evaluating one's own work.

Individualized reading is a resurgence of what was known in the 1920s as *free reading,* that is, children read from a wide variety of materials whatever they like. Reading is never for its own sake, but rather for its content; fiction or nonfiction, books, magazines, newspapers, and textbooks are all considered suitable materials. An early assumption that underlay such programs was that the children would naturally select materials at a level appropriate for them, but this assumption has not been supported empirically (cf. Fleming, 1966). Teachers, however, may give children guidance in the selection of books. Teachers who use the individualized reading format often hold brief conferences with each of the children daily. Word-attack skills are taught to each child as he or she has a need for them. Some teachers supplement individualized reading with other instructional materials, such as phonics workbooks or basal readers. The success of such a program must be evaluated child by child. Certainly many learning disabled children would be able to profit from such instruction, given that they received consistent, extensive, and sympathetic support. Parents may be able to render great assistance to teachers by organizing similar individualized reading programs for their learning disabled children at home.

Multisensory Approaches

A number of systems have been devised that use a variety of senses either in succession or simultaneously in reading instruction. Children do not simply look at the print. They are instead encouraged to trace, write, and say (either aloud or subvocally) the words while reading. Monroe (1932), for example, advocated overt motor responses, because they provide the teacher with an opportunity to observe the child's response; they intensify one of the components of what she assumed is the learning process used by successful beginning readers; they add a kinesthetic dimension to auditory and visual discrimination; and they help to focus the child's attention. Most of the multisensory systems were developed specifically for disabled readers and have enjoyed wide popularity, especially among clinicians and others who have the opportunity to work with dyslexic children in one-to-one situations. Most are phonics programs. Three programs which seem to be among the most widely used will be discussed here: the Fernald method, the Orton-Gillingham-Stillman approach, and the Slingerland method. There are many, many other programs that are based on similar principles, but familiarity with the three programs described here should provide sufficient background to enable a teacher to determine that a program of this type might be worth seeking and exploring for a particular child.

The Fernald Word Learning Technique (1943) is often referred to as the VAKT method, because it involves the visual, auditory, kinesthetic, and tactile senses. Fernald was especially concerned with teaching children who demonstrated emotional problems. She strove, therefore, to devise a system that would be radically different from the one in which the child's failure had occurred. Her teaching strategy begins with having the child write a story. The children write whatever they can and then ask the teacher to help them with any words they do not know. For some children that may be every word. What words the children learn to read, therefore, depend on their interests and spoken language. Fernald recommended that adults refrain from reading to children, because motivation for them to read themselves must be maintained.

When a child asks for a word, that word is printed in black crayon in large letters on a durable piece of paper. The child is instructed to look at the word, trace it with the index and middle fingers, and to say the *syllables* aloud as the tracing occurs. The process is repeated until the child can write the word correctly twice from memory. Children are not permitted to copy the word a few letters at a time. The word must be learned as a unit and written and pronounced without hesitation between segments. If an error is made, the child must begin again at the beginning of the word. Each child keeps a file of words he or she has learned. Later, the child stops tracing and simply looks at the word, says it, and writes it. Later still, the writing (which employs the kinesthetic mode) is stopped. Finally, children become able to recognize new words. Phonics are not taught. Instead, the child's reading ability is generalized by using words and parts of words which were previously known. At this point the child reads for content. The Fernald method is usually employed outside the regular classroom. Children are returned to their regular class for reading as soon as they are capable of reading the appropriate level material.

Myers (1978) in his review of the research literature evaluating the use of the Fernald method has found equivocal results. Even with learning disabled children, it is not clear whether her method has any advantages over a purely visual method. Fernald's approach was, of course, based on the idea that many reading problems were related to difficulties with visual discrimination. This hypothesis no longer seems to be tenable.

The Orton-Gillingham Method was devised by Gillingham and Stillman (1965, 1970; Gillingham, 1936). Their program was based on the work of Orton. J. Orton (1966) wrote that S. Orton's instructions to teachers stressed the importance of careful, daily observation of their pupils and flexible procedures. She listed two basic principles of his work (p. 131):

> 1   Training for simultaneous association of visual, auditory, and kinesthetic language stimuli—in reading cases, tracing and sounding the visually presented word and maintaining consistent direction by following the letters with the fingers during the sound synthesis of syllables and words (Orton, 1928).
>
> 2   Finding such units as the child can use without difficulty in the field of his particular disability and directing the training toward developing the process of fusing these smaller units into larger more complex wholes (Orton, 1937).

S. Orton's work was unquestionably concerned with specific developmental dyslexics. He, as well as others (cf. Gates, 1922; Gray, 1922; Monroe, 1932), felt certain that the difficulties experienced by these children were related only to decoding problems. Chall (1967) described his approach as a "systematic-phonics program buttressed by kinesthetic aids" (p. 169).

Gillingham's (and Stillman's) remedial reading techniques were dependent on individualized instruction with a sympathetic, caring adult. Children were not simply asked to accept the oddities in the orthography of their language: an explanatory history of English was provided before instruction began. Lessons were expected to continue for forty-five to sixty minutes per day for a minimum of two years. During the time that the children were receiving special instruction, they were not permitted to read, write, or spell in class or at home. Gillingham recommended that the child be read to so that he or she could keep up with class work.

Gillingham's procedures are designed to establish associations between how letters or words look and sound and how they feel when they are written. She, therefore, used sensory modes in combinations. Writing, for example, was taught by having the child watch while the teacher wrote a letter and explained its orientation, form, where to put the pencil to begin making the letter, etc. The child then traced and later copied the teacher's model. When tracing was proficient, the child tried to write the word from memory and finally to write it with closed eyes.

Once letter-sound correspondences have been mastered, pupils are introduced to *phonograms,* a letter or group of letters that produce a single acoustical sound. It is the phonograms that are used in subsequent drills. Phonograms are written on cards and the cards are placed in combination to produce words. First each phonogram's sound is produced and then said aloud faster and faster, until the sounds are fluent and blended. Word analysis is carried out auditorally. The teacher says a word and the child responds by saying which letters are being heard. When the children become proficient, they spell (that is, the teacher says the word, the child repeats it, the child names the letters in the word, and writes them). Children do not receive books to read until blending skills are firmly established. Once books are in use, however, phonic rules are taught along with rules for syllabication and accent. Nonphonetic orthography is introduced and these words are simply learned by rote.

The Orton-Gillingham approach has received wide support, especially among clinicians. Although persons using the system seem almost unanimously to have found it beneficial, little research has been carried out to evaluate its benefits when compared to other types of reading instruction (Kline, 1977). Gates (1947) and Dechant (1964) have criticized the method because of its lack of flexibility, its emphasis on reading mechanics apart from meaning, and its tendency to develop laborious readers (perhaps more closely related to the characteristics of the children rather than to the method per se). Recently, however, there has been a resurgence of interest in the technique for classroom use. Enfield and Greene developed a program based on the Orton-Gillingham method for the public elementary and junior high schools of Bloomington, Minnesota (cited in *The Orton Society,* 1978). Enfield and Greene found the program successful in increasing the rate of progress of normally achieving second and third graders. The program was cited by a Presidential Panel as a model for the nation.

Slingerland (1974) has more recently developed an instructional program for use with children who have Specific Language Disability (SLD), a term frequently used to denote those children we have been calling specific developmental dyslexics. Slingerland (1972) recommended that SLD classrooms be self-contained and part of regular, rather than special education services so that no additional teaching staff would be required. Children who needed such services would simply be assigned to the SLD class.

Slingerland's multisensory approach is based on learning first the smallest units of "sight-sound-feel" (a single letter of the alphabet). When a few consonants and a vowel are known as single units and can be translated among sensory channels, they are combined into a phonetic, one-syllable, short-vowel word (p. 22). Encoding or blending precedes decoding. Some tests of the use of the Slingerland method have demonstrated its effectiveness, but the results are not impressive. A study was conducted by East (1969) in which first grade students who received instruction by the Slingerland method were matched against a control group whose instruction was based on a basal reading program. After three years of instruction, the scores on the *Metropolitan Achievement Test* were as shown in Table 13-1.

The author does not discuss statistical significances. He says only that the experimental group scores were higher and that the Specific Language Disability techniques were of significant value. A summarization of these and other findings (Slingerland Study II, no date) suggested that perhaps the progress of these children was masked by their inability to score well on standardized tests. It also suggested that the reading problems of dyslexic children may persist

**Table 13-1   Scores on the *Metropolitan Achievement Test* after Three
Years of Instruction in the Slingerland Method**

	Word knowledge	Word discrimination	Reading comprehension
Experimental group	69.54	69.60	62.66
Control group	67.04	67.76	61.64

Source: East, 1969.

regardless of competent instruction. These may be just claims, but they do not confirm the superiority of the Slingerland Multisensory Method.

One further caution is in order concerning the use of multisensory techniques with learning disabled children. Brown (1976), working with Chapanis, has found that a small number of dyslexic children manifest cross-modal extinction.[5] Since multisensory techniques incorporate simultaneous use of different modes (e.g., tracing while looking and saying), this subgroup of dyslexic children may be suppressing one of the stimulus modes. Perhaps multisensory systems necessitate a greater expenditure of energy than more traditional systems for these children.

Summary and Conclusions

We have examined a number of different strategies used to teach children to read. Some of the techniques described here are more typically used with regular class children than with children who require remedial instruction. It is important for special educators to be conversant with such techniques, however, because children who have failed to learn to read have been taught by one or another of them. Even with the shift from the use of the "whole-word" method generally employed in beginning reading with basal series to a phonics (or linguistic) approach, there has not been a decrease in the numbers of children who fail to profit from classroom reading instruction. Since theorists in reading have begun to conceptualize reading as primarily a language, rather than a perceptual task (Vellutino, 1977), we have some basis for understanding why some programs seem to be less successful. We have, however, no clear evidence to date that one system or even one group of systems appears to be superior to the others in fostering success in all aspects of reading.

COGNITIVE/PSYCHOLINGUISTIC APPROACHES

The reading strategies described above were grouped together under the heading of Conventional Approaches, because they share the conventional wisdom that reading constitutes a process of translating visual symbols to

[5]Cross-modal extinction refers to the condition in which a person is able to perceive a stimulus in any one mode (e.g., visual, auditory, kinesthetic), but when two stimuli are presented simultaneously in two different modes, only one is perceived. The other is said to be *extinguished*.

auditory language. Although there has been some disagreement as to whether a whole-word or phonics method should be used and whether initial reading should be silent or oral, the proponents of those systems generally agree that accuracy in translating the code is important to beginning readers. Furthermore, they argue that since English is an alphabetic writing system, letter-sound correspondences should be taught at some point.

The application of psycholinguistics to the understanding of reading has lead to the development of a second position on the linguistic nature of the reading process. Descriptions of this position have been eloquently and often humorously presented by Goodman (1976a, b, c), Goodman & Goodman (1976), Kolers (1970), and Smith (1971, 1973, 1975a, b, 1977). The following brief summary draws heavily upon these accounts.

The Goodman/Smith Model

These theorists believe that language is *not* the intermediary between print and comprehension. They argue, instead, that meaning is abstracted directly from print. Written language is viewed as parallel to spoken language rather than as subsidiary. The rationale becomes clear if we draw an analogy between written and oral language and functioning in two spoken languages, such as English and French. A person fluent in both languages does not need to translate from one to the other, but understands the meaning directly from either language. Kolers (1970) presented paragraphs to bilinguals in which French and English were intermixed within sentences. For example, they were asked to read, "Son cheval, suivi by two hounds . . ." or "his horse, followed de deux bassets. . . ." He compared the bilinguals' comprehension of the mixed paragraphs with their comprehension of the same paragraphs all in French or all in English when the amount of time they had to read was the same. Kolers reasoned that if the readers had to make all of the words in the mixed paragraphs correspond to a single language before they could comprehend their meaning, reading would take more time and, therefore, comprehension would be poorer. This did not occur. Furthermore, in a second part of the experiment when the bilinguals were asked to read aloud, many of their errors were translations, i.e., if *door* were the first word in English (following French), it may have been read as *la porte.* The same kind of translation occurred when *door,* for example, was the last word in an English sequence (again followed by French). Kolers suggested that these and other studies support the position that meaning is derived directly from print (just as it is derived directly from spoken language), and that spoken language does not mediate between print and meaning.

Consider also the example of: *The none tolled hymn she had scene bear feat inn hour rheum* (Smith, 1975a, p. 350). If the meaning of language were derived from the translation to sound, then the spelling anomolies would be neither so evident nor so troublesome to the reader. In addition, "the anomolies . . . are invariably identified before the alternative meaning associated with the sound, which is then separated from the meaning associated with the spelling" (p. 350).

Goodman defined reading as a "complex process by which a reader reconstructs, to some degree, a message encoded by a writer in graphic language" (1976a, p. 472). Printed language is considered to be different from spoken language. Smith noted that to detect that difference one has only to read a written passage aloud. Furthermore, reading is not thought to be a precise process involving "exact, detailed, sequential perception and identification of letters, words, spelling patterns and large language units" (Goodman, 1976c, p. 497). Reading is instead a process of sampling, predicting, guessing—in short a "psycholinguistic guessing game" (Goodman, 1976c). The meaning is in the mind of the reader rather than in the print. The reader must actively *interact* with the print in order to decode the author's message.

Three sets of cues are involved in that interaction: graphic, syntactic, and semantic. The better the reader knows the topic area in which he or she is reading, the faster and more fluent the reading. Also people who know the topic area well are able to abstract more meaning from the print, because they bring more understanding to it. There is then no stable process of dealing with graphic cues. Their importance depends upon the amount of knowledge the reader brings to the reading situation and on the other cues available.

Knowledge of syntax constitutes another cue in reading. N. Chomsky (1965) distinguished between "deep" and "surface" structure. Deep structure refers to the level of language at which meaning is interpreted, i.e., the semantic level. Surface structure refers to the level at which phonological or graphic representations are realized. The bridge that enables a reader (or a speaker) to move back and forth between the deep and surface structures is syntax (the knowledge of words and grammar). Kolers (1970) argued that any theory of reading that attempts to explain reading by the matching of sounds and letters, discrimination of letters, or other such skills that look at words in isolation is "insensitive" to even the most rudimentary aspects of language processing.

Words must be in context for us to understand them. For example, how should one pronounce *envelope*? (Has the dog been enveloped by the quicksand?) Only by looking at words in relation to other words and by understanding their grammatical functions can we cross the bridge from meaning to pronunciation. Conversely, we can cross the bridge in the other direction, that is from the surface to deep structure. For example, consider the deep structure difference between "the blue boy's horn" and "the boy's blue horn."

Kolers (1970) found that many errors in reading were constrained by syntax. For example, people reading aloud tended to substitute words that were the same parts of speech for words they had misread. When substitutions were not grammatically correct, they usually alerted the readers to their having made an error. Further syntactic information allows the reader to predict what a given word that is not known may be. For example, in the sentence "Mary typed the_____," the missing word could not be *bought, be, beautiful,* or *but.* Knowledge of the grammatical elements of the sentence dictates the use of a noun.

The third type of cueing system that enables the reader to interact with print is the semantic. Our knowledge of the meaning of "Mary typed the_____," allows us to determine that *bouquet, bucket,* and *bicycle* are also inappropriate.

A very limited set of possibilities has been circumscribed. Even though the word has never been read, we know that it has to be a word such as *story, manuscript, list,* or *page.* If we add only a single phonological cue, "Mary typed the b_____," we can predict the word quite accurately without the necessity of seeing it. Theorists who posit that meaning is abstracted directly from print argue that this happens very often in reading. We use the redundancy (Smith, 1971) in the sentence, i.e., the overlap among the cueing systems, to predict what is coming and to derive the meaning of the words we do not know. Because so many cues are available, we need not read every word. Developing fluent reading skills, in fact, means developing strategies for using a minimal amount of graphic information.

Although Goodman (1976c) acknowledged that there is a difference in the reading behavior of beginning and proficient readers, Smith (1977) argued that the difference may be the result of educational strategies rather than the child's spontaneous response to print. He has observed, for example, that children who are just learning to read tend to skip the words they do not know and to guess at their meaning from the context. They make few attempts to sound the words, even though many children know both the alphabet and that "B is for ball" at quite a tender age.

Implications for Instruction in Reading   One major implication of the direct-meaning theories of reading is that reading never constitutes an end in itself. People read and children will learn to read when there is a necessity to do so (Goodman & Goodman, 1976). Instruction in reading, therefore, should always be meaningful. A variety of materials should be used to ensure that the content is interesting and relevant. Children should, at least part of the time, be encouraged to select their own materials. Goodman (1976b) pointed out that reading to learn stimulates learning to read.

These theorists also argue that the only valid goal of reading is comprehension. Children cannot learn to comprehend meaning, i.e., to decode the writer's message, by doing drills and exercises. Smith (1973) drew an analogy between learning to read and learning to ride a bicycle. In neither case, he argued, do lists of rules or emphases on splinter skills help. Riding and reading are integrated processes in which abilities must be used simultaneously, not one at a time. The only way to learn to read, therefore, is by reading. Drills, exercises, and games divert children's attention for long periods of time from what they should be doing—reading!

According to this view, behavioral objectives have no place in reading instruction. Goodman (1976a) argued that the use of behavioral objectives reflects a confusion between competence and performance. Performance is too often accepted as an indication of competence. To emphasize his point he described a study conducted with Burke in which they found that as children became rapid, effective silent readers, they read orally less well. They were distracted and disrupted by the necessity of encoding what they were reading into oral language. Poor oral reading indicated a higher level of competence!

Another issue related to the use of behavioral objectives is that they tend to lead to the isolation of fragmentary skills and to quite limited outcomes. Smith (1973) noted that fractionating the reading process into its constituent parts changes not only the process, but also the nature of the parts. Emphasis on phonic skills, for example, may interfere with the use of syntactic or semantic cues. He also pointed out that the separation of "code-breaking" from meaning is artificial. Language is not simply a set of symbols: it is a system of communication. "Phonemes do not exist outside of the full system of constraints in which they are found" (p. 163). In addition, Smith argued, oral language is no less a code than written language and yet few persons suggest that oral language be taught sound by sound outside a context of meaning.

Finally, behavioral objectives necessitate a hierarchically organized sequence of teaching that is necessarily arbitrary (Goodman, 1976a). Reading cannot be adequately explained in terms of sequential processing of hierarchical skills (LaBerge, 1980). Furthermore, Reid (1979) has argued that when sequences of behavioral objectives are used as the basis for teaching, children must have the flexibility to adapt to someone else's structure—that is not likely to be the children who have learning disabilities. In addition, putting the parts together is a job that is left almost entirely to the children themselves. The assumption is often made that if the parts are taught, the relations between them will become magically clear. This assumption is implicit in the notion that teaching children to decode words will lead to comprehension.

Four additional areas in which the direct-meaning school differs from the decode-to-sound school in their assessment of instructional procedures are in the teaching of skills, the role of error, the concept of readiness, and the problems of dialect differences.[6]

The issues that were raised concerning the use of behavioral objectives grow directly from the objections these theorists have to teaching skills. Goodman is perhaps the most liberal on this issue and says that the teaching of skills may be useful, but only in perspective. Insistence on the correct identification of each word, for example, leads teachers to teach phonics skills. We have seen from our example (Mary typed the book.), however, that we do not need to read every word. We can use a variety of techniques to understand written language. As a more dramatic example, Goodman (1976a) noted that children with visual handicaps can learn to read as well as other children. They learn to rely more heavily on syntactic and semantic cues and to use the graphic presentation only to check their assumptions.

The skills Goodman (1976a, pp. 490, 492) advocated teaching are quite different from the conventional ones and include:

1 The ability to scan
2 Fixing or focusing the eye on a line of print
3 Selecting the most important graphic cues, such as initial consonants

---

[6]It should be noted that although the term "psycholinguistic" is popularly associated with the direct-meaning theory, the decode-to-sound theory is equally deserving of the label. The decode-to-sound model is also often referred to as an "information processing" approach to reading.

4 Predicting the graphic presentation from syntactic and growing semantic constraints

5 Forming an image to check what is actually seen with what one expected to see

6 Searching memory so that language knowledge as well as experience and conceptual level can be brought to bear

7 Formulating a tentative hypothesis or making guesses on the basis of the *minimal* number of cues and relevant knowledge related to syntax and semantics

8 Semantic and syntactic testing, i.e., asking whether what has been read makes sense and whether it sounds like language

9 If the working hypothesis has failed either the syntactic or semantic tests, to recall the graphic image for a match and to gather more graphic information if needed

10 Regressing when an hypothesis has failed so that the point of error may be located and the text can be reprocessed

11 Decoding

In this model decoding refers to the integration of the new and the previously forming meaning through assimilation, accommodation, or both (Goodman, 1976a, p. 492). This approach suggests that remedial instruction should include the teaching of such skills *as needed*. No arbitrary teaching sequence is used. The teacher must be knowledgeable about both the reading process and the children and help them as they need it.

Standardized tests that compare reading ability among children are not needed in this model. Reading is not viewed as a competitive sport. If a variety of materials are available for selection by the children, and if children are given help as they require it, the theory suggests there is no need to designate children as special cases. Smith (1973) suggested that singling out a child probably interferes with his or her reading ability. Children who know that they are not performing up to expectations tend to become anxious, to take fewer chances, and consequently, become tied to the print. Often, too, this child is put through a series of drills in which fewer cues are available, and which take time away from reading. Of course, this model would also eliminate classification of children.

Error in this model is both necessary and useful (see also Chapter 3).[7] Goodman (1976a), for example, stated that regressing is an important strategy in reading, because it enables the reader to self-correct. It is the process of correction that leads the reader to new insights, new strategies, and new words. Smith (1971), arguing on the basis of decision theory, pointed out that making an error can be just as informative as being correct. If a child, for example, is not certain as to whether the word is *was* or *saw,* trying the wrong one and judging its appropriateness tells just as much as trying the right one. (Incidentally, if children are taught to use semantic constraints in reading, the confusion between

---

[7]Miscues are discussed in Chapter 10.

was and *saw* often disappears.) Consequently, opportunity to learn is diminished for children who are afraid of making errors. In this model, therefore, guesses are more than appropriate; they are cardinal.

These models do not admit the concept of readiness in the sense of skills needed prior to beginning reading. Smith (personal communication) believes that what children need to know about reading is acquired as a consequence of having read. No special visual, auditory, or verbal ability is needed beyond that which enables children to acquire spoken language and to distinguish familiar objects. Goodman and Goodman (1976) as well as Smith (1977) suggest that literacy develops as a consequence of need and the understanding that meaning is conveyed through print. The Goodmans suggest further that Halliday's (1975) functions of language are as relevant to learning to read as they are to the oral uses of language (see Chapter 12). Children learn early that written language can be used to regulate people's behavior, e.g., STOP signs and prescriptions. Written language can also be used to tell people what you want, to ask questions about objects and events, to create an imaginative situation, etc. Clay (1972, cited in Goodman and Goodman) found that even five-year-olds are aware of print and its uses. Children often ask "What's that say?" or suggest that they know what a printed message such as an advertisement means, even though they cannot read all the words. The Goodmans, therefore, suggested that initial reading instruction should reconstruct the situations in which children naturally acquired their original ability. One should first try to discover what it is the child can already read and to extend the range of competence. This can be done by creating an environment in which written language, play, and learning by reading hold a prominent position. Further, situations should be constructed to allow children to use written language in each of its functions.

Finally, there are differences in the way the direct-meaning and decode-to-sound theorists view the impact of dialect differences. When one supposes that reading is a mapping of sounds to graphic symbols, any variations in spoken language make that mapping more difficult. Smith (1975b), however, argued that the majority of dialects of spoken English differ from standard English in syntax and phonology, but not in regard to deep structure. Since English orthography is not a direct recording of phonology (see the section in this chapter on phonics), Chomsky and Halle have written that it is an optimal system for all dialects. Written language, Smith argued, "should be regarded as a dialect in its own right, mutually comprehensible with speech, just as dialectical varieties of speech are mutually comprehensible because of underlying consistencies" (1975b, p. 352). He believes that children have problems, not because of the structure of written language, but because of classroom problems, teachers that insist that children read word for word, and intercultural conflicts. Goodman (1976a) noted that not only do blacks and other minority group students have problems with reading, but so do boys in general. He thinks that this problem is related to the failure of the schools to reach these children. Much of what is taught in school is simply irrelevant to them.

Summary and Conclusions

The model presented here as an alternative to the conventional conceptualization of the reading process and of approaches to teaching reading is based on a very different set of assumptions. Reading is seen as a process of deriving meaning. Reading is comprehending directly from print, without the intermediary of oral language. Written language is thought to constitute a parallel to spoken language. The model posits that readers make use of syntactic and semantic as well as phonological and morphological cues. It views reading as a process that requires simultaneous processing on a variety of levels and abhors the splintering of reading into isolable skills. Error is viewed as a necessary and constructive part of learning. Guesses are favored over accuracy. No particular skills are considered prerequisites for reading and the effect of dialectical differences on reading problems is thought to be negligible outside a system of reading instruction that requires word-by-word accuracy.

The present authors could find no evidence that the methods described here had been tested systemmatically with learning disabled children. There are, however, aspects of this theory that are attractive: the lack of concern about errors and the use of three simultaneous cueing systems. Programmed sequences of instruction often decrease the incidence of errors and, thereby eliminate one source of learning. Other, more flexible systems also view errors as things to be avoided. In an atmosphere in which errors are considered important tools of learning, learning disabled children should be less self-conscious and willing to try. The focus on cueing systems provides three means of testing accuracy. Learning disabled children often do not know when they have erred and rely on feedback from teachers. Although feedback is undoubtedly helpful, children must develop means of testing hypotheses for themselves. Asking "Does that make sense?" or "Does that sound like language?" is a beginning in establishing self-check procedures.

A Synthesis: Schema Theory[8]

Rumelhart (1976) offered a compromise to the arguments that reading consisted primarily in breaking the code (Chall, 1967) or that it consisted primarily in mapping previous knowledge onto the printed symbol while utilizing the print as little as possible (Goodman, 1976a, b, c; Smith, 1977). Rumelhart synthesized these two opposing viewpoints by arguing that reading is an *interactive* process which requires both "top down" and "bottom up" processing. Briefly, schema theorists (those who argue that reading is influenced by higher-order as well as perceptual information) contend that neither spoken nor written text, in itself, carries meaning. Listeners or readers must use the cues provided by the writer or the speaker to *construct* the meaning for themselves (Anderson, Spiro, & Montague, 1977).

Perhaps the clearest account of schema theory is that provided by Adams

[8]Adapted from Reid, Knight-Arest, and Hresko (1981).

and Collins (1977). They defined a schema as a description of a particular class of concepts. All schemata are embedded into hierarchical systems. A very general schema which incorporates all aspects of the conceptual class rests at the top of the hierarchy. Adams and Collins give the example (borrowed from the work of Schank and Abelson) of the schema *going to a restaurant.* The top-level schema would include everything known about going to restaurants: that they are commercial establishments; that people select among the choices available; that they eat food that others have prepared for them; that they must pay; and that they do not wash their own dishes. Embedded within this very general schema are more specific schemata which might relate to eating at a fancy restaurant, a stand-up outdoor counter, or a fast-food chain. As one moves down the hierarchy, "the number of embedded schemata multiplies while the scope of each narrows, until, at the bottom most level, the schemata apply to unique perceptual events" (pp. 5–6). The top level, therefore, includes both an abstraction and a conceptual frame of reference for all the particular events that fall within the area comprised by it. Because it must include a sufficiently general description to cover all members of the class, particular data are quite vaguely specified. Because a schema includes the relations among its component parts, elements are understood in context. Mention of an ice cream cone, for example, would be sufficient to rule out the possibility of an exclusive restaurant.

Reading is seen as the simultaneous coordination of schemata at all levels. "Bottom up" processes (e.g., visual features) may lead to higher-level schemata (e.g., letters) which, in turn, may lead to even higher-level schemata (e.g., words), and the process continues upward. At the same time, higher-level schemata are evoked by information obtained from the print and are utilized to fill in (or instantiate) the particular data (lacking from the most general top levels) in a "top down" process. These processes do not occur in a fixed sequence. (See also the Bjork model in Chapter 4.)

Weaver (1978) challenged the popular idea that learning disabled children suffered only from problems of decoding—'bottom up" processing. She indicated that they experience comprehension difficulties even when stories are presented orally and suggested that schema theory offered researchers in learning disabilities a promising framework through which to investigate "top down" processes that affect reading performance. There is currently substantial documentation (cf. Weaver's literature review) to indicate that children with specific reading disability do not always comprehend once they have "cracked the code." Furthermore, Rubin (1977) has delineated differences in both "top down" and "bottom up" processing when written, rather than oral language must be interpreted (e.g., differences in grammar and context). This more complex view of the reading process coupled with our understanding of the difficulties exemplified by learning disabled children suggests a rich area of study. Schema theorists "challenge(s) the wisdom of bottom-up instructional strategies, and . . . all but nullify the generality of empirical findings based on 'isolated' processes" (Adams & Collins, 1978, p. 3).

Summary

We have reviewed a number of techniques for teaching reading, as well as opposing theoretical conceptions of what the process involves. No clear evidence has emerged that supports one program for all the needs of reading. Systems that stress decoding skills appear to be less effective in fostering comprehension, the goal of reading. Those that emphasize comprehension may not develop skills of phonetic analysis and synthesis, especially in learning disabled children. Multisensory programs may be helpful for some children, but do not appear suitable for all or, in some instances, to be more effective than traditional systems. The relevant characteristics of reading problems, themselves, are also at issue.

It appears, then, that there is no simple answer to the question of which instructional program is best for learning disabled children. Learning disabled children with reading problems appear to constitute a heterogeneous group for whom a wide variety of approaches and strategies are useful. Because most instructional systems emphasize one aspect of reading or another, an eclectic approach seems most appropriate. It seems, however, that "bottom up" programs, to borrow Rumelhart's terminology, are not adequate, because they fail to recognize the simultaneous interaction among features, letters, words, syntax, etc. All of these levels must be operating simultaneously for reading to occur. (Recall, for example, the pronunciation of *envelope*.) Systems that take "top down" processes into account seem more appropriate, because they teach reading and reading skills within the context of meaning, and, therefore, use all available aids to decoding written language.

INSTRUCTING LEARNING DISABLED CHILDREN IN READING

The question often asked by practitioners is, "What does all this theorizing mean to me?" Unfortunately, many educators fail to see the implications of research and theory for intervention. Consequently, opportunities for improvement in educational practice are often lost. In fact, intervention is always based on what one thinks about the child's abilities and problems, the nature of the material to be taught, the skills that will need to be utilized, and the nature of learning. When we thought of learning disabilities as perceptual problems, for example, there was a great deal of teaching and remediation emphasizing perceptual skills. When we defined reading as a process of matching visual to auditory cues, again, the conceptions of the reading process influenced the methods selected for reading instruction. Indeed, Harste and Burke (1977) found that both the teaching and learning of reading are theoretically based. If we assume that knowledge is reducible to skills, we teach in sequentially ordered bits. If knowledge is viewed as holistic, we more often employ naturalistic and highly contextualized strategies. Research and theory, therefore, often have a considerable impact on what happens in classrooms—oftentimes, without our awareness.

A variety of techniques have been suggested to incorporate "top down" considerations in instruction, and many seem particularly well suited for the types of individualized instructional programs that severely disabled readers seem to need. Interactive systems also capitalize on the knowledge of spoken language with which the child comes to school. Perhaps, inexpensive and unadorned as they are, language experience approaches incorporating a variety of instructional techniques can constitute as powerful and as comprehensive an instructional system as the most expensive and carefully sequenced commercial series. Furthermore, language experience is also sufficiently flexible to be used with nearly any type of reading series a teacher might prefer.

Instructional techniques that seek to foster fluent, automatic reading, include *reading to, reading with, reading again,* and *reading together.* There are a number of apparent benefits to be gained from *reading to* children. Probably foremost among them is that the child is given opportunity to hear an adult read quickly, accurately, fluently, and automatically. There is, then, no question about what reading is and how it should be done. Reading is from the beginning seen as something one does for fun and/or to gain information—that it has a purpose is clear. Children who listen to stories have the opportunity to learn about important story elements such as plot, character, motive, etc. (Stein & Glenn, 1979) and to begin to develop other necessary comprehension abilities.

Reading with is sometimes referred to as assisted reading (Hoskisson, 1979). The intent of *reading with* children is to enable them to be immersed in print, even though they may not be able to read fluently, themselves. There are three stages in assisted reading. In the first stage, the teacher (or parent) reads aloud to the child (or children) and then asks the child to repeat what is read as he or she follows along in the book. In the second stage, the teacher reads aloud, but skips words that the child knows, so that the child can supply them. Finally, in the third stage, the child reads and the teacher simply supplies any words the child does not know. Assisted reading is not intended to constitute a comprehensive approach to reading instruction. It is, rather, intended as a first approach to be followed by more systematic instruction (including phonics) once the child is able to do some reading and once he or she has acquired the habit of reading. Other means of *reading with* include the use of talking books and taped passages.

Reading again is also an important strategy. In separate studies, both Samuels (1979) and C. Chomsky (1978) demonstrated that repeated readings encourage automaticity—especially for students with learning problems. Typically, we keep pressing students to read at higher and higher levels of complexity. For readers who are having difficulty, that sometimes means keeping them on the edge of failure. Children can read fluently with comprehension only when they can read with approximately 95 percent accuracy. Furthermore, they tend to use *different* strategies in reading easy rather than difficult text (Leslie & Osol, 1978). If our aim is to practice with appropriate strategies, it seems apparent that lateral reading (reading a number of books at the same level of difficulty) and rereading constitute important supplemental instructional alternatives. In addition, rereading suggests that books have value. All of us occasionally reread a favorite book—just for the sheer pleasure of doing so.

Reading together is a large-group variant of *reading with*. Choral reading provides a fluent model and gives the child an opportunity to participate as well as he or she can. Choral reading may be most effective when combined with rereading. The first time a child comes across an unknown word, he or she has an opportunity to hear the other readers read it. By the third or fourth reading, the child will have acquired a new word.

All of these approaches—language experience, *reading to, reading with, reading again,* and *reading together*—provide children with the view that reading is purposeful, meaningful, and rapid. They can all be used as either initial or remedial instructional approaches and can be used with nearly any reading series. But practice in fluent, oral reading is not enough. In fact, as Groff (1979a, b) noted in his criticism of the *Reading Miscue Inventory* (see Chapter 10), oral and silent reading do not appear to access the same linguistic competence (see also Mosenthal, 1976–1977). Practice in silent reading is also crucially (and many would argue supremely) important.

One problem that seems to have plagued teachers is that children tend to forget tomorrow what they learned today. We seem to be very able to teach children so that they appear to understand, but those techniques clearly do not ensure that they will maintain what they have learned. It has been demonstrated repeatedly that, contrary to popular belief, primary rehearsal does not lead to long-term storage. We have traditionally given children drills and exercises that incorporate only simple repetition. As we noted in the chapters on memory, perception, and attention, what leads to long-term storage is the continued processing of information so that new information is related to what the child previously knew. Gagné and Memory (1978) have shown that encouraging the reader to relate old and new information is effective in enhancing comprehension. A number of teaching techniques have been developed that are helpful in fostering the drawing of relationships: the use of contextual (especially visual) information (Sherman, 1976), making comprehension an explicit goal of reading (Schwartz, 1977), the use of a guided lecture in which important ideas are noted (Kelly & Holmes, 1979), problem-solving tasks (Hoffman, 1979), inquiry training (Legenza, 1978), and concept stretching, slicing, and other questioning techniques, previewing techniques, and feedback and modeling strategies (Pearson & Johnson, 1978).

Finally, a considerable amount of the research coming out of the Center for the Study of Reading (a federally funded center designed to clarify the processes involved in reading and to develop better assessment and instructional systems) has indicated that many children have difficulties determining whether they have understood what they have read and in deciding what to do if they have not (cf. Anderson, 1977; Baker, 1979; Brown & Smiley, 1977). Generally, it is the teacher who monitors the child's comprehension, but certainly that is a task that all readers must learn to do for themselves. Schallert and Kleiman (1979) suggested that one of the goals of comprehension instruction should be to help children find ways to check whether they are understanding and to develop strategies for coping when they have not understood. Encouraging children to form associations, to paraphrase, and to make comparisons may be helpful as methods useful in guiding children back to and through a text (Pearson & Johnson, 1978).

Finally, it has been demonstrated repeatedly that instruction in high-achieving schools has the following characteristics (Guthrie, 1978): (1) careful adherence to district policy, (2) formal teaching and evaluation practices, (3) relatively large blocks of time devoted to instruction in reading and mathematics, (4) teachers who stay abreast of children's accomplishments and who keep careful records, (5) the use of many supplemental materials, and (6) the bulk of time spent on instruction rather than management problems. Certainly, to some extent, these are the characteristics of achieving schools because it is in this kind of environment that children learn the skills and abilities that will be on tests. But it is undeniably true—no matter what theoretical stance one takes—that the effectiveness of reading instruction is enhanced when children are given considerable time to read and when teachers are knowledgeable about the abilities the children demonstrate.

SUMMARY AND CONCLUSIONS

In this chapter, we have examined kinds of reading problems and have categorized them under two types: primary and secondary. Those with learning disabilities include persons whose problems are restricted to reading and those whose reading problems are secondary, except where those problems result from a condition that has been given another label within special education (mental retardation, emotional disturbance, etc.). An exploration of a variety of explanations for dyslexia indicated that the most widely accepted explanation is that of maturational lag. This is the preferred etiology because: (1) it is parsimonious in that it can as easily account for other academic difficulties (dysgraphia, dyscalculia, etc.), and (2) it views the problem as *functional* rather than pathological. Children with reading problems are seen as the naturally occurring, lower end of the normal curve. As Rudel (1977) is fond of saying, if schools prized musical ability as highly as they prize reading ability, many of us would have gone through school labeled as "dysmusics" or perhaps (improperly) "musiclexics."

Our review of instructional systems was divided according to the theoretical orientation that gave rise to each: the conventional approaches based on the assumption that reading is decoding to sound, the cognitive/psycholinguistic alternative that argues that meaning is derived directly from print without translation to oral language and, finally, a cognitive synthesizing position that views reading as an interactive process simultaneously integrating "top down" and "bottom up" processing at all levels. To date, we have no evidence that any particular instructional system reduces the incidence of reading problems in the schools. Although phonics programs, for example, have been demonstrated effective (Groff, 1979a), there does not appear to be any improvement in poor readers' comprehension that results from word identification training. Although word identification correlates substantially ($r = .68$, Schwartz, 1977) with overall measured reading ability, careful examination of the nature of children's performances indicated that the relation is a "weak" one and that a number of different types of disabled readers can be distinguished. It appears, therefore, that the most promising instructional systems and programs are those that:

1 Approach reading as an interactive process and employ techniques designed to enable children to understand the nature and function of reading;
2 Regard the outcomes of reading as personal;
3 Recognize that children read better when they are reading material that is interesting to them;
4 Include for those who need it, systematic and structured instruction in a variety of techniques for the analysis and synthesis of the graphic representation.

SUGGESTED READINGS

Kolers, P. A., Wrolstad, M. E., & Bouma, H. (Eds.). *Processing of visible language, Vol. 1.* New York: Plenum Press, 1979.

Pearson, T. D., & Johnson, D. D. *Teaching reading comprehension.* New York: Holt, Rinehart and Winston, 1978.

Singer, H., & Ruddell, R. B. (Eds.). *Theoretical models and processes of reading.* Newark, Delaware: International Reading Association, 1976.

Smith, F. *Understanding reading.* New York: Holt, Rinehart and Winston, 1978.

Chapter 14

Written Language

INTRODUCTION

Disorders of written language have been noted consistently in the learning disabled (Johnson & Myklebust, 1967; Myers & Hammill, 1976). Until recently, however, the magnitude of the problem was not recognized; neither was sufficient research effort expended on determining the parameters of the disabilities. We will address three aspects of written language in this chapter: spelling, handwriting, and composition. Although these topics will be treated as distinct entities, the reader should realize that education is an integrative process, and that the topics included here, along with reading and oral language, form the basis for a total language arts program. Spelling and handwriting are, after all, only tools to be used in composition—the expressive analog of reading. Teachers can profit from considering their interactive nature in instructional planning. Having had uncomfortable or failing experiences with reading, many learning disabled students are likely to be less than enthusiastic about writing compositions, spelling, and handwriting. Furthermore, the reluctant reader, because of a lack of experience with print, is unlikely to be aware of words that do not correspond to phonetic rule generalizations (Otto, McMenemy, & Smith, 1973).

SPELLING

Spelling and handwriting share the distinction of having been virtually neglected in the development of innovative curriculum strategies in both special and regular education. As a consequence, the teacher of the learning disabled has little information to build on regarding types of spelling errors, kinds of instruction available, or strategies for task modifications. In fact, it has not been demonstrated that people actually become better spellers after having had consistent instruction in spelling. Older school children with little or no formal instruction appear to spell as well as children who have had regular instruction. Of course, for learning disabled children who appear to lack a level of linguistic awareness commensurate with that of their peers, it may be helpful to make regularities in spelling explicit. We will provide information from two sources: from the research with learning disabled populations where it is available, and from the research with normal children.

Instruction in Spelling

Both regular class and learning disabled children have difficulties mastering the complexities of spelling. Spelling mastery is almost a universal goal in education, but one that most pupils do not achieve. Learning to spell is complicated by numerous factors. We must learn to spell words which conform to some type of rule structure. We must learn to spell words which are not rule governed, but which vary according to tense change (e.g., choose, chose) or plurality (e.g., woman, women). We must learn to spell so that others view us as competent language users. We must learn to spell automatically so that efforts to write will not prohibit getting thoughts on paper. The sheer number of words with which we must deal makes this an extremely difficult task.

Numerous authors indicate the need to assess and develop spelling "readiness" through discrimination training, memory training, sound blending, and auditory closure. This type of prespelling instruction is inefficient. "Readiness" for spelling consists not of these correlated skills, but rather in exposure to language and to the written language system. Success in spelling depends on facility with language and understanding of the regularities which it has. The best possible spelling readiness system is probably a broad language development program, integrating reading, writing, listening, and speaking skills.

As we have hinted before, the teaching of spelling is best integrated as a part of the entire language arts system so that the experiences the child has with other aspects of the language arts curriculum feed into spelling instruction. What becomes difficult to decide upon is *what* should be taught in a spelling program. Should the spelling program tie directly into the reading program? Should the teacher focus on rule acquisition? Should methods be deductive or inductive? Perhaps the best way to begin to decide what should be taught is to focus on whether the instruction is to be developmental or remedial.

Given that the approach to be chosen is developmental, anyone of a number of basic spelling programs are available. A recent survey by Hammill,

Larsen, and McNutt (1977) indicated that of the basal spelling series available to teachers, the three most often selected for use were *Spell Correctly* (Benthul, Anderson, Utech, Biggy, & Bailey, 1974), *Word Book* (Rogers, Ort, & Serra, 1970), and *Basic Goals in Spelling* (Kottmeyer & Claus, 1968, 1972). There appears to be little to differentiate these programs. Each seeks to improve spelling ability by focusing on the words most often used by children in their writing at various age levels. *Spell Correctly* develops word patterns from both phonological and morphological sources, while *Word Book* focuses on vowel-changing, rhyming, and nonrhyming patterns. *The Basic Goal in Spelling* series appears to be the most phonetically oriented of the group.

It may very well be, however, that teachers do not have these materials available or that they do not wish to use a formal spelling sequence. The scope and sequence chart presented in Figure 14-1 will provide an overview of spelling skills from early kindergarten through grade 10 (Cohen & Abrams, 1976). Although prepared for use in testing for diagnostic purposes, it does give the teacher an idea of what the focus of instruction in spelling might be at each of a number of grade levels.

Scope and sequence charts may give teachers an understanding of what constitutes appropriate content, but they do not give teachers the answer to *how* the content should be transmitted. One possibility is to focus on the teaching of phonics rules as a method of transmitting spelling ability. But then one must ask whether the rules should be taught directly or indirectly. Furthermore, teaching the rules may be an inappropriate endeavor altogether. In order to teach a rule, one must decide upon what rules will be taught, and when the efficiency of a rule drops low enough to be declared unusable. Smith (1971), for example, noted that seventy-nine rules are needed for determining the pronunciation of primary single-letter vowels alone. Consider the immense number of rules that would be needed if all the letter combinations were to be taught! On the other hand, three points in favor of teaching rules are that: (1) there is a rather consistent relationship between sounds and letter representations, (2) there is a pattern and system in the ways words are created, and (3) the number of "spelling demons" is relatively small (Hanna, Hodges, & Hanna, 1971, p. 97). Teaching each word in isolation would clearly be an exceedingly inefficient way to provide even a small core of words for an individual to employ in writing. Since rules are often helpful in understanding the spelling of those words which we do not classify as demon words, perhaps some type of rule-governed teaching is appropriate.[1] Table 14-1 lists widely applicable spelling rules.

Studying the controversy of whether to teach spelling rules or not has led us to conclude that spelling rules are useful, once an individual knows something about both the way words are spelled and the way words sound. To teach spelling rules to a child who cannot write any words or to teach rules apart from writing

---

[1]This is not to minimize the apparent problems of defining the rule structure for the spelling of a given language. C. Chomsky (1970), Smith (1971), and others have stressed the difficulty of predicting spelling from the phonetic representation of the word and the corresponding difficulty of predicting the sound of a word from the spelling.

Test Level	1	2	3	4	5	6	7	8
Avg. Grade Level	K-3	1-4	2-5	3-6	4-7	5-8	6-9	7-10
Consonants	bd l g h l m n p r t v y	s z w	c j k x qu			c: city g: germ		
Beginning Blends	dr- gr- tr- pl- fl-	sw- sp- sl- st- str- spr- spl-						
Ending Blends	-mp -nd -ft -lt -nt	-st -nt -lf -nd -mp	-nk					
Diagraphs		ch sh th ng	wh					ph: phrase ch: ache
Vowels	short a e i o u	short a e i o u	ai, ay, a-e ee, ea, e-e igh, y i-e, ind oa, ow, o-e, old	u-e: cube	u-e: rule -y: envy	ie: field ei: receive schwa (ə)*	y: system	i: stadium i: companion
Vowel Digraphs				oo: pool	oo: hood ea: ready			
Diphthongs				oi: join ou: cloud ow: down aw: claw	oy: joy ew: chew	au: sauce		
"r" & "l" control				ar, er, ir, ur er, ear are, ire, ore all				
Prefixes				un- re-	pre- en- mis- ex- a- in-	con- per- com-		Derivational Doubling; immature
Suffixes		-s: chops	-s: wheels -ing ed -es	-er -est -ly -ful -y	-tion -ive	-ent -en -ant	-ment -ous -ness -sion	-ance -ence -ible -able -fully -ally -ssion
Endings				-et: target -ic: public -al: signal -le: poodle		-ey: kidney	-us: cactus	
Syllables:** open and closed							open: ti-ny closed: gos sip	
Generalizations						ck-k ch-tch ge-dge		
Advanced Phonics								ti: cautious ci: social fu: future
Contractions							mustn't they've	
Rules							1. Dropping e: hope-hoping 2a. Doubling final consonants (monosyllabic): hop-hopping 3. Changing y to i: funny-funnier	2b. Doubling final consts (polysyllabic): open-opening begin-beginner
Sample Words	lap rug flop yet mint	sang chops brush spent bathtub	mean loaded junk painting waxes	refuse smartest fired join loudly	loyal ahead expensive strangle prescribe	loosen freckle computer belief launched	skinny scaring cloudiness sympathy enormous	fortunately immortal forbidden phrase architect
Total Test Words	20	20	40	40	40	40	40	40

* The "schwa" is a neutral vowel sound in an unaccented syllable.
** Open syllable ends in a vowel making the vowel long: mo/ment, pu/pil. Closed syllable ends in a consonant making the vowel short: sad/dle, pup/py.

Figure 14-1　A scope and sequence chart for spelling. (*From Cohen, C. R. & Abrams, R. M. Spellmaster, spelling: Testing evaluating book one. Exeter, N. H.: Learnco Inc., 1976.*)

Table 14-1   Widely Applicable Spelling Rules

Rule 1   Words Ending in *ff, ll,* or *ss*
Words of one syllable, ending in *f, l,* or *s* (sounding /f/, /l/, or /s/ after one vowel, usually end in *ff, ll,* or *ss.* (If the *f* sounds like /v/ or *s* sounds like /z/ the rule does not apply.) The cli*ff* is ta*ll* and covered with mo*ss.*
Rule 2   Doubling the Final Consonant—Monosyllables
Words of one syllable, ending in one consonant, after one vowel, double the final consonant before a suffix beginning with a vowel, but do not double it when the suffix begins with a consonant: *big, bigger, bigness.*
Rule 3   Doubling the final Consonant—Dissyllables and Polysyllables
Words of more than one syllable, ending in one consonant, after one vowel, double the final consonant before a suffix beginning with a vowel, if the accent is on the last syllable: *be 'gin, beginning;* but *o' pen, opening.*
Rule 4   Silent *e*
Words ending in silent *e* drop the *e* before a suffix beginning with a vowel, but do not drop the *e* before a suffix beginning with a consonant: *hope, hoping, hopeful.*
Rule 5   Regular Plurals
The most common way of forming the plural of nouns is to add *s* to the singular: *dog, dogs; elephant, elephants; table, tables.*
Rule 6   Plurals of Nouns Ending in *s, x, z, ch,* or *sh*
Nouns ending in *s, x, z, ch* or *sh* form the plural by adding es to the singular: *gas, gases; tax, taxes; topaz, topazes; thrush, thrushes; torch, torches.*
Rule 7   Plurals of Nouns Ending in *y*
Nouns ending in *y* after a vowel form the plural by adding *s: boy, boys.*
Nouns ending in *y* after a consonant form the plural by changing *y* to *i* and adding *es: lady, ladies.*
Rule 8   Plurals of Nouns Ending in *o*
Nouns ending in *o* after a vowel form the plural by adding *s: studio, studios.*
For the plural of nouns ending in *o* after a consonant, consult the dictionary.
Rule 9   Plurals of Nouns Ending in *f* or *fe*
Most nouns ending in *f* or *fe* form their plurals regularly by adding *s: roof, roofs; fife, fifes.* However, some of them form the plural by changing the *f* or *fe* to *ves: leaf, leaves; knife, knives.*

is simply neither practical nor effective. A beginning spelling program should focus on having children who can do some reading and writing understand that words are composed of sounds and that the sounds have position and sequence.

If rules are accepted as helpful for teaching, how are the rules to be presented? One approach would be to teach the rules deductively. In this method, the child would first be presented with the rule to be learned and given specific exemplars of the rule. The child would be expected to learn to verbalize the rule and, subsequently, to be able to apply it. In contrast, in the inductive method the child is presented with a number of exemplars and is expected to derive the rule from them. There is no need for each child to develop the rule singly. Children may work in groups or may be guided by a tutor or teacher. Children who are required to extract common elements from the words become the *authors* of the rule. Research has shown that rule learning is enhanced when the children are actively engaged in developing the rule themselves.

Table 14-1 *(continued)*

Rule 10 Possesives
The singular possessive of nouns is formed by adding *'s* to the singular: *Tom's* knife, the *child's* toy. The plural possessive is formed by adding an apostrophe to a plural ending in *s:* the *boys'* knives, the *rabbits'* burrow; and by adding *'s* to a plural not ending in *s: men's* voices, *women's* work, *children's laughter.* The possessive of personal pronouns does not require an apostrophe. The form of the word indicates possession: his, her, their.
The passive form of an indefinite pronoun does require an apostrophe: *one's, anybody's, everybody's, somebody's, any one's, no one's, every one's.*

Rule 11 Plurals of Letters, Figures, and Signs
The plurals of letters, figures, and signs are formed by adding an apostrophe *s:* cross your t's.

Rule 12 Rule for *ie* and *ei*
Put *i* before *e*
Except after *c*
Or when sounded like *a*
As in *neighbor* and *weigh.*

Rule 13 The suffix—*ful*
The suffix *ful* differs from the word full. The suffix never has two l's: joy*ful*, harm*ful*, sorrow*ful*.

Rule 14 The Suffix—*ly*
When the suffix *ly* is added to a word, the spelling of this word does not change: *soft +—ly, softly; safe +—ly, safely; hopeful +—ly, hopefully.*

Rule 15 Final *y* before a Suffix
Words ending in a dipthong, the second letter of which is *y,* remain unchanged before any suffix.

Rule 16 The prefixes *dis*—and *mis*—
The prefixes *dis*—and *mis*—are placed before a word without altering its spelling; *dissatisfy, misdeed.*

Rule 17 Prefixes Changed for the Sake of Euphony
The final consonant of a prefix may change to match the following letter or to a letter more easily blended with it, *col lide* instead of *con lide.*

Source: Adapted from Gillingham & Stillman, 1970.

The instructional area most likely to be neglected in the spelling program is that of pupil discovery of the behavior of phoneme-grapheme correspondences in his language and the rules and generalizations upon which the orthography is based. The inductive approach should be given the importance it deserves; and the teacher, rather than initiating the rule or principle to be learned, should encourage the pupil to extract it from close examination of words which illustrate the generalization being presented in a particular lesson (Hanna, Hanna, Hodges, & Rudorf, 1966, p. 129).

The steps to utilizing an inductive approach to learning a rule are given in Table 14-2. There are perhaps times when it is inefficient to employ the inductive method of teaching. Occasionally, it would require an exceedingly long period of time or the child may have incorrectly formulated an idea of the rule. Although some will question the use of inductive techniques with the learning disabled, Freidman (1978) has presented evidence which indicates that learning disabled children are able to benefit more from inductive than from didactic learning.

Table 14-2 Teaching Spelling Inductively: An Example

1 Show the children a picture symbol of a word containing the letters *ay* in final position (hay, tray, pray).
2 Have the children say the word the picture represents.
3 Write the word on the chalkboard.
4 Have the children supply from their own speaking vocabularies words that have the same final sound (ray, delay, relay, sleigh, today, Chevrolet, holiday).
5 Ask the children to observe the spelling of words in which the final sound is *long a*.
6 Have the children verbalize the generalization they observe (when the *long a* sound comes last in a word, it is usually spelled *ay*).
7 Reinforce the generalization (the children might add the letters *ay* to the first letters they hear in picture symbols—picture of pig stimulates *p + ay = pay*

Source: Adapted from Otto, McMenemy, & Smith, 1973, p. 258.

Remedial Approaches

Remedial approaches in spelling are few. They have paralleled the development of remedial reading programs. Of the available programs for remedial intervention in spelling the systems developed by Fernald (1943) and Gillingham and Stillman (1970) are probably the most widely used. Both of these techniques are detailed and structured, and in most cases, are best reserved for those children who are severely disabled in the area of spelling. In both cases, the teaching of spelling is closely integrated with instruction in reading. For an analysis of these techniques, the reader is referred to Chapter 13.

There exists one other approach to the instruction of spelling which focuses on modality matching, that is, finding out the most preferred modality of an individual and then teaching through that modality (Westerman, 1971). The usefulness of this approach, however, is open to question. Recent research (cf. Tarver & Dawson, 1978) on modality preferences (the primary vehicle special educators have used to operationalize the concept of aptitude treatment interaction) suggests that our ability to determine a person's modality preference is severely limited. (For a discussion of the problems inherent in this approach, see Chapter 5.)

Disabilities in Spelling

There are two distinct ways in which special educators have viewed errors: (1) as the demonstration of problems associated with the specific underlying abilities necessary for task completion, and (2) as errors associated with the rules for graphic representations words. Rather than view the omission of the *r* in *bread*, for example, as the omission of the second letter of a blend (a rule error), those who work from a specific abilities model (cf. Mann & Suiter, 1974) tend to view the error as one of a channel deficit, in this case, an auditory-channel deficit related to auditory discrimination. Rule-oriented persons might view the same errors as indicative of specific rule deficits related to the child's knowledge of blends and the use of double consonants. The former may be thought of as an example of the more conventional approach taken to the analysis of errors within the field of learning disabilities. The alternative view, exemplified by the instructional approach of Hanna, Hodges, and Hanna (1971), and the assessment approaches of Larsen and Hammill (1976) and Kottmeyer (1970), attempt to discover the rule that the child has not mastered.

In assessing frequent errors made by children, Edgington (1957) identified several types of errors (see Table 14-3). These are helpful not only for evaluating spelling errors which occur on tests, but also mistakes made during the course of homework or class assignments. Errors are viewed as misapplications of the rule and a lack of understanding about the exceptions to a rule.[2] Another method of determining the extent of spelling problems would be to use techniques of applied behavioral analysis (Chapter 10) to keep a record of the types and frequency of children's errors and develop a program designed to focus on those detected. The most efficient method would probably be to analyze errors through the use of rules, in order to determine whether a child's errors happen in isolation, and to effect change in the child's spelling behavior by influencing the use of rules rather than reinforcing specific words. Of course, steps should be taken wherever possible to modify the child's instruction so that poor spelling does not become a barrier to performance in other academic areas. Children might profit most from being taught to use a dictionary. Other strategies might include having a peer assigned to provide help in spelling or using tape recorders to "write" letters, compositions, and tests. It is never beneficial to let mastery of lower-level functions (such as spelling) interfere with instruction in higher-order abilities (e.g., expository writing).

Assessment of Spelling Ability

In addition to formal tests (see Chapter 10), informal spelling tests may be developed by individual teachers using measures such as the one described in Table 14-4. The assessment of a child's spelling ability can come from the

[2]The use of phonics as the basis for spelling programs may be deceptively simply. Recall that Smith (1971) noted that there are approximately seventy-nine rules for the pronunciation of vowel sounds alone and, given that a child were capable of having at his or her disposal all seventy-nine rules, there would still be the question of deciding whether or not an exception to one of the rules was at hand. Yet, the use of rules as a basis for *analysis* of the child's spelling problems appears to be a useful framework for teachers to employ.

Table 14-3 Frequent Spelling Errors

1   Addition of unneeded letters (for example, dressess)
2   Omissions of needed letters (hom for home)
3   Reflection of dialectical speech patterns (Cuber for Cuba)
4   Reflection of child's mispronunciations (pin for pen)
5   Reversal of whole words (eno for one)
6   Reversal of consonant order (lback for black)
7   Reversal of consonant or vowel directionality (brithday for birthday)
8   Reversal of syllables (telho for hotel)
9   Phonetic spelling of nonphonetic words or parts thereof (cawt for caught)
10 Wrong association of a sound with a given set of letters, such as *u* learned as *ou* in you.
11 "Neographisms" or letters put in a word that bear no discernible relationship with the word dictated
12 Varying degrees and combinations of these or other possible patterns

Source: Adapted from Edgington, 1957.

Table 14-4   Diagnostic Spelling Test

Give list 1 to any pupil whose placement is second or third grade.
Give list 2 to any pupil whose placement is above grade three.
Grade scoring, list 1:

Below 15 correct:	Below second grade
15-22 correct:	Second grade
23-29 correct:	Third grade

Any pupil who scores above 29 should be given the list-2 test.
Grade scoring, list 2:

Below 9 correct:	Below third grade
9-19 correct:	Third grade
20-25 correct:	Fourth grade
26-29 correct:	Fifth grade
Over 29 correct:	Sixth grade or better

Any pupil who scores below 9 should be given the list-1 test.

List 1

#	Word	Illustrative Sentence	Element Tested
1	not	He is not here.	
2	but	Mary is here, but Joe is not.	
3	get	Get the wagon, John.	Short vowels
4	sit	Sit down, please.	
5	man	Father is a tall man.	
6	boat	We sailed our boat on the lake.	
7	train	Tom has a new toy train.	Two vowels together
8	time	It is time to come home.	
9	like	We like ice cream.	Vowel-consonante-e
10	found	We found our lost ball.	
11	down	Do not fall down.	ow-ou spelling of ou sound
12	soon	Our teacher will soon be here.	
13	good	He is a good boy.	Long and short oo
14	very	We are very glad to be here.	
15	happy	Jane is a happy girl.	Final y as short i
16	kept	We kept our shoes dry.	c and k spellings of the
17	come	Come to our party.	k sound
18	what	What is your name?	
19	those	Those are our toys.	wh, th, sh, ch, and ng
20	show	Show us the way.	spellings and ow spelling
21	much	I feel much better.	of long o
22	sing	We will sing a new song.	
23	will	Who will help us?	
24	doll	Make a dress for the doll.	Doubled final consonants
25	after	We play after school.	
26	sister	My sister is older than I.	er spelling
27	toy	I have a new toy train.	oy spelling of oi sound
28	say	Say your name clearly.	ay spelling of long a sound
29	little	Tom is a little boy.	le ending
30	one	I have only one book.	
31	would	Would you come with us?	Nonphonetic spellings
32	pretty	She is a pretty girl.	

Table 14-4 *(continued)*

List 2

	Word	Illustrative Sentence	Element Tested
1	flower	A rose is a flower.	ow-ou spellings of ou sound
2	mouth	Open your mouth.	er ending, th spelling
3	shoot	Joe wants to shoot his new gun.	
4	stood	We stood under the roof.	Spelling
5	while	We sang while we marched.	wh spelling, vowel-
6	third	We are in the third grade.	consonant-e
7	each	Each child has a pencil.	
8	class	Our class is reading.	ch spelling, two vowels
9	jump	We like to jump rope.	together
10	jumps	Mary jumps rope.	Double final consonant, c;
11	jumped	We jumped rope yesterday.	spelling of k sound
12	jumping	The girls are jumping rope now.	
13	hit	Hit the ball hard.	
14	hitting	John is hitting the ball.	j spelling of soft g sound
15	bite	Our dog does not bite.	
16	biting	The dog is biting on the bone.	Doubling final consonant
17	study	Study your lesson.	before adding ing
18	studies	He studies each day.	Dropping final e before ing
19	dark	The sky is dark and cloudy.	
20	darker	This color is darker than that one.	Changing final y to i
21	darkest	This color is the darkest of the three.	before ending
22	afternoon	We may play this afternoon.	er, est endings
23	grandmother	Our grandmother will visit us.	
24	can't	We can't go with you.	
25	doesn't	Mary doesn't like to play.	Compound words
26	night	We read to mother last night.	Contractions
27	brought	Joe brought his lunch to school.	
28	apple	An apple fell from the tree.	Silent gh
29	again	We must come back again.	
30	laugh	Do not laugh at other children.	le ending
31	because	We cannot play because of the rain.	
32	through	We ran through the yard.	Nonphonetic spellings

evaluation of assignments, stories written by the child, answers to test questions, and almost any other source which allows the analysis of the child's written language. To assist in this endeavor, it is useful to know not only the types of errors most commonly made, but also the scope and sequence of spelling elements. The teacher may wish to develop a checklist. Knowing the types of problems to look for facilitates the analysis of errors.

HANDWRITING

Handwriting refers not to the creative aspects of writing which will be referred to as composition, but to the motor act of writing. The topics we will address in this section include a discussion of how one approaches instruction in handwriting, intervenes in remediating handwriting, and evaluates a child's performance. The child who is having reading problems often exhibits handwriting difficulties as well.

Instruction in Handwriting

As with practically every other academic skill, many educators assume that "readiness" skills must be developed prior to instruction in handwriting. Most focus on the development of eye-hand coordination, ocular control, laterality, small-muscle coordination, etc. While it may be that some degree of eye-hand coordination, for example, is necessary for adequate handwriting, the only way to determine whether a child is ready to profit from instruction in handwriting is to teach him or her to write and then evaluate the product. Eye-hand coordination is, after all, developed during the experience of writing. The use of correlated underlying abilities as the means of establishing readiness for handwriting lacks empirical justification (Harris & Herrick, 1963; Wiederholt, 1971). A more appropriate activity would be convincing the child that letters and symbols are useful. If handwriting is to be presented to the child as something worthy of attention, then the child must be offered a reason to be interested. Introducing handwriting within the context of language often provides that motivation. It also prevents teachers from forgetting that handwriting is a tool to permit expressive writing, not a goal in itself (Hammill, 1978; Wallace & Larsen, 1978).

Children are expected to learn manuscript and cursive handwriting during the first four years of school. During first grade, children are expected to learn manuscript and become proficient in using it as a tool. During second grade, children begin the shift to cursive handwriting and by the end of the third grade, woe is the child who has not become proficient in cursive writing! It is amazing to note that the emphasis on handwriting and the shift from manuscript to cursive are based on convention. Not too long ago, a person's social competence was judged by the "flair" and "style" of his or her writing. Today, this sequence of instruction appears a tribute to history rather than a prudent practice.

Whether manuscript or cursive handwriting should be taught is an unresolved controversy. Although the argument has been raised repeatedly in the field of learning disabilities, it is also of concern in regular education. The arguments for teaching manuscript are that it is not only much easier to learn, but that it conforms to print, and is usually much more legible than cursive handwriting. Although opponents of manuscript suggest that it is a slower form of writing than cursive, research suggests that it is not. On the cursive side, the arguments are often made that it is faster and more fluid, that by beginning with cursive, there is no need to transfer, and that it eliminates reversals and inversions. In actuality, it probably does not matter which system is taught. Children have been shown to experience problems either way.

Of the developmental handwriting programs (those structured programs to be used by groups of children) the Noble and Noble (1966) program, *Better Handwriting For You,* and the Zaner-Blosner publications, *Chalkboard Tech-*

niques and Activities for Teaching (1976) and *Creative Growth With Handwriting* (1975), are among the more widely used. Each presents sequenced material, moving from manuscript through cursive handwriting. Each can adequately meet the needs of the teacher interested in handwriting materials.

For the teacher who wishes to develop handwriting materials without becoming involved in sequenced structured texts, scope and sequence charts and materials are available which present material related to the manner in which handwriting instruction should be introduced and developed. Table 14-5 presents an adapted set of sample handwriting skills developed by Stephens, Hartman, and Lucas (1978).

Hofmeister (1973) posited five *instructional errors* to avoid: (1) massed practice without supervision, (2) lack of immediate feedback, (3) emphasis on rote practice instead of use, (4) failure to provide good models, and (5) lack of differentiation between good and poor work samples. Any one of the above could contribute to the lack of success a child may experience in handwriting development.

Remedial Instruction

There are few materials and methods available for the remediation of handwriting difficulties. Our designation of what will be considered as a remedial technique is based on factors such as the focus on specific instructional elements, utilization of techniques not normally used in the regular class, and techniques designed for use with limited numbers of children.

One method of remedial instruction in handwriting is that of Gillingham and Stillman (1970) (see also Chapter 13). Writing in this program is subsumed under the visual-kinesthetic language linkage. Associations are formed as the child watches the teacher make a letter and provides a verbal explanation of the formulation. The child then traces the teacher's model, with the tracing

Table 14-5   Sample Handwriting Skills

	Manuscript skills	
Level 1	316*	To write the straight-line letters I, i, t, when shown models.
	325	To write slant-line letters v, w, k, x, z, when the letter names are given orally.
Level 2	330	To maintain correct alignment in writing words, by having letters of same size equal in height.
	331	To write words that have minimum, intermediate, and tall letters and have those letters be the correct proportion to one another.
Level 3	337	To write the punctuation marks., ,, ?, " ", when shown models.
	338	To write the punctuation marks ., ,, ?, " ", when shown a sentence and given punctuation mark names orally.
	Cursive skills	
Level 3	341	To write the undercurve letters i, t, e, l, u, w, r, s, b, when shown models.
	355	To write the double loop letters J, L, when shown models.
	365	To write the difficult joinings ov, ve, ye, ga, bo, wl, be, yo, when shown models.

Source: Adapted from Stephens, Hartman, & Lucas, 1978, pp. 181-183 Copyright © 1978 Bell and Howell Company.
*Three-digit numbers indicate the skills order in the teaching sequence.

continuing until the model is mastered. The next stages of instruction are copying, writing from memory, and writing with eyes closed or averted. The goal of this program is to develop automaticity in the child's writing.

A second method is that developed from the Montessori language program (Guyer, 1974). With the belief that adequate handwriting depended upon muscular composition, pronouncing the letter and manipulation of the pen or pencil, Montessori's technique depends upon the child's tracing sandpaper letters, then tracing popsicle sticks, the use of metal insets, and finally, the use of a moveable alphabet prior to the use of any writing instrument.

Larson (1968) has presented a remedial program based upon the techniques suggested by Lehtinen. The stages cited by Larson (1968) are: (1) perceptual-motor readiness, (2) duplication of letter forms, (3) spatial organization, (4) combining elements, (5) relating cursive writing to print, (6) relating writing to speech (that is, associating letters and speech sounds), (7) translating meaningful verbal patterns into written forms, and (8) functional writing communication.

Reger, Schroeder, and Uschold (1968) have prepared an extensive sequence for remediating handwriting difficulties where the child is moved through a series of activities from chalkboard through newsprint and lined paper in a sequence designed to develop cursive handwriting skills. The steps are outlined in Table 14-6.

Finally, the work of Johnson and Myklebust (1967) provides yet another framework from which the remediation of handwriting difficulties can proceed. Johnson and Myklebust (1967) provided thorough explanations of educational procedures for both writing difficulties and deficits in revisualization. For the remediation of writing, "it is necessary to begin by presenting visual and kinesthetic patterns separately, gradually working toward integration of the two" (p. 206). Design copying and preletter formation blend movements, whereby letters and numbers are formed. Remedial strategies for revisualization

Table 14-6   Remedial Handwriting

1   Name the letter.
2   Discuss the form of the letter while the child looks at it.
3   On a blank overlay, make the letter for the children.
4   Using the polaroid filter wheel, show the children the direction of the letter.
5   Develop the kinesthetic feel for the form of letters with use of sunken and raised script letterboards (may be purchased from the American Printing House for the Blind).
6   The child makes the letter while he or she looks at the model.
7   The child's eyes are on the model, not on his or her hand.
8   Help the child compare the work with the model.
9   Auditory clues may be given to help the child who has difficulty with the letter, or the child's hand may be held as he or she makes the letter. Some children may need to write the letter in salt or sand (on a salt tray).
10   Have the child write the letter on the chalkboard without the model.
11   Have the child write the letter on newsprint without a model, eyes averted.
12   Have the child write on paper with eyes on the paper.

Source: From *Special Education: Children with Learning Problems* by Roger Reger, Wendy Schroeder, and Kathy Ushold. © 1968 by Oxford University Press, Inc. Used by permission.

focus on improving attention and on progressing from recognition to partial recall to total recall (Johnson & Myklebust, 1967). The rationale "is that the child first requires sufficient opportunity to see and work with the entire stimulus, then with only partial cues, and finally to revisualize them without external assistance" (Johnson & Myklebust, 1967, p. 222). The reader will recognize this technique as *fading* (see Chapter 16). Johnson and Myklebust (1967) have recommended five principles that underlie such remediation for dysgraphics. These principles include moving from gross to fine patterns, developing orderly movements, reinforcement of visual-motor patterns through repetition, using materials with optimal visual feedback to the child (such as finger paints, sand, and stencils), and using verbal directions for the teaching of movements.

We recommend that instruction in handwriting (a) be direct, and (b) take place within a language context. If a child is having difficulty with the formation of specific letters, then it is those specific letters which need attention. Children must be made aware of what the tool of handwriting will allow them to accomplish and the freedom that it will give them. Commitment to learn comes in part from seeing the necessity to learn.

Some children will not be able to master the elements of handwriting, either cursive or manuscript, well enough to allow them to write legibly. For these children, alternative measures must be employed. The use of tape recorders and typewriters is becoming more and more common. Tape recorders can be used for class notes and examinations. Typewriters can be used for homework, reports, and other assignments outside of the classroom.

Assessment of Handwriting Ability

Wiederholt et al. (1978) compiled nine points to note for both manuscript and cursive handwriting. For manuscript writing, the items to evaluate are:

1　Position of hand, arm, body, and/or paper
2　Size of letters: too small, large, etc.
3　Proportion of one letter or word to another
4　Quality of the pencil line: too heavy, light, variable, etc.
5　Slant: too much or irregular
6　Letter formation: poor circles or straight lines, lines disconnected, etc.
7　Letter alignment: off the line, etc.
8　Spacing: letter or words crowded or too scattered
9　Speed: too fast or too slow (p. 183).

With regard to cursive writing, Wiederholt et al. (1978) noted that the teacher should evaluate:

1　Position of hand, arm, body, and/or paper
2　Size of writing: too large, small, etc.
3　Proportion of one letter or word to another
4　Quality of the pencil line: too heavy, light, variable, etc.

5   Slant: too much slanting, too nearly vertical, or wild
6   Alignment of letters off the line in places
7   Letter formation: angular letters, too round or thin, illegible, beginning or
ending strokes poorly made, downstrokes not uniform, letters disconnected, looped
letters, weak, etc.
8   Spacing: margins uneven, letters or words crowded or scattered
9   Connecting lines between letters: improperly executed or placed (p. 184).

It is helpful for teachers to be aware of the more common mistakes that
occur in the development of both manuscript and cursive handwriting skills. For
they can form the basis of evaluation of work samples (see Tables 14-7 and 14-8).

Gillingham and Stillman (1970) noted that left-handed children are very
often referred for instruction in handwriting. One reason for this appears to be

Table 14-7   Most Common Errors of Formation of Manuscript Letters by First-Grade Children

1   The most frequent type of error was incorrect size. The error was most frequent with the
descenders, p, q, y, and j.
2   The letter forms most frequently reversed were N, d, q, and y.
3   Parital omission occurred most frequently in m, U, and I.
4   Additions occurred most frequently with q, C, k, m, and y.
5   Incorrect relationship of parts was generally common, occurring most frequently with k,
R, m, and n.
6   Incorrect placement relative to line was a common error with descenders and a less
frequent error with the other letters.
7   The letter forms most frequently misshaped were j, G, and J.
8   Errors were most frequent in letter forms in which curves and vertical lines merge—J, U, f,
h, j, m, n, r, u; and least frequent in letter forms constructed of vertical lines or horizontal
and verticle lines—E, F, H, I, L, T, i, I, t.

Source: Adapted from Lewis & Lewis, 1965.

Table 14-8   Errors Commonly Occurring at the Elementary School Level in Cursive Writing

1   Failure to close letters (a, b, f, g, j, k, o, p, q, s, y, z)
2   Top loops closed (l like t, e like i)
3   Looping nonlooped strokes (i like e)
4   Using straight-up strokes rather than rounded strokes (n like u, c like i, h like li)
5   End-stroke difficulty (not brought up, not brought down, not left horizontal)
6   Difficulty crossing t
7   Difficulty dotting i
8   Top short (b, d, f, h, k, l, t)
9   Letters too small
10 Closing (c, h, r, u, v, w, y)
11 Part of letter omitted
12 Up-stroke too long
13 Letters too large

Source: Adapted from Newland, 1932.

the general inability of teachers to instruct left-handed children successfully. With the correct instruction, there is no reason why left-handed children should not enjoy success in handwriting. Teachers must identify left-handed writers. Children should be observed prior to instruction in order that the appropriate hand be chosen for instruction. Gillingham and Stillman (1970) noted that some children may choose to begin instruction with the right hand not because that is the one they are most adept with, but because they observe that *most* children use their right hand or that their friends use the right hand.

COMPOSITION

Almost never is curriculum for the learning disabled designed with adequate concern for written expression. This is not to say that mechanics of written expression are not emphasized. Spelling, handwriting, and punctuation are frequently included areas of study. Both creative and expository writing are generally neglected, however.

> Skills will develop if the teacher stimulates the learners to write frequently and confidently, but neither skills nor effective writing will develop if the focus is on isolated skills (Smith, Goodman, & Meredith, 1976, p. 243).

There is no doubt that skills can be taught. Teachers must also, however, realize that children need to be given the opportunity to use these skills in a meaningful, purposeful manner. Since written expression has been virtually ignored by teachers of the learning disabled, this section will list important aspects of understanding and teaching written expression, and will suggest a few methods that can be used to assess the growth of written expression.

Understanding and Teaching Written Expression

At one time or another, all people have the need or desire to write. Such writing may take the form of answering questions on a test, writing a short autobiography on a job application, or filling out one of the countless forms one meets in daily living. As educators become increasingly aware of the needs of secondary learning disabled students, this aspect of writing is beginning to receive attention. The other forms of communication, however, are still not being addressed. These include writing as the communication of events (experiences, feelings, reactions to others) and literary writing. These three categories have been referred to as transactional or functional writing, expressive writing, and literary writing (Britton, 1972), respectively. Although few people gain proficiency in all three, most of us are at least capable of functional and expressive writing.

There appears to be little concensus about the best way to instruct children in written expression. A few points do, however, generate some agreement: (1) children learn to write best when the writing activities they engage in are meaningful and purposeful, (2) children learn to write by writing, not by listening to someone talk about writing or by practicing skill components (Blake, 1971; Cohen & Plaskon, 1980; Ruddell, 1974; Smith, Goodman, & Meredith, 1976), and (3) in the early stages of written expression, mechanics should receive secondary emphasis; the major concern should be for quality and organization of ideas (Ruddell, 1974).

Purpose and meaning are of primary importance. They also reflect the belief that children come to us with a motivation to write which needs to be explored and extended. Meaningless exercises will not encourage a high degree of participation. Smith, Goodman, and Meredith (1976) stress that writing which is not read is not writing, because it ceases to be communication. Children must be given the opportunity to see that their writing is influential and that others view it as having worth.

Instruction in functional writing need not mean boring exercises. Burns and Broman (1979) have listed a number of potentially interesting activities to be included in functional writing assignments. These include not only the traditional forms and applications, but also announcements, letters, reports, diaries, records, minutes, postcards, and newspaper articles. The more children understand the importance of these communications and their effect on those who read them, the more likely they are to develop an interest in writing. Teachers must avoid teaching children functional writing according to a single style or form. Although some conventions must be observed, instruction should not be directed toward the acquisition of rigid formats.

Interest in expressive writing (writing about experiences) develops early in most children. It can be fostered in school by such activities as writing stories and essays, and use of the language experience approach in reading. Unhappily, this ability is inadvertently destroyed in many children by teachers who focus on the *mechanics* of writing rather than on the content. Papers are often returned to children with few comments about the ideas or emotions communicated, but with an abundance of red marks, slashes, and circles pointing out problems with punctuation or spelling. Children need to know that their ideas are as important as the correctness with which they are expressed. Teacher comments, especially for young children's writing, should emphasize the quality of the child's thinking, the clarity with which ideas are expressed, and the adequacy of their organization.

Although some have tried literary writing with mildly handicapped children (Cady, 1975; Nathanson, Cynamon, & Lehman, 1976; Rich & Nedboy, 1977), few teachers engage such children in this activity regularly. Mildly handicapped children, however, are capable of creative, sometimes even poetic writing. Writing about fantasies, desires, feelings, and fears can have the side benefit of allowing a release of emotions. In addition, children can be taught that poetic writing can be fun, beneficial not only for releasing emotion, but just for pleasure. Teachers of the learning disabled can employ the same techniques that are used for teaching normally achieving children. Activities that lead to reflection, feelings, imagining, etc. are useful and fun. Learning disabled children should be exposed to them too. Like other children they can benefit from knowing many different forms of expression.

Few packaged materials have been developed to teach composition. Perhaps the most important factor in developing written composition ability is a conducive atmosphere. Cazden (1971), in discussing the development of language ability in general, focused upon providing "contextual" supports to foster growth. She advocated the use of the child's environment to generate topics for writing lessons. Before children participate in any type of composition program, they must be convinced that they have something to say, and that what they say will be accepted. Since writing a composition is a creative, constructive process, it amounts to sharing oneself. If children feel uncertain about whether what they have to say will be appreciated, they probably will be hesitant about writing.

Teachers may motivate children to write by creating an audience. School newspapers, prose and poetry books, plays, etc. are all appropriate. At the University of Oklahoma, Mandelbaum urges her students who are preparing to become special education teachers to laminate the books written by children in their classes and to have the school library circulate them. What pride children have when their classmates tell them they liked the book! Magazines and commercial programs are often rich sources to help the teacher with creative ideas to foster growth of composition ability. Teachers may also develop writing ability regularly as part of a language experience approach to reading.

Although need for concern for the *content* of writing has been noted in the press (*Time,* May 9, 1980), it is not possible to be totally unconcerned about the need for adequate writing mechanics. Spelling and handwriting have already been discussed, but the development of vocabulary, punctuation, capitalization, and organization are also serious concerns. The scope and sequence chart developed by Hammill and Poplin (1978) is the most complete guide available. Adapted from work by Otto and McMenemy (1966) and Green and Petty (1967), this scope and sequence chart (Table 14-9) covers word usage, vocabulary, punctuation, capitalization, grammar, paragraphs, and sentences from grade 1 through grade 8.

Developing the mechanics of writing is very often badly accomplished. Errors often seen in the writing of adults attest to this failure. With respect to punctuation, some note (Petty, Petty, & Becking, 1976) that these errors are the result of poor instruction, a perceived lack of importance on the part of children, and lack of practice in real writing situations. In order to alleviate these problems, children need practice *writing,* not doing exercises. By motivating children to write and by letting them know what they write is important, teachers can foster the development of skills. The first draft that children do is best attended to for meaning, clarity of thought, purpose, and cohesion. Only secondarily should mechanical errors be noted. In later drafts, when the children are nearing final copy, attention can be given to mechanical problems, i.e., punctuation, spelling, etc.

It is frequently helpful to provide opportunities for students to create their

Table 14-9   A Scope and Sequence for the Development of Conceptual Writing

	Grade 1	Grade 2	Grade 3
Capitalization	The first word of a sentence The child's first and last names The name of the teacher, school, town, street The word "I"	The date First and important words of titles of books the children read Proper names used children's writings Titles of compositions Names of titles: Mr., Mrs., Miss	Proper names: month, day, common holidays First word in a line of verse First and important word in titles of books, stories, poems First word of salutation of informal note, as "Dear" First word of closing of informal note, as "Yours"
Punctuation	Period at the end of a sentence which tells something Period after numbers in any kind of list	Question mark at the close of a question Comma after salutation of a friendly note or letter Comma after closing of a friendly note or letter Comma between the day of the month and the year Comma between name of city and state	Period after abbreviations Period after an initial Use of an apostrophe in a common contraction such as isn't, aren't Commas in a list
Vocabulary	New words learned during experience Choosing words that describe accurately Choosing words that make you see, hear, feel	Words with similar meanings; with opposite meanings Alphabetical order	Extending discussion of words for precise meanings Using synonyms Distinguishing meanings and spellings of homonyms Using the prefix *un* and the suffix *less*
Word usage	*Generally in oral expression* Naming yourself last Eliminating unnecessary words (my father he); use of *well* and *good* Verb forms in sentences: is, are did, done was, were see, saw, seen ate, eaten went, gone came, come gave, given	*Generally in oral expression* Double negative Use of *a* and *an; may* and *can; teach* and *learn* Eliminating unnecessary words (this here) Verb forms in sentences: rode, ridden took, taken grow, grew, grown know, knew, known bring, brought drew, drawn began, begun ran, run	Use of *there is* and *there are; any* and *no* Use of *let* and *leave; don't* and *doesn't; would have, not would of* Verb forms in sentences: throw, threw, thrown drive, drove, driven wrote, written tore, torn chose, chosen climbed broke, broken wore, worn spoke, spoken sang, sung rang, rung catch, caught

Hammill and Poplin, 1978, pp. 186–191.

Table 14-9 *(continued)*

	Grade 4	Grade 5	Grades 6, 7, and 8
Capitalization	Names of cities and states in general Names of organizations to which children belong, such as Boy Scouts, grade four, etc. Mother, Father, when used in place of the name Local geographical names	Names of streets Names of all places and persons, countries, oceans, etc. Capitalization used in outlining Titles when used with names, such as President Lincoln Commercial trade names	Names of the Deity and the Bible First word of a quoted sentence Proper adjectives, showing race, nationality, etc. Abbreviations of proper nouns and titles
Punctuation	Apostrophe to show possession Hyphen separating parts of a word divided at end of a line Period following a command Exclamation point at the end of a word or group of words that make an exclamation Comma setting off an appositive Colon after the salutation of a business letter Quotation marks before and after a direct quotation Comma between explanatory words and a quotation Period after outline Roman numeral	Colon in writing time Quotation marks around the title of a booklet, pamphlet, the chapter of a book, and the title of a poem or story Underlining the title of a book	Comma to set off nouns in direct address Hyphen in compound numbers Colon to set off a list Comma in sentences to aid in making meaning clear
Vocabulary	Dividing words into syllables Using the accent mark Using exact words which appeal to the senses Using exact words in explanation Keeping individual lists of new words and meanings	Using antonyms Prefixes and suffixes; compound words Exactness in choice of words Dictionary work; definitions; syllables; pronunciation; macron; breve Contractions Rhyme and rhythm; words with sensory images Classification of words by parts of speech Roots and words related to them Adjectives, nouns, verbs—contrasting general and specific vocabulary	Extending meanings; writing with care in choice of words and phrases In writing and speaking, selecting words for accuracy Selecting words for effectiveness and appropriateness Selecting words for courtesy Editing a paragraph to improve a choice or words

Table 14-9 *(continued)*

	Grade 4	Grade 5	Grades 6, 7, and 8
Word usage	Aggreement of subject and verb Use of *she, he, I, we,* and *they* as subjects Use of *bring* and *take* Verb forms in sentences: blow, blew, blown drink, drank, drunk lie, lay, lain take, took, taken rise, rose, risen	Avoiding unnecessary pronouns (the boy he . . .) Linking verbs and predicate nominatives Conjugation of verbs, to note changes in tense, person, number Transitive and intransitive verbs Verb forms in sentences: am, was, been say, said, said	Homonyms: *its,* and *it's; their, there, they're; there's, theirs; whose, who's* Use of parallel structure for parallel ideas, as in outlines Verb forms in sentences: beat, beat, beaten learn, learned, learned leave, left, left lit, lit, lit
	teach, taught, taught raise, raise, raise lay, laid, laid fly, flew, flown set, set, set swim, swam, swum freeze, froze, frozen steal, stole, stolen	fall, fell, fallen dive, dived, dived burst, burst, burst buy, bought, bought Additional verb forms: *climb, like, play, read, sail, vote, work*	forgot, forgotten swing, swung, swung spring, sprang, sprung shrink, shrank, shrunk slid, slid, slid

Table 14-9 *(continued)*

	Grade 1	Grade 2	Grade 3
Grammar	Not applicable	Not applicable	Nouns: recognition of singular, plural, and possessive Verbs: recognition
Sentences	Write simple sentences	Recognition of sentences; kinds: statement and question Composing correct and interesting original sentences Avoiding running sentences together with *and*	Exclamatory sentences Use of a variety of sentences Combining short, choppy sentences into longer ones Using interesting beginning and ending sentences Avoiding run-on sentences (no punctuation) Learning to proofread one's own and others' sentences
Paragraphs	Not applicable	Not applicable	Keeping to one idea Keeping sentences in order; sequence of ideas Finding and deleting sentences that do not belong Indenting

Table 14-9 *(continued)*

Grade 4	Grade 5	Grades 6, 7, and 8
Nouns, common and proper; noun in complete subjects Verb in complete predicate Adjectives: recognition Adverbs: recognition (telling how, when, where) Adverbs modifying verbs, adjectives, other adverbs Pronouns: recognition of singular and plural	Noun: possessive; objective of preposition; predicate noun Verb: tense; agreement with subject; verbs of action and state of being Adjective: comparison; predicate adjective; proper adjective Adverb: comparison; words telling how, when, where, how much; modifying verbs, adjectives, adverbs Pronouns: possessive; objective after prepositions Prepositions: recognition; prepositional phrases Conjunction: recognition Interjection: recognition	Noun: clauses; common and proper nouns; indirect object Verb: conjugating to note changes in person, number, tense; linking verbs with predicate nominatives Adjective: chart of uses; clauses; demonstrative; descriptive, numerals; phrases Adverb: chart of uses; clauses; comparison; descriptive; *ly* ending; modification of adverbs; phrases Pronoun: antecedents; declension chart—person, gender, case; demonstrative; indefinite; interrogative; personal; relative Preposition: phrases Conjunction: in compound subjects and predicates; in subordinate and coordinate clauses Interjection: placement of, in quotations Noun: antecedent of pronouns; collective nouns; compound subject; direct object; indirect object; object of preposition Verb: active and passive voice; emphatic forms; transitive and intransitive; tenses; linking verbs Adverb: as modifiers; clauses; comparing adverbs; adverbial phrase, use of *well* and *good* Adjectives: as modifiers; clauses; compound adjectives Pronouns: agreement with antecedents; personal pronoun chart; indirect object; object of preposition; objective case, person and number; possessive form

(Grammar)

Table 14-9 *(continued)*

	Grade 4	Grade 5	Grades 6, 7, and 8
Grammar			Preposition: in phrase Conjunction: coordinate; subordinate; use in compound subjects; compound predicates; complex and compound sentences
Sentences	Command sentences Complete and simple subject; complete and simple predicate Adjectives and adverbs recognized; pronouns introduced Avoiding fragments of sentences (incomplete) and the comma fault (a comma where a period belongs) Improving sentences in a paragraph	Using a variety of interesting sentences: declarative; interrogative; exclamatory; and imperative (*you* the subject) Agreement of subject and verb; changes in pronoun forms Compound subjects and compound predicates Composing paragraphs with clearly stated ideas	Development of concise statements (avoiding wordiness or unnecessary repetition) Indirect object and predicate nominative Complex sentences Clear thinking and expression (avoiding vagueness and omissions)
Paragraphs	Selecting main topic Choosing title to express idea Making simple outline with main idea Developing an interesting paragraph	Improvement in writing a paragraph of several sentences Selecting subheads as well as main topic for outline Courtesy and appropriateness in all communications Recognizing topic sentences Keeping to the topic as expressed in title and topic sentence Use of more than one paragraph Developing a four-point outline Writing paragraphs from outline New paragraphs for new speakers in written conversation Keeping list of books (authors and titles) used for reference	Analyzing a paragraph to note method of development Developing a paragraph in different ways: e.g., with details, reasons, examples, or comparisons Checking for accurate statements Use of a fresh or original approach in expressing ideas Use of transition words to connect ideas Use of topic sentences in developing paragraphs Improvement in complete composition—introduction, development, conclusion Checking for good reasoning Use of bibliography in report based on several sources

own standards for evaluating composition. It often helps them focus on the important aspects of writing. Students generally need help in developing independence in proofreading and dictionary skills (Hammill, 1978; Wiederholt, Hammill, & Brown, 1978).

With respect to sentences, C. Chomsky (in preparation) and others (Hunt, 1969; Mellon & O'Hare, 1973; O'Hare, 1973) have worked on techniques for developing awareness of syntactic structure in children. Sentence combining, phrasing, paraphrasing, sentence comparisons, sentence ambiguity, lexical ambiguity, etc. help make children aware of how they can manipulate words. Children need practice varying the complexity of sentences and with becoming aware of run-on-sentences, sentence fragments. etc. The necessary paragraph knowledge includes developing logical sequences, focusing on the topic, writing related sentences, summarizing, and bridging from one paragraph to another (Burns, 1974).

These mechanical aspects of writing are important. People often determine the worth of ideas by the "cleanness" of the writing. The goal for teachers of the learning disabled is not to develop a cadre of budding authors, but to help children who traditionally have difficulty communicating develop more effective expression. In sum, the instructional activities necessary for inclusion in a composition program are punctuation and capitalization, vocabulary, word usage, grammar, sentence construction, and paragraph construction (Wiederholt, Hammill, & Brown, 1978). The key to success is in remembering that writing instruction is helpful only after children have some idea of the meaning of writing as communication and have done some writing.

Assessment of Composition Ability

In addition to formal evaluation, there are other methods of determining how children are progressing in written language. Cohen and Plaskon (1980) suggested that teachers develop checklists of punctuation usage, capitalization, etc., and that a record be kept of when children successfully demonstrate usage.

T-units are measures of the syntactic maturity of writing. They are essentially clauses. As children mature, they tend to use a greater number of clauses per sentence. Maturity also brings a more sophisticated vocabulary, often measured by the average number of syllables per word. Analyzing student compositions in these ways is useful in documenting growth over time. Another method, borrowed from the oral language realm, is the type-token ratio. In this method the number of different words is divided by the number of total words. The resulting decimal gives an index of whether there is a great deal of redundancy in the writing. For example, the closer the decimal is to 1.0, the more *different* words the writer is using. The closer to 0.0 the ratio is, the more redundancy there is (Cohen & Plaskon, 1980). Work by Cartwright (1969) and Carroll (1938) on the index of diversification offers another alternative. In this method, the number of words in a composition is divided by the number of times the most frequently used word occurs. The more extensive the vocabulary, the higher the resulting value. Again from the oral language area, the average sentence length can be used as an estimate of ability (Cartwright, 1969; Cohen & Plaskon, 1980). In this method, the total number of words in the composition is divided by the total number of sentences. The result gives a gross measure of syntactic ability. O'Donnell (1976) has useful comments for teachers who may want to use these or similar measures of syntactic maturity.

SUMMARY

We have endeavored in this chapter to evaluate three very important areas of functioning: handwriting, spelling, and composition. Each has been presented in conjunction with pertinent material regarding the areas of instruction, remediation, and assessment of potential problem areas. Our review has indicated the need for continued research in written expression, especially in regard to composition and especially with learning disabled children. We have stressed that the components of writing are meaningful only when they are integrated into a total language arts curriculum.

SUGGESTED READINGS

Cohen, S. B., & Plaskon, S. P. *Language arts for the mildly handicapped.* Columbus, Ohio: Charles E. Merrill Publishing Company, 1980.

O'Donnell, R. C. A critique of some indices of syntactic maturity. *Research in the Teaching of English*, 1976, *10*, 31–38.

Smith, E. B., Goodman, K. S., & Meredith, R. *Language and thinking in school.* New York: Holt, Rinehart and Winston, 1970.

Chapter 15

Teaching Mathematics and Arithmetic

INTRODUCTION

Children classified as learning disabled very often have disabilities in mathematics. As Burns (1975) has pointed out, however, a considerable amount of research on mathematics and arithmetic is focused upon curriculum, the attitudes of students, and teacher training. The interaction between student and material (and the resulting problems) is rarely the focus of research (Cawley, 1978). As a result, very little information regarding the characteristics of the learning disabled with respect to mathematics is available. This chapter will include an exploration of problems in mathematics and arithmetic, a discussion of conventional instructional approaches, and some alternatives.

FACTORS RELATED TO MATHEMATICS AND ARITHMETIC DISABILITIES

One of the first to write about the occurrence of mathematical disabilities was Henschen in 1919. He described a case of *number blindness* that occurred in the absence of *word blindness*. He proposed that such a condition could result from brain lesions. By 1925, over thirty articles had been written on the subject. *Dyscalculia* was the term used to refer to "a partial disturbance of the ability to manipulate arithmetic symbols and do mathematical calculations" (Bush & Andrews, 1973, p. 28), while *acalculia* referred to "inability or loss of ability to manipulate arithmetic symbols and do mathematical calculations" (p. 5). Goldstein (1948) and Luria (1966) both described neurological dysfunction characterized by problems in mathematics, including a loss of spatial organization, loss of visual discrimination for numbers and signs, and inability to copy or reproduce numbers and geometric designs. In addition, Luria (1966) defined a form of parietal lobe dyscalculia that was characterized by inability (1) to align rows of numbers, (2) to memorize, (3) to arrange numbers in a sequence, (4) to give a series of numbers, and (5) to respond to operational symbols.

Dyscalculia has been found to be related to the existence of dyslexia, although no one-to-one correspondence exists (Johnson & Myklebust, 1967; Kosc, 1974). Critchley (1970) noted the difficulty some dyslexics have writing numbers from dictation and in confusing numbers containing zero. In addition, he noted difficulties with visualization of numbers, memory for digits, and the ability to commit computation tables to memory. Rabinovitch (1968) among others (cf. Cohn, 1971; Orton, 1937; Rawson, 1968) argued that since spelling, arithmetic, and reading are all symbolic activities, cooccurrence of disabilities should be expected. Many problems in mathematics may be even more directly related to reading disabilities. Recent research has indicated that the level of syntactic complexity of word problems greatly affects student success (Larsen, Trenholme & Parker, 1978). Most research has also shown written material (e.g., directions, word problems, explanations) accompanying appropriate levels of arithmetic and mathematics concepts to vary from three grades below to five or more grades above (Heddens & Smith, 1964; Smith, 1966). Others (Reed, 1965; Stauffer, 1966) have noted that the mathematics and arithmetic curricula reflect a very specific vocabulary.

Chalfant and Scheffelin (1969), in an early monograph on central processing dysfunction, cited five factors related to the occurrence of quantitative disabilities: (1) general intelligence, (2) problem-solving ability, (3) verbal ability, (4) spatial ability, and (5) neurophysiological correlates. Bartel (1975) also attempted to identify general factors related to the development of quantitative disabilities. She identified six potential factors: (1) ineffective instruction, (2) perceptual disorders, (3) directionality problems, (4) difficulties in abstract thinking, (5) memory problems, and (6) reading problems. Reid (1977) speculated that difficulties in seeing regularities in the environment, in making generalizations, and in relating mathematical ideas to past experiences might prevent adequate mathematical growth, because mathematics requires the organization of structures and relationships.

Another factor to consider is early experience (Kurtz & Spiker, 1976). Each child has a unique set of experiences and characteristics that affect cognitive maturity. These may include preschool enrollment, environmental deprivation, cultural diversity, neurological impairment, or retardation (cf. Callahan & Glennon, 1975; Reisman, 1972). All children, however, are expected to have achieved the same level of cognitive development by the first school day. Surely differences due to these factors could affect mathematical learning.

The quality of instruction has also been implicated as a factor in poor arithmetic and mathematics performance. The learning disabled are recognized as profiting only marginally from lecture/paper/pencil presentations. Yet, most instruction in arithmetic tends to be carried out using workbooks and worksheets that focus on skill practice. This practice results in poor numerical reasoning, poor concept development, and poor problem solving. (Cawley, 1970; Cawley & Goodman, 1969). Furthermore, many teachers have poor understanding of both mathematical concepts and arithmetic computation. Few understand the growth of mathematical knowledge during the preschool and early school years and the relevance of this development to instruction. Many are unable to explain adequately the algorithms which they are required to teach. They depend heavily upon teacher guides, tests, and worksheets. Little time is devoted to more activity-oriented or innovative instructional techniques (Cawley, 1978). At the secondary level the problem is more complex because teachers are more specialized. Few have adequate knowledge of the earlier concepts upon which their instruction is based (Cawley, 1978). Since many complex concepts are the result of restructuring and integration of earlier, less complex concepts (Greeno, 1978), it is precisely the more fundamental concepts that often need to be nurtured in learning disabled students.[1]

A recently completed study of teacher effectiveness has demonstrated that teachers can make significant changes in students' learning of mathematics through changes in the way they schedule their teaching time (Good & Grouws, 1979). The findings indicated that instructional behavior on the part of the teachers significantly increased academic gains in students. Table 15-1 presents a summary of the major instructional behaviors incorporated into the program.

The Analysis of Mathematical and Arithmetical Errors

Throughout this chapter, we have been referring to both mathematics and arithmetic. This distinction has been purposeful. Mathematics refers to the study or development of relationships, regularities, structures, or organizational schemata dealing with space, time, weight, mass, volume, geometry, and number. Arithmetic refers to the computational methods used when working with numbers. These computational methods or operations are: (1) commutative property for addition and multiplication, (2) associative and multiplicative property for addition, (3) distributive property for multiplication over addition, (4) multiplicative inverse, and (5) additive inverse. The distinction between mathematics and arithmetic is critical since mathematical understanding underlies arithmetic understanding (*Britannica World Language Dictionary,* 1965). Formal measures of mathematics and arithmetic achievement were presented in

---

[1]The development of the understanding of mathematics is presented in *The Growth of Understanding in Mathematics: Kindergarten Through Grade Three* (Lovell, 1971) and *How Children Learn Mathematics* (Copeland, 1974).

Table 15-1   A Summary of the Key Instructional Behaviors Identified in the Missouri Mathematics Effectiveness Project

Daily Review (first 8 minutes except Mondays)
  (a) Review the concepts and skills associated with the homework
  (b) Collect and deal with homework assignments
  (c) Ask several mental computation exercises
Development (about 20 minutes)
  (a) Briefly focus on prerequisite skills and concepts
  (b) Focus on meaning and promoting student understanding by using lively explana-
       tions, demonstrations, process explanations, illustrations, etc.
  (c) Assess student comprehension
       (1) Using process/product questions (active interaction)
       (2) Using controlled practice
  (d) Repeat and elaborate on the meaning portion as necessary
Seatwork (about 15 minutes)
  (a) Provide uninterrupted successful practice
  (b) Momentum—keep the ball rolling—get everyone involved, then sustain involvement
  (c) Alerting—let students know their work will be checked at end of period
  (d) Accountability—check the student's work
Homework assignment
  (a) Assign on a regular basis at the end of each math class except Fridays
  (b) Should involve about 15 minutes of work to be done at home
  (c) Should include one or two review problems
Special reviews
  (a) Weekly review/maintenance
       (1) Conduct during the first 20 minutes each Monday
       (2) Focus on skills and concepts covered during the previous week
  (b) Monthly review/maintenance
       (1) Conduct every fourth Monday
       (2) Focus on skills and concepts covered since the last monthly review

Source: Good, T.L. & Grouws, D.A. The Missouri Mathematics Effectiveness Project: An experimental study in fourth-grade classrooms. *Journal of Educational Psychology*, 1979, 71(3), p. 355–362. Copyright © 1979 by The American Psychological Association. Reprinted by permission.

Chapter 10. The concern here is to clarify the types of errors that appear to characterize problems in arithmetic (similar analyses of erroneous thinking in mathematics are unavailable) and to explore how these can be assessed for the purpose of instruction. Errors are almost never capricious or random. Children's faulty rules have sensible origins (Ginsburg, 1977). Analyzing the pattern of errors children make can give insight into the thinking the child brings to the task.

One rather large study that attempted to classify arithmetic computation errors was conducted by The Elementary School Mathematics Committee (1975). This study assessed the errors made by children in the fourth, fifth, and sixth grades in the four basic arithmetic algorithms: addition, subtraction, multiplication, and division. Some of the more common errors are listed in Table 15-2.

Lankford (1974) compared differences in the computational practices of good and poor computers. Students who were poor computers depended heavily on a few basic facts and procedures. Counting was employed extensively and

Table 15-2   Common Errors Made by Children in the Fourth, Fifth, and Sixth Grades in the Four Basic Operations

Addition	Subtraction	Multiplication	Division
1 Problems in carrying	1 Symbols disregarded	1 Problems in carrying	1 Digits in the quotient incorrectly placed
2 Inconsistent adding	2 Not always subtracting according to placement of the number	2 Problems with zero	2 The number being borrowed would be added
3 Inability to add to the next tens number	3 Disregarding an additional digit in the minuend	3 Disregarding the second or third digits in a two- or three-digit multiplier	3 Zero omitted either at the end or in the middle of the quotient
4 Problems with zero	4 Renaming a number as though borrowing were done	4 Problems multiplying by tens and hundreds	4 Having a remainder greater than the divisor
	5 Increasing a number without borrowing	5 Not indenting partial products	5 In a two-digit divisor, dividing by the first figure only
	6 When zeros were involved in the minuend, multiple borrowing was difficult	6 Not using the simplest method	
		7 Problems in horizontal multiplication	
		8 Not placing decimal points in the right places, or omitting dollar and cents signs	

Source: Elementary School Mathematics Committee, 1975.

errors often appeared when the counting became too involved. Operations of fractions were too difficult to remember, so students devised systems or procedures which *seemed* logical. Students who were poor in computation also had difficulty with long division.

Using an information processing approach to the analysis of errors, Radatz (1979) described errors in terms of the processing deficits that apparently led to them. These included: (1) language difficulties, (2) inadequate command of spatial information, (3) deficient mastery of prerequisite skills, facts, and concepts (the sole focus of most analyses), (4) incorrect associations or rigidity of thinking, and (5) application of irrelevant rules or strategies. This analysis comes closest to describing problems in mathematical reasoning.

Several strategies for detecting these errors are available to teachers. Cox (1975), for example, has suggested that teachers develop informal diagnostic tests that cover the basic scope and sequence (see Table 15-3). By having children complete at least five problems at each level, a teacher can gain

Table 15-3　Scope and Sequence for Mathematics—Kindergarten through Grade Six

Grade	Counting and comparing	Addition	Subtraction	Multiplication
Kindergarten	1–1 matching of sets (10 objects or less) more, fewer; most, fewest matching sets and numbers (1–10) ordering numbers (0–10)			
Grade 1	counting to 100 before and after comparing: larger, smaller place value through 99 skip counting (10s, 5s, 2s) ordinals (first, second, third, fourth, fifth, last)	sums to 5 sums to 7 (between 2 and 7) sums to 10 or two addends sums to 15 or three addends sums to 18; multiples of 10; sums less than 100 sums 11 to 18	differences minuend 2 to 5 differences minuend 6 to 9 0, subtrahend differences minuend 10 to 12 multiples of 10 minuend 40 to 90	
Grade 2	counting to 999 one more, one less count by 2s, 5s, 10s, 100s >, <, = ordinals to tenths place value to 100s odd and even	sums 11 to 18 (change addends to obtain same sum) sums 11 to 18 or three addends sums 99; four addends multiples of 10 (no regrouping) regrouping as 10+; sums to 19 sums to 99; regrouping sums to 99; no regrouping multiples of 100; no regrouping multiples of 1000	minuend 10 to 18 missing subtrahend and minuend two digits minus one digit two digits minus two digits (no regroup) three digits minus three digits (no regroup) regroup 1s	multiples of 2 (0 to 5) multiples of 3 (0 to 5) multiples of 2 (5 to 9) multiples of 3 and 4 (5 to 9, 0 to 5)

Source: Jerman & Beardslee, 1978.

(continued on following page.)

Table 15-3 *(continued)*

Grade	Counting and comparing	Addition	Subtraction	Multiplication

Grade 3	counting to 10,000
	place value to 9999
	regrouping 10s and 1s
	rounding (one digit only)
	comparing
		regrouping practice
		regrouping 1s to 10s
		regrouping 1s to 10s, 100s
		regrouping 10s to 100s
		regrouping 100s to 1,000s
		regroup two or three places
		adding with dollars and cents;
		  no regrouping
		adding with dollars and cents;
		  regroup to two or three places
		regroup to three places and over
		  zeros
			regroup 1s
			regroup 10s
			  minuend less than 700
			regroup 1s
			regroup 10s
				products to 25
				products 20 to 45
				products 30 to 81 and 20
				  to 51
				products 36 to 81
				products: one digit by two
				  or three digits

Grade 4	counting to one million
	place value to 999,999
	reading numbers to
	  1,000,000
	rounding
	Roman numerals to XXXIX
	regrouping to thousands
	comparing
	decimals to hundreths
	comparing decimals
		regroup (internal)
		two regroups in columns and one
		  internal regroup
		three regroups in columns; one
		  internal
		regroup over zeros; three regroups
		  in columns; two internal
		  regroups
		two regroups in columns; two internal
		  regroups
		two internal regroups
		regroup over zeros
		three internal regroups
		sum of one column 20
		sum of two columns 20
			regroup 100s
			regroup 1s and 10s
			regroup 1s and 10s over 0s
			regroup 1s, 10s, and 100s
			regroup through 100s over
			  one 0
				products: one digit by
				  two or three digits
				multiples of 10
				multiples of 100
				multiplying by multiples
				  of 10 and two-place
				  numbers
				multiplying 1000s

Table 15-3 (continued)

Grade	Counting and comparing	Addition	Subtraction	Multiplication
Grade 5	rounding Roman numerals to C counting in other bases (base 5, 8, or 2) comparing negative integers decimals to thousandths comparing decimals	sums of 10s column 20; two digit; four addends sum of two columns 20; six digit; three addends sum of three columns 20; six digit; three addends sum of all columns 20; five digit; three addends all regroup; six digit; two addends one column sum 20; six digit; four addends two columns sum 20; five digit; four addends three columns sum 20; five digit; four addends all columns sum 20; five digit; four addends all regroup; seven digit; two addends	regroup through 1000s regroup through 1000s over 0s	multiplying by multiples of 10 multiplying 100s by 10s multiplying 1000s and 10,000s multiplying by multiples of 10 and 100 multiplying by two- and three-digit numbers
Grade 6	rounding decimals place value in other bases (base 5, 8, or 2) place value—scientific notation reading decimals	all columns sum 20; six digit; three addends decimals tenth's place; three addends decimals hundredth's place; two addends decimals hundredth's place; three addends decimals thousandth's place; two addends decimals thousandth's place; three addends decimals ten-thousandth's place; two addends decimals ten-thousandth's place; three addends decimals hundred-thousandth's place; three addends decimals millionth's place; two addends	regroup to five or six places	multiplying by two- and three-digit numbers multiplying 10,000s multiplying 1000s by 100s, and 10,000s by 100s multiplying 10,000s by three-digit numbers multiplying 10,000s by four- or-more-digit numbers

(continued on following page.)

Table 15-3 (continued)

Grade	Division	Number theory and numeration systems	Fractions	Problem solving
Kindergarten				
Grade 1			indentifying $\frac{1}{2}$, $\frac{1}{3}$, $\frac{1}{4}$	one-step addition and subtraction finding the weight of objects cross-number puzzles
Grade 2		counting by 10s skip counting by 2s to 10 and by 5s to 25 counting by 100s and 1000s	identifying $\frac{2}{3}$, $\frac{2}{4}$, $\frac{3}{4}$, $\frac{3}{2}$, $\frac{5}{2}$ construction representation of $\frac{1}{2}$, $\frac{1}{3}$, $\frac{1}{4}$	one-step addition and subtraction coin problems cross-number puzzles one-step addition and subtraction with larger sums probability one-step multiplication
Grade 3	dividends to 30 dividends to 81 one-digit divisor, two-digit dividend, no remainder one-digit divisor, two-digit dividend, with remainder one- or two-digit divisor, two- or three-digit dividend with or without	even and odd numbers skip counting by 2s, 3s, 4s, 5s (number patterns) multiples of 10 and 100 multiples of 2, 3, 5 factors of numbers 6 to 24 commutative and associative properties: $+$, $\times$, one-digit numbers	constructing representations of halves, thirds, and fourths using sets comparing pictures to fifths with common denominators comparing fractions to fifths with common denominators comparing fractions to sixths with unequal denominators identifying fractions on a number line	one-step addition and subtraction one-step multiplication and division one-step problems involving larger numbers problems involving units of measure

Grade 4	dividing by multiples of 10 with or without a remainder dividing 1000s dividing 1000s by multiples of 10 dividing 1000s by two-digit divisors finding averages	primes and composites factors (common factors) multiples (common multiples) figurate numbers (squares and triangular) sum and product of primes distributive property; × over +, × over −, (left and right); one-digit numbers identity elements 0 for + 1 for ×	adding and subtracting fractions with same denominator (to 6) equivalent fractions (one denominator twice the other) comparing unit fractions comparing fractions with equal numerators, denominators differ by 1 adding and subtracting, denominators to 12	one-step problems, all four operations two-step problems, same operation at each step, different operations at each step problems with not enough or extra information estimating sums addition problems with several steps numbers, all operations one-step problems using larger numbers challenge problems
Grade 5	division with larger quotients zeros in the quotient dividing 10,000s by one-digit divisors dividing 10,000s by two-digit divisors zeros in the quotient	sum and product of odds and evens divisibility rules for 2, 3, 5, 10 prime factorization GCF of two numbers to 99 (relatively prime) LCM of two numbers to 99 Roman numerals, Egyptian numerals − is inverse of + ÷ is inverse of × commutative, associative +, ×, distributively × over + × over − (left and right) two-digit numbers	unit fractions (to $1/10$) times a whole number reducing fractions and multiplying by 1 in the form of $\frac{c}{c}$ product of unit fractions (to $1/12$) fraction of whole numbers mixed fractions to improper fractions improper fractions to mixed fractions (to $1/12$) adding mixed fractions	one-step problems, all operations short problems involving several steps consumer problems of several steps finding averages problems with not enough, or extra information
Grade 6	dividing 100,000s by two-digit divisors dividing by three-digit divisors division involving decimals division involving decimals division involving divisors in the divisor division involving divisors less than 1	powers, exponents, scientific notation common multiples using set intersection (LCM) divisibility rules for 4, 8, 9 square root modular arithmetic right distributivity ÷ over +, ÷ over −	sums and differences, one denominator a multiple of the other products of proper fractions add and subtract mixed numbers with regrouping sums and differences of proper fractions, denominator not multiples of each other fraction divided by a whole number or a fraction	one- and two-step problems, all operations choosing appropriate number sentences ratio and proportion problems percentage problems area and perimeter problems problems with not enough, or extra information

(continued on following page.)

Table 15-3 (continued)

Grade	Geometry	Decimals and percent	Probability and statistics	Measurement
Kindergarten				
Grade 1	paths and straight paths correspondence between paths and segments size discrimination shape recognition closed curves, inside and outside		interpreting bar and picture graph	nonstandard units centimeter inches pennies (10 or less) time, hours
Grade 2	drawing triangles, rectangles, and squares naming segments in plane figures same size and shape lines of symmetry through folding and drawing activities solid figures: cone, cube, sphere, and cylinder	addition and subtraction of dollar amounts	interpreting bar and picture graph	decimeters, centimeters inch, foot temperature, °F and °C liter, quart kilogram, pound pennies, nickels, dimes time: half hours, quarter hours
Grade 3	center of a circle, radius, and diameter quadrilaterals: rectangles, right angles, and squares perimeter area: counting by square units, multiplying, and measurement angle and angle notation	addition and subtraction of dollar amounts	introduction to probability (two to four outcomes) graphing data	meter, yard half gallon, pint gram, ounce quarters time to the minute

Grade 4	similarity, scale drawing parallel and perpendicular lines ordered pairs, coordinate geometry volume, counting cubic units, multiplying given the dimensions angles: acute, obtuse, opposite, congruent	addition and subtraction of dollar amounts single digit times cents or dollar amounts adding and subtracting decimals to tenths reading and writing decimals to hundredths	probability experiments (frequency tables) making predictions	millimeter, kilometer fractions of an inch (½, ¼), mile milliliters, cups square centimeters, square inch adding and subtracting dollars and cents days, weeks, months, years
Grade 5	classifying triangles: scalene, right, isosceles, equilateral simple construction; congruent figures sum of interior angles of three-, four-, five-, and six-sided polygons solids: face, edge, vertex, diagonal construction with straightedge and compass	adding and subtracting dollar amounts reading and writing decimals to thousandths sums, differences, and products to thousandths writing fractions as decimals and decimals as fractions division of tenths and hundredths	probability as a ratio 0 and 1 probability; impossible and certain events combinations permutations average (mean)	cubic measure: cubic centimeter, cubic inch converting within system interrelations: volume and capacity
Grade 6	construction; review and extend corresponding measure of similar triangles slides, flips, turns volume of prism and rectangular solids, but not spheres or cylinders introduce π, circumference	comparing tenths, hundredths, and thousandths adding and subtracting to thousandths converting common fractions to decimals to ten thousandths multiplication and division of decimals using cross-multiplying to solve percent problems	two-coin toss two-dice toss average (mean) range, median, mode sampling to determine probabilities	dam, hm acre, hectare milligram, ton interrelations: weight and volume

(continued on following page)

Table 15-3 (continued)

Grade	Relations, functions, and graphs	Integers
Kindergarten		
Grade 1	counting objects in a graph form (1 to 10 objects) sums and differences to 10 on the number line equivalent sets (one-to-one correspondence)	
Grade 2	order on the number line to 50 sums and differences to 18 on the number line function machines; sums and differences to 18	
Grade 3	number line multiply to 25; sums and differences to 20 function machine; multiply to 25 complete the tables: addition, subtraction, multiplication function machines; division facts to 25 ÷ 5	

Table 15-3 (continued)

Grade 4	review of facts using tables given a table of values with one part missing adding rationals on a number line complete tables using rationals graphing ordered pairs in the first quadrant	
Grade 5	discover the rule using tables discover the rule using graphs function machines using inverse operations reading ordered pairs on the Cartesian plane rationals on the number line, adding, subtracting, multiplying, and dividing	introduction to negative numbers order of integers
Grade 6	scale drawings graphing ordered pairs using a rule powers and roots using function machine graphing ordered pairs in the plane graphing straight lines	order of integers adding two integers with like signs adding two integers with unlike signs subtracting integers with like signs subtracting integers with unlike signs

information about the error patterns of the pupils. The techniques of applied behavioral analysis (see Chapter 10) have also been suggested (cf. Blankenship, 1978; Dunlap & House, 1976). Individual variations in child development necessitate that a *total* diagnostic approach be taken. Error patterns that give the teacher clues to the child's growth of understanding can also be observed in children's behavior during games, the questions they pose, the way they solve problems, and the class material they complete. Of paramount importance is the careful evaluation of their performances for potential clues to degrees of understanding and the development of misconceptions (Adams, Ellis, & Beeson, 1977; Ashlock, 1976; Erlwanger, 1975; Reisman, 1972).

TRADITIONAL APPROACHES TO TEACHING MATHEMATICS AND ARITHMETIC

Lovell (1971) has suggested that most of the materials available for instruction in mathematics and arithmetic fall within three categories. Some are verbally oriented; others rely upon visual perception and imagery. The last group are activity centered. The first two categories encompass the most common materials currently in use with normally achieving and learning disabled pupils.

Teaching Children Basic Skills

Teaching Children Basic Skills is a curriculum guide (Stephens, Hartman, & Lucas, 1978) that focuses on the content areas, as noted in Table 15-4. It provides sequences of skills, methods for assessment, and teaching strategies. The approach is behavioral and includes both traditional and modern mathematics. It spans pre-first grade through third grade. Preparation of the material has been underway since 1973. The effectiveness of this curriculum has not been formally evaluated.

Brueckner Diagnostic Tests and Self-Helps in Arithmetic

This program consists of a series of screening and diagnostic tests in traditional computation skills (Brueckner, 1965). On the reverse side of each diagnostic test is included self-helps in the diagnostic area. The screening tests include whole numbers, fractions, decimals, and arithmetic operations. The twenty-three diagnostic tests and self-helps are grouped into two areas. The first is the mastery of basic facts and includes addition facts, subtraction facts, multiplication facts, division facts, and uneven division facts. The second area contains eighteen additional tests of the fundamental arithmetic operations: addition, subtraction, multiplication, division by one-place numbers, division by two-place numbers, regrouping fractions, addition of like fractions, subtraction of like fractions, addition of unlike fractions, subtraction of unlike fractions and division of fractions. The *Diagnostic Test of Decimal Fractions* includes addition of decimals, subtraction of decimals, multiplication of decimals, and division of decimals. Although the diagnostic tests appear useful, the effectiveness of the self-helps is untested.

Table 15-4 Arithmetic Skills from Prefirst Grade through Third Grade

Measurement
>geometry
>length/height/distance
>money
>temperature
>time

Operations and properties
>addition
>division
>inverse operation
>multiplication
>subtraction

Numbers/numerals/numeration systems
>cardinal numerals
>numerals
>odd/even
>ordinal numbers
>place value
>rational numbers
>roman numerals

Sets
>comparing
>ordering

Source: Stephens, Hartman, & Lucas, 1978, p. 240.

DISTAR: Arithmetic I, II, III

DISTAR: Arithmetic (Englemann & Carnine, 1972, 1975, 1976) teaches children necessary arithmetic and mathematical knowledge through the use of behavioral principles. DISTAR I teaches children how to go about answering questions, a backward counting strategy for solving subtraction problems, simple story problems, more ($>$) or less ($<$) problems using signs, thirty-five addition facts, and ordinal counting. DISTAR II covers time telling, multiplication, column addition, algebra addition facts, additional addition and subtraction facts, identification of coins, use of metric and standard units, fractions, more than and less than comparisons, and story problems. DISTAR III extends the basic operations, long division, story problems, and formal problem solving. Most of the available research on the success of these programs comes from the publisher. Indications are that the programs succeed, but that conclusion is based upon tests designed to assess what the program teaches. Questions about children's levels of understanding and the generalizability of their learning to real-life problems are still unanswered.

Traditional programs other than the ones cited are available. The intent of this section was not to provide a comprehensive overview of all conventional materials employed, but rather to show a few representative ones. There are some generalizations to be made concerning these types of materials. First, they view computation as the primary goal of instruction. Mastery of computational skills is the overriding concern. Second, the applicability of the program to learning disabled children comes from what many authors call "individualizing instruction." What this actually means is differential pacing of children through the *same* material. Different entry and exit points define this method of individualizing. Third, few of the materials seriously consider children's competence levels before engaging them in formal instruction. Fourth, the available programs do not provide compensatory strategies for children who are not capable of learning through the traditional means (i.e., providing alternative means of recording answers, dealing with computation facts, or reading the instructional material).

A COGNITIVE APPROACH

Most traditional approaches to mathematics instruction emphasize arithmetic computation. Computation is, however, an empty skill if conceptual ability is lacking. Without an understanding of number as a property of objects, computation cannot be understood. Without an understanding of the meaning of classes and relations, of order and magnitude, of form and arrangement, the comprehension of addition is impossible. Cognitive approaches to instruction in mathematics consequently emphasize the development of the mathematical concepts that render computation meaningful.

Furthermore, in a cognitive approach the child is viewed as the central, active figure in learning. Through the child's increasing understanding of sets and subsets acquired through experience with toys and other objects, he or she evidences a growing understanding of what constitutes number. Knowledge of space, an area of deficit for many learning disabled children, depends on progressive development that takes place through the interaction of the child with the environment, not through the drawing of squares to perfection. A cognitive approach is, therefore, activity centered rather than lecture/paper/pencil oriented.

It is through the child's interaction with objects and his reflections about those interactions that time expands to more than the hands on a clock, and dimensions of duration and succession become understood. Although this learning is necessarily gradual, teaching is nonetheless explicit and directed. The goal, however, is a long-term acquisition which will not be forgotten in a week or a month. This kind of acquisition is facilitated by the child's ability to bring appropriate past experience to bear. Although attention is directed in lessons toward numerals, computation, and the hands of the clock, instruction is viewed as an interactive process to which the child must contribute—just as he or she must contribute to the interpretation of text. Specifics are taught only in relation to a larger context. A cognitive approach is holistic.

There are a number of programs that take a more cognitive approach to arithmetic/mathematics instruction than those we have already reviewed. Although no formal evaluation of these programs with learning disabled children has been conducted, they are promising, because they are child centered and activity centered, or have as their goal conceptual understanding.

Stern Structural Arithmetic

The first of these programs is the *Stern Structural Arithmetic* program (Stern & Stern, 1971; Stern, Stern, & Gould, 1965, 1966). The mathematical games of Catherine Stern, brought from Germany in the early 1940s, were the central core from which the later programs were developed. The materials build upon the premise that before numbers are ever introduced, the child must develop an understanding of mathematical relationships. Also incorporating ideas of Montessori, the basic materials employed are those of pattern matrices, number blocks or cubes, and unit blocks. The emphasis is on manipulation, both physical and mental, and upon language and relationships. The child learns through a variety of activities and interactions and is always directed to think about what has been accomplished.

> Slowly and thoroughly, one step at a time, each child experiences and talks about numerical relationships. Later he learns to record his experiences in figures that are filled with reality and understanding. He is on his way, at his own pace, and with enthusiasm, to a satisfying mastery of mathematical concepts and practices. The way of teaching is determined, as in the mastery of language, by the nature of the subject, the way human beings learn, and the particular needs of the individual student (Stern, 1971).

Although there is no formal research documenting the effectiveness of this approach for learning disabled children, M. Stern works regularly with learning disabled children in her continuous program development efforts. As much as any other, therefore, this program is directed toward their needs.

Project MATH

There is another program for exceptional learners. Project MATH, developed by Cawley and his colleagues (Cawley, Fitzmaurice, Goodstein, Lepore, Sedlak, & Althaus, 1976), is an approach to mathematics and arithmetic instruction that includes both a curriculum and assessment devices focusing upon the development of understanding. Project MATH uses a systems approach to move children through various levels of developmental or remedial activities. The components of the model include (1) Mathematics Concept Inventory, a domain-referenced assessment device, (2) Multiple Option Curriculum, to be explained below, (3) Clinical Mathematics Interview, an intensive evaluation that builds upon the other assessment, and (4) Remedial Modules, intensive work on task-analyzed algorithms.

The Multiple Option Curriculum is developed around strands (e.g., fractions), areas (e.g., operations), and concepts (e.g., division of a whole number by a proper fraction). For each of these, the Curriculum lists behavioral objectives, illustrative materials, activities, and evaluative criteria. The Curriculum is much more than skills analysis. Problem solving is stressed. The philosophy of the program is "that students with learning disabilities be taught and helped to discover the principles (rules, ideas, algorithms, and the like) of mathematics in order to increase their own capacity to 'learn to learn' and to transfer and generalize" (Cawley, 1978, p. 217).

Project MATH is one of the few programs that appears to be useful with adolescent learning disabled students. This is primarily because of the flexible manner in which the goals of the Multiple Option Curriculum can be attained. In addition, the Project MATH curriculum is very closely aligned with the regular developmental curriculum. Though the impact of the Project MATH curriculum at the secondary level has yet to be fully assessed, preliminary field testing has supported its use (Cawley, Fitzmaurice, Shaw, Kahn, & Bates, 1978).

Nuffield Mathematics Project

Another program that uses a cognitive approach is the Nuffield Mathematics Project (The Nuffield Foundation, 1967–1974). This program, designed to be implemented with children from the earliest grades through intermediate school, is built around the concept that children need to experience the world before they can question the specifics about it. The curriculum is designed for *active* learning. Children are participants in the learning process and not the recipients of information. The term *activity* should not be misconstrued. The child's engagement in physical activity in and of itself is of little use. It is the child's reflection on the activity, his or her thinking about what has transpired, that is the activity referred to, just as in Piaget's theory.

In the Nuffield laboratory approach, the teacher's role is not direct instruction, but rather setting up activities that: (1) allow for exploration and experimentation, (2) introduce necessary vocabulary, and (3) lead to the emergence of a problem. Both active learning and problem solving are incorporated. In the first of the Nuffield publications, *I do, and I understand* (1967), not only is the philosophy of the program developed, but guidelines are given for selecting materials and structuring the physical environment. It is suggested that materials such as clay, plasticine, bricks, sand, water, dried peas, beans, rice, nails, buttons, matchboxes, thread spools, straws, pipe cleaners, pop beads, and small toys be available. Devices such as balances, scales and weights, rulers, measuring tapes, timers, stop watches, thermometers, watering cans, and containers of varying sizes and shapes are more complex types of materials needed. Yet, the materials and suggested activities are only that. The developers of the program note that exactly what is covered in a class will vary according to the needs and desires of the children.

Like other cognitively oriented approaches, the Nuffield Project stresses that children need to have the opportunity to record the information they develop. Projects such as collecting personal data from the class (sizes of shoes, waists, weights, heights) as well as class data (dates of birthdays, numbers of brothers or sisters, etc.) provide recording opportunities. Activities range from using imitative play (grocery, post office, toy store, etc.) to developing ideas of money or quantity, to sharing the candies in a bag for the development of early understandings of division. Flexibility is one of the key words to using the Nuffield material. For example, in activities based upon quantity, there is no reason that children must use the standard measures or even know the standard measures prior to developing understanding. A child could use an empty bottle, a doll's cup, anything that allows a consistent measure. Recording can be in pictographs rather than numbers. Time concepts can be developed through the use of vocabulary, stories, and activities such as jumping rope, etc. At a higher, more advanced level of the Nuffield program, concepts related to shape and size are explored using flexible outlines of shapes, so that the shape can be changed even though the number of sides remain the same.

The Nuffield Project reflects the work of many individuals whose work is geared toward developing guides to meaningful activity with children. Among the numerous publications available to describe the Nuffield Project are three sets of activity cards (*Problems—Green Set,* 1969; *Problems—Red Set,* 1970; *Problems—Purple Set,* 1970) which are useful in helping teachers become aware of possible activities. The reader is referred to the readings list for the titles of other guides to the Nuffield Mathematics Project.

Mathematics Laboratories

Mathematics laboratories are gaining widespread popularity. Use of the laboratory setting is flexible, and can be used for enrichment, application, or for the total curriculum (Kramer, 1978). Because it is child-centered, the program can easily make provision for individual differences. Materials range from balances and scales, to trundle wheels, to puzzles, sand, and teacher-made materials. Research has indicated success with a number of populations, including the mentally retarded (Tobin, 1973) and underachievers (Kastner, 1975).

The Nuffield Project is a successful venture into laboratory approaches to mathematics and arithmetic. Yet, it is only one approach, using a Piagetian theoretical framework. The basic concepts of the active involvement of children can be employed regardless of the content. The scope and sequence material presented in Table 15-3 tells a teacher only what children are generally expected to know at different grade levels, and the difficulty sequence of the materials. It does not tell a teacher how to go about helping children develop that knowledge. The laboratory approach would seem to be an appropriate strategy.

To develop a laboratory, a room or a portion of a room must be available to house materials. Although it is more convenient to use purchased materials, teachers and children can easily make balance pans and trundle wheels rather inexpensively. Making the equipment which will be used in the mathematics laboratory is a worthwhile learning experience in itself. Problems can be posed verbally, on task cards, or designed by students or groups of students. Group problem solving has the advantage of providing children the opportunity to learn from one another and also encourages social and language learning. Any of the following sources will be useful for suggesting appropriate problems: Copeland (1974), Dumas (1971), Ginsburg (1977), Kramer (1978), and Lovell (1971). Of course, the references related to the Nuffield Math program would also be useful.

SUMMARY AND CONCLUSIONS

This chapter dealt with a number of rather important issues, including the characteristics of dyscalculia, the problems associated with the term, and the intervention strategies employed from both a conventional and cognitive viewpoint. Deciding what mathematics and arithmetic program is appropriate for the learning disabled is critically important. Over the past few years, the term, *back to basics* has been heard by many. It represents a belief that the alternative mathematics and arithmetic programs of the 1960s failed to meet the needs of the children. None are more cogently aware of the shortcomings of these alternatives than mathematics teachers and researchers. Yet, for one of them (Offner, 1978), the term *back to basics* represents a "movement which substitutes rote learning, 'consumer math,' and mindless pencil-pushing for understanding" (p. 217), and represents "an educational crime" (p. 217). Teachers of mathematics have been striving for years to change traditional programs into meaningful curricula, where teaching had real value. After years of debate and searching, many believe (in opposition to computation-oriented educators) that "Problem solving is probably the single most important *basic skill*" (Cowan & Clary, 1978, p. 133). If problem solving is the real basic skill, then mathematics is not only a body of knowledge, but a process of inquiry. To be successful, a student must be able to make observations, organize information, specialize and generalize, express mathematical ideas, and prove conjectures (Hiatt, 1979). Problem-solving strategies span the content areas and allow children the freedom to explore on their own, without restrictive bonds to adults or others who know the "process." The lack of understanding which learning disabled children have of their world and how to learn from that world is well documented and is evident in the cumulative deficit that accrues throughout their lifetimes.

SUGGESTED READINGS

Dumas, E., & Schminke, C. W. *Math activities for child involvement,* 2d ed. Boston: Allyn and Bacon, 1977.

Kramer, K. *Teaching elementary school mathematics.* Boston: Allyn and Bacon, 1978.

Nuffield and The Schools Council Project. *I do and I understand. Mathematics begins; Beginning mathematics; Computation and structure 2; Computation and structure 3; Shape and size 2; Shape and size 3; Pictorial representation 1.* New York: Wiley, 1969.

Chapter 16

Classroom Management

INTRODUCTION

Perhaps one of the most arduous tasks for those who were not "born teachers" is the management of children who are particularly difficult, whether in mainstreamed classes, special classes, or in resource rooms. There are several effective approaches to classroom management which incorporate a variety of techniques. The most widely used management programs in special education employ behavior modification techniques, but most such interventions borrow as much from sound planning and common sense practices as from empiricist principles. Some (cf. Chinn, Winn, & Walters, 1978; Gordon, 1974; Losen & Diament, 1978) advocate both parent and classroom interventions based on principles of nondirective therapy. These approaches run counter to the more traditional notion that teachers, parents, etc. should always be in control.

Several issues are important in management. One is the structure of the school. A second relates to the use of behavior modification principles to control behaviors (both academic and social) of difficult children. Following the discussion of these (approaches that dominate current practice), will be a discussion of one nondirective intervention, Gordon's (1974) method of "teacher effectiveness."

STRUCTURE OF THE SCHOOL DAY

For learning disabled children placed in mainstreamed settings, the first approach to behavioral/instructional management is in the large group. The way the school day is structured, therefore, is of paramount importance. At least three major decisions must be made regarding the structure of the teaching day: when to teach what, pacing, and transitions (Sloane, 1976). Structuring the interaction between the child and the teacher is also important.

Sequencing Activities

There are no hard and fast rules for ordering activities during the school day. Perhaps the best way to develop an appropriate schedule is to have the child or children join in the planning. It is not wise to lead children to believe that they can determine what they will and will not do in school, but choices should be made apparent where they exist and children should help to schedule the sequence of activities they must perform, with careful guidance from the teacher.

Sedentary and lively activities should be alternated to prevent boredom, but limit excitement. Out-of-class activities can be accommodated. Activities children enjoy can be alternated with those they like less, so that completion of a disliked task allows one to move on to an enjoyable one. It is usually a good idea to get the least preferred tasks out of the way early. Favorite activities might be scheduled first thing in the morning, just before lunch, and just after lunch. Once the schedule has been devised, it should be written and followed.

Pacing

Pacing is integrally related to the sequencing of activities and refers to two things: the speed with which each child moves through the curriculum and the speed with which the teacher conducts lessons and activities.

The only way to know when a child is ready to move on to new skills and new concepts is to make certain that he or she has mastered or cannot master the old ones. Using a diagnostic teaching cycle in which the teacher (1) determines what the child knows and does not know, (2) prepares activities for the child, (3) teaches, (4) tests, and (5) reformulates objectives is probably the most efficient way to determine where to go next (also see Chapter 10).

Pacing is also related to the rate at which activities are presented. Lags, periods of time when the children are engaged in no activity, lead to behavior problems. It is very important that every minute of the day be planned. Most teachers find it helpful to keep a file of "fill-in" activities, which take five or ten minutes, have some educational value, and can be implemented instantaneously. What is sometimes forgotten is that it is important to make sure that the children are engaged in activity, not the teacher. Research has shown that behavior is more likely to become disruptive if children have nothing to do (Sloane, 1976).

Each child should have some seat work that needs to be done each day. The problem with exercises is that they are often overused and inappropriately used. Children with learning problems will occasionally do a worksheet and make a huge number of errors. That is inexcusable, since the value of seat work lies in the practice it affords children on a task or skill they have already mastered. When a child gets most of the answers wrong, he or she has practiced an incorrect or inappropriate behavior. Seat work should be assigned—and homework too—only after the teacher is certain that the skill or activity has been mastered. A variety of materials and presentation formats should be used to insure generalizability. The work should also be interesting and meaningful. Seat work can be presented in the form of a game as easily as a ditto sheet. Exercises often amount to busy work and that should be avoided at all costs. Too much practice leads to boredom and boredom means trouble.

It is important for the teacher to appear calm and well-planned. Teachers should not give the impression that they are pressured and hurrying. Research studying impulsivity has shown that impulsive children will respond positively to a more slowly paced, reflective teacher.

Transitions

Transitions between activities often lead to problem behaviors, because children's attention is not focused on any particular activity. For many children, the only time they have to talk to their classmates is during the transition period. Group work has the advantage of fostering social and verbal interactions and reducing the inclination to interact during inappropriate times. Even when children work in groups, however, they must end and begin activities. The best defense against an eruption during transition is to have every child know exactly what he or she is expected to do and how it is to be done. Children should be given or should generate for themselves exact descriptions of acceptable behavior. Rules should be made only where problems exist. Rules should be clear and positive, and should be enforced consistently.

Structuring the Teacher-Pupil Interaction

The teacher has control over a number of variables which can create a comfortable and pleasant school atmosphere. First, is the way an activity will be presented to the child. The choice is determined by the teacher's knowledge of the interface between the child's abilities and the demands of the task. Diagnostic teaching is quite helpful in determining what the child can and cannot do and what he or she needs to learn in order to perform a given task. It may also help the teacher decide how the task might best be presented to the child.

The teacher, in addition, can use the arrangement of furniture in the room to facilitate children's performances and at times even to ensure their safety. When little children are using scissors, it might not be very appropriate to have them clustered closely together. Some arrangements encourage talking, because children are facing each other. Others foster attention to individual work.

Language is also a variable that the teacher can manipulate. Some recommend (cf. Barsch, 1965a) that teachers speak slowly, use only essential words, and avoid ambiguous language. This notion, however, is highly controversial. Since children induce their own linguistic rules from listening to others speak (Bloom & Lahey, 1978), it is important that the teacher provide a rich, appropriate model. Teachers must be accepting of the child's language. Telling a child to stop saying *ain't* or to use an *s* for the third person singular verb form is usually more harmful than helpful. Children do not learn language by being taught a set of rules. Trying to remember rules to please the teacher can only make a child self-conscious and disrupt the fluency of his or her language.

BEHAVIOR MODIFICATION

Behavior modification techniques can be used to increase behavior, decrease behavior, and affect behavior, in a number of other ways. All of these are relevant to the management of learning disabled children at a second level, i.e., when large-group management techniques are ineffective alone. Axelrod (1977) posed and then responded to the question that most opponents of the use of behavior modification raise: "What gives teachers the right to modify student behavior?" (p. 158). He responded by stating that every teacher has an *obligation* to modify child behavior: that is the purpose of schooling. He also argued that ensuring that children are successful pupils enlarges their freedoms, rather than curtails them.

Means of Increasing the Rate of Behavior

Positive Reinforcement   One fundamental principle of behavior modification is that behavior which is followed by positive consequences will be strengthened. These consequences are called *positive reinforcement.* In the common parlance, they are referred to as rewards or incentives. Reinforcers may be tangible (e.g., candies, tokens) or social (e.g., attention, privileges). Of course, one employs tangible reinforcers only when they are necessary, and moves toward the maintenance of behavior through social reinforcers. It may be necessary to reward every behavior initially, but behavior modifiers work gradually toward a variable schedule.

It is important for teachers to recognize that they may be using positive reinforcement when they least expect it. An acting-out child, for example, may receive the teacher's full attention when he or she misbehaves. Since these children typically are seeking attention, the teacher is increasing the rate of their undesirable behavior unknowingly. It is not only important to know what constitutes positive reinforcement; it is also important to know when to use it and when not to.

Reinforcers derive their ability to modify behavior from two sources: motivation and feedback (Gardner, 1978). Certainly, children are willing to increase some behaviors in order to obtain others (e.g., to answer more questions to receive attention from the teacher). Often, however, feedback is the only reinforcer necessary. Children will most often continue a behavior they know to be correct and stop using behaviors they know to be incorrect.

Negative Reinforcement The strengthening of behavior through the removal of unpleasant events is negative reinforcement. Consider the child, let us say Douglas, who talks out-of-turn in class (Axelrod, 1977). The teacher may shout at Douglas (the aversive event). When he stops talking, the shouting stops. The teacher may have increased the amount of Douglas' quiet behavior, but the resultant quality of the classroom climate leaves something to be desired. Negative reinforcement (taking away something that the child finds aversive in order to increase a behavior) can become a trap for many teachers. It would certainly be more productive to reward Douglas when he is not talking than to shout when he is.

Negative reinforcement can, on the other hand, be a powerful tool if used properly. Perhaps a child dislikes spelling drills. The teacher can promise to excuse the child from these drills if he or she masters 90 percent of the weekly spelling list. It is likely that the child's ability to spell words correctly will be increased.

Shaping Shaping is a method for eliciting closer and closer approximations of a desired or "terminal" behavior. If a child, for example, is very shy and never talks in class, the teacher may decide to shape voluntary participatory behaviors. Since the child does not respond spontaneously, the teacher may initially prompt or elicit a response. She may, in fact, ask the child a question. Any attempt at a response would be rewarded, perhaps by a smile. The teacher would continue to reward the child's responding to her questions until the behavior was established. Then she would require a closer approximation of the terminal behavior, voluntary participation. She might choose to reward only voluntary responses to questions which were not directed specifically to this child. This may mean rewarding eye contact or any subtle mouth or hand movement. The teacher would require progressively more complete responses before reinforcement would be given. In this way, the teacher guides the child into making a desired response.

Fading Fading is a technique that is used for changing the conditions under which a target behavior is performed, by gradually reducing the amount of supportive information. Fading assumes that the child has the capacity to make a response, but does not do so.

Means for Decreasing the Rate of Behavior

Reinforcing Incompatible Behaviors One means for decreasing the rate of an undesirable behavior is to reinforce a desirable behavior which is incompatible with it. If a child is often out of his seat without permission, the teacher may decrease the out-of-seat behavior by reinforcing the child when he is working on his assignments.

Extinction Another means for reducing the incidence of undesirable behaviors is simply to ignore them. This technique is referred to as extinction.

Ignoring a behavior can be a very effective technique for withdrawing whatever positive reinforcement was previously maintaining it. The teacher who attends to the child who misbehaves can reduce the number of problems the child exhibits by ignoring that child whenever he or she does misbehave. Axelrod (1977) lists several factors which limit the effectiveness of extinction: (1) even though the teacher may ignore the child, classmates may not and so the child may still receive sufficient reinforcement to warrant the continuation of the behavior; (2) some behaviors may be inherently reinforcing (e.g., talking to a friend) and so may continue after they are ignored by the teacher; and (3) ignored behaviors will initially occur more frequently. Another issue is that there are some behaviors (e.g., disturbing or hurting other children, doing something dangerous) that a teacher simply cannot ignore.

Punishment   Punishment refers to following a target behavior with an aversive consequence. Common forms of punishment used in schools are keeping a child after school, giving a child bad grades, etc. The use of punishment, however, is controversial. Allegations that punishment produces only temporary benefits and that it teaches the punished to be aggressive have not been substantiated. Punishment fails, however, in the sense that it does not teach a desirable behavior in the place of the one which was decreased. In addition, a teacher who punishes a child may find that the child devises a way to avoid the punishment, perhaps by not coming to school.

Time-out is a form of punishment in which the ability to receive positive reinforcement is denied. A child who is acting-out in class, for example, may simply be removed from the class for a period of time. The child would be permitted to return to the group and to the possibility of reinforcement after a time either predetermined (e.g., ten minutes) or determined by the child (e.g., when you are ready to work).

Differential Reinforcement   Differential reinforcement of other behavior refers to the use of reinforcement only when a behavior does not occur. For example, a class may be reinforced if no one talks out for ten minutes. If someone talks out at the end of seven or nine minutes, a new ten-minute period would be begun.

Additional Basic Processes Affecting Behavior

There are four additional means for affecting behavior. These will be described briefly. *Imitation* is a very effective means for teaching a new behavior. It can have a positive or negative outcome, depending on the behavior which is imitated. *Discrimination* is the ability to determine when a behavior is appropriate and when it is not. Discrimination is induced by reinforcing a behavior in some situations and ignoring it in others. *Stimulus generalization* refers to the use of a behavior learned in one situation in another. A very common example of stimulus generalization is the toddler's use of "daddy" to refer to many men. Finally, *chaining* is a process of acquiring a complex response, such that each link in the chain becomes a stimulus for the next. Doing a puzzle, for example, putting one piece in place, provides a cue for putting the next piece in. Using *backward chaining* may, however, be more effective. Backward chaining would refer to the situation in which all the pieces were left in the puzzle except the last one.

The Management of Difficult Children

Behavioral techniques have been listed and described which can be used in increasing and/or decreasing behaviors. Tables 16-1 and 16-2 adapted from Gardner (1978, pp. 327–331) show how these may be used in a program designed

Table 16-1 Developing Curiosity

Curiosity may be fostered by:

1 Exposing the child to new events—toys, foods, textures, shapes, auditory stimuli, people—when the child is relaxed and pleasant. Events should be presented in a positive, enthusiastic manner that doesn't force the child to participate. Reinforce the child for any positive behavior.
2 Encouraging exploration that makes use of a variety of sense modalities. The child should be encouraged to touch, squeeze, smell, see, hear, and taste. Experiences should be described in words—written or oral.
3 Encouraging the child to imitate a model.
4 Encouraging the child to ask questions about experiences.
5 Presenting exploration as a fun activity.
6 Remembering that an adult who is warm and pleased by divergent behavior is likely to get children to demonstrate curiosity.
7 Presenting problems that have many solutions.
8 Encouraging the child to explore various aspects of himself and his feelings.
9 Encouraging free, uninhibited, and even exaggerated expression.

Source: Adapted from Gardner, 1978.

Table 16-2 Developing Self-Confidence

Self-confidence refers to a range of behaviors that can be demonstrated in various settings. Evidence of confidence would include entering into problem situations without undue fear or caution, reacting with curiosity to new or puzzling events, openness to experiencing new situations or events, ability to cope with failure, verbal expressions of positive self-regard, freedom to use skills in an uninhibited manner, and relating easily to others.

The teacher can facilitate the development of self-confidence in children with learning disabilities by:

1 Providing the child with numerous successful experiences;
2 Helping the child to develop a wide variety of skills and the ability to use them in a variety of situations;
3 Praising skill attainment and providing appropriate feedback such as "You are quick," "You did that well," and "I am pleased with the way you did that."
4 Exposing the child to a variety of tasks and social situations and reinforcing both the initial and the continued involvement;
5 Helping children make a realistic appraisal of their capabilities and limitations.

Source: Adapted from Gardner, 1978.

to foster curiosity and in a program to increase self-confidence—two topics of vital importance to teachers of the learning disabled.

Among the learned disabled population there are probably three types of difficult children for whom carefully planned management strategies are important. For children who are aggressive or who throw temper tantrums the problem lies in decreasing behaviors. For children who are withdrawn, an increase in behaviors is required. All of these programs necessitate the initial definition of target behavior and assessment of baseline functioning. For a description of asssessment techniques, see the section on applied behavioral analysis in Chapter 10. Tables 16-3, 16-4, and 16-5 delineate steps in devising management programs for these types of children. The tables have been adapted from Gardner (pp. 355, 354–355, 357). These guidelines will help the interested teacher devise appropriate programs for the particular children with whom he or she works.

The Engineered Classroom

One of the best-known behavioral intervention systems, the Santa Monica Madison School Plan, was developed during the late 1960s as an attempt at designing appropriate educational settings (Hewett, 1968; Hewett, Taylor, & Artuso, 1968). The engineered classroom concept was based upon the belief that children learned at individual rates and that, in order to capitalize upon this

---

Table 16-3   Designing a Program for an Aggressive Child

1 Define the behaviors and describe the time, place, and social settings in which they occur. A program should be designed to deal with the behaviors—hitting, pushing, yelling, smart talk—and not with aggression itself.
2 Obtain measures of the frequency with which the behaviors occur, so that you can later determine whether the rate of aggressive behavior is being reduced. The objective is to lower the rate of aggressive behavior to a tolerable level.
3 Before initiating any interventions, observe what the behavior produces. Does the child get his way? Does he get attention? Do adults become upset? These and similar events may be maintaining the behavior.
4 How frequently does the child receive reinforcement for behaving appropriately? Adults and peers often learn to ignore the obnoxious child. They avoid interaction even when the child is behaving satisfactorily because they fear that a situation might occur in which aggressive behaviors may be renewed. Consequently, the child may be attended to only when behaving aggressively.
5 Avoid giving the child his or her way after aggressive behavior.
6 Gradually introduce the aggressive child to positive social experiences. Frequent pairing of praise and tangible reinforcers is essential as a means of increasing the reinforcement value of these social events.
7 Reinforce desired behaviors in other children while the aggressive child is observing.
8 Be as consistent as possible.
9 Initiate the behavior management program both at home and at school.
10 Demonstrate socially acceptable behaviors to the child.
11 Remain calm. An angry, loud, explosive teacher is providing an aggressive model.

Source: Adapted from Gardner, 1978.

Table 16-4 Designing a Program for a Child with Temper Tantrums

1 Define the behaviors that make up the temper tantrum and the time, place, and social setting in which these behaviors occur. Note what produces or precipitates the temper tantrums.
2 Obtain measures of the frequency of the behaviors.
3 Describe the results the child obtains by using tantrum behaviors.
4 Attempt to get the child involved in behaviors that will reduce the possibility of frustration.
5 Provide no reinforcement during or following the temper tantrums. Let it run its course.
6 Provide reinforcement when the child is involved in appropriate behavior.
7 Do not let the child's temper tantrum arouse your sympathy or guilt.

Source: Adapted from Gardner, 1978.

Table 16-5 Designing a Program for a Withdrawn Child

1 The first step in the development of a management program for a withdrawn child is to define the behaviors the child engages in that led you to think of him or her as withdrawn. Observe the child's specific reactions in social situations.
2 Obtain measures of the frequency of the observed behaviors.
3 Avoid all forms of punishment and begin to use people as positive reinforcers (or as dispensers of positive reinforcers at first, if that is necessary).
4 Introduce new people to the child gradually and in low-anxiety situations.
5 Reinforce approximations of social interactions, if needed, while directly teaching appropriate social behaviors. Shaping and modeling would be appropriate techniques. Be certain, however, that aversive consequences (punishment) are avoided.
6 Reinforce a wide variety of behaviors. It would be important, for example, to listen carefully to the child, to attend, to ease him or her into positive relationships with other children, etc.

Source: Adapted from Gardner, 1978.

variation, an environment was needed which allowed teacher flexibility in determining the time, setting, duration, and extent to which children would work. Behaviorally oriented, the system relied heavily upon the check-mark system for reinforcement. The engineered classroom was designed to allow each child to move through attentional, response, exploratory, social, and mastery levels at an individual pace. The major limitations of this program, however, were the lack of attention given to social interaction, and the lack of systematic training of children for reentry into the regular class curriculum (Hewett & Forness, 1974).

As a result of the limitations of the engineered classroom, and because of a need to continue to explore alternative educational settings, the engineered classroom was expanded to provide the mechanism for training exceptional learners to reenter the regular education mainstream. The system depended upon the child's successful movement through four levels of instruction, Preacademic I, Preacademic II, Academic I, and Academic II. Each of the levels stressed different aspects of the levels of learning, and different uses of curriculum, conditions, and consequences of learning. Each of the four levels of instruction consisted of a different class setting. Figure 16-1 shows the settings.

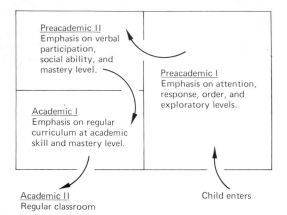

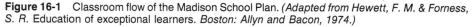

Figure 16-1 Classroom flow of the Madison School Plan. *(Adapted from Hewett, F. M. & Forness, S. R. Education of exceptional learners. Boston: Allyn and Bacon, 1974.)*

Children could move through the levels with ease. The highest level, Academic II, represented attainment of regular grade-level curriculum. As such, the curriculum consisted of the grade-level academic work. The rewards were the regular grading systems, along with satisfaction at the acquisition of knowledge and social praise. The instruction took place in the traditional teacher-large group setting, unless an alternative setting was indicated as being necessary. Academic I consisted of regular class material with remedial work. In this setting, though the regular large group-teacher setting was employed, where possible, small group and individual instruction were also provided. In addition to the grading system employed by the regular school setting, a system was utilized which reflected behavior and work accomplished on an hourly basis. The next level, Preacademic II, focused upon grade-level mastery with extensive and sustained remedial work. The grading system was primarily the check-mark system, with free-time exchange. The instruction at this level took place in teacher-small group settings with provisions for one-to-one instruction. At the most elementary level, Preacademic I, the emphasis was on the level of attention, response, order, and exploration. Neither social nor mastery levels were addressed. The check-mark system was employed for both tangible and free-choice rewards, with additional rewards for work completion and exploratory behavior also being distributed. The condition for learning was primarily teacher-child oriented.

The Santa Monica extension of the engineered classroom grouped learning disabled, emotionally disturbed, and educable mentally retarded together for instruction. Hewett and Forness (1974) imply that the program was successful for all types of learning disabled children, including those classified as hyperactive or having attentional problems. It is, however, open to the same questions as other behavioral programs: the degree to which gains are maintained, the ease with which social consequences are introduced, and the generalization of responses from one setting to another.

AN ALTERNATE APPROACH

An approach to behavior management that is steadily gaining in popularity is *Teacher Effectiveness Training* (TET). This system is predicated on the assumption that the quality of the interaction between the teacher and his or her students is the major factor in teacher-learner relationships. TET's proponents argue that only after an effective relationship has been established is there time for real teaching-learning. This system has been taught to teachers at every level from elementary through high school in every state, often through televised courses.

Gordon (1974), the author of the program, conceptualized conventional classroom management practices in John Holt's terms, i.e., as the "hoop-jump-biscuit" game. In this game, the teacher holds up a hoop and tells the student to jump. If the student makes it, he gets a biscuit. Teachers hold the hoop higher and higher on subsequent trials, thereby requiring more sophisticated performances before rewards are given.

TET strives to help teachers develop better communication skills. The goal is to create classrooms in which the needs of the teacher are respected by the students and vice versa. Gordon believes that one cannot simply say that children should receive praise:

> One kind of praising message will most likely cause students to feel terribly misunderstood and slyly manipulated, while a slightly different message has a high probability of making students see you (the teacher) as a person who is human and genuine, as well as a person who really cares (p. 4)

TET teaches that everyone changes in capacity for accepting other people. What is acceptable in the morning, may not be acceptable in the afternoon. Gordon asserted that it is necessary to communicate one's true feelings to students. This, of course, prohibits the kind of consistency advocated by proponents of behavioral techniques. Gordon insisted that pretending to be accepting when you really are not is fraudulent and that students see through such behavior. This leads, in turn, to mistrust.

Gordon further argued that teachers must be able to establish *ownership* of problems. They must be able to differentiate between circumstances in which the student has a problem and those in which the student's problem causes a problem for the teacher. A problem would belong to the student if the teacher would like the child to act in a different way. The problem is the teacher's, however, when he or she is feeling hurt or damaged by the behavior of the student. There is, of course, a middle ground between the two in which there is no problem for either, i.e., the student is working happily and effectively. Teaching-learning can only be effective when behavior is within the no-problem area.

Gordon listed the following as roadblocks to effective communication: (1) ordering, commanding, or directing; (2) warning and threatening; (3) moralizing, preaching, giving "shoulds" and "oughts"; (4) advising and offering solutions or suggestions; (5) teaching, lecturing, or giving logical arguments; (6) judging, criticizing, disagreeing, or blaming; (7) name-calling, stereotyping, or labeling; (8) interpreting, analyzing, or diagnosing; (9) praising, agreeing, or giving positive evaluations; (10) reassuring, sympathizing, consoling, or supporting; (11) questioning, probing, interrogating, or cross-examining; and (12) withdrawing, distracting, being sarcastic, humoring, or diverting. These behaviors include many that teachers have always believed to be quite effective in helping their students (when the problem belongs to the student).

Gordon said, however, that none of these behaviors is effective, because none shows acceptance of the student's feelings and ideas. He advocated the use of silence, signals that indicate that the teacher is still listening such as uh-hu, or a nod of the head, or the use of door-openers, such as "Do you want to talk about it?" Gordon suggested that only by allowing children to make their own decisions do we show faith in their ability to do so. Clinical experience has shown that children feel safe enough to risk growth when they feel accepted.

The major technique advocated by Gordon is *active listening*. Active listening is reminiscent of Rogerian therapy. In active listening, the receiver sends the message he or she heard back to the speaker. When the student asks the teacher whether there will be a test soon, the teacher guesses that the student is anxious. He feeds that guess back to the student, so that the student is certain that he was understood or he can correct the teacher's guess if the teacher is wrong. The teacher would respond by saying something like, "You are worried that we might have a test soon." Gordon listed the following advantages of active listening:

> (1) Active listening helps the student deal with and defuse strong feelings. . . . (2) helps students understand that they need not be afraid of their own emotions. . . . (3) facilitates problem solving . . . it promotes "talking it out" . . . (4) keeps the responsibility with the student for analyzing and solving his problems . . . (5) makes students more willing to listen to teachers . . . (6) promotes a closer, more meaningful relationship between a teacher and a student (pp. 78–79).

When the problem is the teacher's, TET recommends that the teacher send an "I-message." An I-message is a nonblaming description of a problem that the teacher has. There are three components of an I-message. First, it does not editorialize. It begins with *when* and then describes specific troublesome behaviors. Second, the I-message contains a concrete description of the effect the problem has on the teacher. Third, the I-message describes how the teacher feels about what is happening. An example of an I-message is: "When you have your feet in the aisle (*description of behavior*), I'm apt to trip over them (*tangible effect*) and I'm afraid I'll fall and get hurt (*feeling*)" (p. 144, italics Gordon's).

TET proposed that teachers arrange classrooms and instruction in such a way that conflicts are prevented whenever possible. When they arise, however, one uses the "no-lose method." In the no-lose method, the teacher and the student or students join together to find a solution to the conflict that is acceptable to all parties. Hence, no one loses. If students who are working in a group are disturbing the rest of the class, the teacher and the students would each present their point of view and then seek a mutually satisfying solution. In this case, such a solution might simply be moving the group to a conference room.

Gordon acknowledged that his program is radically different from that taught to most teachers during their university training. So far as the present authors can determine, there is little research evidence to suggest whether the method is effective or ineffective with learning disabled children. The method is, however, gaining wide popularity and many special education teachers are among the students in Gordon's thirty-hour, in-service courses. Since he has published his method in book form, even more teachers are trying the method on their own.

SUMMARY AND CONCLUSIONS

This chapter has focused on ways in which the teacher can effect change in the behavior of children within classroom settings. The major topics covered in the chapter were structuring a school day, using behavior modification principles to manage difficult children, and Gordon's TET approach.

Suggestions for structuring the school day included scheduling activity, using pacing as a structuring strategy, and planning for transitions. The point was made that the teacher has available the necessary techniques to monitor the interaction of children throughout the entire day, and that through the manipulation of the various daily activities, pleasant and effective structure could be maintained.

Behavior modification principles were introduced as useful remedial techniques. The basic techniques for increasing desired behaviors which were introduced were positive reinforcement, negative reinforcement, shaping, and fading. The major techniques for decreasing behaviors were reinforcing an incompatible behavior, extinction, punishment, and differential reinforcement. In addition, it was noted that imitation, discrimination learning, stimulus generalization, and chaining also affect behavior.

The primary strategy employed in TET is that of active listening. With the emphasis on effective communication, TET leads to the understanding and "ownership" of behavior. Evaluations of the program's effectiveness are lacking.

In closing, we recommend that the teacher be familiar with a wide variety of techniques for behavior management. Each has its own uses; some people prefer one, and some another. An effective teacher should be able to intervene in a variety of ways depending upon the individual(s) involved, the setting, and the immediate effect of the child's behaviors on others in the environment.

SUGGESTED READINGS

Axelrod, S. *Behavior modification for the classroom teacher*. New York: McGraw-Hill, 1977.

Gardner, W. I. *Children with learning and behavior problems*. Boston: Allyn and Bacon, 1978.

Gordon, T. *Teacher effectiveness training*. New York: McKay, 1974.

Epilog

The aim of this book has been to describe and advocate a cognitive approach to the conceptualization of learning disabilities and the instruction of learning disabled persons. To accomplish that goal, we have drawn on both the field's history and its current predominant models as contrasts. The basic psychological processes inherent in learning—which are by definition somehow impaired in the learning disabled—were discussed theoretically and empirically to show that attempts at direct training are unwarranted and that many current teaching strategies fail to account for important aspects of those functions. Specifically, we have argued that current models of human thinking emphasize that learning involves much more than the systems of intelligence used for representing information—perception and associative memory. Executive functions, such as the ability to devise, monitor, and execute a plan, are also integral to learning. Yet, much of our instructional methodology, especially the technology developed for remedial interventions, is directed almost exclusively toward the representational system. Two significant problems emerge when the persons to be taught are learning disabled: First, these persons have particular difficulty acquiring and using executive functions. Second, when teachers perform most executive functions for their students, learning disabled persons are necessarily deprived of the opportunity to plan and organize learning experiences for themselves. Although some of the persistence of remedial technology is undoubtedly related to classroom management issues and the need to keep assignments sufficiently well-defined and circumscribed so that the students' gains can be easily demonstrated, recent evidence from the psychology of learning (cf. Smith, 1975) suggests that splintering complex processes (such as reading, speaking) into component abilities changes their nature. Furthermore, there is no assurance that the students will be able to integrate those component abilities successfully and use them appropriately.

A cognitive approach to instruction incorporates at least four principles: First, learning is a personal process in which each person constructs new knowledge. Although the manipulation of external events can influence learning, the most important aspects of the learning experience are internal. As students have experiences, participate in discussions, listen to lectures, observe demonstrations, and so forth, they understand new information by relating it to past experience, drawing inferences and relationships, etc. This process of integrating new information with current knowledge modifies the new information and even changes the nature of what was previously known (cf. Inhelder & Piaget, 1969; Loftus & Loftus, 1980). Second, a cognitive approach acknowledges that learners must be made aware that they are responsible for their own learning. Students must not be allowed to become passive in the educational encounter. One of the difficulties learning disabled persons have is that they are less likely than their normally achieving peers to take an active role in their own learning. They do not work out and apply strategies spontaneously to help themselves learn better. While good readers, for example, ask themselves questions and puzzle over answers to assist in studying difficult text, poor readers simply read the text through once again (Bransford, Stein, Shelton, & Owings, in press). Learning disabled persons must be instructed in the use of study skills, information-gathering techniques, and problem-solving strategies. A third important aspect of a cognitive approach is its emphasis on relationships. Organization and integration of information is a necessary condition if the information is to be retained. Students must be encouraged to use information in relevant ways, to derive metaphors, analogies, rule statements, and to select, summarize, and outline important points. Exercises should be integrative, rather than the practice of isolated information or skills. Activities may be either deductive or inductive, but they are always child-centered. Finally, a cognitive approach to education recognizes that learning in many areas is necessarily holistic. Teaching children to read by practicing letter-sound correspondences is, for example, a more difficult, formal, and abstract task than teaching them to read by reading to them, transcribing their thoughts into print, and assisting them in reading their own communications. The first instructional technique gives children only one set of cues for reading—graphophonemic cues. When meaning is involved, children have two additional cueing systems to assist them—their knowledge of the semantic and syntactic constraints of English. Learning in a cognitive orientation is viewed as the elaboration of past experience, not the acquisition of new bits of skills and understandings.

In keeping with our child-centered orientation, we viewed the process of placement and assessment as requiring information that relates not only to test performance, but also to personal characteristics and changes in behaviors across settings. We consequently advocated that information be gathered from all available sources, including classroom observation—a source regrettably often overlooked because of the time pressures on evaluators. Formal assessment techniques constitute the appropriate basis for classification decisions and give some guidance to broad goals to be considered for IEP development, but only ongoing appraisal through diagnostic teaching can provide teachers with the kinds of information they need for daily instructional planning.

Although there are a number of approaches to both developmental reading and remedial training, none of these has been demonstrated as particularly well-suited to the learning disabled. Most programs have been applauded by those who use them. Controlled studies that evaluate their effectiveness in comparison to other types of programs, however, have failed to demonstrate their superiority over more conventional approaches. That finding probably stems in part from the fact that the learning disabled do not constitute a homogeneous group and it drives home the point that teachers of the learning disabled must be familiar with the whole range of instructional possibilities. One additional point that needs to be made is that outside of reading (for example, in composition, spelling, arithmetic, and science), there is practically no guidance available from controlled research. Only educated guesses and trial and error can determine what strategy or group of strategies will be most effective with any one child. Remedial efforts have been so concentrated on "basic skills" that the learning disabled have a far less rich educational experience than do their normally achieving peers. One plea we have made in a number of sections of this book is that teachers strive to make certain that a child not be deprived of the opportunity to learn because he or she cannot read or do arithmetic. Compensatory strategies directed toward minimizing the effect of the handicap need to be used regularly and intentionally.

We have stressed repeatedly throughout this text that a cognitive approach to educating the learning disabled is not an entirely new one. We have argued that a cognitive approach uses many techniques with which we are already familiar—only the emphases change. Although true, that statement is probably deceptive. Certainly all teachers use hands-on activities, ask children to summarize, deduce rule statements, and draw analogies. Certainly all teachers ask children to work in groups to solve problems. Those are tools of the cognitive approach with which we are all familiar. What is different about the cognitive approach, however, is that the view of the learner and consequently the view of the teacher and of schooling itself, is fundamentally changed. Students are seen as actively in control of their own learning. Learning is regarded as a unique and personal construction. The role of the teacher is not one of imparting knowledge. Rather it is one of selecting and arranging experiences from which students can learn in ways students could not accomplish by themselves. The aim of schooling should be learning how to learn and not the inculcation of some finite set of skills and knowledge. It appears to us that an approach that teaches students to develop strategies for learning is particularly well-suited to the needs of the learning disabled, i. e., persons with problems in learning how to learn.

Finally, this book must come to an end with our reiteration of one important point made in its beginning: that teaching the learning disabled is likely to be influenced by a synthesis of the behavioral and cognitive orientations. Although the cognitive approach has provided us with a richer, more complex view of human learning, much of our educational technology is derived from behavioral principles. How to integrate that technology into interventions that respect the learner as active and his/her learning as personal is the challenge of the future. We hope that this text will stimulate teachers to resolve some of the apparent conflicts and thereby contribute to the advancement of that dialectical synthesis.

References

Abrams, J. Learning disabilities—a complex phenomenon. *The Reading Teacher,* 1970, *23,* 299–303.

Abrams, J., & Kaslow, F. Family systems and the learning disabled child: Intervention and treatment. *Journal of Learning Disabilities,* 1977, *10*(2), 86–90.

Abt Associates, *Education as experimentation: A planned variation model* (Vol. 4). Cambridge, Mass.: Abt Associates, 1977.

Ackerman, P., Peters, J., & Dykman, R. Children with learning disabilities: WISC profiles. *Journal of Learning Disabilities,* 1971, *4,* 150–166.

Adams, M. J., & Collins, A. A schema-theoretic view of reading. Urbana: University of Illinois Center for the Study of Reading, Technical Report No. 32, April 1977.

Adler, S. Behavior management: A nutritional approach to the behaviorally disordered and learning disabled child. *Journal of Learning Disabilities,* 1978, *11*(10), 651–656.

Adrian, E. D., & Mathews, B. H. C., The Berger rhythm: Potential changes from the occipital lobe in man. *Brain,* 1934, *57,* 355–385.

Aiken, L. R. *Psychological testing and assessment* (2d ed.). Boston: Allyn & Bacon, 1976.

Algozzine, B. The emotionally disturbed child: Disturbed or disturbing? *Journal of Abnormal Child Psychology,* 1977, *5.* 205–211.

Algozzine, B., Forgnone, C., Mercer, C., & Trifiletti, J. Toward defining discrepancies for specific learning disabilities: An analysis and alternatives. *Learning Disability Quarterly,* 1979, *2,* 25–31.

Algozzine, R. F., & Sutherland, J. Non-psychological foundations of learning disabilities. *Journal of Special Education,* 1977, *11,* 91–98.

Allen, R., & Allen, C. *Language experiences in reading.* Chicago: Encyclopaedia Britannica, Inc., 1970

Alley, G. Perceptual-motor performance of mentally retarded children after systematic visual-perceptual training. *American Journal of Mental Deficiency,* 1968, *73,* 247–250.

Alley, G. R., Deshler, D. D., & Warner, M. M. Identification of learning disabled adolescents: A Bayesian approach. *Learning Disability Quarterly,* 1979, *2,* 76–83.

Alpert, J. L. Some guidelines for school consultants. *Journal of School Psychology,* 1977, *15,* 308–319.

Altwit, L. Decay of immediate memory for visually presented digits among nonreaders and readers. *Journal of Educational Psychology,* 1963, *54,* 44–45.

American Council on Science and Health. *Diet and hyperactivity: Is there a relationship?* New York: May 1979.

American Psychological Association, American Educational Research Association, & National Council on Measurement in Education. *Standards for educational and psychological tests.* Washington, D.C.: American Psychological Association, 1974.

Anastasi, A. *Psychological testing,* (4th ed.) New York: Macmillan, 1976.

Anderson, B. F. *Cognitive psychology.* New York: Academic Press, 1975.

Anderson, R. C. The notion of schemata and the educational enterprise: General discussion of the conference. In R. C. Anderson, R. J. Spiro, & W. E. Montague (Eds.), *Schooling and the acquisition of knowledge.* Hillsdale, N.J.: Lawrence Erlbaum, 1977.

Anderson, R. C., Spiro, R. J., & Montague, W. E. *Schooling and the acquisition of knowledge.* Hillsdale, N.J.: Lawrence Erlbaum, 1977.

Ansara, A. Maturational readiness for school tasks. *Bulletin of the Orton Society,* 1969, *19,* 51–59.

Aram, S. M., & Nation, J. E. Patterns of language behavior in children with developmental language disorders. *Journal of Speech and Hearing Research,* 1975, *18,* 229–241.

Arter J. A., & Jenkins, J. R. Examining the benefits and prevalence of modality considerations in special education. *Journal of Special Education,* 1977, *11,* 281–198.

Ashlock, R. B. *Error patterns in computation: A semi-programmed approach* (2d ed.). Columbus, Ohio: Merrill, 1976.

Askov, E. N., & Kamm, K. Context clues: Should we teach children to use a classification system in reading? *Journal of Educational Research,* 1976, *69,* 341–344.

Aten, J., & Davis, J. Disturbances in the perception of auditory sequence in children with minimal cerebral dysfunction. *Journal of Speech and Hearing Research,* 1968, *11,* 236–245.

Atkinson, B. R., & Seunath, O. H. M. The effect of stimulus change in attending behavior in normal children and children with learning disorders. *Journal of Learning Disabilities,* 1973, *6,* 569–573.

Atkinson, R. C., & Shiffrin, R. M. The control of short-term memory. *Scientific American,* 1971, *225,* 82–90.

Ausubel, D. P. *Educational psychology: A cognitive view.* New York: Holt, Rinehart and Winston, 1968.

Ausubel, D. P., Novak, J. D., & Hanesian, H. *Educational psychology.* New York: Holt, Rinehart and Winston, 1978.

Axelrod, S. *Behavior modification for the classroom teacher.* New York: McGraw-Hill, 1977.

Bachara, G. Human figure drawing and learning disabled children. *Academic Therapy,* 1975–1976, *11*(2), 217–220.

Baddeley, A. D., & Warrington, E. K. Memory coding and amnesia. *Neuropsychologia,* 1973, *11*, 159–165.

Badian, N. A. Auditory-visual integration, auditory memory and reading in retarded and adequate readers. *Journal of Learning Disabilities,* 1977, *10*(2), 108–114.

Badian, N. A., & Serwer, B. L. The identification of high-risk children: A retrospective look at selection criteria. *Journal of Learning Disabilities,* 1975, *8*, 283–287.

Baker, H. J., & Leland, B. *Detroit Tests of Learning Aptitude.* Indianapolis: Bobbs-Merrill, 1935.

Baker, L. Comprehension monitoring: Identifying and coping with text confusions. Center for the Study of Reading, University of Illinois at Urbana-Champaign. ERIC Document Reproduction Service No. ED 117 525, September, 1979.

Ballard, J., & Zettel, J. J. Fiscal arrangements of Public Law 94-142. *Exceptional Children,* 1978, *44*, 333–337.

Baloh, R., & Strum, R. Neuropsychological effects of chronic asymtomatic increased lead absorption. *Archives of Neurology,* 1975, *32*, 326–330.

Bandura, A. Self-efficacy: Toward a unifying theory of behavioral change. *Psychological Review,* 1977, *84*, 191–215.

Bandura, A., Ross, D., & Ross, S. A. Transmission of aggression through imitation of aggressive models. *Journal of Abnormal and Social Psychology, 1961, 63,* 575–582.

Bandura, A., Ross, D., & Ross, S. A. Imitation of film-mediated aggressive models. *Journal of Abnormal and Social Psychology,* 1963, *66*, 3–11.

Bannatyne, A. The etiology of dyslexia and the color phonics system. In J. Money (Ed.), *The disabled reader: Education of the dyslexic child.* Baltimore: Johns Hopkins University Press, 1966.

Bannatyne, A. *Reading: An auditory vocal process.* San Rafael, Calif.: Academic Therapy Publications, 1973.

Barclay, J. R., & Reed, M. Semantic integration in children's recall of discourse. *Developmental Psychology,* 1974, *10*, 277–281.

Barkley, R. The effects of methylphenidate on various types of activity level and attention in hyperactive children. *Journal of Abnormal Child Psychology,* 1977, *5,* 351–369.

Barkley, R., & Cunningham, C. Do stimulant drugs improve the academic performance of hyperactive children? A review of outcome research. *Clinical Pediatrics,* 1978, *17,* 85–92.

Barsch, R. The concept of language as a visuo-spatial phenomenon. *Academic Therapy Quarterly,* 1965, *1,* 2–11.(a)

Barsch, R. The *movigenic* curriculum. Madison, Wisc.: State Department of Public Instruction, 1965.(b)

Barsch, R. *Achieving perceptual-motor efficiency: A space-oriented approach to learning.* Seattle: Special Child Publications, 1967.

Bartel, N. R. Problems in mathematics achievement. In D. D. Hammill & N. R. Bartel (Eds.), *Teaching children with learning and behavior problems.* Boston: Allyn & Bacon, 1978.

Bartel, N. R., Bryen, D. N., & Bartel, H. W. Approaches for alternative programming. In E. L. Meyen, G. A. Vergason, & R. J. Wheelan (Eds.), *Alternatives for teaching exceptional children.* Denver, Col.: Love, 1975.

Bartel, N. R., & Guskin, S. L. A handicap as a social phenomenon. Unpublished manuscript, Indiana University, 1968.

Barten, H. H., & Barten, S. S. *Children and their parents in brief therapy.* New York: Behavioral Publications, 1973.

Bateman, B. D. *Interpretation of the 1961 Illinois Test of Psycholinguistic Abilities.* Seattle, Wash.: Special Child Publications, 1968.

Bateman, B. Teaching reading to learning disabled children. Paper presented at the Reading Conference sponsored by the National Institute of Education, University of Pittsburg, April, May, June, 1976.

Beatty, J. R. The analysis of an instrument for screening learning disabilities. *Journal of Learning Disabilities,* 1975, *8,* 180–186.

Beatty, J. R. Identifying decision-making policies in the diagnosis of learning disabilities. *Journal of Learning Disabilities,* 1977, *10,* 201–209.

Becker, L. D. Learning characteristics of educationally handicapped and retarded children. *Exceptional Children,* 1978, *44,* 502–511.

Begab, M. Childhood learning disabilities and family stress: Cause and consequence. In J. Hellmuth (Ed.), *Learning disorders* (Vol. 3). Seattle, Wash.: Special Child Publications, 1968.

Bender, L. *Psychopathology of children with organic brain disorders.* Springfield, Ill.: Charles C Thomas, 1959.

Bender, L. Psychological problems of children with organic brain disease. In E. C. Frierson & W. B. Barbe (Eds.), *Educating children with learning disabilities: Selected readings.* New York: Appleton-Century-Crofts, 1967.

Bender, L. Childhood schizophrenia: A review. *International Journal of Psychiatry,* 1968, *5,* 211–221.

Bender, N. Hierarchical semantic organization in educable mentally retarded and learning disabled children. Paper presented at the AERA meeting, San Francisco, April 1976.

Benthul, H. F., Anderson, E. A., Utech, A. M., Beggy, M. U., & Bailey, B. H. *Spell correctly.* Morristown, N.J.: Silver Burdett, 1974.

Benton, A. L. Developmental dyslexia: Neurological aspects. In W. J. Friedlander (Ed.), *Advances in neurology* (Vol. 7). New York: Raven Press, 1975.

Berko, J. The child's learning of English morphology. *Word,* 1958, *14,* 150–177.

Berman, A. Incidence of learning disabilities in juvenile delinquents and nondelinquents: Implications for etiology and treatment. *ERIC,* 1975, *2,* 101.

Berman, A., & Siegal, A. Adaptive and learning skills in juvenile delinquents: A neuropsychological analysis. *Journal of Learning Disabilities,* 1976, *9,* 583–589.

Berman, D. S. Cognitive-behaviorism as a dialectic contradiction. *Human Development,* 1978, *21,* 248–254.

Berry, J. W. Matching of auditory and visual stimuli by average and retarded readers. *Child Development,* 1967, *38,* 827–833.

Bettelheim, B. Bringing up children. *Ladies Home Journal,* 1973, *90,* 28.

Bever, T. G. The cognitive basis for linguistic structures. In J. Hayes (Ed.), *Cognition and the development of language.* New York: Wiley, 1970.

Bhatara, V., Arnold, L. E., Lorance, T., & Gupta, D. Muscle relaxation therapy in hyperkinesis: Is it effective? *Journal of Learning Disabilities,* 1979, *12*(3), 182–186.

Birch, H. G. Dyslexia and the maturation of visual function. In J. Money (Ed.), *Reading disability: Progress and research needs in dyslexia.* Baltimore: Johns Hopkins University Press, 1962.

Birch, H. G., & Belmont, I. Perceptual analysis and sensory integration in brain-damaged persons. *Journal of Genetic Psychology,* 1964, *105,* 173–179.

Birch, H. G., & Belmont, L. Auditory-visual integration in normal and retarded readers. *American Journal of Orthopsychiatry*, 1964, *34*, 852–861.

Birch, H. G., & Belmont, L. Auditory-visual integration in brain-damaged and normal children. *Developmental Medicine and Child Neurology*, 1965, *7*, 135–144.(a)

Birch, H. G., & Belmont, L. Auditory-visual integration, intelligence and reading ability in school children. *Perceptual and Motor Skills*, 1965, *20*, 295–305.(b)

Bjork, R. A. Short-term storage: The ordered output of a central processor. In F. Restle, R. M. Shiffrin, N. J. Castellan, H. R. Lindman, & D. B. Pisoni, (Eds.), *Cognitive theory* (Vol. 1). Hillsdale, N.J.: Lawrence Erlbaum, 1975.

Bjork, R. A., & Whitten, W. B. Recency-sensitive retrieval processes in long-term free recall. *Cognitive Psychology*, 1974, *6*, 173–189.

Black, F. Self-concept as related to achievement and age in learning disabled children. *Child Development*, 1974, *45*, 1137–1140.

Blake, H. E. Written composition in English primary schools. *Elementary English*, 1971, *48*, 605–616.

Blanck, G., & Blanck, R. *Ego psychology: Theory and practice.* New York: Columbia University Press, 1974.

Blank, M., & Bridger, W. Deficiencies in verbal labeling in retarded readers. *American Journal of Orthopsychiatry*, 1966, *36*, 840–847.

Blank, M., Weider, S., & Bridger, W. Verbal deficiencies in abstract thinking in early reading retardation. *American Journal of Orthopsychiatry*, 1968, *38*, 823–834.

Blankenship, C. S. Remediating systematic inversion errors in subtraction through the use of demonstration and feedback. *Learning Disability Quarterly*, 1978, *1*, 12–22.

Bloom, L. *Language development: Form and function in emerging grammars.* Cambridge, Mass.: The M.I.T. Press, 1970.

Bloom, L. M. LD[3]. Paper presented at the New York Child Language Association, 1977.

Bloom, L., & Lahey, M. *Language development and language disorders.* New York: Wiley, 1978.

Bloom, L. M., Lightbown, P., & Hood, L. Structure and variation in child language. *Monographs of the Society for Research in Child Development*, 1975, *40*.

Bloomfield, L. Linguistics and reading. *Elementary English*, 1942, *18*, 125–130.

Blumenthal, A. L. *The process of cognition.* Englewood Cliffs, N.J.: Prentice-Hall, 1977.

Boder, E. Developmental dyslexia: Prevailing diagnostic concepts and a new diagnostic approach. In H. Myklebust (Ed.), *Progress in learning disabilities* (Vol. 2). New York: Grune & Stratton, 1971.

Boder, E. Developmental dyslexia: Prevailing concepts and a new diagnostic approach. *Bulletin of the Orton Society*, 1973, *23*, 106–118.

Boehm, A. E. *Boehm test of basic concepts.* New York: Psychological Corporation, 1971.

Bolstad, O. D., & Johnson, S. M. Self-regulation in the modification of disruptive behavior. *Journal of Applied Behavior Analysis*, 1972, *5*, 443–454.

Bond, G. L., Balow, B., & Hoyt, C. *Silent Reading Diagnostic Tests.* Ardmore, Pa.: Meredith Corporation, 1970.

Bornstein, P. H., & Quevillon, R. P. The effects of a self-instructional package on overactive preschool boys. *Journal of Applied Behavior Analysis*, 1976, *9*, 179–188.

Bortner, M. Phrenology, localization, and learning disabilities. *Journal of Special Education*, 1971, *5*, 23–29.

Bortner, M. Perceptual skills and early reading disability. In L. Mann & D. A. Sabatino (Eds.), *The second review of special education.* New York: Grune & Stratton, 1974, 79–102.

Boyd, L., & Randle, K. Factor analysis of the Frostig Developmental Test of Visual Perception. *Journal of Learning Disabilities,* 1970, *3,* 253–255.

Bracht, G. H. Experimental factors related to aptitude-treatment interactions. *Review of Educational Research,* 1974, *40,* 627–645.

Bradley, C. The behavior of children receiving benzedrine. *American Journal of Psychiatry,* 1937, *94,* 577–585.

Braine, M. On learning the grammatical order of words. *Psychological Review,* 1963, *70,* 323–348.

Braine, M. On the basis of phrase structure: A reply to Bever, Fodor, and Weksel. *Psychological Review,* 1965, *72,* 483–492.

Braine, M. On two types of models of the internalization of grammars. In D. Slobin (Ed.), *The ontogenesis of grammar.* New York: Academic Press, 1971.

Braine, M. Length constraints, reduction rules, and holophrastic processes in children's word combinations. *Journal of Verbal Learning and Verbal Behavior,* 1974, *13,* 448–456.

Braine, M. Modeling the acquisition of linguistic structure. Paper presented at the New York Child Language Association, 1979.

Bransford, J. D., & Franks, J. J. The abstraction of linguistic ideas. *Cognitive Psychology,* 1971, *2,* 331–350.

Braud, L. W., Lupin, M. N., & Braud, W. G. The use of electromyographic biofeedback in the control of hyperactivity. *Journal of Learning Disabilities,* 1975, *8,* 420–425.

Brewer, W. Dyslexia: Neurological and genetic etiology. In E. O. Calkins (Ed.), *Reading forum.* Bethesda, Md.: U.S. Department of HEW, NINDS Monograph No. 11, 1973, 47–54.

Bricker, W. A., & Bricker, D. D. An early language training strategy. In R. L. Schiefelbusch & L. L. Lloyd (Eds.), *Language perspectives: Acquisition, retardation, and intervention.* Baltimore: University Park Press, 1974.

Britton, J. *Language and learning.* Norwich, Great Britain: Penguin Press, 1972.

Broadbent, D. E. *Perception and communication.* New York: Pergammon Press, 1958.

Broden, M., Hall, V., & Mitts, B. The effects of self-recording on the classroom behavior of two eighth-grade students. *Journal of Applied Behavior Analysis,* 1971, *4,* 191–199.

Brown, A. L. Judgments of recency for long sequences of pictures: The absence of a developmental thread. *Journal of Experimental Child Psychology,* 1973, *15,* 473–480.

Brown, A. L. The development of memory: Knowing, knowing about knowing, knowing how to know. In H. W. Reese (Ed.), *Advances in child development and behavior* (Vol. 10). New York: Academic Press, 1975.

Brown, A. L. Knowing when, where, and how to remember: A problem of metacognition. In R. Glaser (Ed.), *Advances in instructional psychology.* Hillsdale, N.J.: Lawrence Erlbaum, 1978.

Brown, A. L., & Campione, J. C. Permissible inference from the outcome of training studies in cognitive development research. *Quarterly Newsletter of the Institute for Comparative Human Development,* 1978, *2,* 46–53.

Brown, A. L., & Smiley, S. Rating the importance of structural units of prose passages: A problem of metacognitive development. *Child Development,* 1977, *48,* 1–8.

Brown, E. Neuropsychological interference mechanisms in aphasia and dyslexia. In R. Rieber (Ed.), *The neuropsychology of language: Essays in honor of Eric Lenneberg.* New York: Plenum, 1976.

Brown, J. R., & Simonson, J. A clinical study of 100 aphasic patients. I. Observations on lateralization and localization of lesions. *Neurology,* 1957, *7,* 777–783.

Brown, L. L., & Hammill, D. D. *Behavior Rating Profile: An ecological approach to behavioral assessment.* Austin, Tx.: Pro-Ed, 1978.

Brown, V. L., Hammill, D. D., & Wiederholdt, L. J. *The Test of Reading Comprehension.* Austin, Tx.: 1978.

Brown, R. *Words and things.* Glencoe, Ill.: The Free Press, 1958.

Brown, R. *A first language: The early stages.* Cambridge, Mass.: Harvard University Press, 1973.

Brueckner, L. J. *Diagnostic tests and self-helps in arithmetic.* Los Angeles: California Test Bureau, 1955.

Bruinincks, R. H., & Weatherman, R. F. *Handicapped children and special education program needs in northeast Minnesota.* Minneapolis: Department of Special Education, University of Minnesota, 1970.

Bruner, J. S. On perceptual readiness. *Psychological Review,* 1957, *64,* 123–152.

Bruner, J. S., Goodnow, J. J., & Austin, G. A. *A study of thinking.* New York: Wiley, 1956.

Bryan, J. H., & Perlmutter, B. Immediate impressions of LD children by female adults. *Learning Disability Quarterly,* 1979, *2,* 80–88.

Bryan, J. H., Sherman, R. E., & Fisher, A. Learning disabled boys' nonverbal behaviors within a dyadic interview. *Learning Disability Quarterly,* 1980, *3,* 65–72.

Bryan, T. S. The effects of forced mediation upon short-term memory of children with learning disabilities. *Journal of Learning Disabilities,* 1972, *5,* 605–609.

Bryan, T. S., & Connors, S. P. Linguistic and cognitive analyses of social communication. In preparation.

Bryan, T. Peer popularity of learning-disabled children. *Journal of Learning Disabilities,* 1974, *7,* 261–268.(a)

Bryan, T. An observational analysis of classroom behaviors of children with learning disabilities. *Journal of Learning Disabilities,* 1974, *7,* 26–34.(b)

Bryan, T. Peer popularity of learning-disabled children: A replication. *Journal of Learning Disabilities,* 1976, *9,* 307–311.

Bryan, T. Learning disabled children's comprehension of nonverbal communication. *Journal of Learning Disabilities,* 1977, *10,* 501–506.

Bryan, T. Social relationships and verbal interactions of learning disabled children. *Journal of Learning Disabilities,* 1978, *11,* 107–115.

Bryan, T. S., & McGrady, H. J. Use of a teacher rating scale. *Journal of Learning Disabilities,* 1972, *5,* 199–206.

Bryan, T., & Pflaum, S. Social interactions of learning disabled children: A linguistic, social, and cognitive analysis. *Learning Disability Quarterly,* 1978, *1,* 70–79.

Bryan, T., Wheeler, R., Felcan, J., & Henek, T. Come on dummy!: An observational study of children's communication. *Journal of Learning Disabilities,* 1977, *9,* 661–669.

Bryant, N. Clinic inadequacies with learning disorders: The missing clinical educator. In J. Hellmuth (Ed.), *Learning disorders* (Vol. 2). Seattle: Special Child Publications, 1966.

Bryden, M. P. Auditory-visual and sequential spatial matching in relation to reading ability. *Child Development,* 1972, *43,* 824–832.

Buchholz, E. Emotional development and controls in learning disabled children. Unpublished manuscript, New York University, 1978.

Burns, M. *The I hate mathematics! book.* Boston: Little, Brown, 1975.

Burns, P. C. *Diagnostic teaching of the language arts.* Itasca, Ill.: Peacock Publishers, 1974.

Burns, P. C., & Broman, B. L. *The language arts in childhood education.* Chicago: Rand McNally, 1979.

Bush, C. L., & Andrews, R. C. *Dictionary of reading and learning disabilities terms.* Matawan, N.J.: Educational and Psychological Associates Press, 1973.

Bush, W. J., & Giles, M. T. *Aids to psycholinguistic teaching.* Columbus, Ohio: Merrill, 1969.

Buss, A. H., & Plomin, R. *A temperament theory of personality development.* New York: Wiley, 1975.

Butterfield, E. C., & Belmont, J. M. Assessing and improving the executive cognitive functions of mentally retarded people. In I. Bialer & M. Sternlicht (Eds.), *Psychological issues in mentally retarded people.* Chicago: Aldine, 1975.

Cady, J. L. Pretend you are . . . an author. *Teaching Exceptional Children,* 1975, *8,* 27–31.

Callahan, L. G., & Glennon, V. J. *Elementary school mathematics: A guide to current research.* Washington, D.C.: Association for Supervision and Curriculum Development, 1975.

Camp, B. W., Blom, G. E., Herbert, F., & Van Doorninck, W. J. Think aloud: A program for developing self-control in young aggressive boys. *Journal of Abnormal Child Psychology,* 1977, *5,* 157–169.

Cantwell, D. P. Psychiatric illness in the families of hyperactive children. *Archives of General Psychiatry,* 1972, *27,* 414–417.

Cantwell, D. P. The hyperkinetic syndrome. In M. Rutter & H. Hersov (Eds.), *Recent advances in child psychiatry.* London: Blackwell, 1975.

Cantwell, D. P. Genetic factors in the hyperkinetic syndrome. *Journal of Child Psychiatry,* 1976, *15*(2), 214–223.

Carrell, J., & Pendergast, K. An experimental study of the possible relation between errors of speech and spelling. *Journal of Speech and Hearing Disorders,* 1954, *19,* 327–334.

Carroll, J. B. Diversity of vocabulary and the harmonic series law of word frequency distribution. *Psychological Record,* 1938, *2.*

Carroll, J. B. The case for ideographic writing. In J. F. Kavanagh & I. G. Mattingly (Eds.), *Language by ear and by eye: The relationships between speech and reading.* Cambridge, Mass.: MIT Press, 1972.

Carrow, E. *Test for Auditory Comprehension of Language.* Austin, Tx.: Learning Concepts, 1973.

Carrow, E. *Carrow Elicited Language Inventory.* Austin, Tx.: Learning Concepts, 1974.

Cartwright, G. P. Written expression and spelling. In R. M. Smith (Ed.), *Teacher diagnosis of educational difficulties.* Columbus, Ohio: Merrill, 1969.

Cawley, J. F. Teaching arithmetic to mentally handicapped children. *Focus on Exceptional Children,* 1970, *2,* 1–8.

Cawley, J. F. An instructional design in mathematics. In L. Mann, L. Goodman, & J. L. Wiederholt (Eds.), *Teaching the learning-disabled adolescent.* Boston: Houghton Mifflin, 1978.

Cawley, J. F., Burrow, W. H., & Goodstein, H. A. An appraisal of Head Start participants and nonparticipants. Research report. Contract OEO4177. Office of Economic Opportunity. Storrs, Conn.: University of Connecticut, 1968.

Cawley, J. F., Fitzmaurice, A. M., Goodstein, H. A., Lepore, A. V., Sedlak, R., & Althaus, V. *Project MATH, Level I.* Tulsa, Oklahoma: Educational Progress Corporation, 1976.

Cawley, J. F., Fitzmaurice, A. M., Shaw, R. A., Kahn, H., Bates, H. Mathematics and learning disabled youth: The upper grade levels. *Learning Disability Quarterly,* 1978, *1,* 37–52.

Cawley, J. F., & Goodman, J. O. Arithmetical problem solving: A demonstration with the mentally handicapped. *Exceptional Children,* 1969, *2,* 83–88.

Cazden, C. B. Evaluation of learning in preschool education: Early language development. In B. S. Bloom, J. T. Hastings, & G. F. Madaus (Eds.), *Handbook on formative and summative evaluation of student learning.* New York: McGraw-Hill, 1971.

Cegelka, P. T., & Phillips, M. W. Individualized education programming at the secondary level. *Teaching Exceptional Children,* 1978, *10,* 84–87.

Cermark, S. A., Stein, F., & Abelson, C. Hyperactive children and activity group therapy model. *American Journal of Occupational Therapy,* 1973, *27*(6), 311–315.

Chalfant, J. C., & King, F. S. An approach to operationalizing the definition of learning disabilities. *Journal of Learning Disabilities,* 1976, *9*(4), 228–243.

Chalfant, J. C., & Scheffelin, M. A. *Central processing dysfunctions in children: A review of research.* NINDS Monographs No. 9. Bethesda, Md.: U.S. Department of Health, Education, and Welfare, 1969.

Chall, J. *Learning to read: The great debate.* New York: McGraw-Hill, 1967.

Chess, S., & Korn, S. Temperament and behavior disorders in mentally retarded children. *Archives of General Psychiatry,* 1970, *23,* 122–130.

Chinn, P.C., Winn, J., & Walters, R. H. *Two-way talking with parents of special children: A process of positive communication.* St. Louis, Mo.: C. V. Mosby, 1978.

Chislom, J. J., Jr., & Kaplan, E. Lead poisoning in childhood—comprehensive management and prevention. *Journal of Pediatrics,* 1968, *73,* 942–950.

Chomsky, C. Reading, writing, and phonology. *Harvard Educational Review,* 1970, *40,* 287–309.

Chomsky, C. When you still can't read in third grade: After decoding, what? In S. J. Samuels (Ed.), *What research has to say about reading instruction.* Newark, Del.: International Reading Association, 1978.

Chomsky, N. A review of B. F. Skinner's *Verbal Behavior. Language,* 1959, *35,* 26–58.

Chomsky, N. *Aspects of the theory of syntax.* Cambridge, Mass.: MIT Press, 1965.

Chomsky, N., & Halle, M. *The sound pattern of English.* New York: Harper & Row, 1968.

Christopolos, F., & Renz, P. Critical examination of special education programs. *Journal of Special Education,* 1969, *3,* 371–379.

Clay, M. M., Sentence repetition: Elicited imitation of a controlled set of syntactic structures by four language groups. *Monographs of the Society of for Research in Child Development,* 1971, *36.*

Cleary, T. A., Humphreys, L. G., Kendrick, S. A., & Wesman, A. Educational uses of tests with disadvantaged students. *American Psychologist,* 1975, *30,* 15–41.

Clements, S. D. *Minimal brain dysfunction in children.* Washington, D.C.: Cosponsored by the Easter Seal Research Foundation of the National Society for Crippled

Children and Adults and the National Institute of Neurological Diseases and Blindness, Public Health Service, 1966.

Clements, S. D., & Peters, J. E. Minimal brain dysfunctions in school-age children. *Archives of General Psychiatry*, 1962, *6*, 185–197.

Cobrinik, L. The performance of brain-injured children on hidden-figure tasks. *American Journal of Psychology*, 1959, *72*, 566–571.

Cogwill, M., Friedland, S., & Shapiro, R. Predicting learning disabilities from kindergarten reports. *Journal of Learning Disabilities*, 1973, *6*, 577–582.

Cohen, C. R., & Abrams, R. M. *Spellmaster, spelling: Testing evaluating book one.* Exeter, N.H.: Learnco, Inc., 1976.

Cohen, J. H., & Diehl, C. F. Relation of speech sound discrimination ability to articulation-type speech defects. *Journal of Speech and Hearing Disorders*, 1963, *28*, 187–190.

Cohen, J. S., & DeYoung, H. The role of litigation in the improvement of programming for the handicapped. In L. Mann & D. A. Sabatino (Eds.), *The first review of special education* (Vol. 2). Philadelphia: JSE Press, 1973.

Cohen, S., Semmes, M., & Guralnick, M. J. Public Law 94-142 and the education of preschool handicapped children. Law Review. *Exceptional Children*, 1979, *45*, 279–286.

Cohen, S. B., & Plaskon, S. P. *Language arts for the mildly handicapped.* Columbus, Ohio: Merrill, 1980.

Cohn, R. Arithmetic and learning disabilities. In H. R. Myklebust (Ed.), *Progress in learning disabilities* (Vol. 2). New York: Grune & Stratton, 1971.

Coleman, J. M. Mothers' predictions of the self-concept of their normal or learning disabled children, *Exceptional Children*, in press.

Collins, A. M., & Quillian, M. R. Retrieval time from semantic memory. *Journal of Verbal Learning and Verbal Behavior*, 1969, *8*, 240–247.

Conners, C. K. A teacher rating scale for use in drug studies with children. *American Journal of Psychiatry*, 1969, *126*, 884–888.

Conners, C. K., & Barta, F. Transfer of information from touch to vision in brain-injured and emotionally disturbed children. *Journal of Nervous and Mental Disease*, 1967, *145*, 138–141.

Conners, C. K., Goyette, G. M., Southwick, D. A., Lees, J. M., & Andrulonis, P. A. Food additives and hyperkinesis: A controlled double blind study. *Pediatrics*, 1976, *58*(2), 154–166.

Connolly, A. J., Nachtman, W., & Pritchett, E. M. *Key Math Diagnostic Arithmetic Test.* Circle Pines, Minn.: American Guidance Service, 1971.

Connolly, C. Social and emotional factors in learning disabilities. In H. R. Myklebust (Ed.), *Progress in learning disabilities* (Vol. 2). New York: Grune & Stratton, 1971.

Conrad, W. G., & Insel, J. Anticipating the response to amphetamine therapy in the treatment of hyperkinetic children. *Pediatrics*, 1967, *40*, 96–98.

Cook, P. S., & Woodhill, J. M. The Feingold dietary treatment of the hyperkinetic syndrome. *Medical Journal of Australia*, 1976, *2*, 85–90.

Copeland, R. W. *How children learn mathematics.* New York: Macmillan, 1974.

Corteen, R. S., & Wood, B. Autonomic responses to shock-associated words in an unattended channel. *Journal of Experimental Psychology*, 1972, *94*, 308–313.

Council for Exceptional Children. What is mainstreaming? *Exceptional Children*, 1975, *42*, 174.

Cowan, R. E., & Clary, R. C. Identifying and teaching essential mathematical skills—items. *Mathematics Teacher*, 1978, *71*, 130–134.

Cox, L. S. Diagnosing and remediating systematic errors in addition and subtraction computations. *The Arithmetic Teacher*, 1975, *22*, 151–157.

Craik, F. I. M., & Jacoby, L. L. A process view of short-term memory. In F. Restle (Ed.), *Cognitive theory* (Vol. 1). Hillsdale, N.J.: Lawrence Erlbaum, 1975.

Craik, F. I. M., & Lockhart, R. S. Levels of processing: A framework for memory research. *Journal of Verbal Learning and Verbal Behavior*, 1972, *11*, 671–684.

Craik, F. I. M., & Tulving, E. Depth of processing and the retention of words in episodic memory. *Journal of Experimental Psychology*, 1975, *104*, 268–294.

Craik, F. I. M., & Watkins, M. J. The role of rehearsal in short-term memory. *Journal of Verbal Learning and Verbal Behavior*, 1973, *12*, 599–607.

Cratty, B. J. *Developmental sequences of perceptual-motor tasks: Movement activities for neurologically handicapped and retarded youth.* Freeport, N.Y.: Educational Activities, Inc. 1967.

Cratty, B. J. *Motor activity and the education of retardates.* Philadelphia: Lea & Febiger, 1969.(a)

Cratty, B. J. *Perceptual-motor behavior and educational processes.* Springfield, Ill.: Charles C Thomas, 1969.(b)

Cratty, B. J. *Perceptual and motor development in infants and children.* New York: Macmillan, 1970.

Cratty, B. J. *Physical expressions of intelligence.* Englewood Cliffs, N.J.: Prentice-Hall, 1972.

Cratty, B. J. Movement in programs for handicapped children: Hysteria and reality. *Conference on Physical Education Techniques and Methods for Handicapped Children and Youth.* May 24, 1973.

Cravioto, J., & DeLicardie, E. R. Environmental and learning deprivation in children with learning disabilities. In W. M. Cruickshank & D. P. Hallahan (Eds.), *Perceptual and learning disabilities in children: Research and theory* (Vol. 2). Syracuse, N.Y.: Syracuse University Press.

Critchley, M. *The dyslexic child.* London: William Heinemann Medical Books, Limited, 1970.

Critchley, M. Developmental dyslexia: Its history, nature, and prospects. In D. D. Duane & M. B. Rawson (Eds.), *Reading, perception, and language: Papers from the World Congress on Dyslexia sponsored by the Orton Society in cooperation with the Mayo Clinic.* Baltimore: York Press, 1975.

Critchley, M. Language. In E. H. Lenneberg & E. Lenneberg (Eds.), *Foundations of language development* (Vol. 1). New York: Academic Press, 1975.

Critchley, M., & Critchley, E. A. *Dyslexia defined.* Springfield, Ill.: Charles C Thomas, 1978.

Cruickshank, W. M. *The brain-injured child in home, school, and society.* Syracuse, N.Y.: Syracuse University Press, 1967.

Cruickshank, W. M. Myths and realities in learning disabilities. *Journal of Learning Disabilities*, 1977, *10*(1), 51–58.

Cruickshank, W. M., Bentzen, F. A., Ratzeburg, F. H., & Tannhauser, M. T. *A teaching method for brain injured and hyperactive children.* Syracuse, N.Y.: Syracuse University Press, 1961.

Cunningham, C. E., & Barkley, R. A. The role of academic failure in hyperactive behavior. *Journal of Learning Disabilities*, 1978, *11*(5), 274–280.

D'Alonzo, B. J., & Miller, S. R. A management model for learning disabled adolescents. *Teaching Exceptional Children,* 1977, *9*(3), 58–60.

David, O. J. Association between lower level lead concentrations and hyperactivity in children. *Environmental Health Perspectives,* 1974, *3,* 17–25.

David, O. J., Clark, J., & Voeller, K. Lead and hyperactivity. *Lancet,* 1972, *2,* 900–903.

David, O. J., Hoffman, S., McGann, B., Sverd, J., & Clark, J. Low lead levels and mental retardation. *Lancet,* 1976, *6,* 1376–1379.

de Avila, E. A., & Havassy, B. The testing of minority children—a neoPiagetian approach. *Today's Education,* 1974, November–December, 72–75.

Dechant, E. V. *Improving the teaching of reading.* Englewood Cliffs, N.J.: Prentice-Hall, 1964.

de Charms, R. *Enhancing motivation: Change in the classroom.* New York: Irvington, 1976.

de Hirsch, K. Learning disabilities: An overview. *Bulletin of the New York Academy of Medicine, 1974, 50,* 459–479.

de Hirsch, K. Cluttering and stuttering. *Bulletin of the Orton Society,* 1975, *25,* 57–68.

Delacato, C. H. *The treatment and prevention of reading problems: The neurological approach.* Springfield, Ill.: Charles C Thomas, 1959.

Delacato, C. H. *Neurological organization and reading.* Springfield, Ill.: Charles C Thomas, 1966.

DeLeon, J. L., Raskin, L. M., & Gruen, G. E. Sensory-modality effects on shape perception in preschool children. *Developmental Psychology,* 1970, *3,* 538–362.

Denckla, M., & Rudel, R. Naming of object drawings by dyslexic and other learning disabled children. *Brain and Language,* 1976, *3,* 1–16.(a)

Denckla, M., & Rudel, R. Rapid 'automatized' naming (R.A.N.): Dyslexia differentiated from other learning disabilities. *Neuropsychologia,* 1976, *14,* 471–479.(b)

Denckla, M. B. Clinical syndromes in learning disabilities. *Journal of Learning Disabilities,* 1972, *5,* 401–406.

Deno, E. Special education as developmental capital. *Exceptional Children,* 1970, *37,* 229–237.

Denson, R., Nanson, J. L., & McWatters, M. A. Hyperkinesis and maternal smoking. *Canadian Psychiatric Association Journal,* 1975, *20,* 183–187.

DeRuiter, J. A., Ferrell, W. R., & Kass, C. E. Learning disabilities classification by Bayesian aggregation of test results. *Journal of Learning Disabilities,* 1975, *8,* 365–372.

Deutsch, J., & Deutsch, D. Attention: Some theoretical considerations. *Psychological Review,* 1963, *70,* 80–90.

Deutsch, J., Deutsch, D., & Lindsay, P. Comments on "selective attention: stimulus or response." *Quarterly Journal of Experimental Psychology,* 1967, *19,* 362–368.

Dever, R. B. Language assessment through specification of goals and objectives. *Exceptional Children,* 1978, *45,* 124–129.(a)

Dever, R. *T.A.L.K. (Teaching the American language to kids.)* Columbus, Ohio: Merrill, 1978.(b)

de Villiers, J. G., & de Villiers, P. A. *Language acquisition.* Cambridge, Mass.: Harvard University Press, 1978.

DiVesta, F. J. *Language, learning, and cognitive processes.* Monterey, Calif.: Brooks/Cole, 1974.

Disabled or disadvantaged: What's the difference? Symposium No. 9. *Journal of Learning Disabilities,* 1973, *7,* 381–421.

Doehring, D. G. *Patterns of impairment in specific reading disability—a neuropsychological investigation.* Indiana University Press, 1968.

Doise, W., & Perret-Clermont, A. W. Social interaction and the development of cognitive operations. *European Journal of Social Psychology,* 1975, *5,* 367–383.

Doll, E. *Measurement of social competence: A manual for the Vineland Social Maturity Scale.* Princeton, N.J.: Educational Testing Service, 1953.

Douglas, V. I. Stop, look and listen: The problem of sustained attention and impulse control in hyperactive and normal children. *Canadian Journal of Behavioural Science,* 1972, *4,* 259–282.

Douglas, V. I., Parry, P., Marton, P., & Garson, C. Assessment of a cognitive training program for hyperactive children. *Journal of Abnormal Child Psychology,* 1976, *4,* 389–410.

Doyle, W. Making managerial decisions in the classroom. In D. L. Duke (Ed.), *Classroom management. The seventy-eighth yearbook of the National Society for the Study of Education,* (Part II). Chicago: University of Chicago Press, 1979.

Duane, D. D. A neurologic overview of specific language disability for the nonneurologist. *Bulletin of the Orton Society,* 1974, *24,* 5–36.

Dubey, D. R. Organic factors in hyperkinesis: A critical evaluation. *American Journal of Orthopsychiatry,* 1976, *46*(2), 353–366.

Duckworth, E. Either we're too early and they can't learn it or we're too late and they know it already: The dilemma of "applying Piaget." *Harvard Educational Review,* 1979, *49,* 297–312.

Dumas, E. *Math activities for child involvement.* Boston: Allyn & Bacon, 1971.

Dunlap, W. P., & House, A. D. Why can't Johnny compute? *Journal of Learning Disabilities,* 1976, *9,* 210–214.

Dunn, L. *Peabody Picture Vocabulary Test.* Circle Pines, Minn.: American Guidance Service, 1965.

Dunn, L. M. Special education for the mildly retarded—Is much of it justifiable? *Exceptional Children,* 1968, *35,* 5–22.

Dunn, L. M., & Markwardt, F. C. *Peabody Individual Achievement Test.* Circle Pines, Minn.: American Guidance Service, 1970.

Dunn, L. M., & Smith, J. O. *The Peabody Language Development Kits.* Circle Pines, Minn.: American Guidance Service, 1968.

Durrell, D. D. *Durrell Analysis of Reading Difficulty.* New York: Harcourt Brace Jovanovich, 1955.

East, R. C. A study on the effectiveness of specific language disability techniques on reading ability of potentially retarded readers. *Bulletin of the Orton Society,* 1969, *19.*

Eaves, L., Kendall, D., & Crichton, J. The early identification of learning disabilities: A follow-up study. *Journal of Learning Disabilities,* 1974, *7,* 42–48.

Edgington, R. But he spelled them right this morning. *Academic Therapy Quarterly,* 1967, *3,* 58–59.

Egeland, B. Training impulsive children in the use of more efficient scanning techniques. *Child Development,* 1974, *45,* 165–171.

Ehrlich, M. F. Cumulative learning and long-term retention of sentences. *Acta Psychologica,* 1975, *39,* 241–250.

Eisenberg, L. Psychiatric implications of brain damage in children. In E. C. Frierson, &

W. B. Barbe (Eds.), *Educating children with learning disabilities: Selected readings.* New York: Appleton-Century-Crofts, 1967.

Eisenberg, L., Gilbert, A., Cytryn, L., & Molling, P. A. The effectiveness of psychotherapy alone and in conjunction with perphenazine or placebo in the treatment of neurotic and hyperkinetic children. *American Journal of Psychiatry,* 1961, *117,* 1088–1093.

Elkonin, D. B. U.S.S.R. In J. Downing (Ed.), *Comparative Reading.* New York: Macmillan, 1973.

Ellis, N. R. The stimulus trace and behavioral inadequacy. In N. R. Ellis (Ed.), *Handbook of mental deficiency.* New York: McGraw-Hill, 1963.

Emery, E. J. Social perception processes in normal and learning disabled children. Unpublished doctoral dissertation, New York University, 1975.

Encyclopaedia Britannica, Inc. *Britannica World Language Dictionary.* Chicago: Encyclopaedia Britannica Inc., 1965.

Englemann, S. *Preventing failure in the primary grades.* Chicago: Science Research Associates, 1969.

Englemann, S., & Bruner, E. C. *DISTAR: An instructional system.* Chicago: Science Research Associates, 1969.

Englemann, S., & Carnine, D. *DISTAR: Arithmetic level III.* Chicago: Science Research Associates, 1972.

Englemann, S., & Carnine, D. *DISTAR: Arithmetic level I.* Chicago: Science Research Associates, 1975.

Englemann, S., & Carnine, D. *DISTAR: Arithmetic level II.* Chicago: Science Research Associates, 1976.

Englemann, S., & Osborn, J. *DISTAR: Language level II.* Chicago: Science Research Associates, 1971.

Engelmann, S., & Osborn, J. *DISTAR: Language level III.* Chicago: Science Research Associates, 1972.

Engelmann, S., & Osborn, J. *DISTAR: Language level I.* Chicago: Science Research Associates, 1976, 1969, 1972.

Epstein, J. R. Body image in learning disabled children as seen in human figure drawings. Unpublished manuscript, New York University, 1978.

Epstein, M. L., Phillips, W. D., & Johnson, S. J. Recall of related and unrelated word pairs as a function of processing level. *Journal of Experimental Psychology: Human Learning and Memory.* 1975, *104*(2), 149–152.

Erlwanger, S. H. Benny's conception of rules and answers in IPI mathematics. *Journal of Children's Mathematical Behavior,* 1973, *1,* 7–26.

Erlwanger, S. H. Case studies of children's conceptions of mathematics, Part 1. *Journal of Children's Mathematical Behavior,* 1975, *1,* 157–283.

Evans, M., Taylor, N., & Blum, I. Children's written language awareness and its relation to reading acquisition. *Journal of Reading Behavior,* 1979, *11,* 7–19.

Farber, B. *Mental retardation: Its social context and social consequences.* Boston: Houghton Mifflin, 1968.

Federal Register, August 23, 1977, *42,* Part B, Education of the Handicapped Act.

Federal Register, December 19, 1977, *42.* Supplemental procedures for evaluating specific learning disabilities.

Feingold, B. F. *Why your child is hyperactive.* New York: Random House, 1975.

Feingold, B. F. Hyperkinesis and learning disabilities linked to the ingestion of artificial food colors and flavors. *Journal of Learning Disabilities,* 1976, *9*(9), 551–559.

Fernald, G. *Remedial techniques in basic school subjects.* New York: McGraw-Hill, 1943.

Ferster, C. B. Clinical reinforcement. *Seminars in Psychiatry,* 1972, *4,* 101–111.

Feshback, S., Adelman, H., & Fuller, W. W. Early identification of children with high risk of reading failure. *Journal of Learning Disabilities,* 1974, *10,* 639–644.

Feuerstein, R. *Instrumental enrichment: An intervention program for cognitive modifiability.* Baltimore: University Park Press, 1980.

Figueroa, J. G., Solis, V. M., & Gonzalez, E. G. The possible influence of imagery upon retrieval and representation in LTM. *Acta Psychologica,* 1974, *38,* 425–428.

Fine, J. R., Deutsch, C. P., Garland, W., & Sorrentino, E. A three year evaluation of "Project Mainstream." Paper presented at the 1977 Annual Meeting of the American Educational Research Association.

Fish, B. The "one child, one drug" myth of stimulants in hyperkinesis. *Archives of General Psychiatry,* 1969, *7,* 393–398.

Flavell, J. H. Developmental studies of mediated memory. In H. W. Reese & L. P. Lipsitt (Eds.), *Advances in child development and behavior* (Vol. 5). New York: Academic Press, 1970.

Flavell, J. H. An analysis of cognitive-developmental sequences. *Genetic Psychology Monographs,* 1972, *86,* 279–350.

Flavell, J. H. *Cognitive development.* Englewood Cliffs, N.J.: Prentice-Hall, 1977.

Flavell, J. H., & Wellman, H. M. Metamemory. In R. V. Kail, Jr. & J. W. Hagen (Eds.), *Perspectives on the development of memory and cognition.* Hillsdale, N.J.: Lawrence Erlbaum, 1977.

Fleming, D. F., & Attonen, R. D. Teacher expectancies or My Fair Lady. In J. Pilder (Ed.), *Abstracts/1:1970.* Annual Meeting, Paper Session, Washington, D.C.: AERA, 1970, *66.*

Fleming, J. The measurement of children's perception of difficulty in reading materials. Unpublished doctoral dissertation, Harvard University, Cambridge, Mass., 1966.

Fletcher, J. M., & Satz, P. Unitary deficit hypotheses of reading disabilities: Has Vellutino led us astray? *Journal of Learning Disabilities,* 1979, *12,* 22–26.(a)

Fletcher, J. M., & Satz, P. Has Vellutino led us astray? A rejoinder to a reply. *Journal of Learning Disabilities,* 1979, *12,* 35–38.(b)

Flynn, R., & Hopson, B. Inhibitory training: An alternative approach to development of controls in hyperactive children. Paper presented at the National Association of School Psychologists Meeting, Chicago, March 1972.

Follansbee, A. Body image expressed in human figure drawings of learning disabled and nonlearning disabled children. Unpublished manuscript, New York University, 1978.

Food Research Institute, Madison: University of Wisconsin, 1976.

Ford, M. P. Auditory-visual and tactual-visual integration in relation to reading ability. *Perceptual and Motor Skills,* 1967, *24,* 831–841.

Forgus, R. H., & Melamed, L. E. *Perception: A cognitive-stage approach.* New York: McGraw-Hill, 1976.

Forman, G. E., & Hill, F. *Constructive play: Applying Piaget in the preschool.* Monterey, Calif.: Brooks/Cole, 1980.

Forness, S. R., & Esveldt, K. C. Prediction of high-risk kindergarten children through classroom observation. *Journal of Special Education,* 1975, *9,* 375–387.

Forness, S. R., Guthries, D., & Nihira, K. Clusters of observable behavior in high-risk kindergarten children. *Psychology in the Schools,* 1975, *12,* 263–269.

Foster, G. G. Teacher expectancies and the label "learning disabilities." *Exceptional Child Education Abstracts,* 1976, *8,* 278.

Foster, G. G., Schmidt, M. S., & Sabatino, D. Teacher expectancies and the label "learning disabilities." *Journal of Learning Disabilities,* 1976, *9,* 111–114.

Frankenburg, W. K., Dodds, J. B., & Fandal, A. W. *Denver Developmental Screening Test.* Denver: University of Colorado Medical Center, 1970.

Frauenheim, J. G. Academic achievement characteristics of adult males who were diagnosed as dyslexic in childhood. *Journal of Learning Disabilities,* 1978, *11,* 476–483.

Freeman, R. D., Controversy over 'patterning' as a treatment for brain damage in children. *Journal of the American Medical Association,* 1967, *202,* 385–388.

Freides, D. Human information processing and sensory modality: Cross-modal functions, information complexity, memory, and deficit. *Psychological Bulletin,* 1974, *81,* 284–310.

Freston, C. W., & Drew, C. J. Verbal performance of learning disabled children as a function of input organization. *Journal of Learning Disabilities,* 1974, 7(7), 424–428.

Friedman, B. Didactic vs. discovery learning in hyperactive and non-hyperactive learning disabled children. Doctoral dissertation, New York University, 1978.

Frijda, N. H. Simulation of human long-term memory. *Psychological Bulletin,* 1972, 77, 1–31.

Friou, D. M. The use of peer rating techniques to identify behavioral groups in the classroom. Unpublished manuscript. University of Texas at Austin, 1972.

Frostig, M. Testing as a basis for educational therapy. *Journal of Special Education,* 1967, *2,* 15–34.

Frostig, M. Disabilities and remediation in reading. *Academic Therapy,* 1972, *4,* 373–391.(a)

Frostig, M. Visual perception, integrative function and academic learning. *Journal of Learning Disabilities,* 1972, *5,* 1–15.(b)

Frostig, M. *Selection and adaptation of reading methods.* San Rafael, Calif.: Academic Therapy Publications, 1973.

Frostig, M., & Horne, D. *The Frostig program for the development of visual perception: Teacher's guide.* Chicago: Follett, 1964.

Frostig, M., & Maslow, P. *Learning problems in the classroom.* New York: Grune & Stratton, 1973.

Frostig, M., Maslow, P., Lefever, D. W., & Whittlesey, J. R. B. *The Marianne Frostig Developmental Test of Visual Perception,* (1963 standardization.) Palo Alto, Calif.: Consulting Psychologist, 1964.

Fuller, P. W. Attention and the EEG alpha rhythm in learning disabled children. *Journal of Learning Disabilities,* 1978, *11,* 303–312.

Furth, H. G., & Wachs, H. *Thinking goes to school.* New York: Oxford University Press, 1974.

Gagne, E. D., & Memory, D. Instructional events and comprehension: Generalization across passages. *Journal of Reading Behavior,* 1978, *10,* 321–335.

Gallagher, J. J. Planning for early childhood programs for exceptional children. *Journal of Special Education,* 1976, *10,* 171–177.

Gallagher, J. M., & Reid, D. K. *The learning theory of Piaget and Inhelder.* Monterey, Calif.: Brooks/Cole, 1981.

Gallagher, J. M. Problems in applying Piagetian theory to reading or "See Jean run." Paper presented at the Twenty-fifth Lehigh University Reading Conference, Easton, Pa., September, 1976.

Gardner, E. *Fundamentals of neurology.* Philadelphia, Pennsylvania: W. B. Saunders, 1975.

Gardner, W. I. *Children with learning and behavior problems.* Boston: Allyn & Bacon, 1978.

Gargiulo, R. M. Arousal level and hyperkinesis: Implications for biofeedback, *Journal of Learning Disabilities,* 1979, *12,* 137–138.

Garrison, M., & Hammill, D. D. Who are the retarded? *Exceptional Children,* 1971, *38,* 13–20.

Gates, A. I. Psychology of reading and spelling with special reference to disability. New York: Bureau of Publications, Teachers College University, 1922. (Contributions to Education, No. 129.)

Gates, A. I. *The improvement of reading.* New York: Macmillan, 1947.

Gates, A. I., & McKillop, A. S. *Gates-McKillop Reading Diagnostic Tests.* New York: Bureau of Publications, Teachers College Press, Columbia University, 1962.

Gattegno, C. *Words in color.* Chicago, Ill.: Learning Materials, 1962.

Gay, G., & Abrahams, R. D. Does the pot melt, boil, or brew? Black children and white assessment procedures. *Journal of School Psychology,* 1973, *11,* 330–340.

Gazda, G. M., Asbury, F. R., Balzer, F. J., Childers, W. C., & Walters, R. P. *Human relations development,* (2d ed.). Boston: Allyn & Bacon, 1977.

Gehring, R. E., Togliz, M. P., & Kimble, G. A. Recognition memory for words and pictures at short and long retention intervals. *Memory & Cognition,* 1976, *4,* 256–260.

Geis, M. F. A developmental study of category, rhyme, and color encoding in a release-from-proactive-interference paradigm. *Dissertation Abstracts International,* 1975, *35*(7—B), 3611.

Geis, M. F., & Hall, D. M. Encoding and incidental memory in children. *Journal of Experimental Child Psychology,* 1976, *22,* 58–66.

Geis, M. F., & Lange, G. Children's cue utilization in a memory-for-location task. *Child Development,* 1976, *47,* 759–766.

Gellner, L. A. *A neurophysiological concept of mental retardation and its educational implications.* Chicago: J. Levinson Research Foundation, 1959.

Getman, G. N. Visual success in reading success. *Journal of the California Optometric Association,* 1961, *29,* 1–4.

Getman, G. N. *How to develop your child's intelligence.* Luverne, Minn.: Author, 1962.(a)

Getman, G. N. *The school skill tracing board.* Minneapolis, Minn.: Programs to Accelerate School Success, 1962.(b)

Getman, G. N., & Kane, E. R. *The physiology of readiness: An action program for the development of perception for children.* Minneapolis, Minn.: Programs to Accelerate School Success, 1964.

Getman, G. N., Kane, E. R., Halgren, M. R., & McKee, G. W. *Developing learning readiness.* Manchester, Mo.: Webster Division, McGraw-Hill, 1968.

Gibson, E. J. *Principles of perceptual learning and development.* New York: Appleton-Century-Crofts, 1969.

Gickling, E. E., & Theobald, J. T. Mainstreaming: Affect or effect. *Journal of Special Education,* 1975, *9,* 317–328.

Giffen, M. The role of child psychiatry in learning disabilities. In H. R. Myklebust (Ed.), *Progress in learning disabilities,* (Vol. 1). New York: Grune & Stratton, 1968.

Gillingham, A. *Remedial training for children with specific disability in reading, spelling, and penmanship.* Cambridge, Mass.: Educators Publishing Service, 1936.

Gillingham, A., & Stillman, B. W. *Remedial training for children with specific disability in reading, spelling, and penmanship.* Cambridge, Mass.: Educators Publishing Service, Inc., 1965, 1970.

Gilmore, J. V., & Gilmore, E. C. *Gilmore Oral Reading Test.* New York: Harcourt Brace Jovanovich, 1968.

Ginsburg, H. *Children's arithmetic: The learning process.* New York: D. Van Nostrand, 1977.

Glass, A. Blocking of the occipital alpha rhythm and problem-solving efficiency. *Electroencephalography and Clinical Neurophysiology,* 1959, *11,* 605.

Glass, A. Motivation and the intensity of blocking to problem-solving. *Electroencephalography and Clinical Neurophysiology,* 1960, *12,* 262.

Glass, A. Mental arithmetic and blocking of the alpha rhythm. *Electroencephalography and Clinical Neurophysiology,* 1964, *16,* 595–603.

Gold, J. Sex as a variable in the identification of children needing special education. Unpublished manuscript, New York University, 1979.

Goldberg, F. Effects of imagery on learning incidental material in the classroom. *Journal of Educational Psychology,* 1974, *66*(2), 233–237.

Goldman, R., & Fristoe, M. *Goldman-Fristoe Test of Articulation.* Circle Pines, Minn.: American Guidance Service, 1969.

Goldstein, K. *Language and language disturbances.* New York: Grune & Stratton, 1948.

Gomez, M. R. Specific learning disorders in childhood. *Psychiatric Annals,* 1972, *2,* 49–65.

Good, T. L., & Grouws, D. A. The Missouri Mathematics Effectiveness Project: An experimental study in fourth-grade classrooms. *Journal of Educational Psychology,* 1979, *71,* 355–362.

Goodglass, H., & Kaplan, E. *The assessment of aphasia and related disorders.* Philadelphia: Lea & Febiger, 1972.

Goodman, H., Gottlieb, J., & Harrison, R. H. Social acceptance of EMRs integrated into a nongraded elementary school. *American Journal of Mental Deficiency,* 1972, *76,* 412–417.

Goodman, K. S. A linguistic study of cues and miscues in reading. *Elementary English Review,* 1965, *42,* 639–643.

Goodman, K. S. Acquiring literacy is natural: Who skilled Cock Robin? Paper presented at the Sixth World Reading Congress, Singapore, August 1976.(a)

Goodman, K. S. Behind the eye: What happens in reading. In H. Singer & R. B. Ruddell (Eds.), *Theoretical models and processes of reading.* Newark, Del.: International Reading Association, 1976.(b)

Goodman, K. S. Reading: A psycholinguistic guessing game. In H. Singer & R. B. Ruddel (Eds.), *Theoretical models and processes of reading.* Newark, Del.: International Reading Association, 1976.(c)

Goodman, K. S., & Goodman, Y. Learning to read is natural. Paper presented at the Conference on Theory and Practice of Beginning Reading Instruction, Pittsburg, April 1976.

Goodman, L., & Hammill, D. D. *The Basic School Skills Inventory.* Chicago, Ill.: Follett, 1975.

Goodman, Y. M., & Burke, C. I. *Reading Miscue Inventory: Manual procedure for diagnosis and remediation.* New York: Macmillan, 1972.

Goodnow, J. J. Matching auditory and visual series: Modality problem or translation problem? *Child Development,* 1971, *42,* 1187–1201.

Gordon, T. *Teacher effectiveness training.* New York: David McKay, 1974.

Gordon, T. *Parent effectiveness training.* New York: David McKay, 1975.

Gorlow, L., Butler, A., & Guthrie, G. M. Correlates of self-attitudes of retardates. *American Journal of Mental Deficiency,* 1961, *67,* 549–555.

Gottlieb, J., Gampel, D. H., & Budoff, M. Classroom behavior of retarded children before and after integration into regular classes. *Journal of Special Education,* 1975, *9,* 307–315.

Gounard, B. Human figure drawings of learning disabled and normal children at three age levels. *Perceptual and Motor Skills,* 1975, *40*(3), 914.

Gozali, J., & Meyer, E. L. The influence of teacher expectancy phenomena on the academic performances of educably mentally retarded pupils in special classes. *Journal of Special Education,* 1970, *4,* 417–424.

Gray, B. B., & Ryan, B. *A language program for the nonlanguage child.* Champaign, Ill.: Research Press, 1973.

Gray, W. S., *Remedial cases in reading: Their diagnosis and treatment.* (Supplementary Educational Monographs, No. 22.) Chicago, Ill.: University of Chicago Press, 1922.

Gray, W. S., & Robinson, H. M. (Eds.), *Gray Oral Reading Test.* Indianapolis, Ind.: Bobbs-Merrill, 1967.

Green, H., & Petty, W. *Developing language skills in the elementary school.* Boston: Allyn & Bacon, 1967.

Greeno, J. G. Understanding and procedural knowledge in mathematics instruction. *Educational Psychologist,* 1978, *12,* 262–283.

Groff, P. A critique of teaching reading as a whole-task venture. *The Reading Teacher,* 1979, *32,* 647–652.

Groff, P. Goodman and his critics. *Reading World,* 1979 (May), 376–383.

Gronlund, N. *Measurement and evaluation in teaching* (3rd ed.). New York: Macmillan, 1976.

Grossman, R. P. LD and the problem of scientific definitions. *Journal of Learning Disabilities,* 1978, *11*(3), 120–123.

Guerin, G. R., & Szatlocky, K. Integration programs for the mildly retarded. *Exceptional Children,* 1974, *41,* 173–179.

Gupta, R., & Ceci, S. J., Slater, A. M. Visual discrimination in good and poor readers. *Journal of Special Education,* 1978, *12,* 409–421.

Guralnick, M. J. Solving complex perceptual discrimination problems: Techniques for the development of problem-solving strategies. *American Journal of Mental Deficiency,* 1976, *81,* 18–25.

Guthrie, J., & Goldberg, K. Visual sequential memory in reading disability. *Journal of Learning Disabilities,* 1972, *5,* 41–45.

Guthrie, J. T. Research: Context and memory. *Journal of Reading,* 1978, *22,* 266–268.

Guthrie, J. T., & Tyler, S. J. Cognition and instruction of poor readers. *Journal of Reading Behavior,* 1978, *10,* 57–78.

Guyer, B. P. The Montessori approach for the elementary-age LD child. *Academic Therapy,* 1974–1975, *10,* 187–192.

Haberman, M. The relationship of bogus expectations to success in student teaching (or Pygmalion's illegitmate son). In J. Pilder (Ed.), *Abstracts/1:1970*. Annual Meeting, Paper Session, Washington, D.C.: AERA, 1970, 66.

Hackett, M. G. *Criterion reading: Individualized learning management system.* Westminster, Md.: Random House, 1971.

Hagen, J. W., Jongeward, R. H., & Kail, R. V. Cognitive perspectives on the development of memory. In H. W. Reese (Ed.), *Advances in child development and behavior,* (Vol. 10). New York: Academic Press, 1975.

Hagen, J. W., & Kail, R. V. The role of attention in perceptual and cognitive development. In W. M. Cruickshank, & D. P. Hallahan (Eds.), *Perceptual and learning disabilities in children,* (Vol. 2). Syracuse, N.Y.: Syracuse University Press, 1975.

Hagin, R. I. In symposium: Perceptual training for children with learning difficulties. New Jersey Association for Brain Injured Children, 1965.

Hall, J. W., & Pierce, J. W. Recognition and recall by children and adults as a function of variations in memory encoding instructions. *Memory & Cognition,* 1974, *2*(3), 585–590.

Hall, R. J. Cognitive behavior modification and information-processing skills of exceptional children. *Exceptional Education Quarterly,* 1980, *1*, 9–16.

Hall, R. J., & Keogh, B. Qualitative characteristics of educationally high risk children. *Learning Disability Quarterly,* 1978, *1*, 62–68.

Hallahan, D. P., & Cruickshank, W. M. *Psychoeducational foundations of learning disabilities.* Englewood Cliffs, N.J.: Prentice-Hall, 1973.

Hallahan, D. P., Gajar, A. H., Cohen, S. B., & Tarver, S. G. Selective attention and locus of control in learning disabled and normal children. *Journal of Learning Disabilities,* 1978, *11*, 231–236.

Hallahan, D. P., & Kauffman, J. M. Learning disabilities: A behavioral definition. Paper presented at the Second International Scientific Conference on Learning Disabilities, Brussels, January 3–7, 1975.

Hallahan, D. P., & Kauffman, J. M. *Introduction to learning disabilities: A psychobehavioral approach.* Englewood Cliffs, N.J.: Prentice-Hall, 1976.

Hallahan, D. P., Kauffman, J. M., & Ball, D. W. Selective attention and cognitive tempo of low achieving and high achieving sixth grade males. *Perceptual and Motor Skills,* 1973, *36*, 579–583.

Hallahan, D. P., Kauffman, J. M., & Ball, D. W. Developmental trends in recall of central and incidental auditory material. *Journal of Experimental Child Psychology,* 1974, *17*, 409–421.

Hallahan, D. P., Lloyd, J., Kosiewicz, M. M., Kauffman, J. M., & Graves, A. W. Self-monitoring of attention as a treatment for a learning disabled boy's off-task behavior. *Learning Disabilities Quarterly,* 1979, *2*, 24–32.

Hallahan, D. P., Lloyd, J., Kosiewicz, M. M., & Kneedler, R. D. A comparison of the effects of self-recording and self-assessment on the on-task behavior and academic productivity of a learning disabled boy. (Technical Report No. 13). Charlottesville, Va.: University of Virginia Learning Disabilities Research Institute, 1979.

Hallahan, D. P., & Reeve, R. E. Selective attention and distractibility. In B. K. Keogh (Ed.), *Advances in special education,* (Vol. 1). Greenwich, Conn.: J.A.I. Press, 1980.

Hallahan, D. P., Tarver, S. G., Kauffman, J. M., & Grabeal, N. L. A comparison of the effects of reinforcement and response cost on the selective attention of learning disabled children. *Journal of Learning Disabilities,* 1978, *11,* 430–438.

Hallgren, B. Specific dyslexia (cogenital word-blindness). *Acta Psychiatrica et Neurologia Scandinavica,* 1950, Supplement #65.

Halliday, M. A. K. Learning how to mean. In E. H. Lenneberg & E. Lenneberg (Eds.), *Foundations of language development,* (Vol. 1). New York: Academic Press, 1975.

Halliday, M. A. K. *Language as social semiotic: The social interpretation of language and meaning.* Baltimore, Md.: University Park Press, 1978.

Hammill, D. D. Training visual perceptual processes. *Journal of Learning Disabilities,* 1972, *5,* 552–559.

Hammill, D. D. Learning disabilities: A problem in definition. *Division for Children with Learning Disabilities Newsletter.* 1974, *4,* 28–31.

Hammill, D. D. Problems in writing. In D. D. Hammill & N. R. Bartel (Eds.), *Teaching children with learning and behavior problems.* Boston: Allyn & Bacon, 1975.

Hammill, D. D. The field of learning disabilities: A futuristic perspective. Presented at the National DCLD Conference on Learning Disabilities. Louisville, Kentucky, October 6, 1979.

Hammill, D. D., Brown, V. L., Larsen, S. C., & Wiederholt, J. L. *The Test of Adolescent Language.* Austin, Tx.: Pro-Ed, 1980.

Hammill, D. D., & Larsen, S. C. The efficacy of psycholinguistic training. *Exceptional Children,* 1974, *41,* 5–11.(a)

Hammill, D. D., & Larsen, S. C. The relationship of selected auditory perceptual skills to reading ability. *Journal of Learning Disabilities,* 1974, *7,* 429–436.(b)

Hammill, D. D., & Larsen, S. C. *The Test of Written Language.* Austin, Tx.: Pro-Ed, 1978.

Hammill, D. D., Larsen, S. C., & McNutt, G. The effects of spelling instruction: A preliminary study. *The Elementary School Journal,* 1977, *78,* 67–72.

Hammill, D. D., & Poplin, M. S. Problems in writing. In D. D. Hammill & N. R. Bartel (Eds.), *Teaching children with learning and behavior problems.* Boston: Allyn & Bacon, 1978.

Hammill, D. D., & Wiederholt, J. L. *The resource room: Rationale and implementation.* Philadelphia: Journal of Special Education Press, Grune & Stratton, 1972.

Hammill, D. D., & Wiederholt, J. L. Review of the Frostig Visual Perceptional Test and the related training program. In L. Mann, & D. A. Sabatino (Eds.), *The first review of special education.* (Vol. 1). Philadelphia: JSE Press, Grune and Stratton, 1973.

Hammons, G. W. Educating the mildly retarded: A review. *Exceptional Children,* 1972, *38,* 565–570.

Hanna, G. S., Dyck, N. J., & Holen, M. C. Objective analysis of achievement-aptitude discrepancies in LD classification. *Learning Disability Quarterly,* 1979, *2,* 32–38.

Hanna, P. R., Hanna, J. S., Hodges, R. E., & Rudorf, E. H. Phoneme-grapheme correspondences as cues to spelling improvement. Washington: Department of Health, Education, and Welfare, 1966.

Hanna, P. R., Hodges, R., & Hanna, J. S. *Spelling: Structure and strategies.* Boston: Houghton Mifflin, 1971.

Hare, B., Hammill, D. D., & Bartel, N. R. Construct validity of selected ITPA subtests. *Exceptional Children,* 1973, *40,* 13–20.

Hare, B. A., & Hare, J. M. *Teaching young handicapped children: A guide for preschool and the primary grades.* New York: Grune & Stratton, 1977.

Haring, N. G., & Bateman, B. *Teaching the learning disabled child.* Englewood Cliffs, N.J.: Prentice-Hall, 1977.

Haring, N. G., & Krug, D. A. Placement in regular programs: Procedures and results. *Exceptional children,* 1975, *4*, 413–417.

Harris, T. L., & Herrick, V. E. Children's perception of the handwriting task. In V. E. Herrick (Ed.), *New horizons for research in handwriting.* Madison, Wis.: University of Wisconsin Press, 1963.

Harste, J., & Burke, C. L. A new hypothesis for reading teacher research: Both the teaching and learning of reading are theoretically based. In P. D. Pearson (Ed.), *Reading: Theory, research, and practice, Twenty-sixth Yearbook of the National Reading Conference.* Clemson, S.C.: National Reading Conference, 1977.

Hawley, C., & Buckley, R. Food dyes and hyperkinetic children. *Academic Therapy,* 1974, *10,* 27–32.

Hawthorne, L. W., & Larsen, S. C. The predictive validity and reliability of the Basic School Skills Inventory. *Journal of Learning Disabilities,* 1977, *10,* 44–50.

Heddens, J. W., & Smith, K. J. The readability of elementary mathematics books. *Arithmetic Teacher,* 1964, *10,* 466–484.

Heilman, A. W. *Phonics emphasis approaches.* Perspectives in reading. Newark, Del.: International Reading Association, 1965.

Hermann, K. *Reading disability: A medical study of word-blindness and related handicaps.* Springfield, Ill.: Charles C Thomas, 1959.

Heron, T. Maintaining the mainstreamed child in the regular classroom: The decision-making process. *Journal of Learning Disabilities,* 1978, *11,* 210–215.

Herson, P. F. Biasing effects of dignostic labels and sex of pupil on teacher views of pupil's mental health. *Journal of Educational Psychology,* 1974, *66,* 117–122.

Hewett, F. M. *The emotionally disturbed child in the classroom.* Boston: Allyn and Bacon, 1968.

Hewett, F. M., & Forness, S. R. *Education of exceptional learners.* Boston: Allyn and Bacon, 1974.

Hewett, F. M., Taylor, F. D., & Artuso, A. A. The Santa Monica project. *Exceptional Children,* 1968, *34,* 387.

Hiatt, A. A. Basic skills: What are they? *The Mathematics Teacher,* 1979, *72,* 141–145.

Hill, F. G. A. A comparison of Words in Color with the basic readiness program used in Washington Elementary School District. *Dissertation Abstracts,* 1967, *27,* 3619-A.

Hobbs, N. *The futures of children.* San Francisco: Josey-Bass, 1975.

Hoffman, S., & Fillmer, H. T. Thought, language and reading readiness. *The Reading Teacher,* 1979, *32,* 290–294.

Hoffman, S. P., Engelhardt, D. M., Margolis, R. A., Polizos, P., Waizer, J., & Rosenfeld, R. Response to methylphenidate in low socioeconomic hyperactive children. *Archives of General Psychiatry,* 1974, *30,* 354–359.

Hofmeister, A. M. Let's get it write. *Teaching Exceptional Children,* 1973, *6,* 30–33.

Hoskisson, K. A response to "A critique of teaching reading as a whole-task venture." *The Reading Teacher,* 1979, *32,* 652–659.

Houghton, R. R., & Tabachnick, B. G. Muller-Lyer illusion in hyperactive boys. *Journal of Learning Disabilities,* 1979, *12*(2), 77–81.

House, E. R., Glass, G. V., McLean, L. D., & Walker, D. F. No simple answer: Critique of the Follow Through evaluation. *Harvard Educational Review,* 1978, *48,* 128–160.

Hresko, W. P. Learning disabled and skill deficient children. *New Realities for Teachers,* Fall, 1977.

Hresko, W. P. Elicited imitation ability of children from learning disabled and regular classes. *Journal of Learning Disabilities*, 1979, *12*, 456–461.

Hresko, W. P., & Reid, D. K. Language and the learning disabled: Models, research, and intervention. *Learning Disabilities: An Audio Journal for Continuing Education*, 1979, *3*, audio cassette.

Hresko, W. P., Reid, D. K., & Hammill, D. D. *The Test of Early Language Development*. Austin, Texas: Pro-Ed, 1981.

Hresko, W. P., Rosenberg, S., & Buchanan, L. Use of the Carrow Test of Auditory Comprehension of Language with learning disabled children. Paper presented at the Council for Exceptional Children, Kansas City, Kansas, 1978.

Huessy, H. R. Study of the prevalence and therapy of the choreatiform syndrome or hyperkinesis in rural Vermont. *Acta Paedopsychiatrica*, 1967, *34*, 130–135.

Hunt, J. V. Review of the Slosson Intelligence Test. In O. K. Buros (Ed.), *The seventh Mental Measurements yearbook*. Highland Park, N.J.: Gryphon Press, 1972.

Hunt, K. W. Teaching syntactic maturity. In G. E. Perren & J. L. M. Trims (Eds.), *Applications of linguistics*. New York: Cambridge University Press, 1969.

Iano, R. P. Shall we disband our special classes? *Journal of Special Education*, 1972, *6*, 167–178.

Iano, R. P. Education theory and evaluation criteria. In *Developing criteria for the evaluation of individualized education program provisions*. United States Office of Education, Bureau of Education for the Handicapped, Division of Innovation and Development, State Program Studies Branch, 1978.

Iano, R. P., Ayers, D., Heller, H. B., McGettigan, J. G., & Walker, V. S. Sociometric status of retarded children in an integrative program. *Exceptional Children*, 1974, *40*, 267–271.

Ingram, T. T. S. Developmental disorders of speech. In P. J. Vinken & G. W. Bruyn (Eds.), Disorders of speech, perception, and symbolic behaviour. (Vol. 4), *Handbook of clinical neurology*. Amsterdam: North Holland, 407–442.

Ingram, T., Mason, A., & Blackburn, I. A retrospective study of 82 children with reading disability. *Developmental Medicine and Child Neurology*, 1970, *12*, 271–278.

Inhelder, B., Sinclair, H., & Bovet, M. *Learning and the development of cognition*. Cambridge, Massachusetts: Harvard University Press, 1974.

Jacobs, W. The biasing effect of the learning disability label on teacher expectancies. Unpublished doctoral dissertation, University of Texas at Austin, 1976.

Jacobs, W. R. The effect of the learning disability label on classroom teachers ability objectively to observe and interpret child behaviors. *Learning Disability Quarterly*, 1978, *1*, 50–55.

James, W. *The principles of psychology*. New York: Dover, 1950. (Originally published in 1890.)

Jansky, J. J., & de Hirsch, K. *Preventing reading failure*. New York: Harper & Row, 1973.

Jastak, J. F., & Jastak, S. R. *Wide Range Achievement Test*. Wilmington, Del.: Guidance Associates, 1965.

Jenkins, J. R., & Pany, D. Standardized achievement tests: How useful for special education? *Exceptional Children*, 1978, *44*, 448–453.

Jerman, M. E., & Beardslee, E. C. *Elementary mathematics models*. New York: McGraw-Hill, 1978.

Johnson, D. J., & Myklebust, H. R. *Learning disabilities: Educational principles and practices.* New York: Grune & Stratton, 1967.

Johnson, M. S., & Kress, R. A. *Informal reading inventories.* Newark, Del.: International Reading Association, 1965.

Jones, K. L., Smith, D. W., Streissguth, A. P., & Myranthopoulos, N. C. Outcome in offspring of chronic alcoholic women. *Lancet,* 1974, *1,* 1076–1078.

Jones, R. Labels and stigma in special education. *Exceptional Children,* 1972, *38,* 553–564.

Jones, R., & Spolsky, B. *Testing language proficiency.* Arlington, Va.: Center for Applied Linguistics, 1975.

Jose, J., & Cody, J. J. Teacher-pupil interaction as it relates to attempted changes in teacher expectancy or academic ability and achievement. *American Educational Research Journal,* 1971, *8,* 39–50.

Kagan, J. The growth of "face" schema: Theoretical significance and methodological issues. In J. Hellmuth (Ed.), *Exceptional infant, the normal infant.* (Vol. 1) Seattle: Special Child Publications, 1967.

Kagan, J. Attention and psychological change in the young child. *Science,* 1970, *170,* 826–832.

Kahn, D., & Birch, H. G. Development of auditory-visual integration and reading achievement. *Perceptual and Motor Skills,* 1968, *27,* 459–468.

Kahneman, D., Tursky, B., Shapiro, D., & Crider, A. Pupillary, heart rate, skin resistance change during a mental task. *Experimental Psychology,* 1969. *79,* 164–167.

Kail, R. V., & Siegel, A. W. The development of mnemonic encoding in children: From perception to abstraction. In R. V. Kail & J. W. Hagen (Eds.), *Perspectives on the development of memory and cognition.* Hillsdale, N.J.: Lawrence Erlbaum, 1977.

Kaluger, G., & Kolson, C. J. *Reading and learning disabilities.* Columbus, Ohio: Merrill, 1969.

Kamii, C., & DeVries, R. *Group games in early education: Implications of Piaget's theory.* Washington: National Association for the Education of Young Children, 1980.

Karlsen, B., Madden, R., & Gardner, E. F. *Stanford Diagnostic Reading Test.* New York: Harcourt Brace Jovanovich, 1977.

Karnes, M. B. *Goal program: Language development.* Springfield, Mass.: Milton Bradley, 1972.

Kaspar, J. C., & Lowenstein, R. The effect of social interaction on activity level in six- to eight-year-old boys. *Child Development,* 1971, *42,* 1294–1298.

Kastner, S. B. An evaluation of the use of mathematics laboratories with underachieving students. Unpublished manuscript, New York University, 1975.

Kastner, S. B., & Rickards, C. Mediated memory with novel and familiar stimuli in good and poor readers. *Journal of Genetic Psychology,* 1974, *124,* 105–113.

Katz, J., & Illmer, R. Auditory perception in children with learning disabilities. In J. Katz (Ed.), *Handbook of clinical audiology.* Baltimore: Williams & Williams, 1972.

Kaufman, A., Baron, A., & Kopp, R. Some effects of instructions on human operant behavior. *Psychonomic Monograph Supplement,* 1966, *1,* 243–250.

Kaufman, K. F., & O'Leary, K. D. Reward, cost, and self-evaluation procedures for disruptive adolescents in a psychiatric hospital school. *Journal of Applied Behavior Analysis,* 1972, *5,* 293–309.

Keele, D. K., Keele, M. S., Huizinga, R. J., Bray, N., Estes, R., & Holland, L. Role of special pediatric evaluation in the evaluation of a child with learning disabilities. *Journal of Learning Disabilities,* 1975, *8,* 40–45.

Keeney, A. H., & Keeney, V. T. (Eds.), *Dyslexia, diagnosis and treatment of reading disorders.* St. Louis, Mo.: C. V. Mosby, 1968.

Keilitz, I., Zaremba, B. A., & Broder, P. K. The link between learning disabilities and juvenile delinquency: Some issues and answers. *Learning Disability Quarterly,* 1979, *2,* 2–11.

Keith, H., Axelrod, S., Anderson, R., Hathaway, F., Wood, K., & Fitzgerald, C. Influence of distributed practice and daily testing on weekly spelling tests. *Journal of Educational Research,* 1973, *67,* 73–77.

Kelly, B. W., & Holmes, J. The guided lecture procedure. *Journal of Reading,* 1979, *23,* 602–604.

Kendall, P. C., & Finch, A. J., Jr. A cognitive-behavioral treatment for impulsivity: A group comparison study. *Journal of Consulting and Clinical Psychology,* 1978, *45,* 330–338.

Kendler, T., Kendler, H., & Carrick, M. Verbal labels and inferential problem solution of children. *Child Development,* 1966, *37,* 749–763.

Kennedy, A., & Wilkes, A. (Eds.). *Studies in long term memory.* New York: Wiley, 1975.

Keogh, B., & Becker, L. D. Early detection of learning problems: Questions, cautions, and guidelines. *Exceptional Children,* 1973, *40,* 5–11.

Keogh, B. K., & Donlon, G. Field independence, impulsivity and learning disabilities. *Journal of Learning Disabilities,* 1972, *5,* 331–336.

Keogh, B. K., & Glover, A. T. The generality and durability of cognitive training effects. *Exceptional Education Quarterly,* 1980, *1,* 75–82.

Keogh, B. K., & Levin, M. L. Special education in the mainstream: A confrontation of limitations? *Focus on Exceptional Children,* 1976, *8,* 1–11.

Keogh, B. K., Major, S. M., Omori, H., Gandara, P., & Reid, H. P. Proposed markers in learning disabilities research. Submitted for publication.

Keogh, B. K., Major, S. M., Reid, H. P., Gandara, P., & Omori, H. Marker variables: A search for comparability and generalizability in the field of learning disabilities. *Learning Disability Quarterly,* 1978, *1,* 5–11.

Keogh, B. K., & Pullis, M. E. Temperament influences on the development of exceptional children. In B. K. Keogh (Ed.), *Advances in special education.* Greenwich, Conn.: J. A. I. Press, 1980.

Kephart, N. C. *The slow learner in the classroom.* Columbus, Ohio: Merrill, (2d ed.), 1971.

Kephart, N. C. Perceptual-motor correlates of learning. In S. A. Kirk & W. Becker (Eds.), *Conference on children with minimal brain impairments.* Chicago: National Society for Crippled Children and Adults, 1963.

Kephart, N. C. *Learning disability: An educational adventure.* Danville, Ill.: Interstate, 1968.

Kephart, N. C. *The slow learner in the classroom.* (2nd ed.) Columbus, Ohio: Merrill, 1971.

Kershner, J. R. Visual-spatial organization and reading: Support for a cognitive developmental interpretation. *Journal of Learning Disabilities,* 1975, *8,* 30–36.

Kershner, J. R. Leeches, quicksilver, megavitamins, and learning disabilities. *Journal of Special Education,* 1978, *12*(1), 7–15.

Kershner, J. R., & Grekin, R. A pilot study of a high-protein and high-vitamin, low-carbohydrate, sugar-free diet with learning disabled children (Special Education Monograph). Toronto: Ontario Institute for Studies in Education, 1976.

Kilma, E. S. How alphabets might reflect language. In J. F. Kavanagh & I. G. Mattingly (Eds.), *Language by ear and by eye: The relationships between speech and reading.* Cambridge, Mass.: MIT Press, 1972.

Kinsbourne, M. Minimal brain dysfunction as a neurodevelopmental lag. *Annals of the New York Academy of Sciences,* 1973, *205,* 268–273.(a)

Kinsbourne, M. Stimulants for insomnia (correspondence). *New England Journal of Medicine,* 1973, *288,* 1129.(b)

Kinsbourne, M. The ontogeny of cerebral dominance. In D. Aaronson & R. W. Rieber (Eds.), *Developmental psycholinguistics and communication disorders.* New York: The New York Academy of Sciences, 1975.

Kinsbourne, M., Swanson, J., & Herman, D. Laboratory measurement of hyperactive children's response to stimulant medication. In E. Denhoff & L. Stein (Eds.), *Minimal brain dysfunction: A developmental approach.* New York: Masson, 1979.

Kinsbourne, M., & Warrington, E. K. Developmental factors in reading and writing backwardness. In J. Money (Ed.), *The disabled reader: Education of the dyslexic child.* Baltimore: The Johns Hopkins Press, 1966.

Kintsch, W. *Learning, memory, and conceptual processes.* New York: Wiley, 1970.

Kirk, S. A. Behavioral diagnosis and remediation of learning disabilities. *Proceedings of the annual meeting of the Conference on Exploration into the Problems of the Perceptually Handicapped Child.* (Vol. 1), 1963.

Kirk, S. A. *The diagnosis and remediation of psycholinguistic disabilities.* Urbana, Ill.: University of Illinois Press, 1966.

Kirk, S. A., & Kirk, W. D. *Psycholinguistic learning disabilities: Diagnosis and remediation.* Urbana, Ill.: University of Illinois Press, 1971.

Kirk, S., McCarthy, J., & Kirk, W. *The Illinois Test of Psycholinguistic Abilities.* Urbana, Ill.: University of Illinois Press, 1968.

Kirp, D. L. Schools as sorters: The constitutional and policy implications of student classifications. *University of Pennsylvania Law Review,* 1973, *121,* 705–797.

Kirp, D. L. The great sorting machine. *Phi Delta Kappan,* 1974, *55,* 521–525.

Kirp, D. L., Buss, W., & Kuriloff, P. Legal reform of special education: Empirical studies and procedural proposals. *California Law Review,* 1974, *62,* 40–155.

Klapp, S. T., Anderson, W. G., & Berrian, R. W. Implicit speech in reading. *Journal of Experimental Psychology,* 1973, *100,* 368–374.

Kline, C. L. Orton-Gillingham methodology: Where have all of the researchers gone? *Bulletin of the Orton Society,* 1977, *27,* 82–87.

Knaus, W., & McKeever, C. Rational-emotive education with learning disabled children. *Journal of Learning Disabilities,* 1977, *10,* 10–13.

Kneedler, R. D. The use of cognitive training to change social behaviors. *Exceptional Education Quarterly,* 1980, *1,* 65–74.

Knight-Arest, I., & Reid, D. K. Peer interaction as a catalyst for conservation acquisition in normal and learning disabled children. *Proceedings of the 9th Interdisciplinary International Conference on Piagetian Theory and the Helping Professions.* 1980.

Knights, R. M., & Hinton, G. The effects of methylphenidate (Ritalin) on the motor skills and behavior of children with learning problems. *Journal of Nervous and Mental Diseases,* 1969, *148,* 643–653.

Kobasigawa, A. Utilization of retrieval cues by children in recall. *Child Development,* 1974, *45,* 127–134.

Kolers, P. A. Three stages of reading. In H. Leven, & J. Williams (Eds.), *Basic studies on reading*. New York: Basic Books, 1970.

Kolers, P. A., & Perkins, D. N. Spatial and ordinal components of form perception and literacy. *Cognitive Psychology*, 1975, *7*, 228–267.

Kooi, K. A. *Fundamentals of electroencephalography*. New York: Harper & Row, 1971.

Kosc, L. Developmental dyslexia. *Journal of Learning Disabilities*, 1974, *7*, 165–177.

Kosiewicz, M. M., Hallahan, D. P., Lloyd, J., & Graves, A. W. The effects of self-instruction and self-correction procedures on handwriting performance (Technical Report No. 5). Charlottesville, Va.: University of Virginia Learning Disabilities Research Institute, 1979.

Kottmeyer, W. *Teacher's guide for remedial reading*. New York: McGraw-Hill, 1970.

Kottmeyer, W., & Claus, A. *Basic goals in spelling*. New York: McGraw-Hill, 1968, 1972.

Koupernik, C., MacKeith, R., & Francis-Williams, J. Neurological correlates of motor and perceptual development. In W. Cruickshank and D. P. Hallahan (Eds.), *Perceptual and Learning disabilities in children*, (Vol. 2). Syracuse, N.Y.: Syracuse University Press, 1975.

Kramer, K. *Teaching elementary school mathematics*. Boston: Allyn & Bacon, 1978.

Krauch, V. Hyperactive engineering. *American Education*, 1971, *7*(5), 12–16.

Kronick, D. Some thoughts on group identification social needs. *Journal of Learning Disabilities*, 1974, *3*, 24–27.

Kronick, D. The importance of sociological perspective towards learning disabilities. *Journal of Learning Disabilities*, 1976, *9*, 115–119.

Kronvall, E. L., & Diehl, C. F. The relationship of auditory discrimination of articulatory defects of children with no known organic impairment. *Journal of Speech and Hearing Disorders*, 1954, *19*, 335–338.

Kroth, R. The behavioral Q-sort as a diagnostic tool. *Academic Therapy*, 1973, *8*, 317–329.

Kroth, R. Parents—Powerful and necessary allies. *Teaching Exceptional Children*, 1978, *10*, 88–90.

Krupski, A. Attention processes: Research, theory and implications for special education. In B. K. Keogh (Ed.), *Advances in special education*, (Vol. 1). Greenwich, Conn.: J. A. I. Press, 1980.

Kuhlman, E. S., & Wolking, W. D. Development of within- and cross-modal matching ability in the auditory and visual sense modalities. *Developmental Psychology*, 1972, *7*, 365.

Kurtz, R., & Spiker, J. Slow or learning disabled: Is there a difference? *Arithmetic Teacher*, 1976, 617–622.

LaBerge, D. Processing in reading. Presentation given at the University of Texas at Dallas, Richardson, Texas, Spring 1980.

LaBerge, D., & Samuels, J. Toward a theory of automatic information processing in reading. *Cognitive Psychology*, 1974, *6*, 293–323.

Lacey, J. I. Psychophysiological approaches to the evaluation of psychotherapeutic processes and outcome. In E. A. Rubenstein & M. B. Parloff (Eds.), *Research in psychotherapy*. Washington: American Psychological Association, 1959.

Ladd, F. Pills for classroom peace? *Saturday Review*, 1970 (November 21), 66–68.

Lambert, N. M., & Windmiller, M. An exploratory study of temperament traits in a population of children at risk. *Journal of Special Education*, 1977, *11*, 37–47.

Lambert, N. M., Windmiller, M., Cole, L., & Figueroa, R. *Manual for AAMD Adaptive Behavior Scale Public School Version (1974 revision)*. Washington: The Association, 1975.

Lambert, N. M., Windmiller, M., Sandoval, J., & Moore, B. Hyperactive children and the efficacy of psychoactive drugs as a treatment intervention. *American Journal of Orthopsychiatry*, 1976, *46*(2), 335–352.

Landrigan, P. J., Baloh, R., Strum, R., & Whitworth, R. H. Neuropsychological dysfunction in children with chronic low level lead absorption, *Lancet*, 1975, *1*, 708.

Langford, F. S. What can a teacher learn about a pupil's thinking through oral interviews? *Arithmetic Teacher*, 1974, *21*, 26–32.

LaPorte, R. E., & Voss, J. F. Retention of prose materials as a function of postacquisition testing. *Journal of Educational Psychology*, 1975, *67*(2), 259–266.

Lapp, D., & Flood, J. *Teaching reading to every child*. New York: Macmillan, 1978.

Larsen, S. C., & Hammill, D. D. The relationship of selected visual perceptual abilities to school learning. *Journal of Special Education*, 1976, *9*, 281–291.

Larsen, S. C., & Hammill, D. D. *Test of Written Spelling*. Austin, Tex.: Pro-Ed, 1976.

Larsen, S. C., & Poplin, M. S. *Methods for educating the handicapped*. Boston: Allyn & Bacon, 1980.

Larsen, S. C., Rogers, D., & Sowell, V. The use of selected perceptual tests in differentiating between normal and learning disabled children. *Journal of Learning disabilities*, 1976, *9*, 85–90.

Larsen, S. C., Trenholme, B., & Parker, R. The effects of syntactic complexity upon arithmetic performance. *Learning Disability Quarterly*, 1978, *1*, 80–85.

Larson, C. Teaching beginning writing. *Academic Therapy Quarterly*, 1968, *4*, 61–66.

Laufer, M. W., & Denhoff, E. Hyperkinetic behavior syndrome in children. *Journal of Pediatrics*, 1957, *50*, 463–474.

Lee, L. L. *Northwestern Syntax Screening Test*. Evanston, Ill.: Northwestern University Press, 1969.

Lee, L. L. *Developmental Sentence Analysis*. Evanston, Ill.: Northwestern University Press, 1974.

Lee, L. L., Koenigsknecht, R. A., & Mulhern, S. T. *Interactive language development teaching*. Evanston, Ill.: Northwestern University Press, 1975.

Legenza, A. Inquiry training for reading and learning improvement. *Reading Improvement*, 1978, *16*, 309–316.

Lenneberg, E. H. *Biological foundations of language*. New York: Wiley, 1967.

Lequerica, M., & Weiner, S. Predicting learning disabilities from WISC—R profiles. Unpublished manuscript, New York University, 1977.

Lerer, R. J., & Lerer, M. P. Response of adolescents with minimal brain dysfunction to methylphenidate. *Journal of Learning Disabilities*, 1977, *10*(4), 223–228.

Lerner, J. W. *Children with learning disabilities*. Boston: Houghton Mifflin, 1976.

Lewis, E. R., & Lewis, H. P. An analysis of errors in the formation of manuscript letters by first-grade children. *American Educational Research Journal*, 1965, *2*, 25–35.

Lewis, J. L. The relation of individual temperament to initial social behavior. In R. C. Smart & M. S. Smart (Eds.), *Readings in child development and relationships*, (2d ed.) New York: Macmillan, 1977.

Lewis, M. The development of attention and perception in the infant and young child. In W. M. Cruickshank & D. P. Hallahan (Eds.), *Perceptual and learning disabilities in children*, (Vol 2). Syracuse, N.Y.: Syracuse University Press, 1975.

Liben, L. S. Memory in the context of cognitive development: The Piagetian approach.

In R. V. Kail & J. W. Hagen (Eds.), *Perspectives on the development of memory and cognition.* Hillsdale, N.J.: Lawrence Erlbaum, 1977.

Liben, L. S. The effect of operativity on memory. Paper presented at the Southeastern Conference on Human Development, Alexandria, Virginia, April 1980.

Liberman, I. Y. Speech and lateralization of language. *Bulletin of the Orton Society,* 1971, *21,* 71–87.

Liberman, I. Y. Segmentation of the spoken word and reading acquisition. *Bulletin of the Orton Society,* 1973, *23,* 65–77.

Lilly, M. S. A training based model for special education. *Exceptional Children,* 1971, *37,* 754–759.

Lin-Fu, J. S. Undue absorption of lead among children—a new look at an old problem. *New England Journal of Medicine,* 1972, *236,* 702–710.

Lipman, R. Government policy on research with hyperactive children. Paper presented at the Council for Exceptional Children. Atlanta, 1977.

Lloyd, J. Academic instruction and cognitive behavior modification: The need for attack strategy training. *Exceptional Education Quarterly,* 1980, *1,* 53–64.

Lockmiller, P., & DiNello, M. Words in Color vs. a basal reading program with retarded readers in grade two. *Journal of Educational Research,* 1970, *63,* 330–334.

Loftus, E. F., & Loftus, G. R. On the permanence of stored information in the human brain. *American Psychologist,* 1980, *35,* 409–420.

Loftus, G. R., & Loftus, E. F. *Human memory: The processing of information.* Hillsdale, N.J.: Lawrence Erlbaum, 1976.

Logan, R., & Colarusso, R. The effectiveness of the MWM and GOAL programs in developing general language abilities. *Learning Disability Quarterly,* 1978, *1,* 32–38.

Loper, A. B. Metacognitive development: Implications for cognitive training. *Exceptional Education Quarterly,* 1980, *1,* 1–8.

Losen, S. M., & Diament, B. *Parent conference in the schools.* Boston: Allyn & Bacon, 1978.

Lovell, K. *The growth of understanding in mathematics: Kindergarten through grade three.* New York: Holt, Rinehart & Winston, 1971.

Lovitt, T. C. Assessment of children with learning disabilities. *Exceptional Children,* 1967, *34,* 233–239.

Lund, K. A., Foster, G. E., & McCall-Perez, F. C. The effectiveness of psycholinguistic training: A reevaluation. *Exceptional Children,* 1978, *44,* 310–319.

Luria, A. R. *The human brain and psychological processes.* (Vol. 1). New York: Harper, 1965.

Luria, A. *Higher cortical functions in man.* New York: Basic Books, 1966.

Lyon, R. Auditory-perceptual training: The state of the art. *Journal of Learning Disabilities,* 1977, *10,* 564–572.

Maccoby, E. E. Selective auditory attention in children. In L. P. Lippsit & C. C. Spiker (Eds.), *Advances in child development and behavior,* (Vol. 3). New York: Academic, 1967.

Maccoby, E. E. The development of stimulus selection. In J. P. Hill (Ed.), *Minnesota symposia on child psychology,* (Vol. 3). Minneapolis: University of Minnesota Press, 1969.

Maccoby, E. E., & Hagen, J. W. Effects of distraction upon central versus incidental recall: Developmental trends. *Journal of Experimental Child Psychology,* 1965, *2,* 280–289.

MacFarlane, A. *The psychology of childbirth.* Cambridge, Mass.: Harvard University Press, 1978.

Mackler, B., & Holman, D. Assessing, packaging, and delivery: Tests, testing, and race. *Young Children,* 1976, *31,* 351–364.

Mackworth, N. H., & Bruner, J. S. Selecting visual information during recognition by adults and children. Unpublished manuscript, Center for Cognitive Studies, Harvard University, 1966.

Madden, R., Gardner, E. R., Rudman, H. C., Karlsen, B., & Merwin, J. C. *Stanford Achievment Test.* New York: Harcourt Brace Jovanovich, 1973.

Magee, P. A., & Newcomer, P. L. The relationship between oral language skills and academic achievement of learning disabled children. *Learning Disability Quarterly,* 1978, *1,* 63–67.

Mahoney, M. J. Cognitive therapy and research: A question of questions. *Cognitive Therapy and Research,* 1977, *1,* 5–16.

Mahoney, M. J., & Kazdin, A. E. Cognitive-behavior modification: Misconceptions and premature evaluation. *Psychological Bulletin,* 1979, *86,* 1044–1049.

Maitland, S., Nadeau, B. E., & Nadeau, G. Early school screening practices. *Journal of Learning Disabilities,* 1974, *10,* 645–649.

Malcomesius, N. *Specific Language Disability Test: Grades six, seven, and eight.* Cambridge, Mass.: Educators Publishing Service, 1967.

Malone, J. R. Single-sound UNIFON: Does it fill the need for a compatible and consistent auxiliary orthography for teaching English and other European languages? Paper presented at the Conference on Perceptual and Linguistics Aspects of Reading, Center for Advanced Study in the Behavioral Sciences, Stanford, Calif., October–November, 1963.

Mann, L. *On the trail of process: A historical perspective on cognitive processes and their training.* New York: Grune & Stratton, 1979.

Mann, P. H., & Suiter, P. *Handbook in diagnostic teaching: A learning disabilities approach.* Boston: Allyn & Bacon, 1974.

Margolis, J., Hill, D., Reid, D. K., West, R., & Hresko, W. P. Mainstreaming: Putting it all together. *Paper presented at the New York State Teachers of the Handicapped,* Lake Kiamesha, New York, 1978.

Marquardt, T. P., & Saxman, J. H. Language comprehension and auditory discrimination in articulation deficient children. *Journal of Speech and Hearing Research,* 1972, *15,* 382–389.

Marshall, N. The structure of semantic memory for text. Paper presented at the meeting of the American Psychological Association, Washington, September 3–7, 1976.

Martin, E. W. Individualism and behaviorism as future trends in educating handicapped children. *Exceptional Children,* 1972, *38,* 517–525.

Marwit, S. J., & Stenner, A. J. Hyperkinesis: Delineation of two patterns. *Exceptional Children,* 1972, *38,* 401–406.

Masters, L., & Marsh, G. E. Middle ear pathology as a factor in learning disabilities. *Journal of Learning Disabilities,* 1978, *11,* 103–106.

Matheny, P. Auditory sequence retention abilities of young children. Unpublished doctoral dissertation. University of Southern California, 1971.

Mattingly, I. G. Reading, the linguistic process, and linguistic awareness. In J. F. Kavanagh & I. C. Mattingly (Eds.), *Language by ear and by eye: The relationships between speech and reading.* Cambridge, Mass.: MIT Press, 1972.

Mattis, S., French, J. H., & Rapin, I. Dyslexia in children and young adults: three independent neuropsychological syndromes. *Developmental Medicine & Child Neurology,* 1975, *17,* 150–163.

Mayron, L. W. Ecological factors in learning disabilities. *Journal of Learning Disabilities,* 1978, *11,* 495–505.

Mayron, L. W., Ott, J., Nations, R., & Mayron, E. Light, radiation, and academic behavior. *Academic Therapy,* 1974, *10,* 33–47.

McCarthy, F. E. Remedial reading and learning disabilities in battle. *The Reading Teacher,* 1978, *31,* 484–486.

McCoulskey, M. Sentence repetition ability of children with language and/or learning disabilities. Unpublished doctoral dissertation, University of Texas, 1971.

McDowell, R. Parent counseling: The state of the art. *Journal of Learning Disabilities,* 1976, *9,* 614–619.

McFie, J. The diagnostic significance of disorders of higher nervous activity. *Handbook of Clinical Neurology,* (Vol. 4). 1969, 1–12.

McGrady, H. J., & Olson, D. A. Visual and auditory learning processes in normal children and children with specific learning disabilities. *Exceptional Children,* 1970, *36,* 581–589.

McGuigan, F. Covert oral behavior during silent performance of language tasks. *Psychological Bulletin,* 1970, *74,* 309–326.

McKay, D. G. Aspects of the theory of comprehension, memory and attention. *Quarterly Journal of Experimental Psychology,* 1973, *25,* 22–40.

McKinney, J. D., & Haskins, R. Cognitive training and the development of problem-solving strategies. *Exceptional Education Quarterly,* 1980, *1,* 41–52.

McNamara, J. J. Hyperactivity in the apartment bound child. *Clinical Pediatrics,* 1972, *11,* 371–372.

McNeill, D. Developmental psycholinguistics. In F. Smith & G. A. Miller (Eds.), *The genesis of language: A psycholinguistic approach.* Cambridge, Mass.: MIT Press, 1966.

McNutt, G., & Heller, G. Services for learning disabled adolescents: A survey. *Learning Disability Quarterly,* 1978, *1,* 101–103.

Medley, D., Schluck, C., & Ames, N. *Assessing the learning environment in the classroom: A manual for users of OSCAR 5.* Princeton, N.J.: Educational Testing Service, 1968.

Meichenbaum, D. *Cognitive-behavior modification.* New York: Plenum, 1977.

Meichenbaum, D. Teaching children self-control. In B. B. Lahey & A. E. Kazdin (Eds.), *Advances in clinical child psychology* (Vol. 2). New York: Plenum, 1979.

Meichenbaum, D., & Goodman, J. Reflection-impulsivity and verbal control of motor behavior. *Child Development,* 1969, *40,* 785–797.

Meichenbaum, D. H., & Goodman, J. Training impulsive children to talk to themselves: A means of developing self-control. *Journal of Abnormal Psychology,* 1971, *77,* 115–126.

Meier, J. H. Prevalence and characteristics of learning disabilities found in second grade children. *Journal of Learning Disabilities,* 1971, *4,* 1–16.

Mellon, J. C. *Transformational sentence-combining: A method for enhancing the development of syntactic fluency in English composition.* Urbana, Ill.: National Council of Teachers of English, 1965.

Mendelson, W., Johnson, N., & Steward, M. A. Hyperactive children as teenagers: A follow-up study. *Journal of Nervous and Mental Disorders,* 1971, *153*(4), 273–279.

Menyuk, P. Comparison of grammar of children with functionally deviant and normal speech. *Journal of Speech and Hearing Research*, 1964, *7*, 109–121.

Mercer, C. D., Algozzine, B., & Trifiletti, J. J. Early identification: Issues and considerations. *Exceptional Children*, 1979, *46*, 52–54.

Mercer, C. D., Algozzine, B., & Trifiletti, J. J. Early identification—An analysis of the research. *Learning Disability Quarterly*, 1979, *2*, 12–24.

Mercer, J. R., & Ysseldyke, J. Designing diagnostic-intervention programs. In T. Oakland (Ed.), *Psychological and educational assessment of minority children*. New York: Brunner/Mazel, 1977.

Messer, S. B. Reflection-impulsivity: A review. *Psychological Bulletin*, 1976, *83*, 1026–1052.

Meyen, E. L., Vergason, G. A., & Whelan, R. J., (Eds.) *Alternatives for teaching exceptional children*. Denver, Colo.: Love, 1975.

Meyer, D. E., Schvaneveldt, R. W., & Ruddy, M. G. Loci of contextual effects on visual word-recognition. In P. M. A. Rabbit & S. Dornic' (Eds.), *Attention and performance V*. New York: Academic Press, 1975.

Miles, N. C., & Miles, T. R. Dyslexia as a limitation in the ability to process information. *Bulletin of the Orton Society*, 1977, *27*, 72–81.

Miller, G. A. Some preliminaries to psycholinguistics. *American Psychologist*, 1965, *20*, 15–20.

Miller, G. A., Galanter, E., & Pribram, K. H. *Plans and the structure of behavior*. New York: Holt, 1960.

Miller, J. F., & Yoder, D. E. A syntax teaching program. In J. E. McLean, D. E. Yoder, & R. L. Schiefelbusch (Eds.), *Language intervention with the retarded: Developing strategies*. Baltimore: University Park Press, 1972.

Miller, J. F., & Yoder, D. E. An ontogenetic language teaching strategy for retarded children. In R. L. Schiefelbusch & L. L. Lloyd (Eds.), *Language perspectives—Acquisition, retardation, and intervention*. Baltimore: University Park Press, 1974.

Milner, A. D., & Bryant, P. E. Cross-modal matching by young children. *Journal of Comparative and Physiological Psychology*, 1970, *71*, 453–458.

Minskoff, E. H., Wiseman, D. E., & Minskoff, J. G. *The MWM program for developing language abilities*. Ridgefield, N.J.: Educational Performance Associates, 1972.

Moletzky, B. Behavior recording as treatment: A brief note. *Behavior Therapy*, 1974, *5*, 107–111.

Molitch, M., & Eccles, A. K. Effect of benezedrine sulphate on intelligence scores of children. *American Journal of Psychiatry*, 1937, *94*, 587–590.

Mondani, M. S., & Tutko, T. A. Relationship of academic underachievement to incidental learning. *Journal of Counseling and Clinical Psychology*, 1969, *33*, 558–560.

Monroe, J. D., & Howe, C. E. The effects of integration and social class on the acceptance of retarded individuals. *Education and Training of the Mentally Retarded*, 1971, *6*, 20–24.

Monroe, M. *Children who cannot read*. Chicago: University of Chicago Press, 1932.

Monteith, M. K. Screening and assessment programs for young children: Reading readiness and learning problems, *Language Arts*, 1976, *53*, 920–924.

Moore, S., & Cole, S. Cognitive self-mediation training with hyperkinetic children. *Bulletin of Psychonomic Society*, 1978, *12*, 18–20.

Morrison, J. R., & Steward, M. A. A family study of the hyperactive child syndrome. *Biological Psychiatry*, 1971, *3*, 189–195.

Mosenthal, P. Psycholinguistic properties of aural and visual comprehension as determined by children's abilities to comprehend syllogism. *Reading Research Quarterly,* 1976–1977, *12,* 55–92.

Muehl, S., & Kremenak, S. Ability to match information within and between auditory and visual sense modalities and subsequent reading achievement. *Journal of Educational Psychology,* 1966, *57,* 230–238.

Mulholland, T. B. The concept of attention and the electroencephalographic alpha rhythm. In C. R. Evans & T. B. Mulholland (Eds.), *Attention in neurophysiology.* London: Butterworth, 1969.

Myers, C. A. Reviewing the literature on Fernald's technique of remedial reading. *The Reading Teacher,* 1978, *31,* 614–619.

Myers, P. I., & Hammill, D. D. *Methods for learning disorders.* New York: Wiley, 1976.

Myklebust, H. R. *Development and disorders of written language.* New York: Grune & Stratton, 1965.

Myklebust, H. R. *The pupil rating scale: Screening for learning disabilities.* New York: Grune & Stratton, 1971.

Myklebust, H. R., & Boshes, B. *Minimal brain damage in children.* (Final report). U.S. Public Health Service Contract 108-65-142. U.S. Department of Health Education, and Welfare. Evanston, Ill.: Northwestern University Publication, June, 1969.

Naiden, N. Ratio of boys to girls among disabled readers. *The Reading Teacher,* 1976, *29,* 439–442.

Nathanson, D., Cynamon, A., & Lehman, K. Miami snow poets: Creative writing for exceptional children. *Teaching Exceptional Children,* 1976, *8,* 87–91.

National Advisory Committee on Dyslexia and Related Reading Disorders. *Reading disorders in the United States.* Washington, D.C.: U.S. Department of Health, Education, and Welfare, 1969.

National Advisory Committee on Handicapped Children. *Special Education for Handicapped Children.* First Annual Report. Washington: U.S. Department of Health, Education, and Welfare, January 31, 1968.

National Assessment of Educational Progress. *Math fundamentals: Selected results from the first mathematics assessment.* Report 04-MA-01. Washington: U.S. Superintendent of Documents, January 1975.

Neisser, U. *Cognitive psychology.* New York: Appleton-Century-Crofts, 1967.

Neisser, U. *Cognition and reality.* San Francisco: W. H. Freeman, 1976.

Neisworth, J. T., Kurtz, D., Ross, A., & Madle, R. A. Naturalistic assessment of neurological diagnosis and pharmacological intervention. *Journal of Learning Disabilities,* 1976, *9*(3), 150–152.

Nelson, T. O., Metzler, J., & Reed, D. A. Role of details on the long-term recognition of pictures and verbal descriptions. *Journal of Experimental Psychology,* 1974, *102*(1), 184–186.

Nelson, W. J. Jr., & Birkimer, J. C. Role of self-instruction and self-reinforcement in the modification of impulsivity. *Journal of Consulting and Clinical Psychology,* 1978, *46,* 183.

Nelson, W. M., III. Cognitive behavioral strategies in modifying an impulsive cognitive style. Unpublished doctoral dissertation, Virginia Commonwealth University, 1976.

Newcomer, P. L. The ITPA and academic achievement. *Academic Therapy,* 1975, *10,* 401–406.

Newcomer, P. L., & Goodman, L. Effects of modality of instruction on the learning of meaningful and nonmeaningful material by auditory and visual learners. *Journal of Special Education,* 1975, *9,* 261–268.

Newcomer, P. L., & Hammill, D. D. *Psycholinguistics in the schools.* Columbus, Ohio: Merrill, 1976.

Newcomer, P. L., & Hammill, D. D. *The Test of Language Development.* Austin, Tx.: Empiric Press, 1977.

Newcomer, P. L., Hare, B., Hammill, D. D., & McGettigan, J. Construct validity of the Illinois Test of Psycholinguistic Abilities. *Journal of Learning Disabilities,* 1975, *8,* 220–231.

Newland, T. E. An analytical study of the development of illegibilities in handwriting from the lower grades to adulthood. *Journal of Educational Research,* 1932, *26,* 249–258.

Newland, T. E. Assumptions underlying psychological testing. *Journal of School Psychology,* 1973, *11,* 316–322.

Nihira, K., Foster, R., Shellhaas, M., & Leland, H. *Adaptive Behavior Scales.* Washington: American Association on Mental Deficiency, 1969.

Noble, J. K. *Better handwriting for you.* N.Y.: Noble & Noble, 1966.

Noelker, R. W., & Schumsky, D. A. Memory for sequence, form and position as related to the identification of reading retardates. *Journal of Educational Psychology,* 1973, *64,* 22–25.

Norman, D. A. *Memory and attention: An introduction to human information processing.* New York: Wiley, 1976.

Norman, D. A., & Bobrow, D. G. On data-limited and resource-limited processes. *Cognitive Psychology,* 1975, *7,* 44–54.

Norman, D. A., & Rumelhart, D. E. A system for perception and memory. In D. A. Norman (Ed.), *Models of human memory.* New York: Academic Press, 1970.

Northern, J. L. (Ed.). *Hearing disorders.* Boston: Little, Brown, 1976.

Northern, J. L., & Downs, M. P. *Hearing in children.* Baltimore: Williams & Williams, 1974.

Novack, H. S., Bonaventura, E., & Merenda, P. F. *Manual to accompany Rhode Island Pupil Identification Scale.* Providence, R.I.: Authors, 1972.

Nunnally, J. C. *Psychometric theory.* New York: McGraw-Hill, 1967.

Nurss, J. R., & McGauvran, M. E. *Metropolitan Readiness Tests: Teacher's manual,* (Part II), *Interpretation and use of test results (level I).* New York: Harcourt Brace Jovanovich, 1976.

Nutrition Foundation. Report of the Advisory Committee on Hyperkinesis and Food Additives to the Nutrition Foundation. New York: The Nutrition Foundation, 1975.

Nyquist, E. B. *Mainstreaming: Idea and actuality: An occasional paper from Commissioner E. B. Nyquist.* Albany, N.Y.: The State Education Department, 1975.

Oakland, T. *Psychological and educational assessment of minority children.* New York: Brunner/Mazel, 1977.

Oakland, T., DeLuna, C., & Morgan, C. Annotated bibliography of language dominance measures. In T. Oakland (Ed.), *Psychological and educational assessment of minority children.* New York: Brunner/Mazel, 1977.

O'Donnell, R. C. A critique of some indices of syntactic maturity. *Research in the Teaching of English,* 1976, *10,* 31–38.

Office of Education. Part B, Education of the Handicapped Act. *Federal Register,* August 23, 1977, *42.*

Office of Education. Supplemental procedures for evaluating specific learning disabilities. *Federal Register,* December 19, 1977, *42.*

Offner, C. D. Back-to-basics in mathematics. *The Mathematics Teacher,* 1978, *71,* 211–217.

O'Hare, F. *Sentence combining: Improving student writing without formal grammar instruction.* Research Report 15, Urbana, Ill.: National Council of Teachers of English, 1973.

Okolo, C., Bartlett, S. A., & Shaw, S. F. Communication between professionals concerning medication for the hyperactive child. *Journal of Learning Disabilities,* 1978, *11*(10), 647–650.

Omenn, G. S. Genetic issues in the syndrome of minimal brain dysfunction. *Seminars in Psychiatry,* 1973, *5,* 5–17.

Ornstein, P. A., Naus, M. J., & Liberty, C. Rehearsal and organizational processes in childrens' memory. *Child Development,* 1975, *46,* 818–830.

Orton, J. L. The Orton-Gillingham approach. In J. Money (Ed.), *The disabled reader: Education of the dyslexic child.* Baltimore: The Johns Hopkins Press, 1966.

Orton, S. T. 'Word-blindness' in school children. *Archives of Neurology and Psychiatry,* 1928, *14,* 581–615.

Orton, S. T. *Reading, writing and speech problems in children: A presentation of certain types of disorders in the development of language faculty.* New York: Norton, 1937.

Osgood, C. E. *Method and theory in experimental psychology.* New York: Oxford University Press, 1953.

Osgood, C. E. A dinosaur caper: Psycholinguistics past, present, and future. In D. Aaronson & R. W. Rieber (Eds.), Developmental psycholinguistics and communication disorders. *Annals of the New York Academy of Sciences,* 1975, *263,* 16–26.

Ott, J. N. The eyes' dual function—Part II. *Eye, Ear, Nose, and Throat Monthly,* 1974, *53,* 377–381.

Ott, J. N. Influence of flourescent lights on hyperactivity and learning disabilities. *Journal of Learning Disabilities,* 1976, *9*(7), 417–422.

Otto, W., & McMenemy, R. A. *Corrective and remedial teaching.* Boston: Houghten Mifflin, 1966.

Otto, W., McMenemy, R. A., & Smith, R. J. *Corrective and remedial teaching.* Boston: Houghton Mifflin, 1973.

Ounsted, C. Hyperkinetic syndrome in epileptic children. *Lancet,* 1955, *2,* 303.

Owen, F. W., Adams, P. A., Forrest, T., Stoltz, L. M., & Fisher, S. Learning disorders in children: Sibling studies. *Monographs of the Society for Research in Child Development.* 1971, *36,* 144.

Ozer, M. N. The assessment of children with learning problems: A planning process involving the teacher. *Journal of Learning Disabilities,* 1978, *11,* 422–426.

Palermo, D., & Molfese, D. Language acquisition from age five onward. *Psychological Bulletin,* 1972, *78,* 409–428.

Palkes, H., Stewart, M., & Freedman, J. Improvement in maze performance of hyperactive boys as a function of verbal-training procedures. *Journal of Special Education,* 1972, *5,* 337–342.

Palkes, H., Stewart, M., & Kahana, B. Porteus Maze performance of hyperactive boys after training in self-directed verbal commands. *Child Development,* 1968, *39,* 817–826.

Paraskevopoulos, J. N., & Kirk, S. A. *The development and psychometric characteristics of the Revised Illinois Test of Psycholinguistic Abilities.* Urbana, Ill.: University of Illinois Press, 1969.

Paris, S. G., & Carter, A. Y. Semantic and constructive aspects of sentence memory in children. *Developmental Psychology,* 1973, *9,* 109–113.

Paris, S. G., & Mahoney, G. J. Cognitive integration in children's memory for sentences and pictures. *Child Development,* 1974, *45,* 633–642.

Parker, T. B., Freston, C. W., & Drew, C. J. Comparison of verbal performance of normal and learning disabled children as a function of input organization. *Journal of Learning Disabilities.* 1975, 8(6), 386–392.

Pascual-Leone, J. On learning and development, Piagetian style: A reply to Lefebvre-Pinard. *Canadian Psychological Review,* 1976, *17,* 270.

Paton, S. M., Walberg, H. J., & Yeh, E. G. Ethnicity, environmental control, and academic self-concept in Chicago. *American Educational Research Journal,* 1973, *10,* 85–99.

Patterson, G. R., Jones, R., Whittier, J., & Whittier, M. A. A behavior modification program for the hyperactive child. *Behavior Research Therapy,* 1965, *2,* 217–220.

Paul, J. L., Turnbull, A. P., & Cruickshank, W. M. *Mainstreaming: A practical guide.* Syracuse, New York: Syracuse University Press, 1977.

Pearson, P. D., & Johnson, D. *Teaching reading comprehension.* New York: Holt, Rinehart & Winston, 1978.

Perfetti, C. A., & Goldman, S. R. Discourse memory and reading comprehension skill. *Journal of Verbal Learning and Verbal Behavior,* 1976, *14,* 33–42.

Perino, J., & Ernhart, C. B. The relation of subclinical lead level to cognitive and sensorimotor impairment in black preschoolers. *Journal of Learning Disabilities,* 1974, *7,* 26.

Peterson, L. R. Search and judgment in memory. In B. J. Kleinmuntz (Ed.), *Concepts and the structure of memory.* New York: Wiley, 1967.

Petty, W. T., Petty, D. C., & Becking, M. E. *Experiences in language: Tools and techniques for language arts methods.* Boston: Allyn & Bacon, 1976.

Piaget, J. *On the development of memory and identity.* Barre, Mass.: Clark University Press, 1967.

Piaget, J. *The grasp of consciousness: Action and concept in the young child.* Cambridge, Mass.: Harvard University Press, 1976.

Piaget, J. *Behavior and evolution.* New York: Pantheon, 1978.

Piaget, J., & Inhelder, B. *The psychology of the child.* New York: Basic Books, 1969.

Piaget, J., & Inhelder, B. *Memory and intelligence.* New York: Basic Books, 1973.

Pick, H. L., & Saltzman, E. *Modes of perceiving and processing information.* New York: Wiley, 1978.

Pitman, J. The future of the teaching of reading. Paper presented at the Educational Conference of the Educational Records Bureau, New York City, October 30–November 1, 1963.

Poggio, J. P., & Salkind, N. J. A review and appraisal of instruments assessing hyperactivity in children. *Learning Disability Quarterly,* 1979, 2(1), 9–22.

Pohl, R. Helping a child with a learning problem feel good about himself. *The Special Education Report,* 1976, 503.

Poplin, M. S. The science of curriculum development applied to special education and the IEP. *Focus on Exceptional Children,* 1979, *12,* 1–16.

Porterfield, J., Jackson, E., & Risley, T. Contingent observation: An effective procedure for reducing disruptive behavior of young children in a group setting. *Journal of Applied Behavior Analysis,* 1976, *9,* 55–64.

Postman, L., Kruesi, E., & Regan, J. Recognition and recall as measures of long-term retention. *Quarterly Journal of Experimental Psychology,* 1975, *27,* 411–418.

Pressley, M. Increasing children's self-control through cognitive interventions. *Review of Educational Research,* 1979, *49,* 319–370.

Proger, B. B., Cross, L. H., & Burger, R. M. Construct validation of standardized tests in special education: A framework of reference and application to ITPA research. In L. Mann & D. A. Sabatino (Eds.), *The first review of special education,* (Vol. 1). Philadelphia: JSE Press, 1973.

Prout, H. T. Behavioral intervention with hyperactive children: A review. *Journal of Learning Disabilities,* 1977, *10*(3), 141–146.

Quay, H. C., & Peterson, D. R. *Manual for the Behavior Problem Checklist.* Unpublished manuscript, University of Illinois, 1967.

Quillian, M. R. The teachable language comprehender: A simulation program and theory of language. *Communications of the ACM,* 1969, *12*(8), 459–476.

Rabinovitch, R. D. Reading problems in children: Definitions and classifications. In A. H. Keeney & V. T. Keeney (Eds.), *Dyslexia: Diagnosis and treatment of reading disorders.* St. Louis: C. V. Mosby, 1968.

Radatz, H. Error analysis in mathematics education. *Journal for Research in Mathematics Education,* 1979, *9,* 163–172.

Rapp, D. J. Does diet affect hyperactivity? *Journal of Learning Disabilities,* 1978, *11*(6), 383–389.

Rappoport, J. L., Lott, I. T., Alexander, D. F., & Abramson, A. U. Urinary nonadrenaline and playroom behavior in hyperactive boys. *Lancet,* 1970, *2,* 1141.

Rawson, M. B. *Developmental language disability: Adult accomplishments of dyslexic boys.* Baltimore: Johns Hopkins Press, 1968.

Rawson, M. B. The self-concept and the cycle of growth. Paper presented at the 24th Annual Conference of the Orton Society, Baltimore, 1973.

Rawson, M. B. Developmental dyslexia: Educational treatment and results. In D. D. Duane & M. B. Rawson (Eds.), *Reading, perception, and language.* Baltimore: York Press, 1975.

Redl, F., & Wattenburg, W. W. *Mental hygiene in teaching.* New York: Harcourt, Brace Jovanovich, 1959.

Rees, N. Auditory processing factors in language disorders: The view from Procrustes' bed. *Journal of Speech and Hearing Disorders,* 1973, *38,* 304–315.

Reeve, R. E., Hall, R. J., & Zakreski, R. S. The Woodcock-Johnson Tests of Cognitive Ability: Concurrent validity with the WISC—R. *Learning Disabilities Quarterly,* 1979, *2,* 63–69.

Reger, R., Schroeder, W., & Uschold, K. *Special education: Children with learning problems.* New York: Oxford University Press, 1968.

Reid, D. K. *Early identification of children with learning disabilities.* Regional Access Project, Community Action Programs, New York University, 1977.

Reid, D. K. Genevan theory and the education of exceptional children. In J. M.

Gallagher & J. A. Easley (Eds.), *Knowledge and development* (Vol. 2): *Piaget and Education*. New York: Plenum, 1978.

Reid, D. K. Some suggested strategies for teaching children with memory deficits. *Special Education '79*. Ontario, Canada: York University Press, 1979. (a)

Reid, D. K. Toward an application of developmental epistemology to special education. *Proceedings of the 8th Interdisciplinary International Conference on Piagetian Theory and the Helping Professions*, 1979. (b)

Reid, D. K., & Hresko, W. P. Thinking about thinking about it in that way and other considerations in the use of test data for instructional planning. *Exceptional Education Quarterly*, 1980, *1*(3).

Reid, D. K., Hresko, W. P., & Hammill, D. D. *The Test of Early Reading Ability*. Austin, Texas: Pro-Ed, 1981.

Reid, D. K., Hresko, W. P., & Margolis, J. Picture-sentence verification in competent and disabled readers. Paper presented at the annual meeting of the Council for Exceptional Children, Kansas City, May, 1978.

Reid, D. K., Knight-Arest, I., & Hresko, W. P. The development of cognition in learning disabled children. In J. Gottlieb & S. S. Strichart (Eds.), *Current research and application in learning disabilities*. Baltimore: University Park Press, 1980.

Reid, G. The etiology and nature of functional articulatory defects in elementary school children. *Journal of Speech and Hearing Disorders*, 1947, *12*, 143–150.(a)

Reid, G. The efficacy of speech re-education of functional articulatory defects in the elementary school. *Journal of Speech Disorders*, 1947, *12*, 301–313.(b)

Reid, J. F. Learning to think about reading. *Educational Research*, 1966, *9*, 56–62.

Reisman, F. K. *A guide to the diagnostic teaching of arithmetic*. Columbus, Ohio: Merrill, 1972.

Reynolds, M. C. Staying out of jail. *Teaching exceptional children*, 1978, *10*, 60–62.

Rich, A., & Nedboy, R. Hey man . . . we're writing a poem. *Teaching Exceptional Children*, 1977, *9*, 90–92.

Richardson, S. A., Birch, H. G., & Hertzig, M. E. School performance of children who were severely malnourished in infancy. *American Journal of Mental Deficiency*, 1973, *77*, 623.

Richie, D. H., & Aten, J. L. Auditory retention of nonverbal and verbal sequential stimuli in children with reading disabilities. *Journal of Learning Disabilities*, 1976, *9*(5), 312–318.

Richmond, B. G., & Dalton, J. L. Teacher ratings and self-concept reports of retarded pupils. *Exceptional Children*, 1973, *40*, 178–183.

Rickards, J. P. Processing effects of advance organizers interspersed in text. *Reading Research Quarterly*, 1975–1976, *11*, 599–622.

Ricks, J. R. Local norms—when and why. *Test Service Bulletin*, The Psychological Corporation, 1971, No. 58.

Ridberg, E., Parke, R., & Hetherington, E. M. Modification of impulsive and reflective cognitive styles through observation of film mediated models. *Developmental Psychology*, 1971, *5*, 369–377.

Ring, B. C. Effects of input organization on auditory short-term memory. *Journal of Learning Disabilities*, 1976, *9*(9), 591–599.

Ringelheim, D. Coming face to face with the impersonal numbers game: A conversation with the late Daniel Ringelheim. *Journal of Learning Disabilities*, 1978, *11*, 11–17.

Ringler, L. H., & Smith, I. Learning modality and word recognition of first-grade children. *Journal of Learning Disabilities,* 1973, *6,* 307–312.

Rist, R. C. Student social class and teacher expectations: The self-fulfilling prophecy in ghetto education. *Harvard Educational Review,* 1970, *40,* 411–451.

Ritter, K., Kaprove, B. II., Fitch, J. P., & Flavell, J. II. The development of retrieval strategies in young children. *Cognitive Psychology,* 1973, *5,* 310–321.

Robbins, M., & Glass, G. V. The Doman-Delacato rationale: A critical analysis In J. Hellmuth (Ed.), *Educational therapy.* (Vol II). Seattle: Special Child Publications, 1969.

Rockowitz, R. J., & Davidson, P. W. Discussing diagnostic findings with parents. *Journal of Learning Disabilities,* 1979, *12,* 2–7.

Rogers, C. M., Smith, M. D., & Coleman, J. M. Social comparison in the classroom: The relationship between academic achievement and self-concept. *Journal of Educational Psychology,* 1978, *70,* 50–57.

Rogers, D. C., Ort, L. L., & Serra, M. C. *Word book.* Chicago: Lyons Y Carnahan, 1970.

Rogoff, B., Newcombe, N., & Kagan, J. Planfulness and recognition memory. *Child Development,* 1974, *45,* 972–977.

Rose, S. A., Blank, M. S., & Bridger, W. H. Intermodal and intramodal retention of visual and tactual information in young children. *Developmental Psychology,* 1972, *6,* 482–486.

Rosenberg, S. Problems of language development in the retarded. In H. C. Haywood (Ed.), *Socio-cultural aspects of mental retardation.* New York: Appleton-Century-Crofts, 1970.

Rosenthal, J. H. A preliminary psycholinguistic study of children with learning disabilities. *Journal of Learning Disabilities,* 1970, *3,* 11–15.

Rosenthal, R., Archer, D., DiMatteo, D., Hill, M. R., & Rogers, P. L. Measuring sensitivity to nonverbal communication. Unpublished monograph, Hartford University, 1977.

Rosenthal, R., & Jacobson, L. *Pygmalion in the classroom: Teachers' expectation and pupils' intellectual development.* New York: Holt, Rinehart, & Winston, 1968.

Rosin, P., Poritsky, S., & Sotsky, R. American children with reading problems can easily learn to read English represented by Chinese characters. *Science,* 1971, *171,* 1264–1267. (Discussion and rejoinder. *Science,* 1971, *173,* 190–191.)

Rosner, J. Language arts and arithmetic achievement, and specifically related perceptual skills. *American Educational Research Journal,* 1973, *10,* 59–68.

Ross, A. O. *Psychological aspects of learning disabilities and reading disorders.* New York: McGraw-Hill, 1976.

Ross, D. M., & Ross, S. A. *Hyperactivity: Research, theory, and action.* New York: Wiley, 1976.

Ross, S. L., Jr., DeYoung, H., & Cohen, J. S. Confrontation: Special education placement and the law. *Exceptional Children,* 1971, *38,* 5–12.

Rost, K. J., & Charles, D. C. Academic achievement of brain injured and hyperactive children in isolation. *Exceptional Children,* 1967, *34,* 125–126.

Rourke, B. P. Issues in the neuropsychological assessment of children with learning disabilities. *Canadian Psychological Review, Psychologie Canadienne,* 1976, *17,* 89–102.

Rubin, A. D. Comprehension processes in oral and written language. Center for the

Study of Reading, University of Illinois at Urbana-Champaign. ERIC Document Reproduction Service No. ED 150 550, April, 1977.

Ruddell, R. B. *Reading-language instruction: Innovative practices*. Englewood Cliffs, N.J.: Prentice-Hall, 1974.

Rudel, R. Neuropsychology and reading. Televised discussion on *Sunrise Semester: Teaching the Learning Disabled*, CBS-TV, February, 1977.

Rudel, R. G., & Denckla, M. B. Relation of forward and backward digit repetition to neurological impairment in children with learning disabilities. *Neuropsychologia*, 1974, *12*, 109–118.

Rudel, R. G., & Teuber, H. -L. Pattern recognition within and across sensory modalities in normal and brain injured children. *Neuropsychologia*, 1971, *9*, 389–399.

Rudel, R. G., Teuber, H. -L. & Twitchell, T. E. Levels of impairment of sensori-motor functions in children with early brain damage. *Neuropsychologia*, 1974, *12*, 95–108.

Rudnick, M. Sterritt, G. M., & Flax, M. Auditory and visual rhythm perception and reading ability. *Child Development*, 1967, *38*, 581–587.

Rumelhart, D. E. Toward an interactive model of reading. (Technical Report No. 56). La Jolla, Calif.: Center for Human Information Processing, 1976.

Ryor, J. 94-142—The perspective of regular education. *Learning Disability Quarterly*, 1978, *1*, 6–14.

Sabatino, D., Naiman, D., & Foster, G. The relationship between independent reward preferences for learning disabled children. *Exceptional Children*, 1976, *10*, 95–96.

Sabatino, D. A., & Ysseldyke, J. E. Effect of extraneous 'background' on visual-perceptual performance of readers and non-readers. *Perceptual and Motor Skills*, 1972, *35*, 323–328.

Salvia, J., & Ysseldyke, J. E. *Assessment in special and remedial education*. Boston: Houghton Mifflin, 1978.

Samuda, R. J. *Psychological testing of American minorities: Issues and consequences*. New York: Dodd, Meade, 1975.

Samuels, M. Scheme influences on long-term recall in children. *Child Development*, 1976, *47*, 824–830.

Samuels, S. J. The method of repeated readings. *The Reading Teacher*, 1979, *32*, 403–408.

Sandler, L., Jamison, D., Deliser, O., Cohen, L., Emkey, K., & Keith, H. Developmental test performance of disadvantaged children. *Exceptional Children*, 1972, *39*, 201–208.

Santogrossi, D. A., O'Leary, K. D., Romanczyk, R. G., & Kaufman, K. F. Self-evaluation by adolescents in a psychiatric hospital school token program. *Journal of Applied Behavior Analysis*, 1973, *6*, 267–287.

Sarason, S. B. Jewishness, blackishness, and the nature-nuture controversy. *American Psychologist*, 1973, *28*, 962–971.

Saunders, R. E. Dyslexia: Its phenomenology. In J. Money (Ed.), *Reading disability: Progress and research needs in dyslexia*. Baltimore: Johns Hopkins Press, 1962.

Savin, H. B. What the child knows about speech when he starts to learn to read. In J. F. Kavanagh & I. G. Mattingly (Eds.), *Language by ear and by eye: The relationships between speech and reading*. Cambridge, Mass.: MIT Press, 1972.

Schaer, H. F., & Crump, W. D. Teacher involvement and early identification of children with learning disabilities. *Journal of Learning Disabilities*, 1976, *9*, 91–95.

Schallert, D. L., & Kleiman, G. M. Some reasons why teachers are easier to understand than textbooks (Reading Education Report No. 9). Urbana: University of Illinois, Center for the Study of Reading, June, 1979.

Schiff, W. *Perception: An applied approach.* New York: Houghton Mifflin, 1980.

Schwartz, R. M. Strategic processes in beginning reading. *Journal of Reading Behavior,* 1977, *9,* 17–26.

Sedlak, R. A., & Weener, P. Review of research on the Illinois Test of Psycholinguistic Abilities. In L. Mann & D. A. Sabatino (Eds.), *The first review of special education,* (Vol. 1). Philadelphia: JSE Press, 1973.

Senf, G. M. Development of immediate memory for bisensory stimuli in normal children and children with learning disorders. *Developmental Psychology,* 1969, *1*(6), [Pt. 2].

Sequential Test of Basic Skills. Palo Alto, Calif.: Educational Testing Service, 1958.

Shankweiler, D., & Liberman, A. M. Misreading: A search for causes. In J. F. Kavanagh & I. G. Mattingly (Eds.), *Language by ear and by eye: The relationship between speech and reading.* Cambridge, Mass.: MIT Press, 1972.

Shavelson, R. J., Berliner, D. C., Ravitch, M. M., & Loeding, D. Effects of position and type of question on learning from prose material: Interaction of treatments with individual differences. *Journal of Educational Psychology,* 1974, *66*(1), 40–48.

Sherman, J. L. Contextual information and prose comprehension. *Journal of Reading Behavior,* 1976, *8,* 369–379.

Shetty, T. Photic responses in hyperkinesis of childhood. *Science,* 1971, *174,* 1356–1357.

Shiffrin, R. M., & Craig, J. C., & Cohen, U. *On the degree of attention and capacity limitations in tactile processing.* (Indiana Mathematical Psychology Report No. 72—8) Bloomington: Indiana University, 1972.

Shiffrin, R. M., & Gardner, R. T. Visual processing capacity and attentional control. *Journal of Experimental Psychology,* 1972, *93,* 72–82.

Shiffrin, R. M., Gardner, G. T., & Allmeyer, D. J. *On the degree of attention and capacity limitations in visual processing.* (Indiana Mathematical Psychology Report No. 72—11) Bloomington: Indiana University, 1972.

Shiffrin, R. M., & Geisler, W. S. Visual recognition in a theory of information processing. In R. L. Solso (Ed.), *Contemporary issues in cognitive psychology.* Washington: Winston, 1973.

Shub, A. N., Carlin, J. A., Friedman, R. L., Kaplan, J. M., & Katien, J. C. *Diagnosis: An Instructional Aid (Reading).* Chicago: Science Research Associates, 1973.

Siller, J. Psychosocial aspects of physical disability. In J. Meislin (Ed.), *Rehabilitation medicine and psychiatry.* Columbus, Ohio: Charles C Thomas, 1976.

Siller, J. Social problems in learning disabled children. Presentation at the New York University Summer Institute in Learning Disabilities, 1977.

Silver, A. A. In symposium: Perceptual training for children with learning difficulties. New Jersey Association for Brain Injured Children, 1965.

Silver, A. A., & Hagin, R. A. *SEARCH.* New York: Walker, 1976.

Silver, L. B. Familial patterns in children with neurologically-based learning disabilities. *Journal of Learning Disabilities,* 1971, *4,* 349–358.

Silver, L. B. Difficulties in integrating child and adolescent training and service in a community mental health center. *Hospital and Community Psychiatry,* 1977, *28,* 26–40.

Silverman, R., Noa, J., & Russell, R. *Oral language tests for bilingual students: An evaluation of language dominance and proficiency instruments.* Portland, Or.: Northwest Regional Educational Laboratory, 1976.

Simpson, D. D., & Nelson, A. E. Attention training through breathing control to modify hyperactivity. *Journal of Learning Disabilities,* 1974, *7,* 274–283.

Sims, H., & Bastian, A. Use of the Meeting Street School Screening Test, and the Myklebust Pupil Rating Scale with first grade black urban children. *Psychology in the Schools,* 1976, *13,* 386–389.

Sinclair-deZwart, H. Language acquisition and cognitive development. In T. E. Moore (Ed.), *Cognitive development and the acquisition of language.* New York: Academic, 1973.

Singer, H., & Ruddell, R. B. *Theoretical models and processes of reading.* Newark, Del.: International Reading Association, 1976.

Siperstein, G., Bobb, M., & Bak, J. Social status of learning disabled children. *Journal of Learning Disabilities,* 1978, *11,* 98–102.

Skinner, B. F. *Verbal behavior.* New York: Appleton-Century-Crofts, 1957.

Slingerland, B. H. *Slingerland Screening Tests for Identifying Children with Specific Language Disability.* Cambridge, Mass.: Educators Publishing Service, 1970.

Slingerland, B. H. Preventive teaching programs in the classroom: A general education responsibility. (Reprint No. 50.) Towson, Md.: The Orton Society Reprint Series, 1972.

Slingerland, B. H. *Why wait for a criterion of failure?* Cambridge, Mass.: Educators Publishing Service, 1974.

Sloane, H. N. Classroom management: Remediation and prevention. New York: Wiley, 1976.

Slobin, D. I. *Psycholinguistics.* Glenview, Ill.: Scott, Foresman, 1971.

Slosson, R. L. *Slosson Intelligence Test.* East Aurora, N.Y.: Slosson Educational Publications, 1971.

Smith, E. B., Goodman, K. S., & Meredith, R. *Language and thinking in school.* New York: Holt, Rinehart and Winston, 1976.

Smith, E. E., Shoben, E. J., & Rips, L. J. Structure and process in semantic decisions. *Psychological Review,* 1974, *81*(3), 214–241.

Smith, F. *Comprehension and learning.* New York: Holt, Rinehart & Winston, 1965.(a)

Smith, F. The readability of junior high school mathematics textbooks. *The Mathematics Teacher,* 1969, *62,* 289–292.

Smith, F. *Understanding reading: A psycholinguistic analysis of reading and learning to read.* New York: Holt, Rinehart & Winston, 1971.

Smith, F. *Psycholinguistics and reading.* New York: Holt, Rinehart and Winston, 1973.

Smith, F. *Comprehension and learning.* New York: Holt, Rinehart, and Winston, 1975.(a)

Smith, F. The relation between spoken and written language. In E. H. Lenneberg & E. Lenneberg (Eds.), *Foundations of language development: A multidisciplinary approach,* Vol. 2. New York: Academic Press, 1975.(b)

Smith, F. Making sense of reading—and of reading instruction. *Harvard Educational Review,* 1977, *47,* 386–395.

Smith, M. D., Zingale, S. A., & Coleman, J. M. The influence of adult expectancy/child performance discrepancies upon children's self-concepts. *American Educational Research Journal,* 1978, *15,* 259–265.

Smith, M. M. Patterns of intellectual abilities in educationally handicapped children. Unpublished doctoral dissertation. Claremont, Calif.: Claremont Graduate School, 1970.

Smith, P. A., Marx, R. W. Some cautions on the use of the Frostig test: A factor analytic study. *Journal of Learning Disabilities,* 1972, *5,* 357–362.

Snyder, J. J., & White, M. J. The use of cognitive self-instruction in the treatment of behaviorally disturbed adolescents. *Behavior Therapy*, 1979, *10*, 227–235.

Spache, G. D. *Toward better reading*. Champaign, Ill.: Garrard, 1963.

Spache, G. D. *Diagnosing and correcting reading disabilities*. Boston: Allyn and Bacon, 1976.

Spitz, H. H. Consolidating facts into the schematized learning and memory system of educable retardates. In N. R. Ellis (Ed.), *International review of research in mental retardation*. Vol. 6. New York: Academic Press, 1973.

Spivak, C., Swift, M., & Prewitt, J. Syndromes of disturbed classroom behavior: A behavioral diagnostic system for elementary schools. *Journal of Special Education*, 1971, *5*, 269–292.

Spradlin, J. E. Assessment of speech and language of retarded children: The Parson Language Scales. *Journal of Speech and Hearing Disorders*, 1963, (Monograph Supplement   10), 8–31.

Spring, C. Encoding speed and memory span in dyslexic children. *Journal of Special Education*, 1976, *10*(10), 35–40.

Spring, C., & Capps, C. Encoding speed, rehearsal, and probed recall of dyslexic boys. *Journal of Educational Psychology*, 1974, *66*, 780–786.

Spring, C., & Sandoval, J. Food additives and hyperkinesis: A critical evaluation of the evidence. *Journal of Learning Disabilities*, 1976, *9*, 560–569.

Sroufe, L. A. Age changes in cardiac decleration within a fixed foreperiod reaction time task: An index of attention. *Developmental Psychology*, 1971, *5*, 338–343.

Sroufe, L. A. Drug treatment of children with behavior problems. In F. Horowitz (Ed.), *Review of child development research* (Vol. 4). Chicago: University of Chicago Press, 1975.

Sroufe, L. A., Sonies, B. C., West, W. D., & Wright, F. S. Anticipatory heart rate decleration and reaction time in children with and without referral for learning disability. *Child Development*, 1973, *44*, 267–273.

Staats, A. W. Behaviorism and cognitive theory in the study of language: A neopsycholinguistics. In R. L. Schiefelbusch & L. L. Lloyd (Eds.), *Language perspectives— Acquisition, retardation, and intervention*. Baltimore: University Park Press, 1974.

Stanley, G., & Hall, R. Short-term visual information processing in dyslexics. *Child Development*, 1973, *44*, 841–844.

Stauffer, R. G. A vocabulary study comparing reading, arithmetic, health and science texts. *The Reading Teacher*, 1966, *20*, 141–147.

Steger, J. A., Vellutino, F. R., & Meshoulam, U. Visual-tactile and tactile-visual paired associate learning in normal and poor readers. *Perceptual and Motor Skills*, 1972, *35*, 263–266.

Stein, N. L., & Glenn, C. G. An analysis of story comprehension in elementary school children. In R. O. Freedle (Ed.), *New directions in discourse processing* (Vol. 2). Hillsdale, N.J.: Ablex, 1979.

Stephens, T. M., Hartman, A. C., & Lucas, V. H. *Teaching children basic skills*. Columbus, Ohio: Merrill, 1978.

Stern, C., & Stern, M. B. *Children discover arithmetic: An introduction to Structural Arithmetic*, (Rev. ed.) New York: Harper & Row, 1971.

Stern, C., Stern, M. B., & Gould, T. S. *Structural Arithmetic workbooks and teacher's guides, K—3*. Boston: Houghton Mifflin, 1965, 1966.

Stern, M. B. Structural Arithmetic and children with learning disabilities. *Bulletin of The Orton Society*, 1977, *27*, 171–182.

Sterritt, G. M., Martin, V., & Rudnick, M. Auditory-visual and temporal-spatial integration as determinants of test difficulty. *Psychonomic Science,* 1971, *23,* 289–291.

Sterritt, G. M., & Rudnick, M. Auditory and visual rhythm perception in relation to reading ability in fourth grade boys. *Perceptual and Motor Skills,* 1966, *22,* 859–864.

Steward, M. Hyperactive children. *Scientific American,* 1970, *222,* 94–98.

Steward, M. A., & Olds, S. W. *Raising a hyperactive child.* New York: Harper & Row, 1973.

Strang, L., Smith, M. S., & Rogers, C. M. Social comparison, multiple reference groups, and the self-concepts of academically handicapped children before and after mainstreaming. *Journal of Educational Psychology,* 1978, *70,* 488–497.

Strauss, A. A., & Kephart, N. C. *Psychopathology and education of the brain-injured child.* (Vol. II). *Progress in theory and clinic.* New York: Grune & Stratton, 1955.

Strauss, A. A., & Lehtinen, L. E. *Psychopathology and education of the brain-injured child.* New York: Grune & Stratton, 1947.

Streufert, S. C. Effects of information relevance on decision making in complex environments. *Memory & Cognition,* 1973, *1*(3), 224–228.

Sutherland, J., & Algozzine, B. The learning disabled label as a biasing factor in the visual motor performance of normal children. *Journal of Learning Disabilities,* 1979, *12,* 17–23.

Swanson, J. M., & Kinsbourne, M. Stimulant-related state-dependent learning in hyperactive children. *Science,* 1976, *192,* 1354–1357.

Tarver, S. G., & Dawson, M. M. Modality preference and the teaching of reading: A review. *Journal of Learning Disabilities,* 1978, *11,* 17–29.

Tarver, S. G., & Hallahan, D. P. Attention deficits in children with learning disabilities: A review. *Journal of Learning Disabilities,* 1974, *9,* 560–569.

Tarver, S. G., Hallahan, D. P., Cohen, S. B., & Kauffman, J. M. The development of visual selective attention and verbal rehearsal in learning disabled boys. *Journal of Learning Disabilities,* 1977, *10,* 491–500.

Tarver, S. G., Hallahan, D. P., Kauffman, J. M., & Ball, D. W. Verbal rehearsal and selective attention in children with learning disabilities: A developmental lag. *Journal of Experimental Child Psychology,* 1976, *22,* 375–385.

Taylor, O., & Swinney, D. The onset of language. In J. V. Marge & M. Marge (Eds.), *Principles of childhood language disabilities.* New York: Appleton-Century-Crofts, 1972.

Templin, M. C. *Certain language skills in children.* Minneapolis: University of Minnesota Press, 1957.

Templin, M. C., & Darley, F. L. *The Templin-Darley Tests of Articulation.* Iowa City, Iowa: Bureau of Educational Research and Service, University of Iowa, 1960.

Teuber, H. -L., & Rudel, R. G. Behavior after cerebral lesions in children and adults. *Developmental Medicine & Child Neurology,* 1962, *4,* 3–20.

Thomas, A. Learned helplessness and expectancy factors: Implications for research in learning disabilities. *Review of Educational Research,* 1979, *49,* 208–221.

Thomas, A., & Chess, S. *Temperament and development,* New York: Brunner/Mazel, 1977.

Thomas, A., Chess, S., & Birch, H. G. *Temperament and behavior disorders in children.* New York: New York University Press, 1968.

Thompson, A. Working with parents of children with learning disabilities. In S. A. Kirk & J. J. McCarthy (Eds.), *Learning disabilities: Selected ACLD papers.* Boston: Houghton Mifflin, 1975.

Tobin, A. The effects of a mathematics laboratory as an intervention for increasing mathematical knowledge. Unpublished doctoral dissertation, Temple University, 1973.

Torgesen, J., & Kail, R. V., Jr. Memory processes in exceptional children. In B. K. Keogh (Ed.), *Advances in special education*, (Vol. I). Greenwich, Conn.: J. A. I. Press, 1980.

Torgesen, J. K. The role of nonspecific factors in the task performance of learning disabled children: A theoretical assessment. *Journal of Learning Disabilities*, 1977, *10*(1), 17–34.

Torgesen, J. K. Performance of reading disabled children on serial memory tasks: A selective review of recent research. *Reading Research Quarterly*, 1978, *14*, 57–87.

Torgesen, J. K. Factors related to poor performance on memory tasks in reading disabled children. *Learning Disability Quarterly*, 1979, *2*, 17–23.

Torgesen, J. K. What shall we do with psychological processes? *Journal of Learning Disabilities*, 1979, *12*, 514–521.

Torgesen, J., Bowen, C., & Ivey, C. Task structure vs. modality of presentation: A study of the construct validity of the visual-aural digit span test. *Journal of Educational Psychology*, 1978, *70*, 451–456.

Torgesen, J., & Goldman, R. Rehearsal and short-term memory in reading disabled children. *Child Development*, 1977, *48*, 56–60.

Treisman, A. M. Monitoring and storage of irrelevant messages in selective attention. *Journal of Verbal Learning and Verbal Behavior*, 1964, *3*, 449–459.

Tucker, J. A. Operationalizing the diagnostic-intervention process. In T. Oakland (Ed.), *Psychological and educational assessment of minority children*. New York: Brunner/Mazel, 1977.

Tulving, E. Episodic and semantic memory. In E. Tulving & W. Donaldson (Eds.), *Organization of memory*, New York, Academic Press, 1972.

Tulving, E., & Donaldson, W. (Eds.). *Organization of memory*. New York: Academic Press, 1972.

Tulving, E., & Madigan, S. A. Memory and verbal learning. *Annual Review of Psychology*, 1970, *21*, 437–484.

Turkewitz, H., O'Leary, K. D. & Ironsmith, M. Generalization and maintenance of appropriate behavior through self-control. *Journal of Consulting and Clinical Psychology*, 1975, *43*, 577–583.

Turnbull, A. P. Strickland, B. B., & Brantley, J. C. *Developing and implementing individualized education programs*. Columbus, Ohio: Merrill, 1978.

Turton, L. J. Developmental and linguistic aspects of learning disabilities. In W. M. Cruickshank & D. P. Hallahan (Eds.), *Perceptual and learning disabilities in children*, (Vol. 1), *Psychoeducational practices*. Syracuse, N.Y.: Syracuse University Press, 1975.

United States Office of Education, *Better education for the handicapped: Annual report, fiscal year, 1969*. Washington: U.S. Government Printing Office, 1970.

Valett, R. E. *Valett developmental survey of basic learning abilities*. Palo Alto, Calif.: Consulting Psychologists Press, 1966.

Valett, R. E. *Programming learning disabilities*. Belmont, Calif.: Fearon Publishers, 1969.

Van Atta, B. A comparative study of auditory skills (sensitivity, discrimination, and memory span) of dyslalic and normal speaking children in grades 1–3. *Aviso*, 1973, *4*, 1–7.

Vande Voort, L., Senf, G. M., & Benton, A. L. Development of audio-visual integration in normal and retarded readers. *Child Development*, 1972, *43*, 1260–1272.

Vaughan, V. C., McVay, R. S., & Nelson, W. E. (Eds.). *Textbook of Pediatrics*. Philadelphia: Saunders, 1973.

Vellutino, F. R. Alternative conceptualizations of dyslexia: Evidence in support of a verbal deficit hypothesis. *Harvard Educational Review*, 1977, *47*, 334–354.

Vellutino, F. R. Toward an understanding of dyslexia: Psychological factors in specific reading disability. In A. L. Benton & D. Pearl (Eds.), *Dyslexia: An appraisal of current knowledge*. New York: Oxford University Press, 1978.

Vellutino, F. R., Pruzek, R., Steger, J. A., & Meshoulam, U. Immediate visual recall in poor and normal readers as a function of orthographic-linguistic familiarity. *Cortex*, 1973, *9*, 368–384.

Vellutino, F. R., Smith, H., Steger, J. A., & Kaman, M. Reading disability: Age differences and the perceptual deficit hypothesis. *Child Development*, 1975, *46*, 493–497.

Vellutino, F. R., Steger, J. A., DeSetto, L., & Phillips, F. Immediate and delayed recognition of visual stimuli in poor and normal readers. *Journal of Experimental Child Psychology*, 1975, *19*, 223–232.

Vellutino, F. R., Steger, J. A., Harding, C. J., & Phillips, F. Verbal vs. non-verbal paired associates learning in poor and normal readers. *Neuropsychologia*, 1975, *13*, 75–82.

Vellutino, F. R., Steger, J. A., Kaman, M., & DeSetto, L. Visual form perception in deficient and normal readers as a function of age and orthographic linguistic familiarity. *Cortex*, 1975, *11*, 22–30.

Vellutino, F. R., Steger, J. A., & Kandel, G. Reading disability: An investigation of the perceptual deficit hypothesis. *Cortex*, 1972, *8*, 106–118.

Vellutino, F. R., Steger, B. M., Moyer, S. C., Harding, C. J., & Niles, J. A. Has the perceptual deficit hypothesis led us astray? *Journal of Learning Disabilities*, 1977, *10*, 375–385.

Vellutino, F. R., Steger, J. A., & Pruzek. Inter-vs intrasensory deficit in paired associate learning in poor and normal readers. *Canadian Journal of Behavioral Science*, 1973, *5*, 111–123.

Verhave, T. A review of Chomsky's "Language and mind." *Journal of Psycholinguistic Research*, 1972, *2*, 183–195.

Vernon, M. D. *Reading and its difficulties*. New York: Cambridge University Press, 1971.

Vernon, M. D. Varieties of deficiency in the reading process. *Harvard Educational Review*, 1977, *47*, 396–410.

von Wright, J. M., Anderson, K., & Stenman, U. Generalization of conditioned GSRs in dichotic listening. In P. M. A. Rabbitt & S. Dornic (Eds.), *Attention and performance*, (V). New York: Academic Press, 1975.

Vurpillot, E. The development of scanning strategies and their relation to visual differentiation. *Journal of Experimental Child Psychology*, 1968, *6*, 632–650.

Walker, D. K. *Socioemotional measures for preschool and kindergarten children*. San Francisco: Josey-Bass, 1973.

Wall, A. Alpha training and the hyperactive child: Is it effective? *Academic Therapy*, 1973, *9*(1), 5–19.

Wallace, G., & Larsen, S. C. *Educational assessment of learning problems: Testing for teaching*. Boston: Allyn & Bacon, 1978.

Wallach, G. P., & Goldsmith, S. C. Language-based learning disabilities: Reading is language, too! *Journal of Learning Disabilities*, 1977, *10*, 178–182.

Wallbrown, F. H., Fremont, T. S., Nelson, E., Wilson, J., & Fisher, J. Emotional disturbance or social misperception? An important classroom management question. *Journal of Learning Disabilities*, 1979, *12*, 645–468.

Wanat, S. F. Relations between language and visual processing. In H. Singer & R. B. Ruddell (Eds.), *Theoretical models and processes of reading* (2d ed.). Newark, Del.: International Reading Association, 1976.

Warren, R. J., Karduck, W. A., Bussaratid, S., Steward, M. A., & Sly, W. S. The hyperactive child syndrome: Normal chromosome findings. *Archives of General Psychiatry*, 1971, *24*, 161–163.

Weaver, P. A. Comprehension, recall, and dyslexia: A proposal for the application of schema theory. *Bulletin of the Orton Society*, 1978, *28*, 92–113.

Wechsler, D. *Wechsler intelligence scale for children—Revised*. New York: Psychological Corporation, 1974.

Weiss, G., Minde, K., Werry, J. S., Douglas, V., & Nemeth, E. Studies on the hyperactive child, (VIII): Five-year follow-up. *Archives of General Psychiatry*, 1971, *24*, 409–414.

Weissenberger, F. E., & Loney, J. Hyperkinesis in the Classroom: If cerebral stimulants are the last resort, what is the first resort? *Journal of Learning Disabilities*, 1977, *10*(6), 339–348.

Weithorn, C. J., & Kagen, E. Training first graders of high-activity level to improve performance through verbal self-direction. *Journal of Learning Disabilities*, 1979, *12*(2), 82–88.

Weithorn, C. J., & Ross, R. Who monitors medication? *Journal of Learning Disabilities*, 1975, *8*, 59–62.

Wender, P. H. *Minimal brain dysfunction in children*. New York: Wiley, 1971.

Wender, P. H. The minimal brain dysfunction syndrome in child. *Journal of Nervous and Mental Disease*, 1972, *165*, 55–71.

Wepman, J. M. Auditory discrimination, speech, and reading. *Elementary School Journal*, 1960, *60*, 325–333.

Westerman, G. *Spelling and writing*. San Rafael, Calif.: Dimensions, 1971.

Wheatley, L. A. Sex bias as a characteristic of learning disabled boys based on reading, language, fine motor, and social/emotional disabilities. *Division for Children with Learning Disabilities Newsletter*, 1972, *2*, 83–89.

Wheeler, R. J., & Dusek, J. B. The effects of attentional and cognitive factors on children's incidental learning. *Child Development*, 1973, *44*, 253–258.

Wickelgren, W. A. Alcholic intoxication and memory storage dynamics. *Memory & Cognition*, 1975, *3*(4), 385–389.

Wiederholt, J. L. Predictive validity of Frostig's constructs as measured by the Developmental Test of Visual Perception. *Dissertation Abstracts*, 1971, *33*, 1556-A.

Wiederholt, J. L. Historical perspectives on the education of the learning disabled. In L. Mann & D. A. Sabatino (Eds.), *The second review of special education*. Philadelphia: JSE Press, 1974.

Wiederholt, J. L., Hammill, D. D., & Brown, V. L. *The resource teacher*. Boston: Allyn & Bacon, 1978.

Wiederholt, J. L., Hammill, D. D., & Brown, V. L. *The resource teacher*. Boston: Allyn & Bacon, 1978.

Wiederholt, J. L., & McEntire, B. Educational options for handicapped adolescents. *Exceptional Education Quarterly*, 1980, *1*, in press.

Wiig, E. H., & Harris, S. P. Perception and interpretation of nonverbally expressed emotions by adolescents with learning disabilities. *Perceptual and Motor Skills,* 1974, *38,* 239–245.

Wiig, E. H., & Semel, E. M. Productive language abilities in learning disabled adolescents. *Journal of Learning Disabilities,* 1975, *8,* 578–586.

Wiig, E. H., & Semel, E. M. *Language disabilities in children and adolescents.* Columbus, Ohio: Merrill, 1976.

Wiig, E. H., Semel, E. M. *Language assessment and intervention for the learning disabled.* Columbus, Ohio: Charles E. Merrill, 1980.

Wiig, E. H., Semel, E. M., & Crouse, M. A. B. The use of morphology by high-risk and learning disabled children. *Journal of Learning Disabilities,* 1973, *6,* 457–465.

Willower, D. J. Special education: Organization and administration. *Exceptional Children,* 1970, *36,* 591–594.

Winick, M. Malnutrition and brain development. *Journal of Pediatrics,* 1969, *74,* 667–679.

Winograd, T. Frame representations and the declarative-procedural controversy In D. G. Bobrow & A. M. Collins (Eds.), *Representation and understanding: Studies in cognitive science.* New York: Academic Press, 1975.

Wittrock, M. C. The cognitive movement in instruction *Educational Psychologist,* 1978, *13,* 15–30.

Wolfensberger, W. Counseling the parents of the retarded. In A. A. Baumeister (Ed.), *Mental retardation: Appraisal, education, and rehabilitation.* Chicago: Aldine, 1967.

Wong, B. Y. L. Increasing retention of main ideas through questioning strategies. *Learning Disability Quarterly,* 1979, *2,* 42–47.

Wong, B. Y. L., & Roadhouse, A. The test of Language Development (TOLD): A validation study. *Learning Disability Quarterly,* 1978, *1,* 48–61.

Woodcock, R. W. *Peabody Rebus Reading Program.* Circle Pines, Minn.: American Guidance Service, 1967.

Woodcock, R. W. *Woodcock Reading Mastery Tests.* Circle Pines, Minn.: American Guidance Service, 1974.

Woodcock, R. W. *Development and standardization of the Woodcock-Johnson Psycho-Educational Battery.* Hingham, Mass.: Teaching Resources, 1978.

Woodcock, R. W., & Johnson, M. B. *Woodcock-Johnson Psycho-Educational Battery.* Boston: Teaching Resources, 1977.

Wright, B. A. An analysis of attitudes—Dynamics and effects. *The New Outlook for the Blind,* 1974, 108–118.

Wright, L. Conduct problems or learning disability? *Journal of Learning Disabilities,* 1974, *8,* 331–336.

Wunderlich, R. C. Hyperkinetic disease. *Academic Therapy,* 1970, *5,* 99–108.

Wunderlich, R. C. *Kids, brains, and learning.* St. Petersburg, Florida: Johnny Reads, 1970.

Yamamoto, K. (Ed.) *The child and his image.* Palo Alto: Houghton Mifflin, 1972.

Young S. Preliminary investigation of sentence repetition ability in children with language and learning disabilities. Unpublished master's thesis, University of Texas, 1971.

Zach, L., & Kaufman, J. How adequate is the concept of 'perceptual deficit' for education? *Journal of Learning Disabilities,* 1972, *5,* 335–356.

Zaner-Bloser, Inc. *Creative growth with handwriting.* Columbus, Ohio: Zaner-Bloser, 1975.

Zaner-Bloser, Inc. *Chalkboard techniques and activities for teaching writing.* Columbus, Ohio: Zaner-Bloser, 1976.

Zaporozhets, A. V. The development of voluntary movements. In B. Simon (Ed.), *Psychology in the Soviet Union.* Stanford, California: Stanford University Press, 1957.

Zeitz, F. The relationship between appraisal of feelings about self in subject areas, perceived to have different degrees of importance, and academic achievement in these areas. *Dissertation Abstracts,* 1976, *35,* 2709A.

Zentall, S. Optimal stimulation as theoretical basis of hyperactiviic achievement in these areas. *Dissertation Abstracts,* 1976, *35,* 2709A.

Zentall, S. Optimal stimulation as theoretical basis of hyperactivi of within-task stimulation for hyperactive and normal children. *Journal of Learning Disabilities,* 1978, *11*(9), 540–548.

Zippel, B. Information retrieval from long-term memory. *Journal of General Psychology,* 1975, *93,* 73–85.

Zurif, E. B., & Carson, G. Dyslexia in relation to cerebral dominance and temporal analysis. *Neuropsychologia,* 1970, *8,* 351–361.

Name Index

Subject Index